A Most Holy War

Americanos
Latin America's Struggle for Independence
John Charles Chasteen

A Most Holy War
The Albigensian Crusade and the Battle for Christendom
Mark Gregory Pegg

Also by Mark Gregory Pegg

The Corruption of Angels
The Great Inquisition of 1245–1246

A Most Holy War

The Albigensian Crusade and
the Battle for Christendom

Mark Gregory Pegg

OXFORD
UNIVERSITY PRESS

2008

OXFORD
UNIVERSITY PRESS

Oxford University Press, Inc., publishes works that
further Oxford University's objective of excellence
in research, scholarship, and education.

Oxford New York
Auckland Cape Town Dar es Salaam Hong Kong Karachi
Kuala Lumpur Madrid Melbourne Mexico City Nairobi
New Delhi Shanghai Taipei Toronto

With offices in
Argentina Austria Brazil Chile Czech Republic France Greece
Guatemala Hungary Italy Japan Poland Portugal Singapore
South Korea Switzerland Thailand Turkey Ukraine Vietnam

Copyright © 2008 by Mark Gregory Pegg

Published by Oxford University Press, Inc.
198 Madison Avenue, New York, NY 10016

www.oup.com

Oxford is a registered trademark of Oxford University Press

Library of Congress Cataloging-in-Publication Data
Pegg, Mark Gregory, 1963–
A most holy war : the Albigensian crusade and the battle for Christendom
/ Mark Gregory Pegg.
p. cm. — (Pivotal moments in world history)
Includes bibliographical references and index.
ISBN 978-0-19-517131-0
1. Albigenses—History. 2. France—Church history—987–1515.
3. Heresies, Christian—France—Languedoc—History—Middle Ages, 600–1500.
4. Languedoc (France)—History, Military—Religious aspects.
5. France, Southern—History. 6. Crusades. I. Title.
DC83.3.P45 2008
944'.023—dc22
2007027108

1 3 5 7 9 8 6 4 2
Printed in the United States of America
on acid-free paper

For Mary Douglas and William Jordan

Contents

Maps

Preface

I first climbed Montségur in the spring of 1995. I was living in Toulouse, researching a dissertation on medieval heresy, and thought it about time I visited this hallowed mountain stronghold of the Cathars, who, wreathed in myth and tragedy, are the most famous heretics of the Middle Ages. I borrowed a tiny Citroën that, if the carcinogenic purr of the engine was anything to go by, smoked at least sixty Gitanes a day, and headed for the Pyrénées. Two hours later the car wheezed into a cul-de-sac below Montségur. Recent rains had washed away most of the nearly vertical track to the top. Scrapes and muddy shins on the way up did, if nothing else, recall why French soldiers had so much trouble assaulting this escarpment in 1243. At the summit I walked around the ruins of a small castle. It was all very picturesque, especially the view of snowy peaks and green valleys. "You feel the sacred aura too?" I turned with a start and saw a woman, handsome, late middle-aged, staring at me. "You were feeling the energy of this place, weren't you?" The vowels were southern Californian. "What do you think of the Cathars? The Cathars threatened the Catholic Church, right? The Albigensian Crusade wiped out the Cathar Church, right?" As abruptly as my interrogator appeared, she vanished among the castle ruins, apparently satisfied that my stunned silence marked me as a fellow traveler in Catharism.

Over the years I've had similar conversations (often as one-sided, frequently as bizarre) about the Cathars. The seductive appeal of these heretics is understandable, as they seemingly represent an alternative, more tolerant Christianity to that of the medieval Catholic Church. Catharism is usually cited as a form of Christian dualism in which the universe was split by a vast cosmic chasm where an active, malign Devil (or bad God) manipulated the earth, and a passive, good God quietly dwelt in heaven. Body and soul, matter and spirit, were irreconcilably divided. Day-to-day existence was an unrequited yearning for an indifferent God, and, if such longing was to be endured, then equanimity in mind and manner had to be practiced. Consequently, thousands of Cathars lived in spiritual and social tranquility (tinged with holy melancholia) between the Garonne and Rhône Rivers, that vast region encompassing all of southern France. This religious idyll was shattered by twenty years of savage holy war during the early thirteenth century. Some Cathars fled as refugees into northern Italy; most stayed behind, furtive and frightened, hunted down by the Inquisition. Montségur was the last heroic stand of the Cathar elite. My spectral Californian probably knew all this and more. Although if she quizzed me now (and stayed for the answer) I would tell her—politely, passionately— that everything about the Cathars is utter fantasy, even down to their name. In fact, I would tell her that more than a century of scholarship on both the Albigensian Crusade and heresy hasn't been merely vaguely mistaken, or somewhat misguided, it has been breathtakingly wrong.

As much as I disavow this learned tradition of misreading and mispri-sion, I do admire it. What I most deplore are the popular attempts to exploit it. I enjoy page-turners—they distract during turbulence, they go with summer holidays—except when they pretend to historical truth. My book-shelves groan with novels and histories dedicated to the "secret history" of the Cathars—which leads directly to the "secret history" of Western civilization itself. *The Da Vinci Code* is the most widely known retelling of this untold story. This *sub-rosa* history usually goes something like this: Jesus survives the cross; He and Mary Magdalene have kids; they all go to southern Gaul; the medieval Church hates this bloodline because it fizzes with the Holy Feminine; the Cathars know the truth; and the Albigensian Crusade was the reactionary, repressive attempt to expunge that knowledge from the world. Swirling around this esoteric tale are troubadours, every dualist heresy under the sun, the Holy Grail, the Templars, the Inquisition, Montségur, Rennes-le-Château, the Priory of Sion, Masonic Lodges, and enigmatic incunabula. What is so astonishing about this unlocking, decoding narrative is that it resembles the standard history to be found in many academic studies. Both accounts argue from silence (the Church suppressed all the evidence); see continuities where none exist (a nod's as good as a wink); rely on documents of dubious provenance (or rather copies of copies of missing documents); and accept *a priori* a Cathar Church.

As clichéd as it now is to see the Albigensian Crusade as a war against the Cathars, such a proposition was new around 1900. Until then the crusade was, rather straightforwardly, regarded as a campaign against the "Albigensians." The legendary eleventh edition (1910) of the *Encyclopaedia Britannica* deftly illustrates (as it does with so much Victorian-into-Edwardian thought) the scholarly metamorphosis of *Albigenses* into *Cathari*. Both heretics have entries (an editorial concession that, even when ideas change, old notions persist), and, while each essay is erudite, "Albigenses" (by a Frenchman) is clearly the musty antecedent that "Cathars" (by an Englishman) so exuberantly supersedes. The Albigensians miraculously appeared in the Limousin (an upland region of the Massif Central) at the beginning of the eleventh century before finally settling in the Toulousain at the beginning of the twelfth. These heretics were basically southwestern French *indigènes* with a dualist bent, a parochial people with a folkloric faith. The crusade against them was a bitter war of national unity. The Cathars, on the other hand, "were the débris of an early Christianity," the remnant of ancient Manichaeans (maybe even Gnostics), who, after a long and hidden Diaspora, reappeared between the tenth and fourteenth centuries as heretical Paulicians and Bogomils in the Balkans and, although scattered throughout western Europe, these dualist immigrants flourished in southern France. These heretics were a venerable and cosmopolitan race with a long and secret history, whose religion was highly ritualistic and textual. The crusade against them was a war of religious persecution, colonization, and racial extermination. The Cathars were very much heretics for a modern age, for a new and turbulent century—which is why they keep on keeping on from one ripped up *belle époque* into another.

Hand in hand with the Cathars (indeed, the intellectual support that allows these centenarian views to keep tottering on) are some equally mistaken notions about religion, which is narrowly defined by abiding doctrines, perennial philosophies, and timeless ideals. Scriptural consistency and theological cogency are what supposedly make religions, not poorly articulated thoughts or anomalous opinions, which get tossed aside as notional (and historical) irrelevancies. The fallacy behind it all is that pure principles form the core of every religion and that no matter how many civilizations rise and fall through the millennia, how many prophets come and go, the principles enduringly persist. Weightless, immaterial, untouched by historical contingency, they waft over centuries and societies like loose hot-air balloons. By combining these untethered beliefs, almost any history (secret or otherwise) can be strung together. Detecting apparently similar ideas (symbols, gods, a certain way with wives) through time and space is only the beginning of an explanation and not the concluding proof. If I chanced upon some heretics from the thirteenth century ostensibly very similar to some heretics living in the very same region in the eleventh, that similarity would be, at best, superficial. Meanings are elusive, resemblances ubiquitous. The reasons I believe two things truly resemble each other, or believe I can safely predict certain continuities from one afternoon to the next, has nothing to do with what medieval people knew about their world. The past isn't simply another country, it's an entirely different universe. At a time when the world is haunted by religiously inspired warfare, religion must be seen as more than floating ideas, more than just ideology with gossamer wings.

A contemporary twist on these idealist assumptions is a high-minded empathy about past beliefs. Analysis isn't based on the interpretation of historical evidence but on the emotional authenticity of a judgment. This posturing easily slips into claiming that only the religious can truly understand religion—and more stridently into insisting that only Christians can fathom Christianity, Jews unravel Judaism, Cathars decode.... This blurring of thinking and feeling (and morality) surrounds us nowadays. Historians must forgo this consoling confusion, for it means taking sides, it means getting even with the past. Insight into the Albigensian Crusade is advanced in no way, shape, or form, if I tell you how religious I am or if I express outrage that the pope in the year 1208 exhorted all Christians to purge heretics from the lands of the count of Toulouse. What happened during the crusade was horrific, as this book will show, but sanctimoniously grieving for the fallen neither comforts the dead nor helps the historian who writes about harrowing events avoid the pitfalls of relativism. A history wrapped in mourning crêpe—whether on the Crusades, the Holocaust, the Gulag, the British Empire, the Inquisition, the Great Leap Forward, the Indian Wars, or Antebellum Slavery—might have its heart in the right place (when not on its sleeve), but its sincerity may be distortingly sentimental.

I have very intense feelings about being a historian, so much so that a rather forthright earnestness frequently overwhelms me (to the amusement of my students, to the despair of my friends). The source of this passion isn't simply a conviction that historians can change the world, it's because I still believe in historical truth. Or rather, I believe in training the imagination at overcoming the sheer incomprehensibility of the past and, by an effort at once intellectual and aesthetic, move closer to a more exacting vision of an expired reality. I aspire to the truth, knowing that I'll never achieve it, knowing that it is (as it must be) just out of my reach. Past worlds (and all their messiness, grandeur, and cruelty) can be understood only if evoked as fully as possible. No half measures, no middies. A world exists from one day to the next, from one decade to another, because of an interweaving of thoughts and actions so individually intimate, so communally strengthening, that the relations a person (or thing) maintains in the material realm entrenches the relations he or she (or it) maintains in the metaphoric, and vice versa. In other words, how a man ploughs his fields, gets dressed, and says hello is inescapably tied to what he knows about heresy, holiness, and the sufferings of Christ. Of course, my skills (such as they are) and my theories (a swag of the functional, interpretative, and pragmatic) add up to nothing unless they coalesce into an aesthetic whole. History is more art than science, striving for the precision of the imagination. Only through imaginative rigor does imaginative sympathy occur. That is why historical prose must experiment with narrative styles and structures. The past is hard enough to imagine without thinking there is only one way to write about it.

Any meditation on the past that starts with the presumption that some things are universal in humans or in human society—never changing, inert, immobile—is to retreat from attempting a historical explanation about previous rhythms of existence. Studies are lauded that argue that there is, say, a pervasive male manner (with other men, with women, with meat) imprinted into masculine genes over a month of prehistoric Sundays. Or that minds always respond in similar ways to tragedy. Or that hereditary behavioral traits impose habits (and occasionally beliefs) from one generation to the next. Or that religion is a primal response to primal fears. Millennia are flattened out, if not totally erased, in essentialism. Historical specificity is either dismissed as irrelevant or seen as epiphenomenal graffiti scratched on (and so disfiguring) unchanging customs and concepts. Arguing for immutable values from biology is no different from arguing for immutable values from theology—selfish genes, selfish doctrines, they both deny history. Assuming that why we do what we do, why we think what we think, is somehow or other beyond our control, and that we would be this way in mind and body whether we lived in Cleveland in 1952 or Toulouse in 1218, forfeits the vitality and distinctiveness of the past to the dead hand of biological determinism, cognitive hotwiring, psychological innateness, liberal pleas for bygone victims, conservative pleas for God-given principles, and amaranthine mush about authenticity.

Three summers ago, when I began thinking about this book, I toured the Lauragais, a rich alluvial plain between Toulouse and Carcassonne, visiting all the villages devastated by the Albigensian Crusade. I again drove the emphysemic Citroën. One blisteringly hot afternoon I stopped at Fanjeaux. This village was torched by crusaders and, according to one survivor, when Dominic de Guzmán (who founded the Dominicans) preached among the charred rubble, a demonic cat hurled itself at an idle bystander, causing the poor man to be promptly burned as a heretic. Eyeing every stray tabby, I walked into a café and ordered a beer. I was carrying a copy of *The Da Vinci Code*. Friends and relatives had been nagging me for an opinion, so I was forcing myself through it. I should've known it was a red rag to whatever Cathar bull was hanging about the bar. Soon enough, a rosé-soused sixty-something Englishman sidled over to where I was sitting. "You know, they deserved it!" "Excuse me?" "The bloody heretics," and he plonked himself down next to me. He actually wasn't too bad and, apart from looking like a goldfish in white slacks, his conversation was witty, even if he argued the pope had no choice but to launch the crusade. "A preemptive strike," he wagged his fin, "that's what it was." Pleased with his formulation, he repeated it a few more times before getting up to go. As he swam out into the sun he said, "Remember, they had it coming!"

The heartfelt woman atop Montségur and the equally sincere fellow whiling away his days in Fanjeaux were never far from my thoughts as I wrote this book. Each one held an oversimplified (if genuine) position about the past; each one reminded me of the continuing fascination with heresy and the Albigensian Crusade. For her, I have attempted to write a history more poignant and moving than the most romantic of myths. For him, I try to offer an account more penetrating and incisive than blunt opinions (and modern analogies) allow. For both, I hope this is a narrative where drama never eclipses learning, where the individual is as vivid as the broadest scenario. As the imagination of readers becomes more precise in the reading of this book, I hope they see, hear, and feel a past world.

The Albigensian Crusade is one of the great pivotal moments in world history, if for no other reason than the fact that a very distinct Christian culture in the lands of the count of Toulouse was accused of being heretical by the Catholic Church, accused of being an apocalyptic plague threatening to destroy Christianity, and that these accusations led to an irrevocable moral obligation for mass murder. The crusade ushered genocide into the West, changing forever what it meant to be Christian, what it meant to be like Christ. The most holy war is a story of grand expeditions, heroic sieges, village insurgents, kings trampled to death, children set on fire, heaven and earth remade—it is the epic story of the battle for Christendom.

Woy Woy, New South Wales, Australia
Sunday, 26 August 2007

Acknowledgments

I would like to thank my agent, Jeff Gerecke, and my initial editor, Peter Ginna, for their abiding enthusiasm for this book. Timothy Bent edited my ultimate draft, and I am indebted to his tact and talent. Robert Moore, Michelle Garceau, Ussama Makdisi, Jennifer Baszile, and Anthony Peck read the entire manuscript and offered much help and insight. Christine Jordan, Sarah Keith, Nandini Chaturvedula, Sara Lipton, Amanda Hingst, Christopher Kurpiewski, Sandra Pott, Elspeth Carruthers, Hannah Johnson, William Bullman, and Amanda Power read various chapters with acumen. Edward Peters, Richard Landes, Marina Rustow, Tamer el-Leithy, Teófilo Ruiz, John Pryor, Walter Wakefield, Malcolm Barber, Malcolm Lambert, Ken Harl, Michael Frassetto, John Ward, John Arnold, Caterina Bruschi, Christine Caldwell Ames, Fiona Somerset, Caroline Smith, Julien Théry, Paul Cobb, and Rachel Mercer shared scholarhip and answered questions. As I was writing this book the Andrew W. Mellon Foundation awarded me a New Directions Fellowship to study Arabic and medieval Islamic culture. I am (as is my work) more thoughtful and nuanced on account of this extraordinary generosity. Alison MacDonald and Jandal Belahnine offered friendship and hospitality when parts of this book were written in Essaouira in Morocco. Joellyn Ausanka deftly oversaw the final editing. My mother, Veronica Seckold, was always encouraging. Margaret and Eva Garb have made me smarter and happier over the past three years, and, as they like to remind me, this book could not have been written without them.

Mary Douglas died just as I was finishing this book. She is one of the two great influences on my life as a scholar. The other is William Jordan. This book is dedicated to them in gratitude and affection.

Dramatis Personae

Innocent III (Lotario di Segni) (1160/61–1216): Elected pope in 1198 and exhorted Christian knights to expunge the *Provinciales heretici*, "Provençal heretics," from the lands of the count of Toulouse in a mighty crusade in 1208. He envisioned himself "below God but above man, less than God but greater than man, who judges all things but who no one judges." The greatest (for good and bad) pope in the Middle Ages.

Folc de Maselha, bishop of Toulouse (1150–1231): Cistercian monk, once married and a notable (if rather mediocre) troubadour, who was elected bishop of Toulouse in 1205.

Dominic (Domingo) de Guzmán (c. 1170–1221): Castilian founder of the Order of Friars Preachers in Toulouse in 1216. These first "Dominicans" (only sixteen) preached against the heretics in the lands of the count of Toulouse.

Bernart de Caux (d. 1251): Dominican inquisitor (perhaps from around Carcassonne) who conducted the largest medieval inquisition (almost six thousand people) from 1245 to 1246 in Toulouse. His body was exhumed in 1281 and reburied beneath a grander tomb so that more pilgrims could visit this "hammer of heretics."

Peire de Castelnau (d. 1208): Cistercian monk, papal legate to *Provincia*, all too easily murdered beside the Rhône River.

Arnau Amalric, abbot of Cîteaux, archbishop (and duke) of Narbonne (d. 1225): Catalan Cistercian monk, papal legate to *Provincia*, ardent leader of the Albigensian Crusade, archbishop of Narbonne in 1212, and who, toward the end of his life, adopted a singularly ambivalent attitude to the most holy war on heresy.

Master Milo (d. 1209): Notary to Innocent III and appointed as papal legate to *Provincia* in March 1209. He was to be the subservient "instrument" of Arnau Amalric.

Master Thedisius, priest and canon of the cathedral of Genoa, bishop of Agde (d. after 1218): Assistant to Milo and appointed legate (and "instrument") when Milo died in December 1209. He became bishop of Agde in 1215 and gave a fierce sermon against the *Provinciales heretici* at the Fourth Lateran Council.

Pierre des Vaux-de-Cernay (c. 1190–d. after 1218): French Cistercian monk who witnessed much of the Albigensian Crusade until 1218 and wrote a *Historia Albigensis* of the crusade.

Guy, abbot of des Vaux-de-Cernay, bishop of Carcassonne (d. 1223): Cistercian monk, uncle of Pierre des Vaux-de-Cernay, and elected bishop of Carcassonne in 1212. He preached the crusade against the "Albigensians" every winter in northern France.

Guilhem, *capellanus* (chaplain) of Puylauren (c. 1200–d. after 1276): In the last years of his life he wrote a chronicle of the crusade so that all persons (high, middle, and low) "may gain understanding of the judgments of God."

Piero di Benevento, cardinal-deacon of Santa Maria in Aquiro (d. 1221): Appointed legate *a latere* in January 1214 by Innocent III.

Honorius III (Cenci Savelli) (d. 1227): Elected pope in 1216, approved three new orders (Dominicans in 1216, Franciscans in 1223, and Carmelites in 1226), and vigorously pursued the most holy war.

Konrad von Urach, abbot of Cîteaux, cardinal-bishop of Porto (c. 1180–1227): Appointed legate to France and *Provincia* in December 1219. He declined the papal throne in 1227.

Romanus Frangipani, cardinal-deacon of Sant' Angelo (d. 1243): Appointed legate *a latere* to both France and *Provincia* by Honorius III in 1225.

Gregory IX (Ugolino, Di Segni) (c. 1170–1241): Elected pope in 1227 and, worried about heresy spreading in France and resurfacing in *Provincia*, asked the Dominicans in 1233 to undertake *inquisitiones heretice pravitatis*, "inquisitions into heretical depravity."

Simon de Montfort (c. 1165–1218): Lord of Montfort l'Amaury in the Ile de France and heir to the English earldom of Leicester through his mother. A lord of moderate means and sanctimonious manner and an appalled participant in the Fourth Crusade, he was acclaimed leader of the most holy war in 1209. As the Athlete of Christ he pursued the crusade with such astounding vigor and talent that by 1215 he styled himself "duke of Narbonne, count of Toulouse, count of Leicester, viscount of Béziers and Carcassonne, and lord of Montfort."

Alice de Montmorency (d. 1221): Wife of Simon de Montfort and often as energetic as her husband in conducting the crusade. Her brother Matthieu was a crusader in the summer of 1215 and helped dismantle the walls of Toulouse.

Guy de Montfort (d. 1228): Younger brother of Simon de Montfort and equally disgusted with the Fourth Crusade. He returned from the Holy Land (after marrying Héloïse de Ibelin) in 1211 and joined his brother in cleansing the Biterrois, Carcassès, Albigeois, and Toulousain of heretics.

Amaury de Montfort (d. 1241): Incompetent and uninspiring eldest son of Simon de Montfort. He succeeded his father in 1218 and conducted the holy war in a determinedly woeful manner. Easily manipulated by the pope, the count of Toulouse, and the king of France.

Baudouin de Toulouse (d. 1214): Younger brother of Raimon VI, count of Toulouse, was raised in France and returned only in 1194. He joined the crusaders the summer of 1211 and was a patron of the troubadour Guilhem de Tudela.

The Counts of Toulouse, Viscounts of Béziers-Carcassonne, Viscounts of Narbonne, and Counts of Foix

Raimon V, count of Toulouse (d. 1194): Became count of Toulouse in 1148 and fought wars with the kings of England and Aragon and the counts of Provence for the next half century. Clever and politically adroit, he was nevertheless unable to persuade popes and other Church intellectuals that his lands were not swarming with the little foxes of heresy.

Raimon VI, count of Toulouse (1156–1222): Succeeded his father as count in 1194 and similarly could not dissuade the Church that his villages and towns were not diseased with heresy. Accused (unfairly) of orchestrating the murder of Peire de Castelnau, he became the target of an apocalyptic holy war in 1208. He quickly signed himself with the cross and became a crusader in 1209. In 1211 he was attacked by Simon de Montfort and the crusaders. Innocent III stripped him of his lands in 1215. He continued fighting the crusaders until his death. He played politics relatively well (he was married five times), but, somewhat surprisingly, his bellicose temperament was as brittle as his martial skills were mundane.

Raimon VII, count of Toulouse (1197–1249): "The brave young count, who verdantly renews the world, who brilliantly colors the darkness with gold," was the eldest son of Raimon VI and his fourth wife, Joanna, sister of Richard the Lionheart, king of England. He was not formally recognized as count of Toulouse by the Church and the king of France until 1229. After 1216 he fought brilliantly successful campaigns against the crusaders, although he eventually surrendered to the French king. At first he despised the Dominican inquisitors, but after 1243 he actively supported them.

Raimon Roger Trencavel, viscount of Béziers and Carcassonne (1185–1209): Nephew of Raimon VI, count of Toulouse, his lands became the focus of the crusade after his uncle yielded to Christ in 1209. An excitable if lackluster leader who swiftly descended into gloomy despondency and death.

Raimon II Trencavel (1207–after 1263): Son of Raimon Roger Trencavel, he spent most of his life in exile at the Aragonese court. He was briefly viscount of Béziers and Carcassonne between 1224 and 1226. In 1240 he launched an ill-conceived rebellion against French rule, and in 1247 he renounced all rights to his familial territories.

Raimon Roger, count of Foix (d. 1222): Simon de Montfort invaded his lands in 1210, and from then until his death he fought with unbridled savagery against the crusaders. He died from an ulcer while besieging Mirepoix.

Roger Bernart, count of Foix (d. 1241): Attacked the crusaders as relentlessly (if not as viciously) as did his father.

*The Kings of France, Count-Kings of Barcelona-Aragon,
and Kings of England*

Philip II Augustus, king of France (1165–1223): Vapidly campaigned with Richard the Lionheart in the Holy Land during the Third Crusade in 1191. In 1208 he was reluctant to commit himself to the crusade against the count of Toulouse, despite repeated appeals from Innocent III. He did allow his son Louis to go on crusade into the south in 1215 and 1219. He efficiently reorganized the bureaucratic structures of France and reconquered Normandy from John, king of England, in 1204. Toward the end of his life he took more interest in the holy war on heresy.

Louis VIII, king of France (1187–1226): As a prince he undertook two holy expeditions, and as king he led a great army into the "Albigensian lands" in 1226. During the siege of Avignon he became ill and died journeying back to France. Louis was mostly a mediocrity (and he was certainly a rather hapless commander), but his royal crusades between the Garonne and the Rhône helped transform the kingdom of France into the kingdom of Christ.

Louis IX, king of France (1214–1270): He was twelve years old when his father died and his mother, Blanche of Castile, became the regent of France. In 1229 (and only two weeks before his fifteenth birthday) he accepted the surrender of the thirty-one-year-old Raimon VII, count of Toulouse. He grew to be a man obsessed with imitating Christ (which frequently made him something of a pious prude). In 1248 (after extraordinary preparations) he went on crusade to the eastern Mediterranean; he failed miserably. In 1270 he again went on crusade; he again failed miserably, painfully dying of dysentery outside Tunis. He was canonized in 1297.

Pere II, count of Barcelona and king of Aragon (1174–1213): He was crowned king by Innocent III in Rome in 1204, promising "to defend the Catholic faith and persecute heretical depravity" as a vassal of the Church. Charismatic, talented in war, and something of a ladies' man, he won a great Christian victory over the grand army of the Almohad Caliph Muhammad al-Nasir on the Andalusian plain of Las Navas de Tolosa in 1212. A year later he crossed the Pyrénées with "the flower of Catalonia and great noble warriors from Aragon" to destroy Simon de Montfort. He had always loathed the Frenchman and distrusted the ambitions of the French crusaders.

John, king of England (1167–1216): His sister was the mother of Raimon VII and he was always sympathetic (if indolent) to his nephew's plight. He too distrusted Simon de Montfort as the crusade was fought right up to (and sometimes just over into) the lands belonging to the English crown in the Agen and Périgord. He promised to aid Pere II and Raimon VII in 1213, but "a great quantity of wind in England" conveniently delayed him. However, he did fund and support both Raimons in exile.

The Troubadours

Guilhem de Tudela (d. after 1223): "He is a cleric from Navarre, who grew up in Tudela then he moved to Montauban," he sang about himself at the beginning of the *canso* (song) he started singing about the crusade around 1218. "In his twelfth year he left [Montauban] because of the destruction he

saw and divined in geomancy. He had read the signs for a long time!"
Although supportive of the crusade, he was no crude panegyrist. Baudouin
de Toulouse was his sometime patron (he gave him a canonry at Bourg
Saint-Antonin in 1211 or 1212), and the loyalties of this lord partially shaped
his outlook. Nevertheless, there was much moral and metaphoric ambiguity in his attitude to the crusaders. He was always trying to sing his way
through events that seemed dictated by a providence too brutal to be
completely benign. He ended the song at the moment Pere II marched
against Simon de Montfort in 1213.

The Anonymous Troubadour (d. 1229): In the final years of the crusade
this unknown troubadour started singing where Guilhem de Tudela ended
his song. He was most likely a soldier of Toulouse or Foix and, after twenty
years of holy war, was furious. He hated the "French from France" and, less
impressed with fate as a despot, saw all terror emanating from Simon de
Montfort. He was intensely nostalgic about the world destroyed by the
crusade. This rage and sentimentality were transformed into sublime and
moving poetry. He ended the song just before Prince Louis besieged
Toulouse in 1219. Guilhem de Tudela's *canso* was transformed by the
anonymous troubadour into one of the great poems of the Middle Ages.

1. The Trencavel

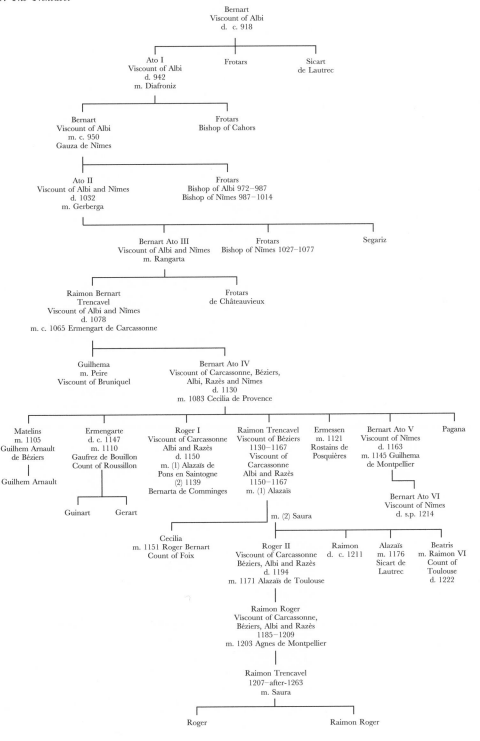

Bernart
Viscount of Albi
d. c. 918

Ato I
Viscount of Albi
d. 942
m. Diafroniz

Frotars

Sicart
de Lautrec

Bernart
Viscount of Albi
m. c. 950
Gauza de Nîmes

Frotars
Bishop of Cahors

Ato II
Viscount of Albi and Nîmes
d. 1032
m. Gerberga

Frotars
Bishop of Albi 972−987
Bishop of Nîmes 987−1014

Bernart Ato III
Viscount of Albi and Nîmes
m. Rangarta

Frotars
Bishop of Nîmes 1027−1077

Segariz

Raimon Bernart
Trencavel
Viscount of Albi and Nîmes
d. 1078
m. c. 1065 Ermengart de Carcassonne

Frotars
de Châteauvieux

Guilhema
m. Peire
Viscount of Bruniquel

Bernart Ato IV
Viscount of Carcassonne, Béziers,
Albi, Razès and Nîmes
d. 1130
m. 1083 Cecilia de Provence

Matelins
m. 1105
Guilhem Arnault
de Béziers

Guilhem Arnault

Ermengarte
d. c. 1147
m. 1110
Gaufrez de Bouillon
Count of Roussillon

Guinart   Gerart

Roger I
Viscount of Carcassonne
Albi and Razès
d. 1150
m. (1) Alazaïs de
Pons en Saintogne
(2) 1139
Bernarta de Comminges

Raimon Trencavel
Viscount of Béziers
1130−1167
Viscount of
Carcassonne
Albi and Razès
1150−1167
m. (1) Alazaïs

m. (2) Saura

Ermessen
m. 1121
Rostains de
Posquières

Bernart Ato V
Viscount of Nîmes
d. 1163
m. 1145 Guilhema
de Montpellier

Bernart Ato VI
Viscount of Nîmes
d. s.p. 1214

Pagana

Cecilia
m. 1151 Roger Bernart
Count of Foix

Roger II
Viscount of Carcassonne
Béziers, Albi and Razès
d. 1194
m. 1171 Alazaïs de Toulouse

Raimon
d. c. 1211

Alazaïs
m. 1176
Sicart de
Lautrec

Beatris
m. Raimon VI
Count of
Toulouse
d. 1222

Raimon Roger
Viscount of Carcassonne,
Béziers, Albi and Razès
1185−1209
m. 1203 Agnes de Montpellier

Raimon Trencavel
1207−after-1263
m. Saura

Roger

Raimon Roger

2. *The Family of Simon de Montfort*

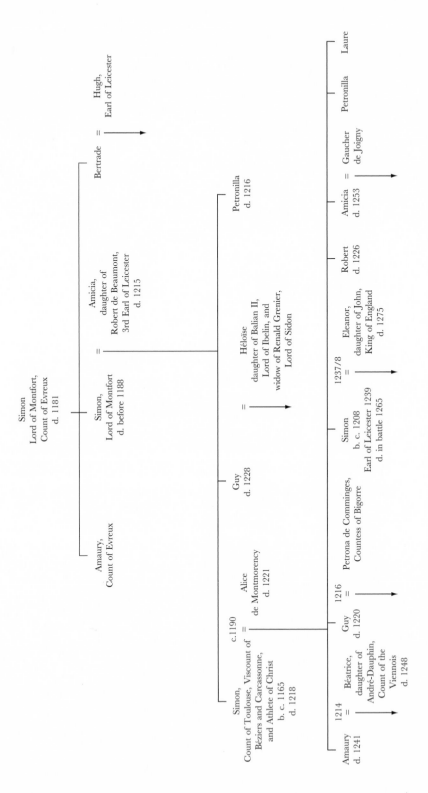

Simon
Lord of Montfort,
Count of Evreux
d. 1181

Amaury,
Count of Evreux

Simon,
Lord of Montfort
d. before 1188

=

Amicia,
daughter of
Robert de Beaumont,
3rd Earl of Leicester
d. 1215

Bertrade
=
Hugh,
Earl of Leicester

Simon,
Count of Toulouse, Viscount of
Béziers and Carcassonne,
and Athlete of Christ
b. c. 1165
d. 1218

c.1190
=
Alice
de Montmorency
d. 1221

Guy
d. 1228

=

Héloïse
daughter of Balian II,
Lord of Ibelin, and
widow of Renald Grenier,
Lord of Sidon

Petronilla
d. 1216

Amaury
d. 1241

1214
=
Béatrice,
daughter of
André-Dauphin,
Count of the
Viennois
d. 1248

Guy
d. 1220

1216
=
Petrona de Comminges,
Countess of Bigorre

Simon,
b. c. 1208
Earl of Leicester 1239
d. in battle 1265

1237/8
=
Eleanor,
daughter of John,
King of England
d. 1275

Robert
d. 1226

Amicia
d. 1253
=
Gaucher
de Joigny

Petronilla

Laure

3. The Counts of Foix and the Counts of Comminges

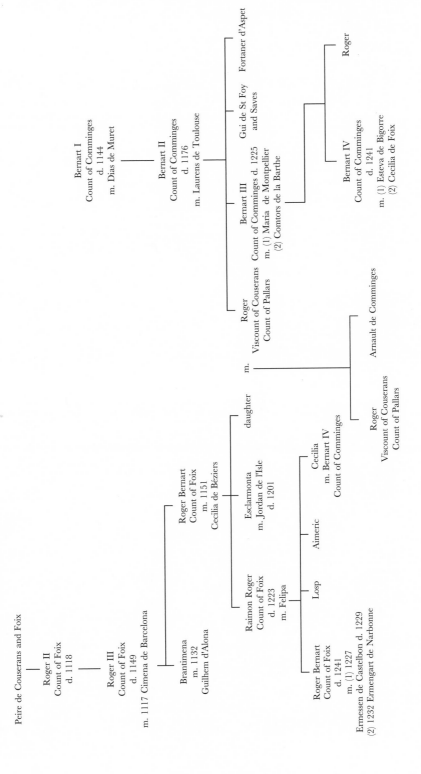

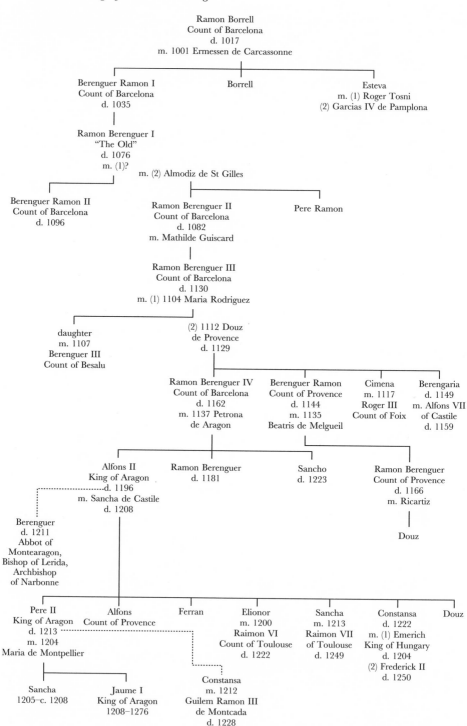

5. *The Counts of Toulouse*

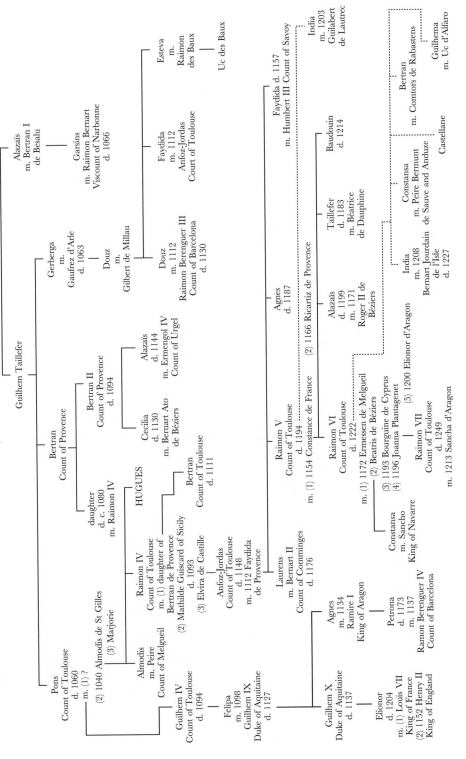

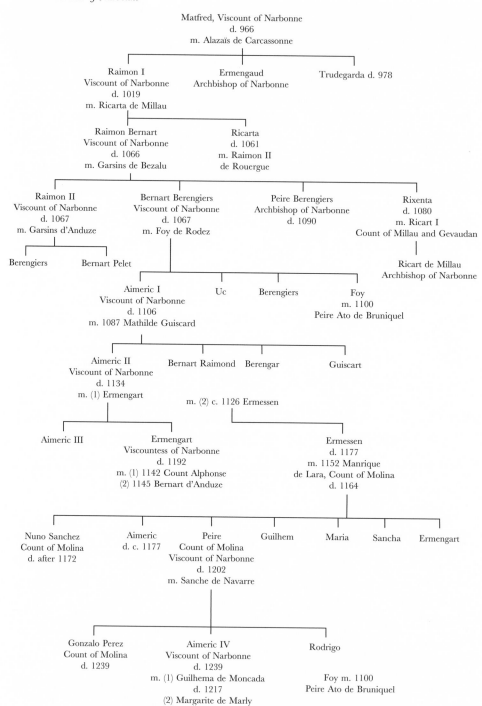

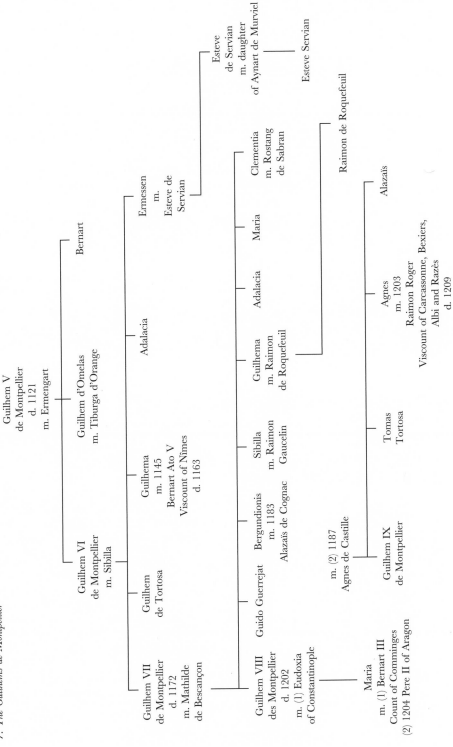

7. *The Guilhems de Montpellier*

Guilhem V
de Montpellier
d. 1121
m. Ermengart

Bernart

Guilhem VI
de Montpellier
m. Sibilla

Guilhem d'Omelas
m. Tiburga d'Orange

Ermessen
m.
Esteve de
Servian

Esteve
de Servian
m. daughter
of Aynart de Murviel

Esteve Servian

Guilhem VII
de Montpellier
d. 1172
m. Mathilde
de Bescançon

Guilhem
de Tortosa

Guilhema
m. 1145
Bernart Ato V
Viscount of Nîmes
d. 1163

Adalacia

Clementia
m. Rostang
de Sabran

Raimon de Roquefeuil

Guilhem VIII
des Montpellier
d. 1202
m. (1) Eudoxia
of Constantinople

Guido Guerrejat

Bergundionis
m. 1183
Alazaïs de Cognac

Sibilla
m. Raimon
Gaucelin

Guilhema
m. Raimon
de Roquefeuil

Adalacia

Maria

Alazaïs

m. (2) 1187
Agnes de Castille

Tomas
Tortosa

Guilhem IX
de Montpellier

Agnes
m. 1203
Raimon Roger
Viscount of Carcassonne, Bexiers,
Albi and Razès
d. 1209

Maria
m. (1) Bernart III
Count of Comminges
(2) 1204 Pere II of Aragon

A Most Holy War

1

"Cousin, do not be afraid," a dead boy told an eleven-year-old girl when he appeared in her house at Beaucaire one night in July 1211. "I come to you by divine permission, drawn by my old abundant affection for you." Three to five days earlier the lad, very much alive, was on his way to visit the little girl when he was attacked and mortally wounded. "In the face of death," he forgave his murderer and repented through confession. "I am allowed to speak to you alone," the ghost now lovingly said to the girl, "and to transmit my replies to others through you." The girl's parents, awake in the same room, were curious about the lively conversation their daughter was having with herself. "Don't you see my cousin Guilhem, who died just recently?" said the girl. The parents crossed themselves in stunned amazement. Guilhem, after that night, visited quite regularly (once with a horned demon spitting fire but most often with his guardian angel, Michael). Indeed, he soon became something of a local oracle, answering questions through his cousin. All this secondhand quizzing was cut short when a pious and learned priest asked if he could talk directly to the revenant. "Why draw things out?" The priest, chasing after the "more abstruse secrets of divine wisdom," listened to a great many things about the horror of death, the torments of purgatory, the ubiquitous sheen of angels—and yet, when all was said and done, he discovered only one specific fact about the mind and mood of God that summer. "Nothing," the dead boy fervently declared, "had pleased God so much" as the "death and extermination of the Albigensians!"[1]

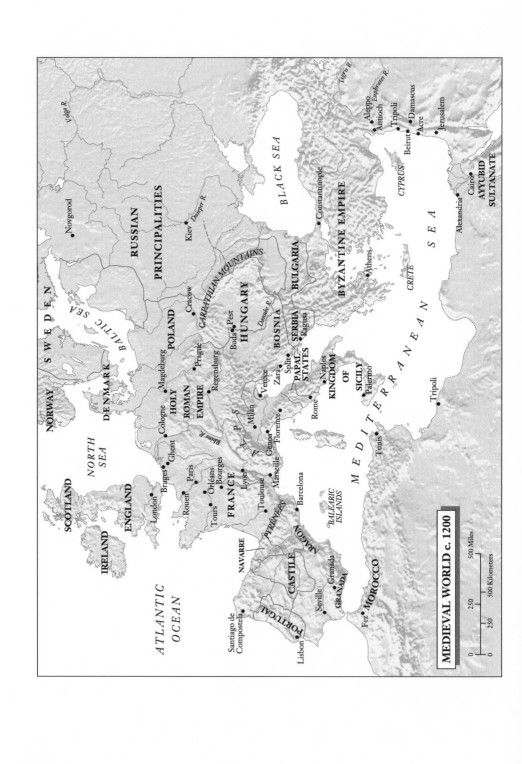

MEDIEVAL WORLD c. 1200

ATLANTIC
OCEAN

NORTH
SEA

SCOTLAND

IRELAND

ENGLAND

London

NORWAY

SWEDEN

DENMARK

BALTIC SEA

RUSSIAN
PRINCIPALITIES

Novgorod

Volga R.

Dnieper R.

Kiev

CARPATHIAN MOUNTAINS

POLAND

Cracow

Magdeburg

Cologne

HOLY
ROMAN
EMPIRE

Prague

Regensburg

HUNGARY

Buda
Pest

Danube R.

BOSNIA

SERBIA

BULGARIA

BLACK SEA

Constantinople

BYZANTINE EMPIRE

Athens

Bruges
Ghent

Paris

Rouen

Orléans
Tours

Bourges

FRANCE

Lyon

Milan

Florence

Genoa

Venice

Zara

Split

Ragusa

PAPAL
STATES

Rome

Naples

KINGDOM
OF
SICILY

Palermo

CRETE

MEDITERRANEAN
SEA

Rhine R.

ALPS

Marseille

Toulouse

PROVENCE

PYRENEES

NAVARRE

Barcelona

ARAGON

CASTILE

Seville

Granada

GRANADA

BALEARIC
ISLANDS

Tunis

Tripoli

Santiago de
Compostela

PORTUGAL

Lisbon

MOROCCO

Fez

Tigris R.

Euphrates R.

Aleppo
Antioch

Tripoli

Damascus

Beirut

Acre

Jerusalem

CYPRUS

Cairo

AYYUBID
SULTANATE

Alexandria

0   250   500 Miles

0   250   500 Kilometers

"Let hearts be awed," wrote Gervase of Tilbury, marshal of Arles, about Guilhem's marvelous appearance two or three years after the fact, "let minds be amazed, let limbs tremble at the wonder of it!"[2] Yet, even with the insight of the dead rewritten through the hindsight of the living, neither ghost nor man could have guessed that the divine pleasure of 1211, a holy ardor unleashed three years earlier, when the pope proclaimed a crusade against the heretics in the lands of the count of Toulouse, was only the beginning of a war that would last, from start to finish, twenty-one years. The Albigensian Crusade, a series of armed pilgrimages in which Christians were guaranteed salvation through the killing of other Christians, savagely reshaped not just the specific holiness flourishing between the Garonne and Rhône Rivers but, and this is no exaggeration, it reconfigured the relationship of divinity and humanity throughout Christendom— indeed, it redefined Christendom itself. What it meant to be a Christian (and, in a certain sense, Jewish or Muslim) would never be the same again. The Albigensian Crusade was a holy war unlike any other before it, a great medieval drama as spiritually subtle as it was crudely brutal and, in its own bloody sibylline way, a terrible prediction of so much sacred violence in the world for the next millennium.[3]

Three years before the dead boy spoke to his cousin—and not all that far from where the lad was killed—a papal legate was murdered. It happened just before sunrise on Monday, 14 January 1208. The Cistercian monk Peire de Castelnau, legate of Pope Innocent III, was about to cross the Rhône near Saint-Gilles when "a squire with an evil heart" trotted up behind and, as the troubadour Guilhem de Tudela sang two years later in his great *canso* (song) on the crusade, "pushed a sharp sword into his spine and killed him." The legate, falling from his pacing mule into the riverine mud, raised his hands to heaven, forgave his murderer, and, receiving communion, died "as the day was dawning." The nameless assassin, "hoping to win the approval of the count [of Toulouse]," escaped on his swift horse to Beaucaire. "When the pope heard of his legate's death," Guilhem de Tudela dryly observed, "you can be sure he wasn't pleased!" Innocent III, servant of the servants of God, "grabbed his chin in anger," yelled an anathema as he crushed out a burning candle and then, "as deliberately as a needle-stitch," chose a course of action that would leave many brave men dead, "their entrails pouring out," and many young girls stripped raw, "with neither covering nor robe." The pope, convinced that all the villages and towns "from beyond Montpellier to Bordeaux" were poisoned by heresy, persuaded that Raimon VI, count of Toulouse, was Peire de Castelnau's killer, and vilifying the count as a protector of heretics, thieves, and murderers, called upon all knights and barons to be "signed with the cross," to be like angels with swords at sunrise, and so "drive the heretics out from amongst the virtuous" in a great crusade.[4]

The youthful Cistercian historian Pierre des Vaux-de-Cernay could, a decade later, "give no better or more authentic account" of the legate's murder, and the fateful papal response, than to simply copy the passionate, apocalyptic, and belligerent letter that Innocent III sent from Rome to six ecclesiastical provinces (Narbonne, Arles, Embrun, Aix, Vienne, Lyon) and (slightly altered) to the king of France, Philip II Augustus, on Monday, 10 March 1208.[5] "News has reached us of a cruel deed," the letter solemnly began, "which must surely bring grief on the whole Church." Peire de Castelnau, although aware "the Devil [had] roused his minister, the count of Toulouse," against him was, despite such antipathy, visiting Raimon VI at Saint-Gilles (a town belonging to the count and from which his family had once derived their name). The legate wanted "complete satisfaction" on a series of accusations from the previous April when, after a long and bitter quarrel, he had excommunicated the count for failing to uproot heresy and for supporting mercenaries. Raimon VI "at one moment seemed truthful and compliant," the pope explained, "while at the next he became deceitful and obdurate," and so the legatine mission, frustrated and fearful, quit Saint-Gilles. "Thereupon the count of Toulouse publicly threatened them with death," accused Innocent III, "and dispatched his accomplices to lay a carefully chosen ambush." Peire de Castelnau, tempting fate like a martyr that chilly morning on the Rhône, expressed no surprise when "one of those mercenaries of Satan, brandishing his lance, wounded him from behind between the ribs." As the legate died he murmured, over and over, "May God forgive you, even as I forgive you."[6]

"Forward then soldiers of Christ! Forward, brave recruits to the Christian army! Let the universal cry of grief of the Holy Church arouse you," exhorted the pope. Peire de Castelnau was transformed (by torturous papal prose) into Jesus Christ; his damp death on the Rhône (by a lance, not a sword) became the redemptive crucifixion on Golgotha; his sacrifice a sign to a corrupt generation. Innocent III, while acknowledging that Raimon VI's guilt for the murder was largely circumstantial, nevertheless thought there was enough evidence—not least "other outrageous actions which have become known to us"—to make all archbishops and bishops publicly declare the count anathematized. All men and women "who are tied to the count of Toulouse by any kind of oath" were to be "released from that oath by our apostolic authority." Crucial, though, was the radical permission for "any Catholic person (provided the rights of the superior lord are respected) to not only proceed against the count of Toulouse in person but also to occupy and possess his lands," in the expectation that the new occupier would "purge those lands of heresy." The only proof Raimon VI could give of sincere repentance for his "many great crimes," and so be reconciled to the Church, was to "expel the followers of heresy from the whole of his dominions." Until that time, all those signed with the cross, the *crucesignati*, "in the name of the God of peace and love" and with "our promise of remission of sins," must strenuously "root out perfidious heresy" and purify the land. "Attack the followers of heresy more fearlessly than even the Saracens," was Innocent III's thundering conclusion, "since heretics are more evil!"[7]

11

ROUND 1030, RODULFUS Glaber, a rather eccentric and somewhat cranky Benedictine monk in his early fifties, writing a grand history "of what happened in the four parts of the globe" in the tiny Burgundian abbey of Saint-Germaine-d'Auxerre, vividly remembered that "just before the third year after the millennium, throughout the whole world, but most especially in Italy and Gaul, men began to reconstruct churches." It was as if "the whole world were shaking itself free, shrugging off the burden of the past, and cladding itself everywhere in a white mantle of churches." This wondrous recollection of temporal impurities being washed away through limestone and mortar did, nevertheless, possess a darker and more apocalyptic significance. In this shimmering white-clothed landscape, hiding behind all those new church columns were, after centuries of silence, insidious demonic heretics. "All this accords with the prophecy of Saint John, who said that the Devil would be freed after a thousand years." The lonely Benedictine was inspired by all the paradoxical, seemingly contradictory, elements that make a millennial vision. No matter what he read, no matter what he heard, he saw a terrible and exhilarating pattern in all events. The Fatimid Caliph, deceived by the Jews of Orléans, destroyed the Holy Sepulchre in Jerusalem; Vesuvius exploded in sulfuric fire; young women and grown sons, starved into savagery, devoured babies and mothers; in Orléans a crucifix softly wept; and a poor man named Leutard, after dreaming that bees had swarmed into his body "through nature's secret orifices," woke up a heretic.[1] Rodulfus

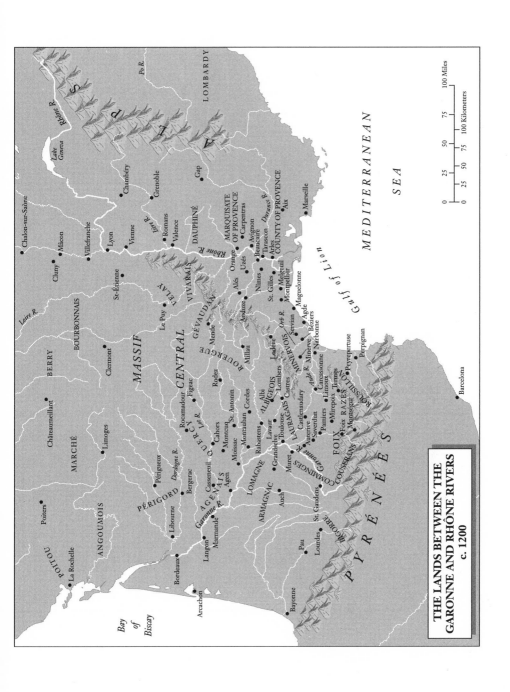

THE LANDS BETWEEN THE GARONNE AND RHÔNE RIVERS

c. 1200

Glaber wanted the world to be purified and yet, at the same time, he knew that such purity could come about only through famine, war, destruction and, in a new chiliastic twist, "having long flourished in secret," an evil abundance of heretics.[2]

Rodulfus Glaber was arguably the first of a strange, disparate, and small group of eleventh-century Latin Christian intellectuals writing (and worrying) about heresy for the first time since Late Antiquity. In 1022, for instance, "Manicheans were discovered and destroyed at Toulouse," noted the Benedictine Ademar of Chabannes in the chronicle he wrote at the abbey of Saint-Cybard in Angoulême (and who in 1010, at the age of twenty, saw a great crucifix weeping in the southern night sky). These Toulousain heretics, far from being historically alone, were the heirs of the third-century dualist heresiarch Mani and the corrupt allies of other "messengers of the Antichrist who appeared in various parts of the West."[3] The disturbing problem about this new intellectual awareness of heresy—and a question that must be asked, even if the answer remains elusive—is whether such heterodoxy actually existed independently of the apocalyptic (and so historical) necessity of populating the world with heretics from the millennium onward. "There must be heresies," Rodulfus Glaber agreed with (and quoted) Saint Paul, so "that they who are of the Faith may be proved."[4] The apparent emergence of heresy in the eleventh century was, more than anything else, the initial articulation of a learned conceit that saw all heretics as linked to each other through time and space, as hellish individuals connected to the divinely marvelous, and as an essential Christian phenomenon perpetually tinged with an apocalyptic hue. This intense eschatological vision shaping the histories and chronicles of some rather quirky intellectuals in the eleventh century would, within two hundred years, become the absolute heresiological truth inflaming thousands of crusaders.

"Most beloved brethren," preached Pope Urban II outside the city of Clermont (in the Auvergne by the thin Tretaine River) on Tuesday, 27 November 1095, "by God's permission placed over the whole world with the papal crown," to His servants an admonition, to His sons an exhortation. His servants were the "salt of the earth" who preserved the faithful with measured saltiness, so that His sons "might not be rotten with sins and stink whenever the Lord might wish to exhort them." God tossed the maggoty man on the dung heap. The right pinch of salt was "wise, provident, temperate, learned, peace-making, truth-seeking, pious, just, equitable, pure." Sadly, the world was rancid with violent iniquities, "perhaps because of the weakness of your justice," perhaps the impurity of your salt—either way, it needed purification through pacification. "The Truce, as it is commonly called"—warfare suspended from Wednesday evening to Monday morning, all violence banned on holy days—"must be renewed." Any person who broke the Truce would be excommunicated. "O, sons of God"—and suddenly, with an apocalyptic jolt, the pope shifted from divine disapproval to divine invitation, from the Massif Central to the eastern Mediterranean, from a limited truce to a sweeping expedition. O Sons of God, "you must help your brothers living in the East, who need your aid for which they have already cried out many times!" The Turks (Seljuqs) have conquered Christian lands (Byzantine Empire) from *Romania* (Anatolia) to the Arm of Saint George (Bosporus). O Sons of God, no matter your status, no matter your wealth, "strive to help expel that wicked race from Christian lands before it is too late!" All who went on this expedition were granted the remission of sins. "Let those who previously waged private war improperly against the faithful go against the infidels in a war that should be started now and should end in victory! Let those who were once robbers now become soldiers of Christ! Let those who formerly fought against their brothers and relatives now fight justly against barbarians! Let those who were once mercenaries for a few shillings now obtain eternal rewards!" Go forth; go forth, "with the Lord going before you."[5]

This somewhat awkward sermon, in the words and rhythms recollected by the chronicler Fulcher of Chartres five years later, elicited such fierce passions among those who heard it and those who heard of it that roughly seven thousand horsemen, thirty thousand footmen, and twenty to sixty thousand other persons ventured upon this holy expedition—an *expeditio*, a *peregrinatio*, an *iter*, now known as the First Crusade. The bellicose pilgrims embroidered the symbol of the cross on their clothing as a sign of victory. "They imprinted the ideal so that they might attain the reality of the ideal."[6] Four years, three thousand kilometers (by foot, by horse), six sieges, two visions of the dead, one holy lance (unearthed), and countless penitential torments later, the soldiers of Christ, ragged and exhausted, captured Fatimid Jerusalem on Friday, 15 July 1099.[7] The holy expedition, pushed and prodded along by apocalyptic anger and utopian exhilaration, metamorphosed into a holy war following "in the footsteps of Christ"—where each step, more sanguine than the last, ultimately led to the violent cleansing of His city and sepulchre. "In our time," wrote the Benedictine historian Guibert, abbot of Nogent, twelve years after the capture of Jerusalem, "God has instituted holy warfare so that the knightly order and the errant mob," rather than engaging in mutual slaughter, "might find a new way of deserving salvation."[8] More than a century later—and three more expeditions to the eastern Mediterranean (the Second,

Third, and Fourth Crusades)—what it meant to be a warrior pilgrim who journeyed to fight "where He walked in bodily form" was a familiar social and moral category. Yet, the first martial pilgrimage to fight Christians within Christendom in 1209 was surprisingly similar to the first armed expedition to the Holy Land in 1096: each one, though a peregrination based on precedent, was an excursion into chiliastic unpredictability.

Corpses, sealed in coffins or in tarred casks, commonly drifted down the Rhône in the early thirteenth century and, though tormented by crosscurrents where the river forks below Beaucaire, so that a few occasionally sailed aimlessly past Saint-Gilles into the Mediterranean, most swam into the spiraling waters just beyond Arles, where, twirling in ever wider circles, they were eventually thrown onto the riverbank (exactly as their relatives intended) for burial in the cemetery of "the Elysian Field," Aliscans.[9] The Garonne, lacking such predictable currents, was slower, more sullen, and, though easily shocked into flooding when the snows melted in the Pyrénées, sluggish with shifting sediment, fallen trees, and mud slabs clotted with offal and blood from the butchers and tanners of Toulouse. Between these two rivers, one dissolving in the Atlantic, the other in the Mediterranean, lay a vast region framed by the Massif Central in the northeast and the Pyrénées in the southwest. A great thick ribbon of alluvial plains, chalky plateaus, saline marshes, and granite mountains that, by the end of the thirteenth century, was known as Languedoc but, during the decades of the crusade, was labeled *Provincia* by the papacy and, by adapting fourteenth-century toponyms, is called *Occitania* by modern scholars.

Provinicia derived from what was thought to have been the Roman imperial province of *Gallia Narbonensis* (and, to a lesser extent, the province of *Gallia Lugdunensis*). It absorbed, as a consequence, all of the ecclesiastical province of Narbonne (containing the bishoprics of Toulouse, Carcassonne, Elne, Béziers, Agde, Lodève, Maguelonne, Nîmes, and Uzès), some of Bourges (Albi, Cahors, and Rodez), elements of Arles (Avignon and Orange), with bits of Auch (Couserans), Vienne (Viviers), and Bordeaux (Agenais).[10] It marked out an entity that, despite the theoretical suzerainty of the French kings to large parts of it, was not northern *Francia* or *Gallia*, in other words, was not France. Its inhabitants were *Provinciales* rather than *Francigenae*. Its "mother tongue" was *lenga d'oc* (from which the French derived Languedoc) rather than *langue d'oïl*; each linguistic tag a variation on the affirmative particle *oc* or *oïl*. This *materna lingua* was (in the modern designation adapted from *Occitania*) Occitan or (in the older cognomen adapted from *Provincia*) Provençal. Occitan was (still is) very similar to Catalan, somewhat like Castilian, and comparable to some northern Italian dialects. Famously, then and now, Provençal was the *lenga romana* or simply *roman* (as opposed to Latin) of the troubadours.[11] *Provincia*, somewhat confusingly, was also the name of the lower Rhône valley, especially the eastern side, where there was a marquisate of Provence and a county of Provence, the former possessed by the counts of Toulouse, the later belonging to the count-kings of Barcelona-Aragon; both required fealty to the Holy Roman Emperor.[12] *Provincia*, in the broad sense of "Province" rather than "Provence," embraced, with some give and take, what has become modern southern France, *le Midi de la France.*

A single tree, "with many branches and leaves, and miraculously large," was suffocating the whole earth in 1145. "I cannot travel anywhere," sang the sublime troubadour Marcabru, "without seeing two or three of its boughs." This tree, "grown tall and spreading in all directions," south over the Pyrénées, north through the lands of the count of Toulouse into Aquitaine, then along the western edge of the Massif Central into France, was so deep-rooted that no one could fell it—the root, unfortunately, was wickedness itself. The origin of the tree lay in "protected territory" and, though Marcabru never specified this region, the branches and leaves implicitly followed (and flourished alongside) the Garonne until, reaching Catalonia and France, they spread throughout the world. The only region along the river accused of being overgrown with malevolence, the only possible terrain where the tree had "established its entire greenery in it," was the territory of Anfoz Jordas, count of Toulouse.[13] This evil thrived in the Toulousain throughout the twelfth century, fervid and febrile, eventually poisoning all of *Provincia* with its infectious roots and shoots.[14] There was something grotesque, amorphous, and feculent about the valleys, mountains, and fields caught between the Garonne and the Rhône. Dante Alighieri recalled this Provençal stew of filth and heresy when, in his early fourteenth-century *Commedia*, he compared the cemetery of Aliscans— and the squalid water swirling before it—to the stifling sepulchres of the arch-heretics in hell.[15] *Provincia* was an old corrupt space at the very heart of Europe. The pesthole perpetuating this corruption was the county of Toulouse. "The errors of the Albigensians," because of this fetid topography, "infected more than a thousand towns" and, without the "swords of the faithful" hacking it back, then unquestionably, argued the Rhineland Cistercian Caesarius of Heisterbach around 1220, "I think this infection would have corrupted the whole of Europe," and so all of Christendom.[16]

Rodulfus Glaber concluded the third book of his world history with a tale of demonic depravity seeping into France from the humid lands to the south. "About the year 1000," he recalled, "men of all the vainest frivolity" began to flood north "with perverted customs and dress, with armour and horse equipment badly put together." Quite shockingly, "they shaved their hair from half-way down their heads, going beardless like jongleurs." On their legs they wore "disgusting yellow boots and leggings." All of this fashion, in a leap from affectation to anarchy, proved these men "were entirely devoid of any law of faith or peace." "Alas," the Benedictine sighed, "the whole of the French people, until recently the most decent of all," refused to persecute these fancy men; instead, "they seized avidly on their abominable example, until at length everyone came to conform to their wickedness and infamy." Sadly, these frivolous trappings were, like the vain errors of heretics, "nothing more than the brand-marks of Satan." Rodulfus Glaber, horrified at the wicked behavior flourishing between (and poisoning the world beyond) the Massif Central and the Pyrénées, felt compelled to stigmatize it "with a few heroic verses." He scorned persons who mix "pleasure and debauchery and call them manners." He fretted about "tyrants with strange bodies" and no honor. He lamented faithless men who wore "clothes too short for them." Already in this bitter prose and poetry were characteristics that later authors associated (sometimes benignly, mostly belligerently) with *Provinciales*. Rodulfus Glaber even seemed to predict the future crusade against such sinners when he warned, with his usual apocalyptic fervor, that as soon as God's great pity no longer stalled His wrath, "Hell would engulf them in its frightful mouth."[17]

"Nowadays, however, with the changes in fashion brought by time," Gervase of Tilbury wrote two hundred years later in the second book of his world history, "the people of the province of Narbonne, men and women alike," and here he meant all those living between the Garonne and the Rhône, "wear very tight clothes in the manner of Spaniards and the Gascons." This sartorial anecdote was, as the marshal of Arles observed in his dedicatory preface to the Emperor Otto IV, "something for your hearing to refresh you in the midst of your worldly cares." The misanthropic millennialism of Rodulfus Glaber may have faded over the centuries, but the disturbing strangeness of Provençal clothing still gave "the impression that their bodies have not just been dressed in their clothes, but have actually been sewn into them." Gervase, in a narrative of more subtlety and power than the elegant (albeit serious) play of the courtier might suggest, knew the "sacred ears" of his imperial listener would instantly connect material appearance, no matter how whimsical, to spiritual attributes. This notion that all things in the world were forever proving the unbreakable intimacy of matter and spirit, that the perceptible was always revealing the imperceptible, underscored all the historical evidence that the marshal of Arles collected and collated "from the books of ancient authors or established from eye-witness testimony."[18] There was no dualism in the Christian cosmos; there was no separation of body and soul; there was no chasm between heaven and earth. The only persons disagreeing with this absolute truth were *Provinciales heretici*, "Provençal heretics"—men and women who, not surprisingly, wrapped their perverted souls and bodies in very tight clothes.

"Before the coming of the crusaders," Bernart Amielh confessed to the Dominican inquisitors Bernart de Caux and Joan de Sant Peire on Monday, 3 July 1245, in the Romanesque cloister of the abbey church of Saint-Sernin in Toulouse, "I saw heretics publicly walking through the streets of Mas-Saintes-Puelles." Less than a year later, the knight Bertran de Quiders told the same inquisition on Monday, 12 March 1246, that "before the crusaders first came," around 1209, "when I was five years old, or thereabouts, I frequently ate nuts, bread, and other foods given to me" by the heretics na Garsenda and na Gualharda, his widowed grandmother and aunt, "who lived publicly at Mas-Saintes-Puelles in their own house."[19] Almost six thousand other men and women were questioned at Saint-Sernin between May 1245 and August 1246. All of them were summoned from their *castra* (fortified villages) and hamlets in the Lauragais (a slim fertile plain between Toulouse and Carcassonne) to "tell the full and exact truth about oneself and about others, living and dead, in the matter of the fact or crime of heresy or Waldensianism."[20] Twelve years earlier, Pope Gregory IX, worried that heresy was spreading in France and resurfacing in *Provincia*, issued two letters (Wednesday, 20 April, and Friday, 22 April 1233) asking the Friars Preachers to eliminate this insidious serpent through *inquisitiones heretice pravitatis.*[21] These inquisitions into heretical depravity were a direct and lasting consequence of the crusade. (Medieval inquisitions are not to be confused with the Inquisitions of the sixteenth and seventeenth centuries. The former were always *ad hoc* investigations, whereas the latter were institutional courts.)[22] Apart from the great inquiry at Saint-Sernin—which was the largest inquisition in the Middle Ages—very few testimonies exist from other inquisitorial tribunals during these years. Nevertheless, the confessions that have survived (usually as seventeenth-century copies of lost originals) reveal, with rare intimacy, how thousands of men, women, and children lived their lives before, during, and after a brutal holy war.

"When I was seven years old," the twice-widowed na (from *domna*, "lady") Maurina Bosquet informed Bernart de Caux and Joan de Sant Peire on Saturday, 10 March 1246, "I stayed at Cabaret in a house of female heretics with my aunt, na Carcassona Martina, from Lent to August." This sojourn happened, she stressed, "when the crusaders first came" into the land. Na Maurina ended her testimony by noting that she had already discussed her aunt and heresy with the Dominican inquisitor Guilhem Arnaut three years earlier and, a year later, with the Dominican inquisitor Ferrer. As a man or a woman confessed to the inquisition—usually with stilted decorum, occasionally with nervous chattiness—his or her first-person vernacular words were instantly translated by scribes into third-person Latin. An individual's transcribed testimony was then read to him or her, with the scribe translating his Latin translation back into the vernacular, so that he or she could confirm the veracity of what was recorded of what was testified. Na Maurina, four days after her first confession at Saint-Sernin, was again questioned about her aunt and heresy. Once more, what she remembered about herself as a little girl was so mundane, so clearly lived without sinful implication, that she did not understand how any thought or deed from four decades ago was evidence of conscious guilt one way or the other. Na Maurina had lived in a blameless past where heretics, "openly coming and going through the streets," were a common sight in 1201.[23] It was a world of remembered innocence, especially if one were only a child, destroyed forever by the coming of the crusaders.

III

A MONGST THE EVENTS recorded in history over the last hundred years in Europe," reflected the elderly Toulousain priest Guilhem de Puylaurens around 1270, "there is one event which is especially worth recalling," and that, without a doubt, was the crusade "taken to defend the Catholic faith and extirpate heretical depravity in the province of Narbonne and in the dioceses of Albi, Rodez, Cahors, Agen, and certain territories of the count of Toulouse beyond the Rhône." Guilhem de Puylaurens, born only a few years before the crusaders came and, throughout the war, a young cleric in the entourage of the Cistercian bishop of Toulouse, Folc de Maselha, "thought it well to record in writing, for the benefit of posterity, what I myself witnessed, or heard from close sources," so that all people, whatever their rank, might gain some insight into the judgment of God and the divine decision "to scourge these unhappy lands" with such an effusion of human blood.[1] "My intention in this history, my sole purpose in writing it," stressed Pierre des Vaux-de-Cernay fifty years earlier, at the beginning of his book on the crusade, "is to ensure that all the nations will be aware of God's marvellous works." The Cistercian described only what he had been able to "witness personally" or learn from "reliable persons," confident that, in the end, "all I have written is true." The old priest and the young monk, so very different in narrative style, one restrained and unadorned, the other bursting with passion and rhetoric (despite a promise "to tell the plain truth in plain fashion"),[2] nevertheless epitomized in their histories the temporal paradox of all medieval heretical historiography. As heretical events were narrated, as heterodox stories were told, time itself was flattened by the timeless audacity of heresy. A kind of heretical essentialism, immune to historical change, was actually confirmed, over and over again, by the very act of writing a history of heresy. The historical truth revealed, and proved in each and every specific anecdote, was the knowledge that heresy had always been with us—an eternal plague that could be eliminated only by the shattering event of a great crusade.

"It is said that Toulouse," wrote Pierre des Vaux-de-Cernay, "deeply duplicitous since its first foundation has rarely, if ever, been free of this plague, this detestable pestilence of heretical depravity." Indeed, the "poison of superstitious unfaithfulness was passed from father to son, one after the other." Proof of the unchanging heretical nature of Toulouse, and so the consequences of sin, was explicitly demonstrated seven centuries earlier when the city was destroyed—"to the degree that the ploughed fields extended to the very centre of the city"—by the Frankish Catholic king Clovis because it was ruled by the Visigothic Arian heretic Alaric II. (This fifth-century heretical ruler of Toulouse "suffered the supreme dishonour of being hanged from a gibbet at the city gates" in a prediction of what did happen to some Toulousain lords fighting the thirteenth-century crusaders.) Even with this memory of destruction, so "infected with this ancient filth were the people of Toulouse" that nothing seemed capable of persuading the current "generation of vipers" to shed "their essential heretical tendencies" or overthrow their natural disposition to embrace heresy. "How hard it is to break with evil customs!" exclaimed the young Cistercian. The "marvellous achievement" of the crusade was that, unlike other episodes of violence, it became one of the "Lord's mighty acts," an event above and beyond the flow of time and so, more divine than human, a most holy war able to purge this dreadful pestilence from the history of the world.[3]

Verfeil, a *castrum* (fortified village) in the Lauragais to the east of Toulouse, was visited by the great and severe Cistercian, Bernard, abbot of Clairvaux, during the summer of 1145. The abbot, aware that the Toulousain and Lauragais were "greatly infected by the disease of faithlessness," thought that if he could extinguish heretical depravity at Verfeil, "which had been especially infected," then "he would find it easier to prevail elsewhere." The abbot started to preach in the tiny village church against the "high" persons of Verfeil. These important men and women, not wishing to hear themselves condemned, walked out of the church, followed by the rest of the village. "The holy man went after them and began to preach the word of God in the public square." The higher individuals of the village, whose houses framed the square, quickly escaped behind closed doors, while everyone else stood around and listened to the abbot. Inside the houses a crescendo of banging doors began reverberating through the square, so much so, that no one could hear the Cistercian. The abbot, angry and upset, "shook the dust from his feet" as a testament that all in Verfeil were dust "and would return to dust." Bernard of Clairvaux immediately left the village, glancing back only to curse, "Verfeil, may God wither you." This malediction—punning on Verfeil, *viridefolium*, "greenleaf"—came to pass according to Guilhem de Puylaurens. All the village knights, living in a hundred houses with a hundred blazons, rich in horses and oats, crumbled into poverty when, year after year, Verfeil was lacerated by hailstorms and war.[4]

"O unhappiest of people!" grieved Bernard of Clairvaux about the Toulousain and Lauragais in a letter he sent to Anfoz Jordas, count of Toulouse, announcing his visit in the summer of 1145. Although the Cistercian's body was sickly, "I am undertaking a hurried journey to those places where that singular wild beast is ravaging," that is, an itinerant heretical preacher named Henri, "since there is no one to resist him or offer protection from him." Henri had wandered through Lausanne, Le Mans, Poitiers, and Bordeaux before he reached Toulouse. "He is an apostate who cast off his religious habit—for he was once a monk—and returned to the filth of the flesh and the world." The fractious lands of the count of Toulouse, unlike the kingdom of France, were wide open to him.[5] Henri had been preaching for almost thirty years; in 1116 he was barefoot and unshaven, "a young man always ready to preach," sleeping in the doorways and gutters of Le Mans.[6] He argued what it meant to be a Christian with humor, scripture, and the manner of his life. Churches, sacraments, and priests were not needed to achieve holiness. Baptism, especially for children, was unnecessary for salvation. "Why, I ask," cried Bernard, "why does this man begrudge to children the child Saviour who was born to them?" This man, "with amazing and truly Jewish blindness," could not see the truth "so blatantly obvious to all." The abbot (as fond of arborical-biblical metaphors as any troubadour) scoffed, "Do you really hope to collect good fruit from such a bad tree as this?"[7] Henri never debated Bernard; indeed, he was later accused of fleeing such a contest. When autumn came, the bishop of Toulouse captured him; within a year, he was never heard of again.[8]

Bernard of Clairvaux, despite the fiasco at Verfeil, prevailed over the charismatic Henri (who, certainly, had "the appearance of piety" but, just as certainly, had "rejected its excellence"). Yet, this was no enduring

Cistercian victory; it was merely the favorable outcome of one season of warm-weather preaching. The abbot of Clairvaux, aware of the ephemeral nature of his success, promised to return despite his weak and sickly body, as the Toulousain and Lauragais were still infested with heretics. He advised Toulouse, in an open letter to the city, not to "receive any outside or unknown preacher, unless he be sent by the supreme pontiff, or have permission to preach from your bishop." False preachers always mixed poison with honey; the words of heretics putrefy innocent Christians, "imperceptibly, just like cancer."[9] The enthusiasm of ordinary men and women to hear and debate what it meant to be holy was not a demonstration of zeal for the divine; on the contrary, it was a symptom of alacrity (at best docility) for heresy. Indeed, thirty years later, another abbot of Clairvaux, Henri de Marcy, went to Toulouse in the summer of 1178 (at the request of the pope, the count of Toulouse, and the kings of France and England) to investigate whether the city really had become "the mother of heresy and head of error." He was shocked to find a "city so diseased that, from the soles of its feet to the top of its head, there was not a healthy piece of it." Henri de Marcy urged radical, and rather ominous, surgery: the evil head must be stunned, severed, and raised up on its own sword.[10]

"Readers should know that the heretics of Toulouse and other cities and villages, as well as their defenders, are generally called 'Albigensians' in this book," Pierre des Vaux-de-Cernay clarified when he dedicated his history to Innocent III, "since this is the name that other nations came to use for all Provençal heretics." A few folios later, despite some comments about "various heresies and heretical sects," he looked back to the years before the crusade and described only two groups of *Provinciales heretici*. The first sect seduced simple hearts with the dualist mendacity of two creators: "one of things invisible whom they called the 'benign' God and one of things visible whom they named the 'malign' God." The other sect, though still evil, were "very much less perverted" and went by the name of *Valdenses* from "*Valdes*, a citizen of Lyon." The worst error of these "Waldensians" was (out of four) wearing "sandals in imitation of the Apostles." The young Cistercian, after conceding that *Albigenses* could be an omnivorous category, only tagged heretics spreading the cancer of dualism with the term.[11] Guilhem de Puylaurens, by comparison, swiftly glossed (in the incipit of his chronicle) that "Albigensian" was what the French commonly called the whole enterprise of the crusade and, with no more clarity than that, never used the word again; instead, "Arians, Manichaeans, and Waldensians (or Lyonnais)" were the heretics infesting the lands of the count of Toulouse.[12] The naming of heretics by medieval intellectuals was rarely whimsical or arbitrary; it was a serious (if sometimes confused and contradictory) exercise at classifying malevolence in the world.

The Benedictine chronicler Geoffroi du Breuil, prior of Saint-Pierre de Vigeois in the Limousin, recorded that, in early summer of 1181, Henri de Marcy, now cardinal and papal legate to France, marched "with a great army against the Albigensian heretics" festering at Lavaur (a *castrum* on the west bank of the Tarn river) around Roger II Trencavel, *vescomte* of Béziers, Carcassonne, Razès, and Albi.[13] Henri, at the end of his visit to Toulouse in 1178, traveled through the Albigeois—a "damnable region, which is like a great cesspool of evil, with all the scum of heresy flowing into it"—to rebuke Roger II for imprisoning the bishop of Albi. The viscount of Béziers, with casual indifference, ignored the abbot of Clairvaux. A furious Henri "declared Roger a traitor, a heretic, and a perjurer for having violated the peace," and condemned him to public excommunication. "It is clear from this that a fine door is open to Christian princes to avenge the wounds of Christ," pleaded the Cistercian as he envisioned armed pilgrimages against the heretical viscount.[14] Henri, three years later, finding the bright door still open, sought his revenge in a tiny (not quite holy) war. Lavaur was besieged until na Alazaiz, wife of Roger II and daughter of Raimon V, count of Toulouse, quickly surrendered the *castrum*. The viscount sued for peace, promising, "along with many lords, to renounce heretical depravity," and, as proof of his new piety, he delivered two heresiarchs to the legate for questioning. One of the heresiarchs, Bernart Raimon, became a canon at the cathedral church of Saint-Etienne (Sant-Esteve) in Toulouse and, as Guilhem de Puylaurens recalled hearing as a child, he was forever known as "the Arian." Geoffroi du Breuil ended his report of Henri de Marcy's Albigeois campaign with the frustrated observation that, as soon as the Catholics left, "the pigs returned to the filth of their ancient sty."[15]

Geoffroi du Breuil was the first person to use *Albigenses* as a heretical appellation. Yet, it was not an all-encompassing category to him or, significantly, to Henri de Marcy; it meant, quite specifically, heretics and mercenaries living in the Albigeois under the jurisdiction of (and so supported by) Roger II. These heretics (according to a lost letter of Henri that the prior of Vigeois inserted into his chronicle) desired lives of evangelical simplicity; dismissed baptism, marriage, and the sacraments of the Church; scorned priests and Mosaic law; denied that the Lord God made heaven and earth; and believed that Christ, having no human birth, possessed no physical body. Geoffroi added a touch of the fantastically lurid with an anecdote about a noblewoman, na Vierna de Boissezon, who left her husband for the heretics and, as part of her initiation into a new holy life, was "lustily debauched by fifty of the more religious of the sect."[16]

The lasting importance of this enigmatic little war against Albigensians—consisting of a sharp summer siege by a small and far from great army whose origins remain obscure and whose divine sanction was decidedly vague—lies in what happened to a different viscount of Béziers in the first horrific summer of the great crusade three decades later. It was only after a year of holy war that "Albigensian" acquired a general purchase on all heretics between the Garonne and the Rhône, and then, almost exclusively in the chronicles, poems, sermons, and letters of northern Europeans. Unquestionably, heretical nomenclature is confusing; undeniably, it can be sorted out; unfortunately, so many modern scholars do not seem to care.

The story of the Cathars begins quietly, furtively, in the eleventh century, their presence faint and uncertain; then, halfway through the twelfth, there they are, loud and visible, from the Mediterranean to the North Sea; until, at the threshold of the thirteenth, a "Cathar Church" exists with systematic dualist doctrines and an elaborate episcopate. Sometime during this hundred or so years Bogomil missionaries covertly travel from the Balkans and influence (if not totally shape) the dualist theology of the Cathars. The regions where the Cathars thrive are the Toulousain, Lauragais, Albigeois, and Carcassès, although substantial populations live in the northern Italian towns and villages of the Trevisian March. This grand narrative reaches its tragic crescendo in the bloody violence of the Albigensian Crusade and, thereafter, the unremitting persecutions of inquisitors until the Cathars disappear, for all intents and purposes, sometime in the early fourteenth century. Occasionally, the Cathars are seen in later centuries, secretly surviving, their influence wide and promiscuous: from the Templars to early Protestants to the occult descendants of a Christ who survives the cross. A saga of spiritual freedom and religious intolerance, a warning and a lesson from the past, always worth telling—except, of course, that none of it is true.[17]

Only a handful of heretics were actually named *Cathari* in the Middle Ages and, most important, no Provençal heretic was ever styled "Cathar" (by choice or accusation) during the years of the crusade. The Benedictine canonist Yves, bishop of Chartres, in a treatise on ecclesiastical jurisprudence from around 1100, reproduced a fifth-century letter of Pope Innocent I to the bishops of Macedonia about "those who have given themselves the name of 'Cathars,' that is 'the pure,' and who sometimes return to the Catholic Church"; and this old papal letter largely replicated the eighth canon of the First Council of Nicaea of 325.[18] Yves de Chartres seized on these half-forgotten schismatics as examples of the eternal nature of dissent and reconciliation within the Church. Sixty-three years later, the

Benedictine Eckbert, abbot of Schönau, preached thirteen sermons against some Cologne heretics—a sect of grubs that "undoubtedly owes its origin to the heresiarch Mani"—known as the "Church of God" to one another but whom other men (with uncommon erudition) "commonly call *Cathari*." The abbot, by way of explaining this ancient sobriquet, simply copied what the bishop copied from the pope—ditto Nicaea.[19]

The naming of some heretics as "Cathars" by Latin Christian intellectuals was, like so much medieval heresiology, a studious adaptation of the glossaries of Late Antiquity.[20] Still, the learned Cistercian Alain de Lille was so unfamiliar with heretical etymology at the end of the twelfth century that, merging wit with ignorance (and heresy with demonism), he quipped that *Cathari* derived from *catus* because "they kiss the hind parts of a cat, in whose likeness, so they say, Lucifer appears to them."[21] "Cathar" was an obscure term that mostly meant (despite the odd Manichaean mannerism) a schismatic of indeterminate heterodoxy who eventually returned to the Church. It was (and is) no more precise or worthy a designation for a heretic than any other—less so, in fact. Regrettably, the name is used with such an appalling lack of discrimination by modern scholars—it gets thrown about like so much Cathar-confetti, lazily adorning almost all heretics before the fourteenth century—that it is an epithet of confusion rather than clarity.

"I do not recall having heard anything new or extraordinary in all their assertions," Bernard of Clairvaux preached about heretics and their doctrines spreading throughout the world in 1144, "but only trite commonplaces long vented amongst the heretics of old." This sermon by the abbot of Clairvaux—his sixty-fifth inspired by the *Song of Songs* and his third on the verse "Seize for us the little foxes that are destroying the vineyards"—was, in the first instance, a soothing reply to a fretful letter from Eberwin, prior of the Premonstratensian abbey in Steinfield, about two new (unnamed) groups of heretics in Cologne; more generally, though, it was a vibrant study of the eternal "vine of the Lord" and the heretical foxes trying to destroy it. This vine "has filled the earth and which we, too, are a part—a far-spreading vine planted by the hand of the Lord, purchased with His blood, watered by His word, propagated by His grace, made fruitful by His spirit." It was a vine always ready for harvest, always fully grown, always sweet and ripe. It existed before the world was created and will be luxuriant when time ends. The foxes of heresy lurked in the shadows of the vineyard. "Recent damage to the vine, in truth, shows that the fox has been at work," and although the cunning animal covered his tracks so that it was almost impossible to discover him, "the Church from the beginning has always had her foxes," and all of them were discovered and taken. As the vine was infinitely perfect and unchanging, so the vulpine attacks against it were tiresomely repetitive and unoriginal. The foxes recycled ancient ideas and thought them modern; little beasts, so trapped in time, they could not transcend it; and who, by imitating the heretics of history, metamorphosed into these malicious animals of the past.[22]

As so much has already been said and done in the history of the world, "it is impossible to say anything new," mused the Benedictine Wibald of Corvey in 1147; heretics, conspicuously lacking any novelty of thought, "do not invent new things but repeat old ones."[23] It was the apparent similarity of heretical ideas through time that demonstrated to medieval intellectuals the historical continuity (and cyclical iniquity) of heretics. The heresies of the past (as revealed in the condemnations of ancient ecclesiastical councils and, especially, in the voluminous writings of Augustine of Hippo against the Manichaeans) provided templates into which the heretical ideas of the present could be fitted and, as a consequence, explained. It was a historical and analytical method that necessitated finding coherence in the beliefs of heretics, no matter when, no matter where, so that not only were all heresies continuous over the centuries but, as all heretical thoughts were perceived as similar from Toulouse to Cologne, from London to Jerusalem, deep and secretive connections must exist among all heretics throughout Christendom. This heretical historicism, in which heretics were the enduring and persistent witnesses to the immortal and infinite Church, was crucial to the making of medieval Latin Christianity. Such a model for understanding heresy was hardly surprising in a world where, at least from the eleventh century onward, Latin Christians endeavored to imitate the Christ of history (as revealed in the New Testament) and were judged holy by the veracity of their imitation. Heretics, despite the divine potential inherent in imitative practices, never copied the life of the Savior, even if, in their perversity, they thought they were doing so. Instead, they replicated (remorselessly, impenitently) the lives and ideas of venomous men like Arius and Mani.

"The bride never forgets the poisoned stings that so often the enemies of the faith have sharpened against her," preached the Cistercian John, abbot of Ford, about the Church as the bride of Christ and serpentine heretics in 1206. This sermon by the English abbot—his eighty-fifth inspired by the *Song of Songs* and his third on the verse "And your breasts will be like clusters of the vine, and your perfumes, or the perfume of your mouth, like the scent of apples"—while certainly resonating with all the heresiological assumptions of the previous century, had a distinctly shrill timbre, an apocalyptic quiver, not heard in Bernard of Clairvaux.

The bride, when the first Arian plague arose, instantly took out her sword, "forged by the Spirit of God," flashed the blade, then sheathed it. "All true," said John, "but then there was the execrable impiety of the Manichaeans." These heretics, fleeing the sword of the Spirit, escaped into darkness and, embracing "the people of darkness," survived the centuries in silence. The bride for too long "has pretended to ignore this incurable wound." Emollients and tourniquets will not save a body completely ravaged by a leprous head. The sword of the Spirit, "which is the Word of God," was now useless against the heretics—it skipped on their throats of brass. "No!" cried the abbot, "it must be a sword of gold, the kind Maccabeus accepted from God," and used immediately by the bride to protect her little ones. Already, though, it might be too late, "for now we find this heresy sending its roots deep and wide into the towns, castles, and territories close to France, even stretching to Italy." Tragically—and astonishingly only two years before the crusade—John lamented that, even if the bride unsheathed her golden sword, "there is now faint hope, if any, of eradicating this most evil seed."[24]

Ironically, the medieval method for understanding heresy is almost exactly the same as that adopted (with little or no reflection) by many modern scholars in their studies of heterodoxy in the eleventh, twelfth, and thirteenth centuries. A pervasive intellectualist and idealist bias assumes that heresies are nothing more than religious doctrines, abstract thoughts, or lucid philosophies. This methodological tendency presupposes that heresies have an intellectual purity and theological coherence in which it is possible to neatly sift out other, less coherent ideas; most crucially, it is a technique that effectively ignores historical and cultural specificity. Consequently, an extraordinary (and often stunning) superficiality permeates many modern interpretations of medieval heresiology. These analyses possess an inexcusable simplicity that, if nothing else, misses the sophisticated intellectual struggle of medieval thinkers into the nature and meaning of heresy before and after the Albigensian Crusade. What is so disturbing about the modern manner in which heresy is commonly studied is that the medieval heretic is taken to be such a coherent and concrete figure in the history of the Middle Ages, particularly in the great scheme of things, that the whys and wherefores of heresy get lost in a kind of intellectual determinism in which certain ideas have an inevitability about them because someone, sooner or later, thought them (or was accused of thinking them). Such hindsight applied to the *Provinciales heretici*, almost always called "Cathars" since the late nineteenth century, has so predetermined these heretics to be what they supposedly became, that the vital importance of why individuals and communities thought or did things at specific times and places vanishes into generalizations that are either trivially true (the Church feared heterodoxy) or obviously false (there was a "Cathar Church").

"Son," na Matuez Vidal gently told her boy, the knight Gardoz, as he lay badly wounded in a house at Toulouse during the crusade, "it's been said to me that you gave yourself to the good men, that is, the heretics." The son survived the war and, three decades later, on Friday, 7 July 1245, he recalled his mother's worried question (and her terminological precision) for the inquisitor Bernart de Caux. "I didn't strongly believe the heretics to be good men," na Flors del Mas told the inquisitor the next day, "quite the contrary, I thought them good as frequently as I didn't." "Likewise, I never believed that the heretics were good men," testified the leatherworker Peire de Garmassia the following spring, "although, I believed their behaviour to be good, even if their faith was bad."[25] Gardoz Vidal, na Flors de Mas, and Peire de Garmassia, like thousands of other men and women interrogated in the aftermath of the crusade, never mentioned Albigensians, Manichaeans, Arians, or Cathars. Instead, in each and every interrogation, in each and every testimony, the only heretics inquired after, the only heretics remembered—apart from a handful of Waldensians—were the "good men," the "good women," and their "believers." Beneath all the layers of heretical nomenclature of the twelfth and thirteenth centuries, beneath all the names used by Catholic polemicists as a way of understanding and condemning heresy between the Garonne and the Rhône, lived these good men and good women. These were the heretics that Bernard of Clairvaux preached against and whose diseased head Henri de Marcy wanted lopped off. These were the men and women that the crusaders, whatever those signed with the cross may have thought before they arrived in the Biterrois or Carcassès, joyously burned and slaughtered as the enemies of Christ.

Na Flors de Mas and Peire de Garmassia, in their precise reflections on naming and morality, testified to the discriminating use of "good man"— *bon ome* in Provençal, *bonus homo* in Latin—as an epithet. The significance of this simple name, while obvious to a lady or artisan of the Toulousain, was mostly ignored (or misunderstood) by a century of ecclesiastical observers. Pierre des Vaux-de-Cernay, even as he acknowledged that some heretics were called "good men," saw no purpose or design in the term.[26] The most surprising aspect of this sobriquet, and perhaps so simplistic as to be overlooked by a Cistercian preacher or historian, was that it was an honorific applicable to any Provençal man (high or low) from around 1140. A few references to "good men" exist from the tenth and eleventh centuries; although the title implied honor and privilege, it was not a distinction (or a compliment) applicable to all men. It was a transient status conferred upon an already important individual by his lord and used only when seigneurial authority required representative vassals as witnesses to charters or faithful men making judgments at once "public" and "just." In the tempestuous decades at the end of the eleventh century and the beginning of the twelfth, long years when the habitual violence inherent in lordship between the Garonne and Rhône became ever more immoderate and anarchic, when the right to protect (and to be protected) coalesced around castles and fortified villages, the good men disappear from the records.[27]

The return of the "good men" in the middle of the twelfth century was the recognition that this fractured and fragmented world had reached some sort of equilibrium. These new good men, far from embodying deference to a superior person, represented only themselves, each other, and their communities. Occasionally, a "prudent [or proven or tested or perfected] man"—*prodome* in Provençal, *probus homo* in Latin—was honored, and, though a less frequent term, the name was simply another way of saying "good man."[28] The prestige and pervasiveness of the good men derived from an intense localism focused on a particular village or town or even a city like Toulouse, where fourteen "prudent men of Toulouse and the bourg" shared authority with the comital court as early as 1120.[29] These villages and towns were like tiny looking-glass cages, with all the men constantly watching one another, unable to escape their own reflected similarity as good and prudent men. Yet, far from being an illusion of temporal and moral equivalence, this courteous resemblance of all men to each other, this moderate exercise in imitation, was the very thing that gave meaning and order to these small communities. In the maintenance of this communal harmony, a fluid and episodic rhythm secured by day-to-day courtliness, one or two good men exemplified not just the routine sameness of all men but how, in periodic variations on this mundane theme, the holy could flare and flicker in a human. It was these very special good men, denounced by preachers, murdered by crusaders, and hunted by inquisitors, whose holiness was transformed into heresy.

IV

A MAN WHO KNOWS well how to observe moderation can pride himself on possessing *cortezia*," Marcabru sang of courtliness in 1148. Any man in any town, village, or castle "who wants to hear everything that is said or aims to possess all that he sees must need moderate this 'all'—or he will never be very courtly." Moderation, the troubadour advised, "lies in noble speech, and *cortezia* comes from loving; and a man who does not want to be misjudged should guard against all base, deceitful, and excessive behaviour." Even though such measured restraint, such *mezura*, "might not make him any happier, he will be wise." Marcabru, with ironic simplicity abating his usual virulent charm, smartly summarized the essence of (and the tension within) the new courtliness framing the lives of all Provençal men and women in the twelfth century. This *cortezia* was not a stylish pastime, a mannerism without meaning; on the contrary, it organized time and space, governing them, controlling them, through prudent speech and behavior, through loving words and actions. Most important, it was in modest variations and improvisations of quotidian courtliness that individuals tested, interpreted, and so made sense of each other and their world. These courteous variations (as precise interpretations of precise social moments) were frequently more vital than the theme of *cortezia* itself. The honor and prestige of being a good man (holy or otherwise) was such a profound demonstration of wisdom through moderation, of the achievement of communal stability through individual restraint, that these men really were (and were thought

to be) the ideal embodiments of *cortezia*. It was not in the great courts of the counts of Toulouse or Poitiers that the courtly ethos of the troubadours was perfected; instead, and this would not have surprised Marcabru, it was in the hundreds of fortified villages and castles between the Garonne and the Rhône that the tempo of *cortezia* truly possessed an intensity, an intimacy, so meaningful, so powerful, that it shaped (and honored) the relationship of heaven and earth.[1]

Courtliness allowed men and women to survive the extraordinarily complex and fastidious system of Provençal land tenure. All the arable land, with the possible exception of some marshy soil along the Garonne above Toulouse and the "rich marshes" of the Camargue at the mouth of the Rhône, was not only cleared and cultivated by the middle of the twelfth century but, in an erratic pattern of florid busyness and extreme detail, was splintered into thousands upon thousands of fields, vineyards, gardens, pastures, and olive groves. A man, noble or not, rarely possessed two or more contiguous shards of this fragmented terrain, and what properties he did claim were mostly scattered around his village or castle (usually no further than seven hundred meters). These pieces of earth were small, often so small as to be visibly worthless, and yet the rights to these minutiae were shared among all brothers, occasionally sisters, frequently other men (not always of the same status), and sometimes an institution or two (churches, monasteries, leprosaria, or the military orders). Along with this visible landscape of claims and rights to hold and possess fields and vineyards there existed, simultaneously, an invisible landscape of claims and rights to the rents and dues on these fields and vineyards. This implicit domain of exactions and gifts was, if anything, even more fractured than the explicitly physical one. Every now and then a man held both these seen and unseen rights on a piece of land, or at least fractions of each right; either way, it made no difference, as each proprietary claim was as authentically possessive as the other. The possessory reality of this world was a constantly swirling tempest of these rights and claims, all too easily misjudged, all too easily forgotten, and with thousands of men essentially impoverished though desperately acquisitive, all too easily prone to dispute and violence.[2]

Villages were as fractured by claims and rights as the fields and vineyards around them. A *castrum* or *vila* usually straddled a small hill and, from outer wall to outer wall, covered no more than a hundred meters. Anywhere between two hundred and five hundred persons (nobles, artisans, peasants, clerics, lepers, diviners, vagabonds, barbers, notaries, good women, good men) lived in a village. The communal square—a swatch of dirt that was a market one day, a venue for sermons the next—was framed by a lordly castle, a stone box of a church, and the houses of high and noble individuals. A slim and wispy street sauntered in and out of the square, up and down the hill. The castle or fortified farm of a local lordly family was the castral *clou*—with a small courtyard, tower, stable, hall, and cellar—and fractions of these structures (and fractions of the land on which they were built) were commonly possessed by numerous siblings, other nobles, and various ecclesiastical institutions. A lord walking from his stable to his hall walked through an ornate proprietary pattern in which he was not always the possessor of the ground where he trod or the owner of the rooms within his walls; occasionally, the castle walls themselves (sandstone, limestone, schist) did not belong to the lord who lived within them. This same principle of possession sliced through all village houses, often no more than a room with an earthen floor, as they splayed outward (and downward) from the lordly *castel*. It even sheared through the little church (and so the petty parish tithes) and was why the village priest was, more often than not, penurious and without honor. Indeed, village priests were so poor and pathetic that, according to Guilhem de Puylaurens, they were commonly mocked in village oaths. "I would rather be a priest," nobles and peasants laughed, "than do this or that."[3]

As men and women owned parts (and parts of parts) of a field or a vineyard, so they owned snippets of rents or morsels of earth or bits of mortgages (and snippets of snippets and morsels of morsels and so on) throughout a village. These tight castral communities, honeycombed by claims and rights, simmered with cupidity, resentment, and proprietorial conceit.

The honor of a man lay in the protection, discreet accumulation, and communal recognition of his proprietary claims and rights. Indeed, as honor was composed of these possessory pieces—to the point where Latin *honor* and Provençal *onor* were synonyms for land rights—it too was partible into fees, transactions, or bequests. "In the year of Our Lord 1169," the gravely ill noble Raimon de Albas bequeathed to the Templar preceptory at Douzens (a *castrum* east of Carcassonne), "my soul, my body, and all my honour and everything I possess or will possess" around the village of Cabriac. Raimon's bequest included "a piece of land that borders the honour of Roger de Cabriac and his brothers to the east, the honour of Raimon Izarn to the south, the honour of the children of Ermengart de Roquenégade to the west," and a road to the north; a third part of a field known as *de Palerio* "that borders the honour of Guilhem Bernart de la Redort to the east" and a hill to the south; "the fourth part and the ownership I hold in the vineyard that Bernart Cil holds from me, namely a half"; in Montauban, "on the southern side a strip of land that borders the honour of Raimon Izarn," the honor of the children of Ermengart de Roquenégade to the west, and an irrigated strip of land to the south; "at the place called *ad Vassa* I give you a third part of all the olive groves there, and I have 16 shillings pledged in another third part that borders the honour of Raimon Izarn to the east," a stream to the south, and the honor of Roger de Cabriac to the west and north. Finally, "if in the aforesaid lands it should happen that some honour be found that was owed to me," the knights of Jerusalem were to possess these claims and rights too.[4] The fragmentation of the very thing that gave a man his identity—so that even personal *valor*, at once innate and acquired, was another synonym for land rights and, as such, partible—meant that questions of individual honor and prestige were forever circulating around a man, moving in and out of focus, depending on what he possessed or was thought to possess (now or in the future).

It was only through the day-to-day, moment-to-moment performance of *cortezia* that questions of honor were answered and a man's identity affirmed. Courtliness—given, received, withdrawn, or demanded—was as precise an exercise in accounting a man's *onor* and *valor* as a testament or contract. What added to the astonishing complexity of this system was that a nobleman might easily sell, lease, even briefly exchange some of his honor with a peasant, or vice versa, effectively rendering the transaction honorable as well. This circulation of honor among all men, and so the rights of courtesy that went with honor, meant that nobles and peasants were frequently, if only for a courtly moment, socially and morally equivalent. There were, Marcabru laughed, "peasant-like lords and lordly peasants" because of this courteous (and proprietary) phenomenon.[5] "I don't know what to do about it," the troubadour sang, "I am so perplexed, for around the plough peasants are putting on courtly airs." As honor must be respected no matter who possessed it, honest men repeatedly said and did things they knew to be false. "By my faith, you can hear a thousand of such men braying that it was never thus."[6] It was this intermittent equivalence of all men, let alone the sometime occurrence of a noble deferring to the honor of a peasant, and so the dissipation (almost dissolution) of authority throughout a village, that necessitated good and prudent men as arbiters in conflicts of honor. Intriguingly, although all men could be good men, the men called on to be moderately wise—judging boundaries, adjudicating fractional rents, deciding fights over houses between claimants—varied from dispute to dispute. This recognition of the possessive cat's-cradle that knotted some men together in one place and time and released them elsewhere, a recognition that deference and loyalty were in constant flux, meant that no man could honorably arbitrate every dispute. It may have been a world in which nobles and peasants all had honor, all had a measure of wisdom, but the older transient notion of being a *bonus homo* in very specific situations for very specific decisions still persisted. The holy good men, by contrast, were always good men.

"Bless me," said ten-year-old Guilhem Aimeri, followed by three bows, and then, "good men, pray God for me." The boy repeated this courtesy many times throughout 1206, when he stayed for a year in the Montmaur house of the holy good man Bernart de Vilanova and another unnamed good man. The inquisitor Bernart de Caux heard of this courtliness, and of the boy eating bread blessed by the good men, when fifty-six-year-old Guilhem Aimeri recalled his childhood "before the crusaders first came" in the verandahs of Saint-Sernin. The elderly Bernart Gasc told the same inquisitor on Saturday, 27 May 1245, that seventy years earlier, when he lived with his mother, Marquesia, in the village of Fanjeaux, "Guilhem de Carlipac, heretic," was their neighbor, "and I often ate in his house, as he gave me bread, wine, and nuts." Bernart Gasc never asked for a benediction from his kind neighbor; neither did he see any other person, young or old, perform any courtly act toward Guilhem de Carlipac in 1175. Thirty years later, though, Bernart Gasc was in the Fanjeaux house of the good man Arnaut Clavel and his unnamed companion when he, along with ten other men and two women, genuflected, saying, "Bless us, good men, pray God for us."[7] All testimonies to the inquisitors acknowledged or denied the courtliness of men like Guilhem Aimeri and Bernart Gasc. Any courtesy (now or in the past) to a holy good man was a confirmation to the inquisitors that the courtly individual was (now or in the past) a "believer" in the heretics. The inquisitions into heretical depravity collected and classified the *cortezia* given to the good men as "adoration"—a designation recalling the false worship and spurious liturgies of ancient heretics. The inquisitors in their rigid codification of measured speech and behavior obscured the complexity, variability, and sheer ubiquity of courtliness in the villages and towns between the Garonne and the Rhône.

Bernart Gasc, after his courteous exchange with Arnaut Clavel, encountered seven other good men on three separate occasions in 1205: once in a house in the village of Caraman, where he bowed and asked for a blessing, and twice in houses at Fanjeaux, where everyone, "except me," adored the heretics.[8] The septuagenarian offered the inquisition no explanation for why he was courtly to some good men but not others, even though he thought all "the heretics to be good men, to have good faith, and to be the friends of God." In all the confessions to the inquisition by any man or woman over forty, in all the memories of existence before the crusade, every person recalled being courteous to the holy good men. Similarly, each person remembered their holy *cortezia* as contingently episodic—sometimes in a house, in a field, at the threshold of a door, at the beginning of day, in the middle of the night, alone, in a group, before menarche, all throughout the year, only twice in a decade, when seriously ill, and so on. Although the times and places when an individual chose to be gracious to a good man were variable, the words and bows offered were less mercurial. This courtly constancy arose not from written doctrinal rules or some systematic ritual; rather, it was the natural outcome of the inescapable courtliness dictating the rhythms of life. It was the coherent and stable holiness of the very special good men, their fixed identities in a universe of flux, that allowed for the coherence and stability of the honors and love they received. The decorous language and genuflections of Guilhem Aimeri and Bernart Gasc were demonstrations of how through simple oscillations in pedestrian *cortezia* the piety of particular men was affirmed. The holy courtliness given to the good men was the idealized version of mundane courtliness.

In a world where the holy was as fragmented as honor, where the sacred ebbed and flowed through (and around) all humans, questions of holiness as much as questions of honor were answered through *cortezia*. The holiness of a good man lay in the constant protection and communal recognition of his possessive claims and rights to the holy. The vernacular term for precisely modulated speech and behavior to the good men was *melhoramen*, transcribed by inquisitorial scribes as *melioramen* or *melioramentum*, and it meant, at one and the same time, improvement, betterment, perfection, moderation, accumulation of honor, the accretion of wisdom, and the reciprocal process of giving and receiving holiness. The "melioration" was the exemplification of all the potential variations of *cortezia*. It epitomized how the capriciousness of a fractured cosmos could be ameliorated through courtliness. Jordan de Sais, the old lord of Cambiac, illustrated the fluid nature of the holy, and how it could be entrenched through the *melhoramen*, when he told Bernart de Caux on Tuesday, 12 December 1245, that thirty-five years earlier, "I genuflected thrice, saying 'bless me,'" to two good men who were his *homines proprii*, that is, peasants over whom he had "bodily" rights. Yet, even as the lord of Cambriac meliorated the holiness of "his owned men" through courtly words and bows, he was himself fractionally improved and perfected, even made a bit more honorable, in the performance of the *melhoramen*. The holy eccentricity of the universe, a moody motility all too visible in the world, was moderated and measured, restrained and secured, through courtliness to men who balanced heaven and earth within themselves.

The ten-year-old Raimon de Eclezia became a good man in 1205. The boy, weak and infirm, was carried by his father to the Montmaur house of the holy good man Guilhem Teissier and another unnamed good man. The sick child, left with the good men, was made into a holy person. "I stayed with those heretics for ten years," Raimon de Eclezia confessed to Bernart de Caux on Saturday, 1 July 1245. During that decade, the youthful good man, along with countless other men and women, performed the *melhoramen* to the older good men "so many times so often, that I can't remember." Good men, despite the mutability of holiness and honor that allowed them to be peasants or nobles, were rarely small boys like Raimon de Eclezia. Good women, by contrast, were always nobles and frequently little girls. "I was not yet ten years old," na Comdorz sorely remembered her transition from little girl to good woman, when "my mother violently forced me to be made into a heretic" and, though only a "clothed heretic" for nine months in 1199, she believed in the good men all her life until the bishop of Toulouse, Folc de Maselha, around 1220 reconciled her to the faith with the penance of wearing two yellow crosses. Little na Audiardiz from the village of Villeneuve-la-Comptal was made a good woman by the good man Izarn de Castres in the house of the good man Bernart Recort in 1206. Audiardiz was a good woman for only a year, "praying, fasting," offering the good men "meliorations," listening to their preaching, "doing other things which heretics do and understand must be observed," and then, as she informed the inquisition on Tuesday, 3 July 1246, "I took a husband." In the half century before the crusade thousands of noble pre-pubescent girls were made into good women for as short a time as a few weeks or for as long as three or four years. All these moderately holy children, after their months or years of being good women, married upon reaching their majorities at twelve. Raimon de Eclezia, after leaving Guilhem Teissier's house, immediately married an adolescent girl who had been a child good woman for two years.[9] The only other good women during these decades were older noble matrons, women beyond the years of fertility, no longer able or willing to marry, sometimes widows, sometimes separated from elderly husbands, quietly living together in twos or threes in tiny houses, nursing and teaching noble little girls like Comdorz and Audiardiz how to be good women.

"When I was seven years old," fifty-two-year-old na Saura told Bernart de Caux on Saturday, 15 April 1245, "I was made a heretic and I stayed a clothed heretic for three years" in a house with other good women in the same village as na Audiardiz. In this holy seclusion no one visited the good women, young or old, and no one offered them any courtly words or bows—"that I recollect," said Saura. "When I was eight years old," reminisced na Bernarta Veziana, another noblewomen from Villeneuve-la-Comptal, "I stayed with my aunt Bernarta Recort," a good woman living with other good women, eating, drinking, and sleeping in their house all through 1205. The child Bernarta, though housed with her aunt for twelve months, was, unlike Audiardiz and Saura, not made into a good woman. "When I was four years old" na Crivessenz from the village of Plaigne went to live with her grandmother na Alazaiz, a good woman residing with other good women in a house at Laurac, and she stayed there from 1206 to 1211, eating and drinking, yet never adoring the good women or becoming one herself.[10] All noble little girls before adolescence stayed with their aunts or grandmothers in houses shared with other old ladies and, though the aged inhabitants were almost always good women, whether a niece or granddaughter was made into a good woman varied from village to village, family to family. (Some of this variability was because only a good man, at least before 1220, could transform a child or a matron into a good woman.) What was similar about all these houses of women at the beginning and end of their lives was their intense isolation, however brief, however long, from the moral and social instability of the world. Inside these houses the good women did not offer each other decorous speech or genuflections: granddaughters did not bow to grandmothers; nieces did not ask for benedictions from aunts. The restraint and moderation that a good man exemplified in his person, that nevertheless needed to be affirmed and perfected through the performance of the *melhoramen*, was replicated through the deliberate creation of holy spaces where the ameliorative power of *cortezia* no longer applied because, in these quiet gaps in the universe, it was not needed.

In 1206 the adolescent Dulcia ran away from her husband Peire Faber to a house of good women in her village. Despite sheltering in this house and in two other houses of good women in two other villages for four years, she never became a good woman herself, "on account of my youthfulness."[11] No woman was a good woman during her years of fertility, the years of her youth, the years when she married, had children, and lived openly as a wife. Marriage was an episode in the lives of all women, a fecund season to be survived, and yet it was an interlude when the powerful constraints of *cortezia* struggled to contain and smother the inherent wantonness and capriciousness of women. The *fin'amor* of the troubadours was, when all was said and sung, less the perfect love given to and received from a noble lady than an overripe and overdone possessive *passement* entwining and entrapping a lady and her property. "Arnaut has made and will make a long attentive wait," sang the troubadour Arnaut Daniel about a certain Lady Better-Than-Good, "for by waiting attentively a good man wins a rich conquest."[12] The seclusion of little girls and widows in houses of good women was a way for hundreds of noble fathers and brothers, clinging tenuously to their proprietary rights, to enclose and regulate the rents and lands embodied in the honor of daughters and sisters. All child good women married, frequently more than once, and throughout their years of marriage they (and their families) struggled to maintain their dotal properties until, as was often the case, they again became good women as widows. A bride, of course, accrued some of her husband's honor in marriage and, more troubling to his family and heirs, might keep it after his death. The prudery and censoriousness behind so much of the dashing wit and well-groomed vulgarity of troubadour songs—especially in the hatred of fractious sluts and adulterous husbands engaged in, as Marcabru suavely put it, "the cunt game"[13]—was an obsession about the alienation and dissipation of honor by a noble woman during her "youthfulness."

The houses of good women, sanctuaries where feminine worth was preserved and where a young runaway bride could be protected from her husband, were nevertheless houses for noble women—and Dulcia Faber was not noble. The simple epithet "good woman"—*bona femna, bona molher* in Provençal, *bona femina, bona mulier* in Latin—was deliberately incongruent and unequal, as a woman known by this humble name was, in the small hierarchies of her village, one of the higher women. The sobriquet "good woman" only faintly echoed the social and moral complexities that resounded within "good man." A good woman, far from relying on holiness secured through courtesy, relied on her inherent honor as a noble for her measured claim to the sacred. It was this intrinsic (if lackluster) divinity that allowed noble little girls, whether good women or not, to remain inside a house when the good men visited, while other little girls waited outside.[14] A youthful noble woman, though, always departed a house as soon as the good men crossed the threshold. By the second decade of the crusade, when children no longer became good women and all older good women were forced to flee the seclusion of their houses, more and more fugitive holy women started to stress their innate nobility by preferring "good lady"—*bona domna* in Provençal, *bona domina* in Latin—as their honorific of choice. It was Dulcia Faber's lack of nobility, as much as her youth, that denied her the honor of being a good woman before, during, and after the crusade. Holiness, at least for a woman between the Garonne and the Rhône, was the property of noble infants and widows.

The boy Guilhem went to live with his father Bernart de la Grassa, "a heretic for a long time," and some other good men in 1195. He was raised by his widowed father for two and half years in a house at Lavaur and then for an unspecified time at another house until, no longer a child, he became "a clothed heretic" sometime in his adolescence. Guilhem de la Grassa, with Bernart de Caux listening, confessed he was a good man for five years before he understood, six or seven years into the crusade, that men like his father were "evil and damned." As a boy he performed the melioration to his father "so many times that he could not remember," and, when he was a good man, he received this courtesy wherever he went. In 1199 the good man Arnaut Jocglar made his small son, Peire, into a good man. "I stayed a clothed heretic with my father at Labécède for six years or more," the son recalled four decades later, eating and drinking "the food of the heretics." During these years Peire Jocglar offered the *melhoramen* to all older good men, including his father, "so many times that he could not remember." Na Ermengart Boer had two good women staying in her house at Mas-Saintes-Puelles during the first year of the crusade and, far from being unable to recall her meliorations to these women, testified that, in "any one week, I adored the female heretics in three or more exchanges."

The *melhoramen* was an honor rarely given to a woman before 1220 and never to small children. (Indeed, children younger than three, boys or girls, were not required to participate in *cortezia*, holy or otherwise, as they possessed no individual courtly identities separate from their mother.) Dulcia Faber explicitly remembered that the good women never "instructed her to honour them" during her four years sheltering in their houses.[15] The seclusion of good women in houses of similar women deliberately eliminated the need for their holiness to be meliorated and, in those few instances when they left their houses, the courtesies traded were paltry and only with other women who, like na Ermengart Boer, were good women as little girls. The divinity of a good woman, deprived of *cortezia*, remained inert, mediocre, and imperfect. A good man, constantly engaged in face-to-face courtliness, perpetually exchanging meliorations, was a living study of holiness being made and perfected.

The humanity of a good man was tempered, and so his divinity enhanced, through dress and food. In the hundreds of inquisitorial references to "clothed heretics" before the crusade, no person specified the cut and color of heretical cloth. The white-robed Cistercian Pierre des Vaux-de-Cernay, having no idea what the good men wore before the crusade, drolly dressed his heretics in the black habits of Cluniac monks.[16] In this world of subtle aesthetic modulations, where bows were counted and courtesies closely watched, a little modesty in dress was significant. All the more so as the Toulousain, Lauragais, and Albigeois were famous for fabrics of bright vermilion red (dyed from dried and crushed female kermes insects) and deep indigo blue (dyed from powdered and fermented woad).[17] A noble wearing undyed cloth, a young girl in a loose shirt tied with a leather cord, an old matron in coarse woolen hose, were all modest variations on mundane attire that, by disguising the human, enriched the sacred. Likewise, their diet was a humble menu of what other men and women ate; and, in many ways, no different to the diet of a Cistercian monk. Pierre des Vaux-de-Cernay, extrapolating from Augustine of Hippo on the ancient culinary habits of Manichaeans, falsely stated that the good men "renounced meat, eggs and cheese."[18] Although the consumption of meat from domesticated animals (cattle, sheep, pig, goat) was limited for good men, and the eating of animal meat (domesticated and wild) was variable and inconsistent for all persons between the Garonne and the Rhône, there was no interdiction on eggs and cheese. Poultry possibly was avoided, in the way a Cistercian avoided bird flesh, although duck and other waterfowl were probably eaten.[19] It was a cuisine where foods cooked and uncooked were equally acceptable; with a fondness for fish and legumes, pâtés and terrines, soups and stews, all based around bread (especially flat *fogassa*), olive oil, and red wine.[20] Foodstuffs (eel pies, salmon pastes, bean soups, jugs of wine, bowls of olive oil, dishes of chestnuts, sacks of grain, purses of salt) were common gifts given to the good men by their neighbors.[21] The appetite of a good man, conditioned by occasional fasts, was meant to be, like everything about him, moderate and balanced.

The improvement and enhancement inherent in the *melhoramen* meant that some good men were holier than others. The more words and bows a good man received, the more holiness he possessed, and, as such enrichment led to more courtesies, his divinity was incrementally amended and revised, day in, day out, by the relentless cycles of *cortezia*. "Now, it should be understood," and Pierre des Vaux-de-Cernay glossed what he heard of this ameliorative process with an invented epithet, "that some of the heretics were called 'perfected' [*perfecti*]."[22] Paradoxically, although the good men exemplified moderation and restraint, a remarkable amount of collective activity went into making them the embodiments of calm and equilibrium. A good man, unlike a good woman, could not live a secluded life and stay a holy person. He lived openly as a tradesman, artisan, farmer, or noble, supporting himself through his work, landholdings, or rents. Older men in this social and spiritual meliorism were favored over younger. Indeed, almost all holy good men before 1210 were widowers, mature men who, at earlier points in their lives, had been ordinary good and prudent men. In the summer of 1153, as the noble widower Piere Raimon de Barbaira gave himself to the Templars at Douzens, he gave the protection of "my youngest and greatly loved son" to six knights, the *viguier* (viscomital official) of Carcassonne, and "all the other knights of Barbaira and the rest of the men from the least to the greatest of the prudent men [*probi homines*] of Barbaira."[23] All the men of this village were good and proven men, all of them equivalent to the local nobles, and yet a spectrum of honor and prestige clearly differentiated one good man from another. The greatest of the prudent men were the holy good men, individuals whose honor and status had progressed and improved within this communal register, although, even in this perfected group, there were men of lesser worth. A dying boy or a man could circumvent this fitful hierarchy of holiness and honor and, without ever receiving the *melhoramen*, end his life as a blessed "friend of God."

In 1205 na Garzen, a good woman living alone in the village of Mas-Saintes-Puelles, carried her dying grandson, n'Ot, into her house and made the child into a good man. Three days later, and now a "friend of God," the little boy died. The child's mother, na Guilhema Meta de Quiders, never visited her son during those last days, although she did see the boy's corpse. (The feminine honorific "na" signified that Ot was so small as to still be identified with his mother and grandmother.) Na Fauressa, a decade later in the same village, was so gravely ill that she could not speak, see, or hear. With death only a breath away, she was carried to a house of good women and made into one of them. "Yet, I quickly recovered speech, so that I was carried back to my own house," and to her husband, Guilhem, lord of Mas-Saintes-Puelles.[24] The transformation of n'Ot and na Fauressa into holy persons and their seclusion within houses of good women or good men were common courtesies for noble girls and women, boys and men, "in the face of death." Raimon de Eclezia only became a good man as a boy because his father thought he was dying (although, unlike the married na Fauressa, he stayed a holy person when he recovered). This sacred metamorphosis of a man or woman *in extremis*, and the days and hours that followed until death, was known as the *consolamen*, the "consolation" or "comforting." The early inquisitors into heretical depravity quite deliberately (and confusingly) classified "consolations" and all other occasions when holy persons were made, such as little girls becoming good women, as acts of "heretication." Unquestionably, consolations imitated the divine transitions that men and women experienced at other, less terminal times and places. Yet, even with the inquisition imposing similarity on all "hereticating" episodes, hundreds of testimonies argued for differences and distinctions in the making of good men and good women.

Around 1200, "at Montmaur, Mirepoix, Laurac, and many other places throughout the land, I saw heretics not only dwelling openly, just like other men, but also openly preaching," remembered Guilhem de la Grassa. "And truly, nearly all men throughout the land would gather together and go hear, and adore, the heretics." Guilhem never preached when he was an adolescent good man; his father, Bernart, though, was a frequent preacher in the public squares of towns and villages. The composition and performance of general sermons before large communal audiences was a fundamental responsibility of mature good men. The good women almost never preached before 1220; if they did, it was always in the seclusion of their own houses before other good women. The necessity to hear and evaluate sermons on the relationship of humanity and divinity, while common to all Christians from the Mediterranean to the North Sea in the twelfth century, was unusually intense between the Garonne and Rhône. Crowds traveled from village to village to hear good men, monks, priests, and other holy persons explain the meaning of existence, either alone or in debate with one another. In 1208, for instance, the good man Izarn de Castres and the Waldensian Bernart Prim debated in the public square of Laurac.[25]

Two years earlier, Diego de Acebes, the bishop of Osma, accompanied by Dominic (Domingo) de Guzmán, the subprior of the cathedral at Osma and future founder of the Dominicans, and the papal legates Peire de Castelnau and Raoul preached and debated for eight days in the public square of Servian (a notable *castrum* north of Béziers) with a good man named Baudois and an itinerant preacher from France called Thierry, "although previously he was known as Guillaume."[26] The talent and skill that a good man displayed in his preaching, always judged and appraised by his audience, complemented and enhanced his accumulated honor and holiness.

A successful sermon resembled a memorable song. Speaking and singing in public were similar in the Middle Ages and, while such harmony applied to all preachers throughout Christendom, the good men (and Cistercians) were assessed and valued by the standards of the troubadours in the lands of the count of Toulouse. "I unhesitatingly consider wise the man who can divine in my song what each word means, as the theme unfolds," sang Marcabru, "for I myself have difficulty in clarifying obscure speech." Childish and clumsy troubadours "make trouble for good men and turn into strife what truth grants" when they deliberately interweave words with fractured and broken thoughts. Yet even limpid songs, like lucid "sermons and preaching, are not worth a jot" when wicked men mock what they hear as banal: "Folly is vile, a belt is leather."[27] The master troubadour Girault de Borneil, singing sometime after 1160, denounced all melodic platitudes, preferring songs with "meaning, rich and rare, bringing fine reputation," rather than unbridled nonsense.[28] Once, when he wanted a song to be just like a sermon, he sought "out fine, tractable words which are all loaded and full of strange, natural meanings," at once extraordinary and ordinary, even if, at first, "not everyone knows what they are."[29] No matter, "I firmly believe that a song is not worth as much to begin with as later when a man understands it."[30] A sermon, as much as a song, "has an imperfect reputation when all are not able to share it."[31] All preachers, whether good men or Cistercians, preached before lay audiences in the vernacular, usually decorating a sermon with Latin words and phrases. (If a preacher was unfamiliar with the mother tongue of his audience, like Bernard of Clairvaux in the Toulousain, then a monk or notary simultaneously translated the Latin into the vernacular.) A good sermon, with preacher and audience in courtly rapport, was a communal "dance for God." Frequently, in such stylized performances, what was said was less important than how it was said.[32] A skilled preacher, fine-tuned in word and manner, aimed for vivid clarity, with novelty reinforcing tradition, fantasy confirming faith, and passing ambiguity leading to lasting revelation—in short, the truth without being trite.

"In the year of the Lord 1165," Guilhem, the bishop of Albi, debated with those "who chose to be called 'good men' " in the public square of Lombers (a fortified village fifteen kilometers south of Albi). In the audience were the archbishop of Narbonne; the bishops of Toulouse, Nîmes, Lodève, and Agde; the abbots of Castres, Adorel, Candeil, Saint-Pons, Cendras, Fontfroide, and Gaillac; numerous other ecclesiastical officials; Raimon I Trencavel, viscount of Béziers, Agde, and Carcassonne; Constance, wife of Raimon V, count of Toulouse, and daughter of Louis VI, king of France; Sicart, viscount of Lautrec; Izarn de Dourgne; "and many other persons, almost the whole population of Albi and of Lombers, together with people of other towns." Gaucelis, the bishop of Lodève, at the command of the bishop of Albi, began the debate with a series of routine questions. Do you accept "the law of Moses, the Prophets, the Psalms, the Old Testament, and the doctors of the New Testament?" What about your faith and the preaching of it? What about the baptism of children? What about the consecration of the body and blood of Christ? What about marriage and if a husband and wife could be saved if they joined carnally? What about repentance and confession? Did repentance at the moment of death lead to salvation? What of mortally wounded knights repenting at the last moment? Should men and women confess their sins to a priest or a minister of the Church? Or to any layman? Or to those persons of whom Saint James said, "Confess your sins to one another"? Is contrition of the heart and confession by the mouth enough penance? Or can men and women make atonement "by fasts, flagellations, and almsgiving, lamenting their sins if they were capable of doing so?" The bishop of Lodève, pausing after each question, allowed those "who chose to be called 'good men,' and who had the support of the knights of Lombers," to respond.

"Before the whole gathering," sitting and standing around the public square of Lombers, the good men answered "that they did not accept the law of Moses, nor the Prophets, nor the Psalms, nor the Old Testament, but only the Gospels, the Epistles of Paul, the seven canonical Epistles, the Acts of the Apostles, and the Apocalypse." They would not expound their faith "unless forced to do so." They did not wish to discuss the baptism of children. The consecration of the body and blood of Christ could be "performed by any good man, cleric or layman." On this point they would say no more, "because they should not be forced to answer questions about their faith." The good men of Lombers "were not willing to reply" on the question of marriage, "except to say only that a man and a woman were joined together to avoid lewdness and fornication, as St Paul said in his Epistle." It was sufficient for the sick "to confess to whomever they chose." They had no opinion about dying warriors, "since St James only speaks of the sick." The apostle "said no more than that they should confess and so be saved." They had no wish to be better than the apostle, or to add anything of their own, "as bishops do." The good men "also made many unsolicited statements." They affirmed that they would never swear any oath, "as Jesus said in the Gospel and James in his Epistle." All bishops and priests who acted contrary to the commands of Christ (as specified in the Epistle of Paul) were "ravening wolves, hypocrites, and seducers," lovers of bows and salutations in streets and squares, desirous of being called "rabbi" and "master." All the clerics now crowding the public square of Lombers were like those priests who betrayed Christ and like traitors whose fingers gleamed with rings of gold. The good men "owed them no obedience, for they were wicked, not good teachers, but mercenaries."

Pons d'Arsac, the archbishop of Narbonne, Azalbertz, the bishop of Nîmes, Peire, the abbot of Cendras, and Anfoz Vidal, the abbot of Fontfroide, stung by the public contempt of bishops and priests, started vehemently arguing with the good men of Lombers. The good men, far from being cowed, fought back with equal vigor. All of them, bishops, abbots, and good men, tossed quotations from the New Testament back and forth; *Johannes* proving a point here, *Marcus* checking it there. The bishop of Lodève, after listening to both sides, called for silence and, on the basis of law and the New Testament—as the good men "would accept no decision except on the basis of the New Testament"—he pronounced a definitive sentence. "I, Gaucelis, bishop of Lodève, by the command of the bishop of Albi and his assessors, do adjudge those who call themselves 'good men' to be heretics. I condemn the sect of Olivier and his companions, and those who adhere to the sect of the heretics of Lombers, wherever they may be." (The good man Olivier was either the holiest good man in Lombers during the summer of 1165 or the first such prudent person in the village twenty or thirty years earlier.) The good men instantly "retorted that the bishop who delivered the sentence was a heretic, not them!" The false prophet Gaucelis was "a ravening wolf, a hypocrite, an enemy to God," whose judgment was deceitful and preordained; the debate at Lombers was a dishonorable farce. The bishop snapped back "that the judgement found against them was based on law," and he was willing to test his decision before the pope, the king of France, the count and countess of Toulouse, and the viscount of Béziers. He swore to charge the good men "with heresy in any Catholic court and that he would submit himself to the decision of a trial." Lord Gaucelis, pettish and swollen with anger, once more proclaimed the good men of Lombers to be "manifestly heretics and notorious for heresy!"

"Listen, O good men," and the good men of Lombers, recovering their poise (for they too had been petulant), spoke courteously to the audience around them, "our faith we will declare." They were doing this now, "out of love for you and for your sake," as the holy good men of their *castrum*. "You do not say that you will speak for the sake of the Lord," mocked the bishop of Lodève, still peevish, "but for the sake of the people." The good men ignored him. "We believe in one God, living and true, triune and one, the Father, the Son, and the Holy Spirit. The Son of God took on flesh, was baptised in the Jordan, fasted in the wilderness, preached our salvation, suffered, died, and was buried, descended into hell, arose on the third day, and ascended into heaven." This orthodox theology, delivered with stiff formality, continued in its unexceptional way for another two minutes until the somewhat prickly conclusion: "If there be anything further in the Church that can be shown from the Gospels and Epistles, we will credit and confess it." The faith of the good men of Lombers—as they told it, as the scribe recorded it, as later scribes rewrote it—was blandly conformist, almost to the point of parody, except for the sharp focus on the New Testament and the utter dismissal of the Old. "I, Gaucelis, bishop of Lodève," having exhausted the standard repertoire of censure and complaint against persons accused of heresy, eventually condemned the good men for holding the wrong opinions on oath taking. Guilhem, the bishop of Albi, reluctantly approved this insipid judgment. The debate at Lombers drew to an inconsequential close, neither here nor there, bathetic at best. Similar debates with similar outcomes happened in many villages and towns before the crusade. The good men of Lombers, like the good men of Fanjeaux and the good men of Carcassonne, did not think of themselves as heretics and, though aware that some Church officials accused them of heresy, were neither cowered nor frightened by the accusation. The good men, while scathing in debate about vainglorious bishops and priests, never assumed that divinity was denied to worthy clerics, such as honorable monks and prudent priests; it was just that holiness was a gift given, more frequently, more deservedly, to them.[33]

In 1173 Valdes, "who had amassed a great fortune through the iniquity of usury," was walking through the streets of Lyon one Sunday in spring when, coming across a crowd listening to a *joglar* singing, he lingered to hear the minstrel's song. The *joglar* was performing the story of Saint Alexis and, having already sung about the saint as a wandering monk in the Syrian desert, was ending with Alexis traveling to Rome, bedraggled and holy, to die peacefully in his father's house. Valdes, deeply moved by the saint's death, invited the itinerant minstrel to his house so that he could hear the song from start to finish. The next morning, Valdes "hastened to the school of theology to seek counsel for his soul's welfare and, when he had been instructed in the many ways of coming to God, he asked the master which was the most sure and perfect way of all." The theologian replied with the words of Christ: "If you would be perfect, go and sell what you have, give all to the poor, and come follow me and you will have treasure in heaven." These holy words—the very same words that inspired Anthony of Egypt around 270 to abandon his farm in the Nile delta and retreat to the waterless desert as the first monk—became the ideal by which Valdes would now model his life. Immediately, he offered his wife "the choice of keeping for herself all his possessions in either movable goods or in property, that is, lands and water, woods, meadows, houses, rents, vineyards, mills, and ovens." His wife, confused and upset at having to do this, chose the property. Valdes, out of his remaining wealth, "returned what he had acquired unjustly," bestowed a large portion on his two little daughters, "whom he placed in the order of Fontevrault without his wife's knowledge," and gave the greatest part to the needs of the poor. "No man can serve two masters, God and Mammon," Valdes cried out on the Assumption of the Blessed Virgin as he cheerfully "scattered money to the poor in the streets."[34]

Three years later, despite being mocked as mad throughout the Lyonnaise, Valdes had acquired a following who gave all they possessed "to the poor and willingly devoted themselves to poverty." Little by little, the followers of Valdes began to preach, publicly and privately, "against their own sins and the sins of others." Valdes—learning parts of the Gospel by heart, always singing songs—preached and sang in the streets and broadways. In March 1179, during the Third Lateran Council summoned by Pope Alexander III, the English courtier-cleric Walter Map "saw simple and illiterate men called Waldenses, after their leader, Valdes, who was a citizen of Lyon on the Rhône." These grubby men, these puddles in the street, presented the pope "with a book written in French which contained a text and a gloss of the Psalms and many of the books of both Testaments." They sincerely requested the pope to authorize them to preach, "although they were nothing more than dabblers." These Waldenses "go about two by two, barefoot, clad in woollen garments, owning nothing, holding all things common like the apostles, naked, following a naked Christ." Walter Map mostly laughed and sneered at the Waldensians, except for one serious comment amid the laughter: "If we admit them, we shall be driven out."[35] An anonymous chronicler, however, had Alexander III warmly embracing Valdes at the council, "approving his vow of poverty but forbidding preaching by either himself or his followers unless welcomed by the local priests."[36] This partial approval was removed in 1184, when Pope Lucius III decreed at the Council of Verona that any persons, especially "the Poor Men of Lyon," who preached without the permission of pope or bishop were condemned to perpetual anathema. (The pope also condemned Cathars, Paterenes, *Humiliati*, and the even more exotic *Passagini*, *Josephini*, and *Arnaldistas*).[37] Valdes and his followers ignored such decrees and condemnations. This disobedience, wrote the Dominican Étienne de Bourbon in the middle of the thirteenth century, forced the Church to judge "them most hostile, infectious, and dangerous heretics, who wander everywhere, assuming the appearance but not the reality of holiness and sincerity."[38]

Peire Jocglar, eighty years after the debate at Lombers, told Bernart de Caux about the preaching of the good men in 1205. "I heard the heretics saying errors about visible things," he confessed on Tuesday, 4 July 1245; namely, "that God didn't make them." The sacred host, he remembered hearing, "isn't the body of the Lord." There was no salvation in baptism or matrimony, and "the bodies of the dead will not be resurrected." It was around this time that Peire, after six years as a youthful good man, married the adolescent na Ava when her seclusion as a child good woman ended (and whom he recalled glimpsing, every so often, during her last three years as a "clothed heretic"). Despite marriage, children, holy war, and "leaving the sect of the heretics" forty years earlier, he still believed in the faith of the good men, "just as though I were a heretic."[39] The early inquisitors focused much less on ideas than habits; no overtly elaborate doctrines were recorded. Nevertheless, their questions still presupposed an intellectual coherence, especially a Manichaean dualism, that never existed before the crusade. Peire, even within the constraints of the inquisition, was not alone in describing the beliefs of the good men as rather sparse, and far from dualistic, at the beginning of the thirteenth century. The ideas of the good men before the crusade—one of the most vexing historical problems about them—should not be confused with, or assumed to be the same as, the heretical notions that Catholic polemists accused them of believing. The world in which the good men had meaning and purpose was so changed by the crusade—slowly at first, then quite drastically—that the thoughts and actions of the good men in 1200 scarcely resemble, except in the most superficial way, the thoughts and actions of the good men after 1230. Peire Jocglar (with some inquisitorial prompting) might have believed in certain continuities over half a century—he thought the man still thought the same as the boy—but the modern historian should be wary of doing the same.

"The world has turned from *cortezia* to villainy and corruption," sang Girault de Borneil about a universe unrestrained by courtliness. The earth was visibly ruined by boorish landowning peasants, and the honor of heaven, immaterial but all around, was dissipated through wickedness, deceit, and worthless flattery. As the good men lost their proven "superiority," or rather "vile wretches and cackling slanderers have stolen it with their sly, stubborn, hard hearts," these holy persons disappeared, "so for one good man" there were now a hundred of the worst. "What will these good men do if God takes no revenge?" In village after village, would the good men cease to be models of heavenly honor, "will they cease to show forth His will," His love, His caprice? Listen, "I advise them against this." A man "who dies a good man" not only cultivated God's honor, enhancing His divine wealth, but merited some of His brilliant treasure—a treasure forever flickering and changing, difficult to see, hard to hold. Girault, in imagining a world without good men, faithfully described the universe that needed them. There was no immutable divide separating heaven and earth. Quite the contrary: the border was supple and changeable, with spirit and matter swirling around each other in a maelstrom of confusion and capriciousness. The sacred was as fragmented as the profane, heavenly honor fluctuated as much as earthly honor—with one profound and re-demptive difference. Holiness, the honor and treasure of God, could be fixed and secured, possessed and exchanged, through *cortezia*, especially in the decorous words and bows given to the good men. The trouble with terrestrial honor was that there was no measured and guaranteed way of maintaining it, let alone sharing it, short of fractious litigation, thuggery, and violence. This raw cycle of instability and uncertainty, perpetually feeding upon itself, was all the work of men. This false and imperfect honor, unable to be ameliorated, was a solvent upon the holy, corroding and degrading the honor of God.[40]

The good men, sharing God's honor and showing His love in the world, followed the Apostles and imitated His Son. This holy mimesis defined Latin Christendom from the end of the eleventh century until the beginning of the sixteenth.[41] "Let us imitate this man," said Bernard of Clairvaux about the Son of God, "since He came for this purpose to give us the form and to show us the way."[42] The splendor and sorrow of Christ in the New Testament was, more than anything else, a narrative about the ebb and flow of the divine and the human in the living of a life. "In My life you may know your way," He spoke through the abbot of Clairvaux, "so that just as I held the unswerving paths of poverty and obedience, humility and patience, love and mercy, so you too will follow these footsteps."[43] The good men modestly conformed to this model of the

Savior. Nevertheless, His footstep to a good man and His gait to a Cistercian, though similar, were still distinct. The history of Christ's existence on earth was resiliently linear to a Catholic intellectual. The testament of His life was a seamless forward flow of unique thoughts and actions. The crawling child led to the crucified adult. The boy of five related to the man at thirty. His compassion for all persons, living or dead, derived from His sequent human experiences. "This is why He was born an infant and advanced to manhood through all the stages of life, so that He might be lacking in no age," preached Bernard of Clairvaux (in his sixty-sixth sermon inspired by the *Song of Songs*) against vulpine heretics who denied the holy empiricism of His continuity as a man. As the Son of God used His humanity to save the world, so ordinary men and women could use their humanity to imitate His divinity and so save themselves.[44] To a good man, though, the story of Christ was an episodic narrative, fitful, startling, veering forward, lurching backward, where divine salvation—the seizure and perfection of holiness—was secured through human moderation.

The life of Christ, the rule by which the good men measured their existence, was nevertheless a story without an obvious apotheosis: His crucifixion was not the culmination of His sojourn on earth or the historical event around which all time (what had happened, was happening, or would happen) pivoted. The Son of God did not save the world through His suffering as a man, bleeding painfully, dying dishonorably, where all His terrestrial moments were determined by, and imbued with, His tragic and climactic spectacle on the cross. Rather, the Son of God saved the world by showing how He mollified His humanity, that visibly transient and wayward property of all persons, through cultivating, maintaining, and enhancing the divine honor given to Him by His Father. He demonstrated an art to living in the world, a holy and honorable aesthetic, where men and women resembled Him not through succumbing to their humanity, not through experiencing birth and death as a path to the afterlife, but through the courtly artifices they built to restrain and moderate the visibly human. Existence was a constantly shifting and changing labyrinth and not a straight line. The boy or girl at ten was not accountable to the man or woman at forty in this nonlinear universe. A person's life was made from innumerable transient and mutable episodes that, while meaningful and intense at specific times and places, did not necessarily proceed, sequentially, one into the other. Baptism was not, in and of itself, wrong—indeed, the good men thought it benign—just the notion that the ceremony had any continuous redemptive worth for an individual. Similarly, marriage—which happened sooner or later to all men and women during adolescence—was not a threshold to salvation. A resurrected body—evidence of individual continuity from life into death—simply made no sense. The New Testament with Christ was not related to the Old without Him. These beliefs, widespread among ordinary Christians before the crusade, were never thought of as heretical. The Son of God, after all, believed them too.

I N OUR LANDS the little foxes destroy the vineyards planted by the right hand of the Lord," lamented Raimon V, count of Toulouse, as he petitioned the abbot of Cîteaux, Alexander, in the late autumn of 1177. The count, drawing upon three decades of Cistercian rhetoric and obsession, described rivers of filth harrowing his province, flooding their banks, uprooting trees, making pools of poison—a peccant domain dying from the cancer of heresy. "So far has this putrefying plague of heresy spread that nearly all who believe it think they are serving God!" Faithless sons pretend to be angels of light. "Priests perverted by this fetid heresy will administer it to the faithful and churches once venerated in the past will lie as untilled fields," forever barren, forever ruined, so that "baptism will be denied, the Eucharist abominated, penance judged insignificant, the creation of man and the resurrection of the flesh scornfully repudiated, and all sacraments of the Church annulled and," most sinful of all, "even the two principles will be introduced." The count, girding himself with the temporal sword, "claim as my own the wrath of God and confess that God has made me His servant to put an end to such faithlessness." Yet, "my powers are inadequate to the task, indeed, the nobles of my land, satiated with this pestilence of faithlessness, cultivate the heresy," and with the faith ploughed under, great masses of men support them. "I dare not nor am I able to confront them." The count begged the Cistercians, through their prayers and, most important, their influence with Louis VII, the king of France, to aid him "with the strong fist of God" in the destruction of his unfaithful nobles. "I am convinced the king of France should be summoned, as I believe his presence will put an end to this evil." Raimon V promised that if the king marched south, "I will open cities to him, hand over towns and fortified places to his punishment, show him the heretics and," quite shockingly, "help him wipe out all the armies and enemies of Christ."[1]

Raimon V, couching his blunt political fears in the soaring apocalypticism of rebellious heretics poised to destroy his lands, charged the Cistercians to exhort the French monarchy to a crusade against heresy in all but name. An astonishingly brazen proposition—and so the reason for comital appeal to the abbot of Cîteaux—as the count had renounced the suzerainty of the French king four years earlier. On Friday, 25 February 1173, Raimon did homage for Toulouse as a hereditary fief—along with an annual payment of 100 marks of silver, ten warhorses, and a promise of military service when summoned—to Henry II, king of England and duke of Normandy, his eldest son, Henry, "the young king," and his second son, Richard, count of Poitou and duke of Aquitaine.[2] This act of obeisance satisfied—or rather, briefly suspended—the dynastic claims of Henry II upon the county of Toulouse, which, beginning with a long summer war throughout the Agenais and Quercy in 1159, the king waged on behalf of his wife na Elionor (Eleanor), daughter of Guilhem X, duke of Aquitaine and count of Poitiers. This proprietorial conflict originated two generations earlier, when Guilhem IV, count of Toulouse, died around 1096 leaving no male heirs. Although the late count's crusader brother Raimon IV of Saint-Gilles easily succeeded to the county, the rights of a daughter, na Felipa, were vigorously advocated by her husband and Elionor's grandfather, Guilhem IX, the famous troubadour-duke of Aquitaine.[3] The homage of Raimon V to the Plantagenets turned Louis VII into a shadow king, "not only in Toulouse but in all our region from the Garonne to the Rhône," complained na Ermengart, viscountess of Narbonne.[4] The French monarch, indolent and weak—and married to na Elionor of Aquitaine himself for fifteen years until 1152—dismissed all worries, ignored all complaints. Raimon V, always the opportunist, seized Narbonne from the forlorn viscountess in 1177 and, always the irritant, excited new wars with old enemies for another thirty years.[5]

Roger II Trencavel, viscount of Béziers, his young nephew Bernart Ato de Nîmes, and Guy Guerrejat, lord of Montpellier, quickly swore oaths to defend na Ermengart and to bring "evil war" upon Raimon V and his son. The viscount, bitterly regretting his youthful marriage (arranged by na Ermengart) to Raimon's daughter in November 1171, realigned himself with Alfons II, king of Aragon and count of Barcelona, ordering all "prudent men and magnates of my lands to attend upon you with the honors and castles they hold from me."[6] The count of Toulouse, apart from the seasonal hostilities along the Garonne with the Plantagenets, routinely skirmished along the Rhône with the Aragonese over the county of Provence. This conflict with Alfons II, somewhat reduced when Henry II arbitrated a peace between count and king in 1173, now resumed with bestial ferocity. The little foxes in the vineyard were the knights and mercenaries of Alfons II and Roger II, along with hundreds of petty nobles whose loyalties waxed and waned from *senhor* to *senhor*. Raimon V, as devious in rhetoric as in war, slandered his enemies with the stain of heresy in the vain hope that Louis VII would overlook the recent past—including the count's divorcing the king's sister to marry the widowed countess of Provence—and undertake the sacred slaughter of faithless nobles. The shadow king, despite the appeals of Cîteaux, was not to be "the strong fist of God." The lands of the count of Toulouse, though spared the apocalyptic crusade he wished upon them, were instead slowly mutilated by one fierce little war after another. Every day in 1179, "the madness of heresy increases," cried Pons d'Arsac, archbishop of Narbonne, to his suffragan bishops, because "Brabançons, Aragonese, Coterels, Basques, and other foreign mercenaries and thieves" ravage the domains of the faithless princes (Raimon V, Roger II, Bernart Ato) who hired them.[7] Two years later, Étienne, abbot of Saint-Germain-des-Prés, traveling through the Toulousain, saw "nothing but burned villages," deserted fields, holy places in ashes—"the very image of death."[8]

"In Gascony and the lands of Albi and Toulouse, and in other places, those heretics, whom some call Cathars, others the Patarenes, others the *Publicani*, and others by different names," decreed the ultimate canon of the Third Lateran Council, "we declare that they and their defenders and those who receive them are under anathema." Now, "regarding Brabançons, Aragonese, Coterels, Basques, and Triaverdines," laying waste those lands like pagans, "we likewise decree that those who hire, keep or support them," especially pernicious princes, "should be subject in every way to the same sentence and penalty as the aforementioned heretics." Importantly, "we receive under the protection of the Church, as we do those who visit the Lord's sepulchre," all men who would expunge such faithless persons. Alexander III saw no difference between heretics, mercenaries, and the princes who nourished them: they all lacerated Christendom as schismatics. The privileges of fighting schismatics in the Toulousain were the same as fighting Saracens in the Holy Land. The pope was tormented by schism as three successive (and successful) antipopes had challenged him from 1159, when he was elected by a majority of the cardinals, until the year before the Lateran Council. The powerful Emperor Frederick Barbarossa created and sustained these other popes. All three antipopes were "heresiarchs" and "schismatics" to the Lateran Council.[9] It was during this long schism that Raimon V supported the second of these imperial popes and, blessed by this pliable pontiff, had his marriage to the sister of Louis VII annulled. The count even expelled the clerical allies of Alexander III from his lands—which, not surprisingly, were then placed under interdict by the pope.[10] The Lateran Council was animated by a visceral hatred of schism and schismatics. The recondite naming of the heretics infesting the Agenais, Toulousain, and Albigeois—abstruse then and absurd now—damned them as schismatics who, if they did not return to the Church as did the Cathars of old, must be brutally purged from Christendom.

The archbishop of Narbonne's *cri de coeur* was largely a recitation of what he had heard at the Lateran Council a few months earlier, except, knowing that the council's arcane heresiology was meant only for Roman canonists and Parisian intellectuals, he saw no need to mention Cathars, Patarenes, or *Publicani.* His complaint was no less heartfelt through repetition, even if the swarming mercenaries were perhaps less virulent than the rhetoric about them. Unquestionably, itinerant bands of routiers and mercenaries existed and, as Raimon V joined the rebellion of the "young king" Henry against his father in 1183, the count and the Plantagenets began another series of wars that attracted ever more Coterels (from the small mail coats they wore) and journeymen-warriors from Brabant. These new hostilities, the last half of a debilitating "forty-years war" according to the English chronicler William of Newburgh, ended only when Raimon VI, count of Toulouse, married Joanna, sister of Richard the Lionheart, king of England, in 1196.[11] Yet, so many of the thieves and mercenaries condemned as rapine foxes were no more than local pettifogging nobles who, despite the mantle of courtliness and the moderation of good men, were always eager to seize honor from their neighbors. The turmoil of war and the rhetoric of heresy provided more than enough chances and excuses for such attacks and sieges. The ecclesiastical bromides for this erratic ferocity were oaths of peace.[12] In April 1207 Peire de Castelnau excommunicated Raimon VI for his unwillingness to swear to a peace along the Rhône and, as one went with the other, for employing mercenaries.[13] Innocent III, when he confirmed this excommunication, warned the count that if he did not cease his acts of war, "then we enjoin all the princes around you to rise against you as an enemy of Christ," and here the words of the father haunted the son, "lest they become even more infected by the stain of heresy under your rule."[14] Ten months later "one of those mercenaries of Satan" murdered the papal legate.

Arnau Amalric, the abbot of Cîteaux, was at the Lateran palace when Innocent III heard of Peire de Castelnau's death. "Brother, go to Carcassonne and to great Toulouse on the Garonne," the pope ordered the Cistercian, "and lead the crusading host against the heretical traitors." The abbot, standing by a marble column, nodded. "In the name of Jesus Christ, pardon the soldiers of all their sins." Arnau Amalric immediately left Rome and, galloping hard all summer, arrived at Cîteaux on Sunday, 14 September 1208, for the Cistercian general chapter. There, surrounded by "all the white monks who wore mitres," the abbot proudly displayed a letter from Innocent III that named him legate and leader of the *crucesignati*.[15] "Go here and there about the world," Arnau Amalric commanded all Cistercians, "over the whole length and breath of Holy Christendom," and, armed with speech sharper than a sword, preach that all Christians take the cross against the pestilence of heresy. The weeping wounds of Christ must be stanched and avenged by a great and holy war.[16]

"I'm so tough that all the scraps and shreds of war cling to me," sang the troubadour Bertran de Born, lord of Autafort, around 1180. "A stye in your eye if you want my scraps!" War was joyful, capricious, and noble; peace was aberrant, gutless, and villainous. "If I start a war in the lead," he laughed, "then peace is no consolation!" He was at one with war, with *guerra*, "since I don't keep or know any other creed!"[17] He cherished April and May as the months when trees hummed with singing birds and meadows bawled with knights and horses in armor. Bird songs and battle cries were the tidings of spring. "Nothing, I tell you, is as delicious (neither eating nor drinking nor sleeping) as hearing the cry 'At 'em!' go up from both sides and the clamour of riderless horses in the shadows and hearing men cry 'Help! Help!' " Let every *ome de paratge*, let every man of honor, think only of war, "think only of hacking heads and arms, since a dead man is more valorous than an unscathed victor."[18] The lord of Autafort celebrated and satirized the grasping bellicosity that thousands of Provençal nobles, great and small, honored as the very essence of their existence. "All day I struggle and fight," his lands ravaged, his villages burned, "as there isn't a scheming or cowardly enemy who doesn't attack me!"[19] He lauded with extravagant wit, bitter parody, and candid affection the rampant warfare that popes and preachers, counts and kings, denounced as the succor of heresy. "I see many a beggarly baron suffering war and turmoil and anguish. I care little about their grief and less about their hurt—so I'll be jolly with a song!"[20] Dante acclaimed him as the most illustrious vernacular poet on war (along with Arnaut Daniel on love and Girault de Borneil on integrity).[21] "War pleases me," Bertran sang in 1198, "because I see courts and gifts and pleasure and song all enhanced by war."[22] A sardonic hymn no less truthful, no less blissful, even though the troubadour was now a monk in the Cistercian abbey of Dalon (on the River Dalon near Autafort), where, seventeen years later, he died amid the scraps and shreds of holy war.

Every spring and summer hundreds of small wars erupted between the Garonne and the Rhône. These wars were short-lived local affairs: gangs of village notables raiding and burning the fields and vineyards of neighboring villages; a hundred or so men assaulting and besieging a castle for a fortnight; headlong charges by little armies across tiny meadows; and savage mêlées of a few dozen horsemen. This warfare was no less violent or bloody for being so parochial, and yet, as with courtliness, the vital importance of these seasonal hostilities lay in the affirmation or denial of individual honor. War was especially important for an impoverished noble who, if judged as no better than a peasant by the *cortezia* of his village, might gain valor in battle, gain possessions in a raid, and so amend his honor and prestige. Indeed, while the proprietary rewards were mostly meager—bags of oats, wine, piglets, goats, sheep, iron helmets, pillowcases, and a hundred-shilling horse, if fortunate—the honorific compensations were abundant. Warfare had the same powerful ameliorative quality as courtliness. "War," even Bertran de Born conceded, "makes a peasant courtly."[23] Although nobles acted as if the rights of *guerra* were restricted only to themselves—troubadour songs repeatedly emphasized this point—artisans or farmers habitually participated in forays and sieges and, through such participation, were enhanced in status. As these small wars flared from village to field to castle the various armies crossed and crisscrossed the fractured and frag-mented possessory rights and claims of other men and women with whom they were not (at present) fighting. The risk of a skirmish in a vineyard inadvertently leading to war with one or more persons who possessed fractions of the trampled vines demanded not only surprising spatial precision in these small wars but also necessitated an astonishing variety of agreements (*covinens* in Provençal, *convenientia* in Latin) between persons about the possibility (accidental or not) of such martial infrac-tions.[24] These small wars, while distinct from the larger wars of the kings of England and Aragon and the counts of Toulouse, were routinely absorbed into the greater conflicts, sometimes only for a battle, sometimes all summer long. More often than not, the great Provençal lords were frustrated by their inability to control these seemingly mercurial and mutable wars.

Paradoxically, although this volatile warfare was condemned as nour-ishing the little foxes and serpents of heresy, it was the very phenomenon that caused so many Provençal nobles to become soldiers of Christ in the summer of 1209. As much as they feared the cancer of heresy poisoning their villages and fields, they feared being attacked as pestiferous by neighbors signed with the cross. As much as they wanted to walk like Him in their own lands, they wanted to seize the goods of neighbors who had not yielded to Him. The easy rapport of greed and sanctity, violence and divinity, though common to all medieval crusaders, was distinctly avid and covetous, prudent and ravening, among the Provençal *crucesignati*. "So many thousands will depart for battle in poverty," promised a popular troubadour song on the First Crusade, "all will return rich men."[25] (This crusade *canso* was in fact so well known that Guilhem de Tudela openly copied its cadence and structure in his *crozada* song.)[26] The crusade against the *Provinciales heretici* guaranteed a summer of exuberant war-making and the opportunity for sacred and martial honor. It would be similar, if grander and more exultant, to the small summer war that Henri de Marcy waged against the "Albigensian heretics" at Lavaur in 1181. These assumptions about warfare were shattered within a year of the holy war on heresy, especially after the first horrific summer. The joy of war that Bertran de Born mocked and adored, with its discrete pleasures and pains, was little more than esteemed nostalgia when he died. Dante, out of his high regard for the dead troubadour, damned him to the ninth *bolgia* of hell as "a sower of scandal and schism." Bertran as the celebrant of dissension when alive, especially between sons and fathers, vassals and lords, was torn apart in death. He circled a "sad road" holding his severed head before him like a lamp. One of his shredded companions on the road was the quintessential Christian schismatic: Muhammad, split from groin to chin.[27]

"A just war is waged by an authoritative edict to avenge injuries," stated the canon lawyer Gratian (citing Augustine of Hippo) around 1140.[28] The hypothetical example of a *justum bellum*: Catholic bishops violently compelling heretical bishops (and the faithful they had poisoned) to return to the Church. The pope, deriving his civil jurisdiction from the emperor, had the authority to order Catholic and obedient bishops of a particular region to summon knights to fight heretical and schismatic bishops within that region. (Gratian, though mostly using "schismatic" and "heretic" interchangeably, at one point quoted Saint Jerome's ancient distinction that "schism" was episcopal dissent from the Church, whereas "heresy" was the perversion of dogma.)[29] In this speculative scenario the soldiers of the orthodox bishops clashed in open battles with the heterodox. Some of the heretics were unavoidably killed (it was not murder to kill an excommunicated person); some had their properties confiscated (a heretic *qua* heretic inherently lacked the spirit of justice, *ergo*, he was legally unable to possess property and so all his goods were to be confiscated by a

Catholic); and some were coerced through imprisonment back into the Catholic faith. All possible avenues to victory must be followed in a just war; all possible weapons must be used in rendering justice to the unjust. Soldiers who obeyed divine exhortations to kill the faithless were the avenging hands of God and instruments of His wrath. A just war was fought by a faithful warrior with an inward "precept of patience" that compassionately guided and legitimated his outward bellicosity. An act of violence against a heretic was actually an act of benevolence that lovingly released the sinner from his sin. A just war always pleased Him. Gratian, whose warm smile greeted Dante in paradise,[30] never considered the crusades to the eastern Mediterranean as just wars. Legally, ethically, the epitome of a *justum bellum* was a holy war against heretics within Christendom.[31]

Innocent III augmented this jurisprudence in 1199 when he instructed the people and clergy of Viterbo (northwest of Rome at the foot of the Cimini mountains) that heresy was "lese-majesty" against Christ as head of the Church. The little foxes in the Lord's vineyard—who, despite motley physiognomies, were all entwined at the tail—"injured" His sovereignty over heaven and earth. A heretic committed treason when he turned away from the faith, and so all his goods were to be confiscated and all his descendants disinherited. All "defenders, harbourers, supporters, and believers in heretics" were as treasonous as heretics themselves and were to be similarly punished.[32] Three years later the pope discussed an "injured" region of Bosnia with the archbishop of Split. "A multitude of certain men, strongly suspected of being guilty of the heresy of the Cathars," lived unmolested and unpunished in the lands of the noble Ban Kulin. This Bosnian lordling pleaded ignorance and innocence about these men; "he believed them not to be heretics but to be Catholics." The pope told him he was wrong; these men were treasonous schismatics uprooting the faith, cutting down His vineyard. Ban Kulin, scolded by the pope, threatened by the king of Hungary, must "suppress those kind of men from all lands subject to him, confiscating all of their goods."[33] Innocent III explicitly used *Cathari* in his letter to the archbishop of Split as a synonym for schismatics; he never implied that dualism existed in Bosnia or that the heretics of Ban Kulin corresponded with (as theologians or immigrants) the heretics of Raimon VI. (Gratian briefly mentioned the *Cathari*, though only as one more schismatic sect in a long inventory of ancient Christian heresies he copied from the seventh-century encyclopedist Isidore, archbishop of Seville.)[34] The greatest wounds inflicted by the little foxes were in the lands of the count of Toulouse. A war to avenge these injuries would be—as Raimon V pleaded, as Alexander III decreed—most just, most holy, and most pleasing to Him.

On Saturday, 15 August 1198, seven months after his elevation to the papal throne at the age of thirty-seven, Innocent III sent an impassioned letter to all the prelates in all provinces of Latin Christendom. He lamented the history of the Holy Land since Saladin (Salah al-Din Yusuf ibn Ayyub), sultan of Egypt and Syria, slaughtered a crusader army at the Horns of Hattin (two hills overlooking the Sea of Galilee) and reconquered Jerusalem in 1187. "Following the pitiable collapse of the territory of Jerusalem, following the shameful massacre of the Christian people, following the deplorable invasion of that land upon which the feet of Christ once stood," the Apostolic See was wretched with grief. "It cried out and wailed to such an extent that due to incessant wailing, its throat was made hoarse, and from excessive weeping, its eyes almost failed." Jerusalem was still "imprisoned by the impious," in spite of the great crusade led by a dazzling Richard the Lionheart and a vapid Philip II Augustus in 1191. "Where is your God? He can neither deliver Himself nor you from our hands," taunted His enemies. "How, brothers and sons, are we to refute the insults of insulters?" A new crusade to the Levant was the apostolic answer. Come to the aid of Him, "as it was for you that He emptied Himself, accepting the form of a servant, was made in the form of a man and appeared in human likeness." The pope ordered cities and nobles to ready soldiers for a two-year pilgrimage beginning next March. He granted a full pardon of sins for any man who endured the rigors and expense of this journey in person. Significantly, he granted a full pardon to those who merely sent (at their own expense) other men. A pilgrim's debts and interest payments were suspended, and interest already charged by Jews was to be reimbursed. "Therefore, let no one withhold himself from this labour," from this holy expedition into the land of His birth.[35]

Four years later a crusade consisting mostly of French and Venetian pilgrims, and ostensibly sailing to Palestine, violently seized the Christian city of Zara (belonging to Imre, king of Hungary) on the Dalmatian coast. Innocent III was outraged: the Crucified One was "injured" when Christians attacked Christians without apostolic approval. The French begged forgiveness; the Venetians argued that Zara belonged to them and denied culpability; the pope absolved the former and excommunicated the latter. The crusaders then intervened in the politics of the Byzantine Empire. Alexios Angelos, whose aunt was married to the brother of the leading crusader, Boniface, marquis of Montferrat, promised the return of the Greek Church to Rome, 200,000 silver marks, and Byzantine support invading Ayyubid Egypt, if the pilgrims overthrew his uncle, Emperor Alexios III Angelos. The crusader nobility agreed and, with a poorly coordinated plan, assailed Constantinople by land and sea in June 1203.

A quixotic enterprise, considering the magnificent urban walls and fortifications, yet a small fire set by the Venetians soon blasted through the city, devouring fifty thousand square meters. The citizens of Constantinople renounced the uncle and acclaimed the nephew as *basileus*. Innocent III was saddened by the further debasement of the crusade when he heard the news. Alexios IV Angelos was strangled in a palace coup eight months later as a pretender subservient to the crusaders, those loathsome schismatics polluting the Queen of Cities. On Monday, 12 April 1204, the crusaders responded by looting Constantinople with irredeemable vandalism and savagery. A month later they elected their own *imperator* and proclaimed a Latin Empire of Constantinople. Innocent III was initially elated that the Greek and Latin Churches were seemingly reunited, seeing it as a sign of the Second Coming. As more details reached Rome, his mood changed, and the sack of Constantinople was "nothing other than an example of pestilence and the works of hell." Such depravity by His soldiers was a sign that Christendom itself was diseased, and the more unrestrained this plague, the more unattainable was Jerusalem.[36]

On Friday, 28 May 1204, Innocent III tried to coax Philip II Augustus into an armed pilgrimage against the little foxes destroying His vines in the lands of the count of Toulouse. Raimon VI and those subject to him were, as always, unwilling to eliminate these beasts; indeed, repined the pope, some clerics in these injured lands were "rapacious wolves in sheep's clothing," ripping apart the Church. These wild animals and those who protected them were traitors to the Son of God; as betrayers of His sovereignty they were to be proscribed, expelled from the royal domain by royal force, with all their goods confiscated. (Intriguingly, while the ubiquitous foxes scampered under the vines, uprooting the faith, the pope never specifically mentioned heresy or heretics.) "So that the material sword can be seen to compensate for the deficiency of the spiritual sword," the pope concluded with a marvelous gift, "you may obtain the same indulgence of sins which we grant to those who cross over to aid the Holy Land."[37] Philip, who endured a miserable summer at Acre in 1191, was not tempted to "walk where He walked" in his own realm. Four years later, when Innocent III exhorted all Christians to avenge the death of Peire de Castelnau with a holy expedition against the count of Toulouse, the king was no more enthusiastic about this universal summons to kill the little foxes than the previous uniquely French invitation. In particular, "concerning the matter of your declaring the count's lands open to occupation," the king curtly told the pope, "I must tell you that I have been advised by learned and illustrious men that you cannot by law do this until he is condemned for heresy." The count, as far as the king was informed, was not accused of heresy. "We say this not to excuse him, since we would rather accuse than excuse him." Needless to say, if the accusation arose, Philip II Augustus would—God willing—act on it.[38]

Throughout the summer and autumn of 1208 Innocent III failed to cajole Philip II Augustus into purifying the villages and towns of Raimon VI with a martial pilgrimage. The king, frustrated by papal perseverance, reluctantly allowed two French barons (the duke of Burgundy and the count of Nevers) to participate in a discreet expedition (only five hundred knights) into the lands of the count of Toulouse. The pope, frustrated by royal indifference, issued a separate general exhortation in October to all the archbishops, bishops, and clergy of France to preach and enjoin Christian knights "to contribute to this most holy work" of exterminating the serpent and cancer of heretical depravity in *Provincia*. All who marked themselves with the "life-giving sign of the cross" were to "know that remission of sins has been granted by God and His vicar to all who, fired by zeal for the orthodox faith, take up arms for this work of piety." The same privileges accruing to an armed journey to His sepulchre in the Holy Land were to be given all warriors "walking in the way of Christ" between the Garonne and the Rhône. The family and property of a man who "yielded to Christ" were protected from the time he took the cross until he died or returned, so that all claims to his property were suspended, so that all interest on his debts ceased. If funds were needed for his journey, lands and other possessions could be pledged (without interest). Clerics who took the cross were able to fund their Provençal pilgrimages by mortgaging two years' worth of revenue from their benefices. The French ecclesiastical establishment was to support and, most especially, copy the preaching of Arnau Amalric and his Cistercians.[39] In promulgating a crusade to eradicate heretics and mercenaries in the lands of the count of Toulouse, Innocent III finally merged a century or more of Latin Christian thought on heresy and holy war that, from the moment the first warrior pilgrim walked like Him between the Garonne and the Rhône, inexorably led to the loving necessity of slaughtering the little foxes.

Innocent III, "namely the vicar of Jesus Christ, the successor of Peter," imagined himself in the middle between God and humanity, "below God but above man, less than God but greater than man, who judges all things but who no one judges."[40] No pope had ever envisioned himself with so magnificent a mandate over the world; no pope had ever experienced the sublime tension of existing simultaneously on earth and in heaven; no pope had ever been able to see all things visible and invisible. (More modestly, the holy good men experienced the same divine tension as the pope.) Innocent III saw that the little foxes and serpents of heresy were, after centuries of concealment, now poised to massacre Christians. He saw that these rabid beasts, though scattered throughout the Lord's vineyard, swarmed in the lands of Raimon VI. The tempestuous world between the Garonne and the Rhône willfully conflicted with his vision of Christendom, and, as so much of his papacy was about making all Christians resemble Him and each other, this virulent difference must be eliminated. All persons between these rivers were pestiferous (or soon would be), and the livid symptoms of this plague were grand malignant ambitions. "Indeed, such pestilential Provinçales not only strive to devastate all we possess but they strive to annihilate us! Truly, not only are they sharpening their tongues to annihilate our souls, they are raising their hands to annihilate our bodies!"[41] The leprosy of these "perverters of souls and putrefiers of bodies," though a malady always festering within the Church, had so feverishly escalated in recent memory that if it were not obliterated— immediately, swiftly—then all Christian existence would come to an end. Christians should cry out for the Lord of Vengeance to descend from heaven and aid them in this mighty struggle. Christians must attack the perverters and putrefiers before they themselves were attacked, and so perverted and putrefied. The crusade against heresy in the lands of the count of Toulouse was a holy war for the very survival of Christendom.

VI

RAIMON VI SENT a succession of emissaries to Rome throughout the summer and autumn of 1208. Bernart de Montaut, archbishop of Auch, and Raimon de Rabastens, former bishop of Toulouse, were the last of these ambassadors. These two men—"excretal and wicked" to Pierre des Vaux-de-Cernay; "eloquent" and "generous" to Guilhem de Tudela—stayed throughout the Roman winter pleading the count's innocence concerning the murder of Peire de Castelnau. The pope was far from persuaded. They complained that Arnau Amalric treated the count harshly and unjustly in the ferocious enthusiasm of his preaching. The pope dismissed all criticism of the abbot. They argued that the excommunicated count was more than ready for reconciliation, and if the pope sent a legate *a latere* (more autonomous, more powerful, and so, hopefully, more impartial than an ordinary legate), then the count would obey him completely. The pope gratified this request—"just as if the count were a deserving petitioner," hissed Pierre des Vaux-de-Cernay—by appointing his own notary, Master Milo, as legate on Sunday, 1 March 1209. Milo, known for his Latin eloquence, was an honest man "neither daunted by fear nor won over by bribery." Master Thedisius, a priest and a canon of the cathedral of Genoa, was to assist him. Raimon was apparently delighted with Milo's appointment. "It has turned out well for me, I have a papal legate after my own heart. Indeed, I shall be legate myself!" The pope ordered Milo to consult with Arnau Amalric on all matters relating to the crusade, especially anything to do with the count of Toulouse, as the abbot truly understood the cunning comital mind. "The abbot will do everything, you will be his instrument," Innocent III bluntly told his new legate. "The count is suspicious of the abbot—you, he will not suspect."

Milo and Thedisius immediately journeyed to France and, toward the end of March, found Arnau Amalric at Auxerre (in the Bourgogne by the turbulent Yonne River). The legate consulted with the abbot on a number of specific points about the progress of the crusade. "The abbot gave his advice in writing and under seal, giving him detailed instructions on all points." Arnau Amalric, Milo, and Thedisius then traveled north to see Philip II Augustus at Villeneuve (in the Sénonais by the Yonne), where the French king was presiding over an assembly of his barons. Milo asked the king about a private letter the pope had sent him two months earlier. The pope, in a slight variation of his now familiar appeal, urged and prayed that the king would, as a most Christian prince, exterminate the *Provinciales heretici* by leading the coming crusade himself or appointing "a strong, wise, and faithful man" such as his son Louis. Philip informed Milo that two great and dangerous lions, the Emperor Otto IV and King John of England, were about to savage him and so he and his son were unable to leave France. The king, with no variation in his now familiar response, thought it more than sufficient that he was allowing some of his barons to undertake the martial pilgrimage. Innocent III, aware that the royal response would be the usual royal ambivalence, issued a separate universal summons to all Christian knights on the same day as his letter to the most Christian prince. "Oppose the Antichrist who walks before you," the pope majestically exhorted, "and fight his ancient mercenary serpents!" Up until this moment, you fought and battled for nothing, you died for no purpose. "As you fought for ephemeral glory, now fight for everlasting glory! As you fought for the body, now fight for the soul! As you fought for the world, now fight for God!"[1]

Milo and Thedisius, disappointed (though hardly surprised) by the king at Villeneuve, departed for *Provincia*. A few weeks later the legatine mission arrived at the *castrum* of Montélimar (in the Drôme by the confluence of the Roubion and Rhône). Milo solicited the opinions of all Provençal archbishops and bishops about the crusade and Raimon VI. He desired each prelate to give him, "in writing and under seal," their views on Arnau Amalric's instructions regarding the count. "His wishes were carried out and—incredibly!—the recommendations of the abbot and the prelates were in agreement on all points without exception. No doubt, this was the work of the Lord!" Milo then wrote to Raimon and ordered him to come to the city of Valence (further north along the Rhône) to hear the instructions of the abbot. The count, expecting such an invitation, dutifully arrived at Valence. He listened to the abbatial mandates and promised to follow all of them. Milo, distrustful and wary of such comital contrition, required Raimon to hand over seven fortified villages to the Church as a pledge of good faith and future obedience. The count did as he was told. (These *castra* were Roquemaure and Fourques on the west bank of the Rhône; Oppède, Mornas, Beaumes de Venise on the east bank; Montferrand in the county of Melgueil; and Largentière in the county of Vivarais.) Thedisius quickly occupied these villages in the name of the Holy Roman Church. A penitent Raimon made the legate even more suspicious, and so Milo directed him to relinquish to the Church all of the county of Melgueil (which the count had held as a fief of the Holy See since 1172). The count again did as he was told. Milo then demanded that the consuls of Avignon, Nîmes, Orange, Montpellier, Valence, Saint-Gilles, and numerous other cities swear oaths that if the count went against the dictates of the abbot, then, instantly, all ties of homage and fealty to the count were severed. Raimon VI, "who once said the abbot of Cîteaux was *hard*, now said the legate was by far *harder*."

On Thursday, 18 June 1209, a naked Raimon VI was led by Milo through the streets of Saint-Gilles in a final act of repentance. This humiliating procession ended beneath the tympanum of the church of Saint-Gilles.[2] There, before a large crowd that included three archbishops and nineteen bishops, the fifty-three-year-old count swore on the body of Christ and the relics of various saints that he would obey all the mandates of the Holy Roman Church. He recited the all-too-familiar list of accusations embraced by his excommunication. "I am said to be unwilling to swear to keep the peace when others swore to it; likewise, I am said to be ignoring my oath regarding the expulsion of heretics and their believers." Further, he was said to have cherished heretics, possessed dubious faith, hired mercenaries, employed Jews, attacked monasteries, assaulted villages, stole episcopal monies, knew more than he was saying about Peire de Castelnau's murder, and, if he did not cause the legate's death, then he certainly caused other religious persons to suffer at the violent hands of mercenaries.[3] Milo placed a coarse robe around Raimon's shoulders. He scourged him as He had been scourged. The count, reconciled and absolved, passed beneath the tympanum into the church. The crowd outside began to cheer and surged toward the church doors. The count, unable to leave by the way he entered, went down into the crypt and, briefly bowing to the recently interred body of Peire de Castelnau, left through a side portal. Four days later Raimon VI—unexpectedly, cleverly—asked Milo to bless him as a crusader against the *Provinciales heretici*. The legate agreed and allowed the count (with two of his knights) to wear the cross on his breast and avenge the injuries done to the crucifix. As Raimon V once thought he could manipulate a holy war in his own lands, so now his son thought the same—and though political adroitness was a family trait, bloody irony clearly was not.[4]

"Lords, from now on there's vigour in my song!" Only a few days after Raimon VI signed himself with the cross, "all the crusaders who had been making their way from various parts of France converged on Lyon—once the first city of Gaul—in accordance with previous decisions and arrangements." Lyon, a city of the Holy Roman Empire in 1209, was the entrepôt on the Rhône for all travel and trade between France and the Mediterranean. In and around the city, gathering in the fields and valleys of the Lyonnais, other martial pilgrims soon joined the French crusaders. "God never made a cleric who could write them all down," Guilhem de Tudela sang of the rallying crusaders, "however hard he tried, not in two months, not in three"—except, of course, himself. He counted "French from France," Poitevins, Gascons, Rouergats, Saintongeais, Burgundians, Auvergnats, Limousins, *Ties* (northern Germans), *Alamans* (southern Germans), all who lived in Provence, all who lived in Vienne, and all who lived from the passes of Lombardy to the plains of Rodez. "If I started right now, not stopping 'till dark, not stopping 'till first-light tomorrow, I couldn't even begin to tell you the names of those Provençals who joined the *crozada*." Guilhem de Tudela's final crusade tally was, not surprisingly, more flourish than fact. "Twenty thousand horsemen, all armed to the hilt! And more than two hundred thousand other men! Some countryfolk, some peasants; and some I'm not even counting, like clerics, like townsmen." The holy expedition that mustered at Lyon was, even with prosaic accounting, an impressive gathering of three thousand horsemen, eight thousand foot soldiers, and an astonishing ten to twelve thousand other men, women, and children who wanted to walk like Him in bodily form. Only the armed pilgrimage of 1096 elicited such an enthusiastic response from so many ordinary Christians. "Lords, upon my faith, the host was marvellous and great!"[5]

"Another host of crusaders journeyed from the Agenais," along the Lot and the Garonne toward Toulouse, seemingly unaware that Raimon VI was reconciled to the Church. This armed pilgrimage was so small and short-lived—less than a thousand men campaigning throughout June—that only Guilhem de Tudela mentioned it. The leaders of this crusade were Gui II, count of Clermont and Auvergne; Raimon III, viscount of Turenne (in the Dordogne); the bishops of Limoges and Bazas; Guillaume, archbishop of Bordeaux; Guilhem de Cardaillac, bishop of Cahors and Agen; Bertran, lord of Cardaillac (and the nephew of the bishop of Cahors and Agen);

Bertran, the lord of Gourdon; and Ratier, lord of Castelnau (who was a follower of Bertran de Gourdon). The troubadour, with his usual embellishment, added that these lords were accompanied by "all of Quercy." This crusade immediately tried and failed to capture Casseneuil, a strong *castrum* on the Lot defended by archers, noble horsemen, and tough "light-footed" Gascon mercenaries who were skilled with the javelin. The crusaders then laid siege to Casseneuil, and, with the village soon exhausted and ready to surrender, Gui II unexpectedly ended the attack. The count of Clermont, who owned properties around Casseneuil, came to an agreement with the good men of the *castrum*. The villages of Puylaroque, Gontaud, and Tonneins were less fortunate; the soldiers of Christ sacked and destroyed these *castra*. "And the host condemned many heretics to be burned and tossed many fair women into the flames (because they wouldn't convert despite pleas for them to do so)." This holy expedition dispersed after these atrocities and was not heard of again—except, once more, as a frightening rumor. The villagers of Villemur, a tiny *castrum* on the Tarn, heard about the cruelty of the crusaders from a runaway boy and, fearful that the soldiers of Christ were marching on them from Casseneuil (more than a hundred kilometers away), promptly set fire to their village at dusk and, as it burned to the ground, escaped into the fields by moonlight.[6]

The great holy expedition departed Lyon at the end of June 1209. All cumbersome baggage—siege equipment, tools, and a variety of other matériel—were loaded into boats (shallow-draft barges or river galleys) for transport down the Rhône. The martial pilgrims initially kept pace with the boats by riding and walking along the eastern riverbank road. All eminent crusade leaders, lay and ecclesiastical, rode together, their bright banners flying. The great secular lords were Eudes III, the duke of Burgundy; Hervé IV, count of Nevers; Gaucher de Châtillon, count of Saint-Pol; Milo IV, count of Bar-sur-Seine; Pierre de Courtenay, count of Auxerre (a cousin of Raimon VI); Peire Bermonz, lord of Sauve (married to Raimon's daughter na Constanz); Aimar, count of Valentinois and Diois (friend and vassal of Raimon); Guichard IV de Beaujeu; Guillaume de Roches, seneschal of Anjou; Humbert, count of Genevois; Gaucher de Joigny, lord of Châteaurenard; and Simon IV, lord of Montfort l'Amaury in the Ile de France (and heir to the English earldom of Leicester through his mother). The great ecclesiastical lords were Pierre, archbishop of Sens; Gautier, bishop of Autun; Robert, bishop of Clermont; and Guillaume, bishop of Nevers. All other men and women "signed with the cross"— squires, sergeants, foot soldiers, crossbowmen, mercenaries, farriers, siege engineers, notaries, blacksmiths, jongleurs, butchers, prostitutes, priests, clerics, beggars, monks, cooks, carpenters, preachers, servants, wives, armorers, troubadours, thieves, muleteers, noble ladies, and ribald boys— meandered as an amorphous millennial mass behind these grand notables. All of these martial pilgrims, whatever their status, whatever their talents, were to be wielded by Arnau Amalric (and his instrument Milo) as the Lord's mighty and invincible blade of gold.[7]

A cross of cloth was stitched by all the *crucesignati* on their shirts, jackets, pelisses, surcoats, and dresses. These crosses (of various sizes and colors) were made from ribbons of silk embroidered with gold for the great nobles—"What they must have cost!"—and, for the thousands of lesser crusaders, strips of cotton or wool. These fabric crosses were, as the preacher Jacques de Vitry affirmed in the aftermath of the crusade, "the sign of the living God." As Christ was signed by God on the cross, so now He signed His soldiers with the cross. "The cross that is fixed to your coats with a soft thread was fixed to His flesh with iron nails." The sign of the cross distinguished His people from the "unfaithful and reprobate." The cross of cloth was no different from the cross of water at baptism; it separated the Christian from the heretic. All persons unwilling to be signed by Him were so weak and rotten that the cross, in any event, could not be sewn onto them: "Like old pieces of cloth worn out by age and no longer useful for anything, they cannot hold a seam." All persons who never yielded to Christ, who never suffered the cross to be sewn upon their shoulders by "the needle of the fear of God" or allowed the cross to be tied on them "with the thread of God's love," were stamped with the symbol of the beast, "as they imitate the devil." All those signed with the cross were the standard-bearers of the highest king and the key-bearers of His house. "It is a custom among noble and powerful men to invest their vassals with precious fiefs by a glove or some other object of little worth; similarly, the Lord invests His vassals with the heavenly kingdom by a cross of modest thread or cloth." Heaven and earth, body and soul, were joined in two strips of overlapping fabric and in the stitches that replicated each of His wounds. A cross of cloth instantly transformed the man (or woman) it was sewn on into an individual who fought for God and suffered as Christ—at once a holy soldier and a holy sacrifice.[8]

Raimon VI, a cross of cloth neatly sewn on the right shoulder of his coat, joined the crusaders outside the walls of Montpellier toward the end of July. He found them eager for battle and relatively well rested. The soldiers of Christ, though excited about walking as He walked, ambled a mere seven kilometers a day between Lyon and Montpellier. The number (and the needs) of so many animals and humans dictated the slow expeditionary rhythm. Around three thousand warhorses (measuring thirteen to fifteen hands, weighing five hundred to six hundred kilograms) were accompanied by twenty thousand roncins (smaller pack horses) and mules. The horses carried riders, saddles, weapons, and feed—that is, no more than one hundred and ten kilograms per animal. The roncins and mules carried everything else, roughly one hundred kilograms (including pack saddle) per animal. They transported tents, wine, nails, horseshoes, boiled hides, ropes, crossbow bolts, arrows, clothing, olive oil (food and lubricant), cooking pots, blankets, and hard fodder (barley and oats for the warhorses and themselves). Every day the horses dined on hard fodder (two to three kilograms) and grazed five or more hours on grass (seven to ten kilograms). Roncins and mules consumed a third less than the horses. All of them, though, required twenty-two to thirty-six liters of water each day. They occupied twenty kilometers of the Rhône when watered together; when they moved away from the river, leather buckets were fetched and hauled from wells and streams throughout the day by thousands of boys. The relentless din of snorts, whinnies, and brays was complemented by yaps, bleats, and squeals from the barely tamed menagerie—goats, dogs, cats, chickens, pigs, sheep, cows, monkeys—pressed into the crusade column. This spectacle of sight and sound extended more than fifteen kilometers on the march. It was an expedition of such magnificent ungainliness that even when those in the van began marching just after sunrise, those in the rear only began marching just before noon; in other words, beasts and pilgrims strolled three to four hours a day before setting up (or reaching) camp. The baggage boats, with considerably more dash, were swept into the Mediterranean and, after coasting westward for a few days, moored amid salt marshes and warm lagoons near Montpellier.[9]

King Pere II of Aragon was lord of Montpellier. He had married na Maria de Montpellier four years earlier and the town was her dowry. The king, despite swearing never to renounce his wife or expend her dotal property, signed away Montpellier in 1205 and asked the pope to annul his marriage in 1206. He gave the town as dowry when he betrothed his eight-week-old daughter na Sancha to eight-year-old Raimon, son of the count of Toulouse, in October 1205. His sister na Elionor had conveniently married the count five years earlier. (The younger Raimon's mother was Joanna, sister of Richard, king of England, whom the older Raimon married in 1196 and who died in childbirth in 1199.) In an open letter to the king, the count, and the consuls of Montpellier, Maria denounced the marriage and dowry of her child, saying she was bullied into the agreement, tricked into acquiescence, and "crucified" by her husband. "Why did he wish to cheat me?"[10] Pere's plans came to nothing when little Sancha died before Christmas. Maria's anger became more furious (and disillusioned) when her husband promptly began annulment proceedings and negotiations to marry the heiress of Jerusalem, Marie de Montferrat. Innocent III was sympathetic to Pere (and to the wants of the Holy Land) and appointed Peire de Castelnau, the legate Raoul, and Juan, bishop of Pamplona, to judge and rule on the case. The consuls and community of Montpellier, however, detested the overbearing monarch and, after rioting twice during the summer, forced him to flee the town in July 1206. Guilhem, bishop of Maguelonne, who shared proprietary rights in Montpellier with Pere—the small episcopal bourg was known as Montpelliéret—arbitrated a compromise between king, queen, and consuls. Two years later, after a tryst of convenience in the *castrum* of Miraval, a son, Jaume, was born on Friday, 8 February 1208. The marriage annulment, though seemingly inert, was still desired by Pere. The queen, with renewed vigor, lobbied against it. They attacked each other with lawyers and mercenaries. At one point the husband even besieged his pregnant wife in one of her castles. This marital turmoil waned within the year, largely because Pere was busy on the other side of the Pyrénées, and so the crusaders camped around a Montpellier at peace.[11]

Around two thousand Provençal crusaders (and about eight thousand horses, roncins, and mules) joined the expedition at Montpellier. Northern crusaders, with sly whispers and knowing nods, cautiously welcomed these southern *crozatz*. Tight clothes, middling armor, foppish courtesy, and an obvious familiarity with heretics were all reasons to be wary. Raimon VI wryly saluted these village warmongers as fellow pilgrims—and almost everyone, from beggar boys to papal legates, hailed him as liar and fraud. "The enemy of Christ," scoffed Pierre des Vaux-de-Cernay about the count as *crucesignatus*, deceitfully "allied himself to the soldiers of Christ."[12] The enmity toward Raimon was understandable—he certainly understood it—as all those who had signed themselves with the cross had done so weeks and months earlier with the fierce intention of assailing him and expunging heretics from his territories. Yet—remarkably, importantly— even though the count was apparently no longer the enemy of Christ, the thrill and purpose of the crusade was no less dampened and no less focused. Raimon as a crusader did not change the fact that the serpents and little foxes were invading Christendom from his cities and *castra*. A landscape of pestilence still existed between the Garonne and the Rhône that needed to be cleansed through holy war and, while the peccant roots of heresy were momentarily beyond His sword, the shoots and branches of the plague could be sheared and hacked. Arnau Amalric, with this in mind, surveyed the horizon and, gauging what stood between him and His eventual victory over the *Provinciales heretici*, decided to attack the lands of the twenty-four-year-old Raimon Roger Trencavel, viscount of Béziers, Carcassonne, Razès, and Albi, whose overlord (as count of Barcelona) was Pere II.

Raimon Roger was the nephew of Raimon VI, and, according to Guilhem de Tudela, he and his uncle discussed what to do about the crusade at the beginning of summer. The count wanted his nephew to stand with him and defend their lands from the "evil destruction" that was about to happen to them. "His reply wasn't 'yes,'" sang the troubadour, "his reply was 'no.'" Raimon Roger soon changed his mind, especially after his uncle was signed with the cross, and tried to become a crusader himself. Milo refused; the legate, Guilhem de Tudela alleged, loathed the viscount. He always intended to attack Raimon Roger sooner or later, as he (and so Arnau Amalric) despised the nephew almost as vehemently as they did the uncle.[13] Guilhem de Tudela's excursus into why the Trencavel territories were targeted by the crusaders, a contrary tale that blamed (and praised) everyone, was no more than songful supposition about a fateful decision he did not understand. The troubadour was not alone in his ignorance. There can be no doubt—despite arguments to the contrary, then and now—that Raimon was startled by the selection of his nephew as the new objective of the holy expedition. The count, of course, wanted to deflect the crusade away from himself, but, as to where or to whom, that is far from clear; he never suggested Raimon Roger. Arnau Amalric, of course, was not willing to let the crusade be deflected or dissipated without a target. The crusade was a "holy game" to the abbot; in this hazard of the die, God invited him to risk all or nothing. "If you hold you win! If you throw away you lose! Watch out what you do! You are given the choice!"[14] The abbot took his chance, made his choice, and, very quickly, very violently, won.

VII

RAIMON VI, WHATEVER his misgivings about the strategy of the crusade, acquiesced to the legatine plan and agreed to guide the *crucesignati* from Montpellier to the city of Béziers on the Orb. The crusaders departed Montpellier on Monday, 20 July, and, with little or no resistance, reached the walls of Béziers two days later on the feast of Saint Mary Magdalen. The baggage boats slipped through the gentle tidewaters of the Orb and, steadily, arduously, maneuvered upriver until, lying off a sandbar near Béziers, horse-boys and muleteers unloaded the cargo. "As the army approached the city, the lords of some neighbouring *castra*, uneasy in their hearts, fled before the crusaders," Arnau Amalric and Milo told Innocent III a month later, "but some knights and other faithful men from these *castra* boldly approached the army and handed these *castra* over to the crusaders, promising loyalty and homage."[1] Servian, where Peire de Castelnau and Dominic de Guzmán debated the good man Baudois three years earlier, was simply abandoned (though not incinerated) by all who lived there. Many other Biterrois villages (including some small *castra* subservient to Servian) swiftly surrendered to the soldiers of Christ. "It was on the day of the feast of the Magdalen," sang Guilhem de Tudela, "that the abbot of Cîteaux delivered his great host," his mighty army of God, to the sandy flatland around Béziers. The martial pilgrims surrounded the city, a kidney-shaped enclave eight hundred meters long and five hundred meters wide, with their tents and kiosks, banners and blazons. "I dare say that those within were greatly tormented and anguished because

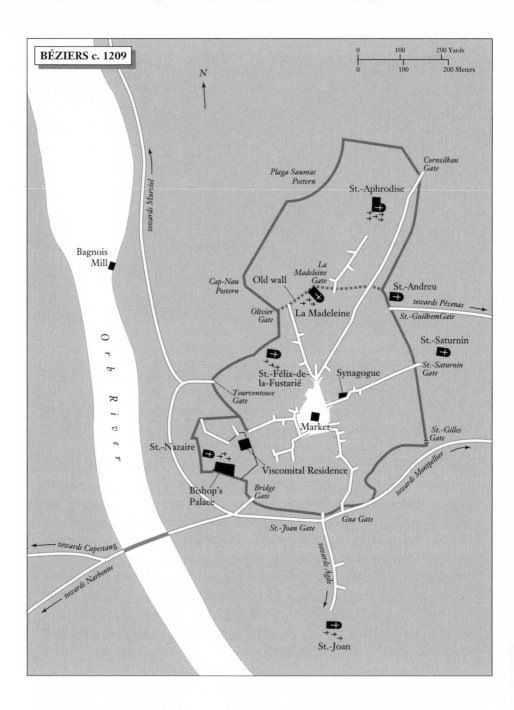

BÉZIERS c. 1209

N

0   100   200 Yards
0   100   200 Meters

towards Murviel

Bagnois
Mill

Plaga Saumas
Postern

Corneilhan
Gate

St.-Aphrodise

Cap-Nau
Postern

Old wall

La
Madeleine
Gate

St.-Andreu

towards Pézenas

St.-Guilhem Gate

Olivier
Gate

La Madeleine

O r b   R i v e r

St.-Saturnin

*St.-Saturnin
Gate*

St.-Félix-de-
la-Fustarié

Synagogue

Tourventouse
Gate

*St.-Gilles
Gate*

Market

St.-Nazaire

Viscomital Residence

towards Montpellier

Bishop's
Palace

*Bridge
Gate*

Gua Gate

St.-Joan Gate

towards Agde

towards Capestang

towards Narbonne

St.-Joan

even the host of Menelaus (from whom Paris stole Helen) never pitched so many tents before the gates of Mycenae nor pitched so many rich pavilions as those put up in a single night, out in the open air, by the French."[2] The holy expedition that enclosed Béziers was, in the proud vision of the legates, "greater, we believe, than has ever before been gathered together amongst Christian people."[3]

Guilhem de Tudela, even as he sang the praises of the crusade, was sympathetic to the forlorn Raimon Roger Trencavel. "In the whole wide world there is no better knight; not one so prudent, not one so generous, not one so courteous or fair." Unfortunately, "because he was very young, he happened to love everyone." Among his nobles and his knights, "not one looked away from him in dread, not one was fearful." Instead, "they caroused before him as if he were a companion." Regrettably, "all his knights and other vavasors supported the heretics (living in their castles, living in their towers) and so they caused their own destruction and their own deaths with dishonor." Inevitably, inescapably, "the viscount died in very great pain, sorrowful and pitiful, because of this grave error." The young *vescomte*, for all his honor and courtliness, deserved to be attacked as much as the *comte* of Toulouse for his failure to eradicate heresy from his domain. The troubadour, once again, half-heartedly justified the approaching tragedy his geomancy never predicted. Pierre des Vaux-de-Cernay had no such prescient qualms and not a shred of pity for a youth who mimicked an evil uncle. The nephew allowed priests to be jostled, beaten, and pissed upon. The nephew never avenged the murder of Raimon I Trencavel by the people of Béziers four decades earlier. The nephew was an incompetent coward. Raimon Roger, who clearly never envisioned being engulfed by a holy war, belatedly reacted with urgency and haste to the looming host. He worked "without end, night and day," readying his lands in the Albigeois, Carcassès, and Biterrois against the crusaders. ("You are defending the city against the pilgrims," a mysterious old man mocked those digging ditches around Béziers, "but who will defend you from above?") As soon as Raimon Roger heard that the holy expedition left Montpellier for Béziers—a destination that, somehow or other, took him by surprise—he galloped through the night on his *milsoldor* ("thousand-shilling") horse from Carcassonne to his city on the Orb.[4]

"The townspeople of the city, the old and the young, the little and the great," came out to greet Raimon Roger when they heard of his arrival. The viscount, though exhausted, sat steady on his strutting horse and tried to calm the men, women, and children who crowded the square in front of his residence. He told them to defend themselves with all their strength and vigor and that soon, very soon, reinforcements would arrive. "As for me," he said to them, "I must take the great road over there to Carcassonne, since they have already waited too long for me." Raimon Roger, on that supremely tepid note, bolted westward over the Orb bridge and back to Carcassonne. The only persons allowed to accompany him were the Jews of Béziers. Everyone else, not surprisingly, "was angry and in great distress." The sun was barely up and the city was hysterical. No one seemed to be in command; no knights seemed ready to fight. At this very moment, the elderly Rainaut de Montpeyroux, bishop of Béziers, careened into the square on his modest (though spritely) mule, dismounted, and hurried the frightened crowd into the cathedral-church of Saint-Nazaire (behind the viscomital residence, overlooking the Orb). In this vast cool space, "rich in relics," the bishop told the assembled multitude that he had just returned from the soldiers of Christ and that "through him they said that they had come to destroy the heretics and they ordered any Catholics amongst the citizens to hand over the heretics." He informed his audience that he knew who all the heretics were "and even had them listed in writing." As lord of their souls and bodies—for he shared high justice in the city with the viscount—he warned them to comply with his demands.[5] If the townspeople of Béziers were hesitant about sacrificing the men and women on the episcopal list, then "they should quit the city and leave the heretics behind, so as to avoid perishing with them." If they refused to hand over the heretics, if they refused to leave the city, then there was nothing the bishop could do to save them from being stripped, harried, and "sliced apart with swords of steel."[6]

Rainaut de Montpeyroux, in one last effort at averting the wholesale butchery of Béziers, pleaded that an agreement be reached between the townspeople, the clergy, and the crusaders. "But most of the people dismissed his advice," saying they would rather be "drowned in the salt sea" than let the crusaders pocket so much as a penny of their possessions. The bishop's dedication to the crusade and his acceptance that some killing was unavoidable—selective bloodshed if possible but, for all his pleas, he countenanced indiscriminate slaughter—shocked his audience into supporting their truant viscount and his uninspiring lordship. The sorrow and wretchedness of the early morning promptly dissolved, and the townspeople of Béziers dismissed all parleys with the crusaders. Everyone left the cathedral-church of Saint-Nazaire and, climbing the city walls, looked out at the myriad tents and pavilions of the army of God. Thousands of pilgrims were still pouring into the Biterrois plain, a straggling horde "as long as a great league," a shambles overflowing roads and paths, slowly drowning the crusader camp in chaos. The townspeople started to "believe that the host could not hold together," and, as it was too ponderous to endure, "in less than fifteen days it would disband." Béziers, they flattered themselves, was so strong and its walls so well defended that, even if it were besieged for a month, it would be impossible to take the city by force. The bishop, saddened that the townspeople wanted to fight, exasperated that they treated his advice as if it were "a peeled apple," got on his mule and trotted back to the crusaders. He told Arnau Amalric that the townspeople of Béziers had chosen to die as heretics rather than live as Christians. "Fools and madmen, they considered them, as they knew very well that what awaited them was suffering, pain, and death."[7]

After Rainaut de Montpeyroux departed Béziers a throng of men and boys, parading back and forth on the Orb bridge, taunted and jeered the crusaders. "Listen to what they did, these villainous men, foolish and more senseless than whales." These men and boys shouted and waved white flags of coarse cloth, "as if they thought they could frighten away the host as birds are scared off a field of oats." They ran further and further along the bridge, shooting arrows and throwing rocks, yelling and challenging the soldiers of Christ. A few crusaders accepted the challenge and rushed onto the bridge. These reckless knights were easily thrown back. A French crusader, slower than his comrades, was tackled to the ground, sliced into pieces, and hurled (arms, legs, and torso) into the Orb. The noble leaders of the crusade ignored this scuffle on the bridge—they were still debating tactics—but the thousands of ribald boys who accompanied the crusade as servants, beggars, and thieves did not. "Come on, let's attack!" screamed the "king of the beggar boys." All the lads near him grabbed clubs—"they had nothing else, I guess"—and, "with not a pair of shoes between them," raced round and round Béziers, their ranks swelling as other boys joined them. The frantic sprint of a few soon spiraled into the frenzied stampede of thousands. Suddenly, the ribalds and their king jumped in and out of the defensive ditches and, clambering over each other, swarmed the walls and gates. They scratched and clawed the walls, loosening stones and rocks; they charged and charged the gates until the wood splintered and the iron frames buckled; they clubbed to death the taunters on the Orb bridge. "What a crush you would have seen as they tried to get into the town!"[8]

The townspeople of Béziers, awed and terrified by the ribald fury, unable to comprehend what was happening around them, succumbed once more to the hysteria and confusion of the early morning. They abandoned their walls and ramparts and, crying and weeping, returned to the cathedral-church of Saint-Nazaire. "It was their only refuge." The beggar boys and their king, with what little opposition there had been in retreat, irrupted through hundreds of holes in the walls and quickly opened the damaged city gates. They climbed the ramparts and bawled at the soldiers of Christ, "To arms! To arms!" Until this moment, the crusaders, whether great lords or humble foot soldiers, watched the zealotry of the ribalds with incredulity and contempt. "Come on, let's get our arms!" Knights mounted horses, crossbowmen shouldered quivers, and sergeants secured swords. The army of God, in no particular order, moved against Béziers. The ribalds, elated by their success, encouraged by the sight of the crusaders, surged through the empty streets of Béziers, kicking in doors, stealing what they liked, murdering everyone they met. "Rich for all time, if they can keep it!" No matter how much they stole, no matter how much they stuffed in their shirts, they killed and killed without respite. All the men, women, and children crowded inside Saint-Nazaire were beaten to death. A smaller gathering in the church of the Magdalene (adjacent to the old northern wall) were slain by knives and cudgels. "No one was protected by cross, altar, or crucifix." Priests were strangled while saying masses *de mortuorum*. "I doubt if anyone came out alive," sang Guilhem de Tudela. "God receive their souls—if it is His pleasure—in paradise. Such vicious carnage has not happened since the time of the Saracens, nor known to have happened nor allowed to have happened until now." The Orb slowly darkened as rivulets of gore spilled down the streets and washed off the bridge.[9]

The soldiers of Christ entered Béziers and, discovering the delirious boys rummaging through houses and hoarding treasure, "went nearly mad with rage and hounded the ruffians with clubs, like dogs," into the streets. The knights stabled their horses and roncins in the vacated houses and seized the spoils of the ribalds for themselves, "because rapine reaps meadows." The beggar boys and their king, thinking they were rich forever, expecting a modicum of praise for their efforts, were outraged and, running yet again through streets and alleys, howled, "Burn it! Burn it!" On corners and in squares they quickly accumulated corpses and kindling and, with huge blazing torches, set each heap alight, "as if it were a funeral pyre." Béziers, with no one to extinguish these bonfires, was soon an inferno. Houses and towers, as hot as ovens, as incandescent as ten thousand candles, glowed and guttered into the sky. One church "cracked down the middle and fell in two parts." Glass windows blistered and shattered. The air was so torrid that helmets cauterized foreheads and chain mail broiled the skin. The crusaders, startled and panicked by the conflagration, unable to breathe, unable to see, fled the city as best they could, abandoning horses, weapons, "and many other fine things." All persons within Béziers—old men, women, children, clerics—who survived the earlier massacre were consumed by the fire. Many of the arsonists themselves, blinded by smoke, scalded by ashes, suffocated. The Orb bridge fractured and collapsed into the river. All in all, from the first shout of the ribald king to the last martial pilgrim escaping the burning city, less than three hours elapsed. Béziers and all the people who lived there were annihilated in an afternoon.[10]

A decade after the immolation of Béziers, Caesarius of Heisterbach encapsulated the murderous eschatology of the crusaders in an *exemplum* praising the wisdom of Arnau Amalric. The soldiers of Christ, though exulting in the capture of Béziers, worried that they could not sort out the faithful from the heretics among the men and women of the city. "Lord," the crusaders asked the abbot of Cîteaux, "what shall we do?" The abbot, thinking for a moment, replied, "Kill them! Truly, God will know his own!"[11] Whatever the truth of this anecdote—and there is only the report of Caesarius—it nevertheless lauded a homicidal ethic that, while shifting and changing through the decades, was an essential principle of the holy war on heresy. "If it can be shown that some heretics are in a city," lectured the Bolognese legal scholar Johannes Teutonicus (in a commentary on Gratian) around 1217, "then all the inhabitants can be burnt."[12]

"The ribalds, as well as other villainous and unarmed persons, attacked the city without waiting for orders from their noble leaders," Arnau Amalric and Milo wrote to the pope. "To our wonderment," the abbot and his instrument enthused, "within the space of two or three hours they surmounted ditches and walls and the city of Béziers was captured and these ribalds of ours spared no order of persons (whatever their rank, sex, or age) and put to the sword almost twenty thousand people. After this great slaughter the whole city was despoiled and burnt, as divine vengeance raged marvellously." The legates, in their bloody joy, exaggerated the number of men, women, and children killed by about five thousand. The murderous frenzy of the beggar boys and their king was, in hindsight, a holy and wondrous gift from Him. "As rumours of so miraculous and terrifying an event steadily disseminated far and wide, everyone thereabouts sought refuge in the mountains and inaccessible places and, between Béziers and Carcassonne, more than a hundred notable *castra* were abandoned." Many of these villages were so well fortified and, "by virtue of their natural location and their strength in men and matériel, it seemed they would easily have been able to withstand the attack of our army for a very long time."[13] The terror inspired by the ribalds lasted through the summer; though more atrocities were to come, the destruction of Béziers enduringly epitomized the cruelty and grandeur of divine vengeance to medieval Christians. Yet what the ribalds did, though unexpected and unauthorized, was near enough to what the soldiers of Christ always intended for the cities and villages of *Provincia* from the beginning of the most holy war on heresy. Arnau Amalric and Milo never doubted that the lands between the Garonne and the Rhône were to be purified by holocausts.

An irrevocable obligation to mass murder existed from the very start of the crusade. All the crusading exhortations of Innocent III exalted the necessity of cleansing Christendom of *Provinciales heretici* through expurgation and extermination. All those signed with the cross were motivated by this apocalyptic exigency. This moral imperative starkly differentiated the holy expedition of 1209 from all crusades to the eastern Mediterranean. Pierre des Vaux-de-Cernay, although comparing purged Béziers to redeemed Jerusalem, looked past recent purifications of the Holy City to the first century after Christ, when the Roman Emperor Vespasian and his son Titus destroyed the Temple and expelled the Jews.[14] There was a distinct ferocity and pitilessness among the pilgrims, especially those from northern France, who walked like Him in the Biterrois. Almost half a century of ecclesiastical admonitions warned, over and over, that most persons who lived in and around the county of Toulouse were wholly or partially diseased with heresy and did not know it. A plea of ignorance was no more than a sign of willful complacency and, in all probability, a symptom of infection. What appeared Catholic and correct on the surface was, so very often, so very cleverly, a façade hiding rampant heretical pestilence. Unless men and women ostentatiously announced themselves opposed to heresy, in the manner of Raimon VI and hundreds of lesser nobles becoming crusaders, then by default they were either heretics or supporters of heretics. The crusaders never thought they were fighting a heretical Church, and they never thought of themselves as fighting, in any coherent sense, the good men and good women. They were, without a doubt, fighting for the survival of Christendom. What added to their ardor and so their murderousness was the conviction that if heresy were not erased root and branch, then, sooner or later, they too would be surreptitiously corrupted by this plague. It was only through the precautionary killing of all and sundry in a city like Béziers that the soldiers of Christ avenged Him and so saved themselves.

VIII

THE CRUSADERS REMAINED for three days before the smoldering ruins of Béziers. Thousands of lost and frightened horses were reclaimed and their singed flesh soothed with honey and rose oil. The tents and pavilions were spotted with ash. The surviving ribald boys were (divine inspiration aside) cuffed and kicked. Black vultures and ravens circled the human remains. The soldiers of Christ, though shaken by their hasty departure from the city, were delighted with the ethical and strategic blessings of the massacre and incineration. "The barons from France and those from the environs of Paris, as well as the clerics and the laymen, the princes and the marquises," agreed that all persons in a village or castle who did not instantly surrender were, once the *castrum* or *castel* was captured, "to be killed without delay." In this way, observed Guilhem de Tudela, "they would meet no resistance anywhere, as everyone would be so terrified at what had already happened." The crusaders, ready to put this plan into practice, impatient to attack Raimon Roger, departed for Carcassonne (sixty kilometers away) on Sunday, 26 July 1209. The army of God was a vast sprawling spectacle on the great road to Carcassonne. This old Roman road (*via Domitia*) veered south along the Mediterranean littoral toward Narbonne before turning west into the Aude valley. The young viscount of Narbonne, Aimeric IV, and the archbishop of Narbonne, Berenguer II, horrified that the soldiers of Christ seemed to be marching toward them—and there was nothing to suggest otherwise—approached Arnau Amalric on the great road and surrendered. The holy expedition,

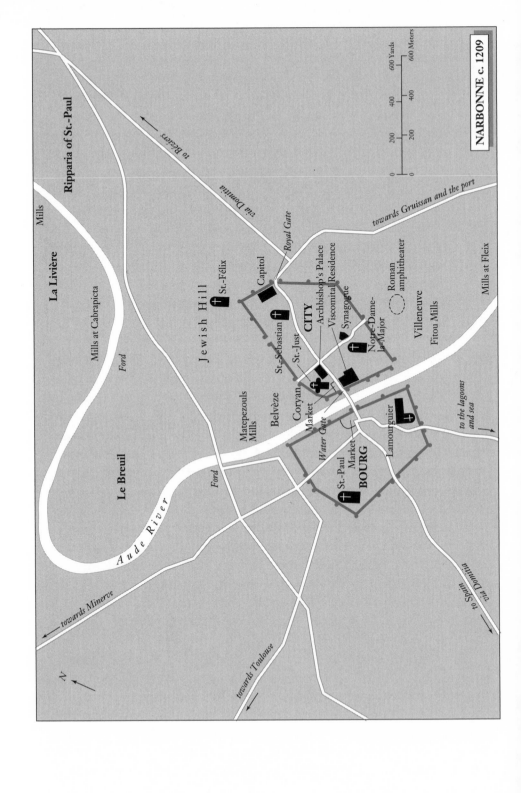

NARBONNE c. 1209

600 Yards

600 Meters

Ripparia of St.-Paul

Mills

La Livière

to Béziers

via Domitia

Royal Gate

towards Gruissan and the port

Mills at Cabrapicta

Ford

St.-Félix

Capitol

Archbishop's Palace

Viscomital Residence

Roman
amphitheater

Jewish Hill

St.-Sebastian

CITY

Synagogue

Mills at Fleix

St.-Just

Notre-Dame-
la-Major

Villeneuve

Le Breuil

Matepezouls
Mills

Belvèze

Coryan

Market

Fitou Mills

Ford

Water Gate

Lamourguier

to the lagoons
and sea

Ford

St.-Paul

Market

BOURG

A u d e   R i v e r

towards Minerve

towards Toulouse

to Spain
via Domitia

N

pleased with the providential submission of the Narbonnais, continued to Carcassonne "with banners held high and flapping in the wind."[1]

On Tuesday evening, "just as the bells were ringing for vespers," a small contingent of horsemen, galloping ahead of the crusaders, was seen from the towers of Carcassonne. Raimon Roger, striding the strong walls of his city, assumed all the martial pilgrims were just behind these knights. He had heard what happened at Béziers and, full of righteous anger, wanted to punish the crusaders immediately. "Come on, barons," he cried to his knights and vavasors, "mount your *alferans* [swift horses]!" The viscount's stratagem was simple: four hundred of his knights astride their best and fastest horses would charge, there and then, routing the soldiers of Christ in the hazy light of dusk. The knights and vavasors around him did not move. "Lords," he implored, "get your equipment, put on your armour, and mount your horses! All of us together against the host in a common attack!" The knights and vavasors around him did not move. The viscount stared blankly at his lords; they stared silently back. "By my faith," Peire Roger, the lord of Cabaret, finally said, "by my counsel, if you follow it, you should not attack." He advised Raimon Roger to stolidly guard and defend Carcassonne. The crusaders, he argued, will undoubtedly advance on the city tomorrow morning—of course, "after they have eaten"—and, edging closer and closer to the defensive ditches and trenches, attempt to cut off the drinking water from the Aude River. If the viscount wanted a fight, he should prepare the city and wait until tomorrow; "then there will be plenty of strong blows given and received!" The oldest and wisest noblemen agreed with this advice. Raimon Roger, crestfallen, assented. He posted armed knights all through the city and along the walls. He even allowed, according to Pierre des Vaux-de-Cernay, the stalls of the cathedral-church of Saint-Nazaire (near the southwestern wall) to be broken up and used to fortify the walls. "The houses of peasants get preserved," fumed the young Cistercian, "while the houses of the servants of God get pulled down!"[2]

Carcassonne was not attacked the next morning—or on the next four mornings. The army of God, straggly as usual, arrived Saturday evening during the feast of Saint Peter in Chains. Admittedly, the eerily deserted villages discovered throughout the Carcassès delayed the curious (every village was searched for inhabitants) and the covetous (every village was ransacked for food and treasure). Roncins and mules, overloaded with baggage from the boats and chaperoned by weary horse-boys and muleteers, slowed the pace even further. The actual city (*cui*) of Carcassonne—the old Visigothic *civitas*—was a lozenge-shaped space roughly three hundred sixty-five meters long and one hundred eighty-three meters wide. It sat on a modest rocky spur of the Corbières mountains, which, despite a lopsided plateau inclining from an eastern height of one hundred forty meters to a western fifty, commanded views of the surrounding fields and villages. The great road from Narbonne and Béziers was visible from the east; the churning confluence of the Aude was visible from the west. It was this ancient urban core that the great walls of Carcassonne enclosed. These walls (sandstone, limestone, brick) were between eighteen and thirty-five meters high, two to three meters thick, and capped with protective wooden parapets. Thirty stone and wooden towers were interspersed along them. (Eugène-Emmanuel Viollet-le-Duc restored the walls in the middle of the nineteenth century and, more inclined to visionary medievalism than historical verisimilitude, erected the magnificent fortifications that still shield the old city.)[3] Two suburbs lay directly outside the walls: the rectangular bourg to the north and the five-sided *castelar* to the south. Shallow ditches and low dry-built rock walls surrounded these suburbs. Another suburb, Saint Vincent (*Sant Vinzet*), squatted five hundred meters below the walls of the old city near the reed beds and marshes of the Aude's eastern confluent. This suburb was defenseless, and all those who lived there—which included the hundred or so Jews of Carcassonne—withdrew inside the urban walls. Before dusk faded into night, the crusaders pitched their tents and pavilions around the city and the suburbs.

The next morning the crusaders—after they had eaten—swiftly occupied Saint Vincent and the nearby Aude bridge. Raimon Roger observed these opening maneuvers from his viscomital residence (whose western wall was woven into the city wall that overlooked the river). He expected as much and, though impatient to fight, continued to watch and wait for the forthcoming assault on his fortifications and water supply. Some crossbowmen in the western towers fired a series of feathered bolts at the crusaders. One or two bolts soared in grand futile arcs over the river, but, as the range of a well-aimed straight-flying bolt was around sixty meters, the rest fell short.[4] The crusade leaders then paused the attack for three days and, without any attempt at stealth, surveyed the city and suburbs of Carcassonne for weaknesses. They decided that the northern bourg was not as strongly fortified as the southern *castelar* and that siege machines would not be needed in an assault. Accordingly, the foot soldiers of His army rushed the northwestern wall of the bourg during sunset on Thursday, 6 August. Arnau Amalric and all the other crusade clergy supported the charge by loudly chanting *Veni Sancte Spiritus*. The knights and crossbowmen defending the suburb, dazzled by the red sun, rattled by the holy chorus, quickly retreated into the city. This abandonment of the bourg, though slightly faster and more erratic than intended, was part of a larger defensive ruse. Raimon Roger, well aware of the crusader plan of action since midmorning,

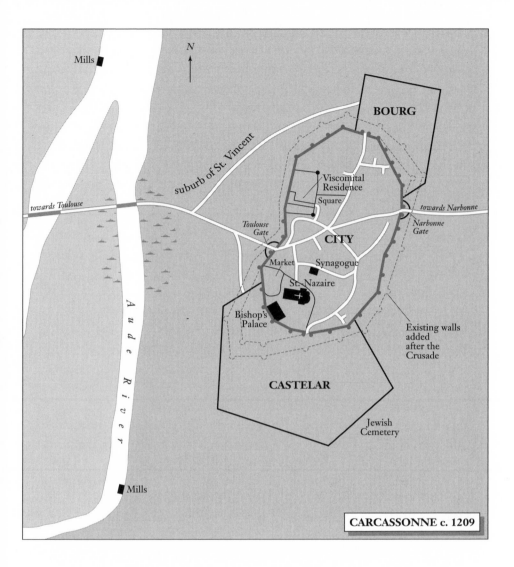

Mills

N

BOURG

suburb of St. Vincent

Viscomital
Residence

Square

towards Toulouse

towards Narbonne

Toulouse
Gate

Narbonne
Gate

CITY

Market

Synagogue

St. Nazaire

Bishop's
Palace

Existing walls
added
after the
Crusade

A u d e   R i v e r

CASTELAR

Jewish
Cemetery

Mills

CARCASSONNE c. 1209

hoped the attackers, thrilled by facile success at the low suburban walls, would be foolhardy enough to press on and assail the high urban walls. He envisioned mowing his assailants down with bolts and arrows as they became boxed in the narrow streets and alleys of the bourg. The soldiers of Christ did not fall into the trap; instead, they again paused their offensive and, throughout the night, demolished the walls and houses of the suburb as thousands of unseen voices jubilantly intoned, "Come, Holy Spirit."[5]

The crusaders, far from relaxing after their nighttime exertions, were so invigorated by the ease with which the bourg was captured that, soon after sunrise, soldiers and knights raced up the clayey southern slope against the better fortified *castelar*. This assault faltered as Raimon Roger and his men defended the suburban walls with unexpected fierceness. Rocks and stones were hurled at the crusaders; bolts and arrows sliced through the air. The crusaders stumbled down the hill, slipping and sliding on the parched ground, falling in and out of ditches, until finally collapsing, dusty and clammy, back where they began. "After this exploit," wrote Pierre des Vaux-de-Cernay, "our men then built machines, which are called 'petraries,' to destroy the wall of the suburb." The petraries, quickly constructed from the holm oaks dispersed throughout the Carcassès and Toulousain in copses and groves (and on whose leaves the kermes insects thrived), were small wooden catapults whose considerable talent for launching rocks and stones belied their lightweight build. These trestle-framed catapults utilized a hefty stone counterweight, as well as a gang of forty men vigorously pulling on ropes, to hurl thirty-kilogram missiles as far as one hundred and fifty meters.[6] An afternoon of petrean battering loosened masonry along the top of the suburban wall. A four-wheeled wagon, covered in layers of cowhide, was then pushed and dragged by some of His more enterprising soldiers right up against the weakened wall. These crusaders, protected by the wagon's tough leather canopy, started digging at the foundations of the wall. The defenders, although exposed on the fractured upper rampart, dropped heavy rocks and flaming torches on the wagon until, crushed and on fire, it crumpled into a blazing heap of leather and wood. The sapping men evaded the rising flames and falling missiles by huddling inside their half-dug tunnel. "What more?" The tunnelers burrowed all night and, crawling back to the crusader camp just before dawn, watched as a deftly sighted petrary brought the sapped wall tumbling down in the early morning light. The soldiers of Christ, shouting and cheering, rushed the *castelar*. The men of Carcassonne plunged into the yawning breach and lashed out with swords and spears at the crusader onslaught. "On that day many blows were given and received; on either side many were dead and bleeding." A lull in the fighting occurred when the boiling sun, directly above, forced the warriors to a standstill. During this martial respite, Raimon Roger acknowledged that the suburb was lost. After setting some houses alight, he and his men withdrew into the city. The tired and thirsty crusaders returned to their tents and pavilions. The *castelar*, soon aflame on every street and alley, burned throughout the afternoon and into the night.[7]

At dusk the crusaders encircled the city with petraries and, complementing these machines with larger and heavier catapults, battered the thick urban walls night and day. These heavier catapults were large, trestle-framed, gravity-powered, counterweight trebuchets that required fewer men to work them and launched formidable projectiles weighing as much as three hundred to five hundred kilograms. Crossbowmen in the towers wasted feathered bolts trying to hit the men working the siege machines. Apart from ribald boys gathering rocks, mostly porous limestone and crystalline granite, for the petraries, the soldiers of Christ rested inside their tents and pavilions. Food, olive oil, and wine were plentiful. Raimon Roger neglected to hoard (or burn) the recent grain harvest, and, as the villages that collected and stored the cereal crop were now uninhabited, the cooks and bakers of His army never wanted for flour. The crusaders were treated to a surfeit of cakes and bread. (Raimon Roger incapacitated his water-powered mills on the Aude, but, after a few repairs, this inconvenience was overcome.) Those persons so egregious as to sell bread to the martial pilgrims—and some villagers further along the Aude tried—were punished with sales of "thirty loaves for a penny." Guilhem de Tudela and Pierre des Vaux-de-Cernay interpreted the abundance of bread as a divine gift signifying His pleasure in the conduct of the holy expedition. A week or so after the assault on the *castelar*, just as the crusaders were about to enjoy an evening repast of warm bread and roast meat, Pere II galloped into the crusader camp with a hundred of his knights. The king offered the great nobles and ecclesiastical lords a courtly greeting. "You are very welcome," they replied. The king and his men cantered through the camp until they came to the rich pavilion of Raimon VI, shaded by a grove near the river. The king dined with his brother-in-law. At the end of the meal, Pere mounted his elegant palfrey, "a bay with a beautiful mane," and, with only three companions, rode unarmed toward the city of Carcassonne. The petraries and catapults paused.[8]

Raimon Roger and his men quickly and joyfully opened the western Toulouse gate for the king of Aragon. The viscount was so excited that he embraced Pere with boyish delight rather than vassalic decorum. Of course, of course, the king was here to help the viscount and his people, "as they were his men, his friends, his dear ones." The king regretted he was not there to help his people. An incredulous Raimon Roger pleaded for aid. He evoked the horror of Béziers; he described the destruction of his lands. Pere became angry and exasperated as he listened to the viscount. "Baron!" he interrupted his vavasor. "By the Lord Jesus, you cannot blame me for any of that, since I told you to expel the heretics; indeed, I commanded you!" The young man was silent. "Viscount," the king continued, "I am greatly worried about you." He softened his tone. "Since such tribulation and such peril as has happened to you was a consequence of these foolish persons and their foolish error." He forgave the youth. "Now, right here, let me suggest something." He came to the point of his visit. "A compromise more or less, if we can get one, with the barons of France." He noted that there were simply too many crusaders and that Raimon Roger would never defeat them all. He contended that trust in the strong walls of Carcassonne, though usually quite sensible, was eroded by the hungry and thirsty multitude (especially the women and children) crowded inside the city. He saw no hope without a compromise. Raimon Roger reluctantly approved some sort of accord with the crusaders. "Lord," said the viscount, "you may do as you wish with the town and everything in it, as we all belong to you, as we once did to the king, your father, who greatly loved us." Pere trotted back to the crusader camp on his fine palfrey. He opened negotiations with the French lords and Arnau Amalric—and was promptly rebuffed. The crusade leaders were intransigent about Carcassonne; everyone (residents, refugees) and everything (houses, money, clothes, pots, buttons) must be surrendered to the soldiers of Christ. The viscount, as a mocking compromise, could flee as a coward with eleven companions. "That will happen," said the king between clenched teeth, "when asses fly in the sky." Pere returned to Raimon Roger and repeated the crusader fiat. The viscount—aghast, appalled—said he would rather kill himself than accept these disgraceful terms. He would rather his men be skinned alive than be so dishonored. He politely asked the king to leave. A grieving Pere and his hundred knights galloped away. The petraries and catapults renewed their thudding cacophony.[9]

"Following these events," wrote Pierre des Vaux-de-Cernay, "our leading men took counsel as to how they should capture the city, bearing in mind that if matters turned out as they had at Béziers, the city would be destroyed." The crusade leaders, while they again surveyed Carcassonne for vulnerabilities, had the ditches around the city filled and movable wooden siege towers known as "cats" constructed. The bishops, monks, and abbots, including Arnau Amalric, were frustrated with what they saw as martial procrastination. "Come on! Why do you delay? Forgiveness?" The French lords ignored the clerical sarcasm and continued planning their offensive. Crossbowmen on the walls of Carcassonne loosened feathered bolts at any crusader who came within range. The fifteen thousand to twenty thousand men, women, and children inside the walls were collapsing in despair and dehydration. The streets and alleys were littered with their miserable and desiccated bodies. The fetor of swollen unburied corpses mingled with the stench of rotting animal carcasses. Black vultures and ravens circled the city. All fortitude and hope departed with the king of Aragon. Water from the Aude was now unattainable and the urban wells were dry. The temperature was around forty degrees Celsius and, as the radiant heat from the buildings and walls was two to five degrees hotter again, the city seethed and simmered throughout much of the day. Indeed, it was so searing hot that saline marshes near Carcassonne, soggy and muddy as long as anyone could remember, partially evaporated and, aside from enticing a few flamingos further inland, exposed salt crystals to be scraped and sold by resourceful villagers. Women and little children, tormented by heat and flies, cried and shrieked in every part of the city. The soldiers of Christ heard the cries, retched at the stink, and counted the carrion birds. (They also purchased some dirty salt.) The crusade leaders diagnosed Carcassonne as moribund and decided an assault was unnecessary. All they had to do was wait a week, perhaps two, and the city would surrender.[10]

After eight days an eminent noble crusader and thirty knights approached the Toulouse gate. The noble crusader suggested a parley and promised to safely escort the viscount to the rich pavilion of Hervé IV, count of Nevers. Raimon Roger agreed and, accompanied by a hundred knights, rode into the crusader camp on his *milsoldor* horse. "Lord," said the noble crusader, "I am a relative of yours." The viscount was unmoved. "Make some sort of agreement with the pope and the barons of the host," implored the older man to his younger relative, "because if they take you by force then, truthfully, all of you will get the same judgement as they got at Béziers." Raimon Roger—broken, emotionless—walked into the rich pavilion of the count of Nevers and, in front of all the crusade leaders, surrendered his city and his lands. He even offered himself as a hostage on the condition that the men, women, and children of Carcassonne would be spared. "He acted like a fool," sang Guilhem de Tudela, "allowing himself to become a captive!" The French lords, as Arnau Amalric and Milo later informed the pope, mercifully agreed to refrain from killing everyone in the city—at least for the rest of the day. Otherwise, the same uncompromising terms addressed to Pere II still applied: all possessions, from buttons to buildings, were forfeited to the soldiers of Christ. In the early afternoon the Toulouse gate was opened and thousands of people charged out, helter-skelter, "each one as if in a battle." Nobles and merchants, knights and sergeants, men and women, boys and girls, all of them dressed only "in shirts and breeches," fell over each other as they surged down the hill and across the Aude bridge in confusion and fear. They carried nothing except what was on their backs and, "upriver, downriver," dispersed into the scorching countryside. "Some went to Toulouse, some others to Aragon, and some others to Spain." The city of Carcassonne was soon desolate. The soldiers of Christ cheered and cheered His victory and His glory. The petraries and catapults were still. Raimon Roger remained a hostage.[11]

"Come on! The abbot of Cîteaux wishes to give a sermon! Forgiveness!" cried heralds as they moved through the cheering crusaders. The light-hearted soldiers followed the heralds into Carcassonne and, sidestepping all the decomposing bodies, crowded into the square in front of the viscomital residence. Arnau Amalric climbed some marble steps and addressed the army of God. "Lords," shouted the abbot, "pay attention to what I say!" The crusaders went quiet. "You see what miracles the king enthroned on high does for you, so that nothing stands against you!" The crusaders murmured agreement. "At God's request I forbid you to keep any spoils for yourselves, not even the value of a piece of charcoal, because if you do keep anything of value from the town, we will immediately excommunicate and curse you!" The crusaders were dismayed. "We will immediately give everything to some strong baron who, with God's grace, will hold and keep this terrain so that the wicked heretics can never retake it!" Almost all the crusaders granted the wisdom of what was said. Arnau Amalric—pleased, satisfied—sang a mass, preached a sermon on the birth of Christ, and promptly offered the lands of Raimon Roger to Hervé IV, the count of Nevers. The count refused. The legate then offered the lands to Eudes III, the duke of Burgundy. The duke refused. The legate glanced at Gaucher de Châtillon, count of Saint-Pol. The count shook his head. The abbot then asked the assembled crusaders for their choice of a new viscount of Béziers and Carcassonne. Some pilgrims suggested Simon IV, lord of Montfort, as the new "prince and lord of the lands." Unfortunately, he too refused the lands of Raimon Roger. "Lord," implored Arnau Amalric, "by God Almighty, accept the honour that they wish to give you!" The offer was again refused. The abbot and the duke of Burgundy threw themselves at Simon's feet "and begged him to accept what was both a burden and an honour." The army of God was wearying of this drawn-out charade. Arnau Amalric finally "made use of his authority as papal legate" and ordered that the honor be accepted. "I will do it!" said Simon. The crusaders acclaimed the new viscount and, as soon as the last hurrah was yelled, thankfully crossed the river to roast meat and warm bread.

"O what foresight in the choice of the prince! O what feeling in the acclamation of the pilgrims!" wrote Pierre des Vaux-de-Cernay. The forty-four-year-old Simon de Montfort was, according to the youthful Cistercian, "tall, with a splendid head of hair," vigorously handsome, "broad-shouldered with muscular arms," physically agile, eloquent, friendly, humble, scrupulously chaste, "prudent in counsel, just in giving judgement," and wholly dedicated to God. "I dare say that no man will ever be found in whom such great gifts (either of nature or of grace) have come together so completely." It was fortuitous that Christ assigned the lord of the "Strong Mountain" to safeguard His shipwrecked Church from the persecution of heretics. Simon had been a pilgrim on the French and Venetian crusade of 1202. However, when this holy expedition wantonly attacked the Christian city of Zara, he denounced the crusaders as wicked mercenaries, proclaiming,

"I have not come here to destroy Christians!" He withdrew from this "company of sinners" and, sailing to the Holy Land, "achieved many victories against the pagans." (A very young Pierre accompanied his uncle Guy, abbot of Vaux-de-Cernay, on the crusade at least as far as Zara.) He was blessed with a wife, Alice de Montmorency, who was as much a paragon as her husband. Simon was saved from excessive pride in his abundant gifts—and from excessive parody in Pierre's giddy portrait—by God thoughtfully burdening him with "such a weight of poverty that he never had a chance to rest and become vain."

Arnau Amalric and the French lords decided on Simon de Montfort as the new viscount of Béziers and Carcassonne soon after Raimon Roger surrendered. Simon, while frequently honored as count of Montfort in recognition of being nominal count (or earl) of Leicester, was an impecunious adventurer who just happened to be more pious if no less avaricious than other nobles like himself. Arnau Amalric, even as he rejoiced in the immolation of Béziers, decided the walls, buildings, and wealth of Carcassonne deserved preservation—unlike the men, women, and children of the Carcassès—because he envisioned the city as a shining citadel, "fortified by men of Catholic faith," from which present and future crusaders would campaign against other cities and *castra* poisoned with heresy. He now realized that the crusade, however glorious the beginning, was a holy war of years and not months. A lord of moderate means, good martial skills, and a sanctimonious manner was needed to make this lasting commitment—and Simon de Monfort was that lord. The count of Nevers, the duke of Burgundy, and the count of Saint-Pol, though sincere about being signed with the cross, were simply unwilling to walk in the way of Christ year in, year out. They applauded Simon's willingness to be a martial pilgrim in perpetuity. The army of God, though, had to be persuaded that a new viscount was necessary and, more important, that it should be Simon. After the pell-mell exodus from Carcassonne, most crusaders wanted to loot and burn the city; they were, as Arnau Amalric later told the pope, "with us in body but not in spirit." The seemingly endless performance of the abbot and the French lords before the viscomital residence was as much artful politicking as the exhaustion of greedy and incendiary passions. Simon de Montfort, after the last hurrah of his acclamation, thankfully adopted the (slightly vain) title of "count of Leicester, lord of Montfort, and viscount of Béziers and Carcassonne."[12]

Hervé IV and Eudes III started preparations for returning to France after Simon de Montfort became the viscount of Béziers and Carcassonne. It was late August and, as far as they were concerned, they were no longer signed with the cross. Arnau Amalric begged the count of Nevers and the duke of Burgundy to stay a little longer in the service of Christ, especially as the weather was still warm, and help Simon besiege the strongly fortified *castra* and castles of Minerve, Termes, and Cabaret. Eudes cheerfully yielded to Christ for a few more weeks. Hervé angrily refused. The count resented the duke's friendship with Simon and, the more he thought about it, he regretted endorsing the piddling lord of Montfort as the new viscount. He never really liked Eudes and, the more he thought about it, he never really liked Simon either. This animosity worried everyone so much that they feared the count and duke might kill one another. It was a relief when Hervé departed for Montpellier; it was a misfortune that he took most of the crusaders with him. Nevertheless, the next day Simon and Eudes journeyed with the remaining soldiers of Christ into the Aude valley. As they marched westerly into the Lauragais plain they came across one empty village after another. Fanjeaux, rakishly perched on a dazzlingly white limestone hill, was already occupied in Simon's name by the *maisnier* (mercenary) Pere Aragon; as this hireling waited for the viscount, he ransacked the deserted village for money. Simon, as a salve for the feelings of some crusaders and as a concerted policy of intimidation, allowed a few uninhabited villages to be set on fire. Raimon VI, in a separate northerly expedition, cordially burned some villages and castles in the Carcassès. He even suggested some pestiferous villages near his own lands that could be destroyed by Simon. Almost four decades later an elderly noblewoman, na Guilhelma Marti, recalled these ominous bonfires when she told the inquisition that some letters of penance Dominic de Guzmán had given her before the crusade, letters regarding an adolescent gift of bread and nuts to the good men, were incinerated when, without warning, without provocation, "Fanjeaux was burnt by the count of Montfort."[13]

The leading men of Castres in the Albigeois traveled south to see Simon de Montfort and, finding him in the Aude valley, petitioned that they were willing to receive the new viscount as their lord. Eudes advised Simon to immediately seize such an important *castrum*, and so, after a swift fifty-kilometer gallop through the Lauragais into the Albigeois, Simon and a small contingent of crusaders occupied the village. As the knights and prudent men of Castres were paying homage to their new viscount, knights and prudent men from Lombers approached the castral walls and offered to be men of the viscount as well. Simon, anxious to rejoin the army of God, declined to accompany the knights back to their village for an act of homage; nevertheless, he took Lombers under his protection. (Lombers, of course, was the same fortified village where the bishops of Lodève and Albi inconclusively debated the holy good men "of the sect of Olivier" in 1165.) The viscount, impatient to return to the Carcassès, stayed long enough in Castres to burn two heretics. "One of them was 'perfected' in the sect of heretics," wrote Pierre des Vaux-de-Cernay in his contrived nomenclature, "and the other was a sort of novice and disciple of the other." One was a mature holy good man and one was a much younger *bon ome*, probably the adolescent son or nephew of the older man. Their fellow villagers (and other good men) betrayed them. The youth, though, repented and promised to abjure heresy. "A great dispute broke out amongst our people when they heard this." Some argued that the lad no longer deserved death; others dismissed his repentance as frightened mendacity. Simon decided the young man must burn; if his contrition were true, the fire would expiate his sins; "if he was lying, he would receive a just reward for his lying." The two men, swathed in heavy iron chains, were torched in the village square. "I abjure heretical depravity," cried the youth amid the smoke, "I want to die in the faith of the Holy Roman Church." The chains girdling him instantly fell apart and—miracle of miracles—he escaped with only scorched fingertips.[14]

Simon de Montfort returned to the army of God after securing (and cleansing) Castres. Eudes recommended that the crusaders undertake one last expedition against Cabaret in the rugged Montagne Noire. Peire Roger, the lord of Cabaret, had retreated to his castle with other knights of the Carcassès. Simon agreed with the duke, and so the soldiers of Christ advanced warily into the chalky mountainous terrain north of Carcassonne. The castle of Cabaret was built on a rough knuckle of black and white limestone protruding out of a stubbly ridge. It was supported by two smaller towers (Surdaspina and Chertinos) on similar jagged knurls. The castle surveyed the Grésilhou River to the west and the Orbiel River to the east. A small fortified village nestled three hundred fifty meters below the castle alongside the Grésilhou. The crusaders pitched their tents and pavilions in the dark narrow ravine watered by the Grésilhou. A feeble and desultory morning assault on the castle's western walls was easily repulsed. The crusaders refrained from further attacks; they were tired of fighting, and the eerie rugous landscape unnerved them. "The mountains are savage and the passes treacherous," sang Guilhem de Tudela, "and no one wished to be killed in that land." The next morning the duke loaded his mules and roncins and prepared to leave the crusade; he lingered one more day and, after promising to help Simon if he ever needed aid, returned to France. Almost every other martial pilgrim departed with the duke of Burgundy. "Very few knights remained with me," Simon complained to Innocent III, "and I am nearly alone amongst the enemies of Christ as I wander through mountains and dangerous precipices."[15]

"Indeed, although the greater part of the army has departed," Arnau Amalric and Milo informed Innocent III, "the expedition, through the grace of God, has achieved as much in two months as it might have hoped to achieve in two or three years of campaigning."[16] It was this sense of so much accomplished so quickly, as well as the waning of summer, that caused most crusaders to depart after the surrender of Carcassonne. Paradoxically, the wonderful successes of the crusade shattered the chiliastic enthusiasm for walking as He walked between the Garonne and the Rhône. The millennialism that had driven and inspired the crusaders largely vanished when Simon de Montfort became viscount of Béziers and Carcassonne. The apocalyptic edge that was so sharp in the ribald boys at Béziers and still fierce among other crusaders at Carcassonne was dulled and finally blunted by the suppression of promiscuous savagery and by Arnau Amalric's wearisome conviction that the crusade would not exterminate the little foxes in one summery expedition. Most crusaders genuinely believed that heresy would be erased from the world, once and for all, by their pilgrimage. The revelation that this was not going to happen, that heresy, though restrained was still rampant, and that the crusade was metamorphosing into other variations of sacred belligerence, so diluted the fervor of the crusaders that all they wanted to do was leave the Carcassès as soon as possible. (The duke of Burgundy merely stifled his desire to leave by a couple of weeks.) Holy wars, for all their bloodshed and brutality, are surprisingly fragile endeavors. The lasting necessity of the holy war on heresy seemed, at least to the soldiers of Christ gathered before Carcassonne and Cabaret, more a disappointment than an opportunity.

"The Lord in His Compassion did not wish this most holy war to end soon," wrote Pierre des Vaux-de-Cernay, "because it providently provided forgiveness for sinners and the enhancement of grace for the just. I say that He wished His enemies to be subjugated successively and gradually so that, as sinners successively and gradually armed themselves to avenge the injuries of Jesus Christ, the prolongation of the time of war would prolong the forgiveness of sinners."[17] There were twenty more summers of this most holy war, and thousands of crusaders, princes, and kings among them rejoiced in the perennial opportunity of forgiveness. Yet the astonishing multitude of ordinary Christians who walked like Him during that first summer, a multitude unmatched except by the First Crusade, never happened again. The mass of Provençal nobles who yielded to Christ in 1209 was not replicated either. Most of these crusaders retreated to their own villages and castles either after the burning of Béziers or the emptying of Carcassonne. The holy war on heresy was not at all what they expected and not at all what they wanted; it was warfare that lacked *onor* in every meaningful sense. The crusade was not an opportunity for courtly melioration; rather, it disregarded and mocked *cortezia*, and its continuation and escalation was greeted with deep apprehension in thousands of villages between the Garonne and Rhône, especially in the Toulousain and Lauragais. Arnau Amalric and Milo, while exulting in the lands captured by the crusaders, loudly lamented that Toulouse was still beyond their reach. At the time they conspicuously condemned Raimon Roger as the "worst defender of heretics." Yet, as was obvious to everyone all along, the abbot and his instrument thought the count of Toulouse much much worse.[18]

IX

IN SEPTEMBER 1209, while the duke of Burgundy was preparing to return to France, and just before the great army of God finally dissolved, Arnau Amalric and Milo sent a small delegation of French knights to Toulouse to demand—with an audacity worthy of the "holy game"—that the citizens compromise at once with the crusaders regarding the heretics in their midst. Raimon VI may have signed himself with the cross, but that did not kill the serpents slithering through the streets of Toulouse. The legates, though clearly thinking the count had more power over his city than he did, understood that Toulouse was largely an independent entity within the county. In the century before the crusade the counts of Toulouse gave away many of their rights and privileges within and without the city to an oligarchy of eminent and courtly men known as the "good men of Toulouse and the bourg." The counts fragmented or forfeited taxes on wine, salt, and other valuable commodities; they partitioned or relinquished certain forms of high justice; they divided up or gave away tolls on roads, bridges, and rivers; and they even shared urban defense with the "greater good men" after 1158. In the middle of the twelfth century the "good men of Toulouse and the bourg" became the "common council of the city and the bourg," and, within twenty years, these "common councillors" were "consuls." Fifty years later these twenty-four consuls, though elected only from the "greater good men," were mostly wealthy mercantile arrivistes rather than honorable patrician scions. (Artisans, tradesmen, and Jews, though frequently good men, were never consuls.) The consuls were so autonomous between 1202 and 1204 that they waged twenty-three small wars of coercion and conquest throughout the Toulousain, a region they grandly (and greedily) labeled "the Fatherland of Toulouse" in 1205. These small wars were fought by a citizen militia commanded by the consulate. Consequently, it was a consul of Toulouse who told the French knights that, though willing to do whatever Innocent III requested, he and his colleagues wished to go and see the pope first. The knights nodded and returned to the crusader camp at Montpellier. A consular mission immediately traveled to Rome.[1]

The city and bourg of Toulouse, shaped like a vast butterfly wing spread out upon the Garonne's eastern embankment, were two entwined spaces that, while separated by an old "Saracen" wall, spanned two thousand three hundred meters from the southern Narbonne gate in the city to the northern Lascrosses gate in the bourg and, from the eastern Saint-Étienne gate in the city to the western Bazacle gate in the bourg, one thousand five hundred meters. Almost twenty thousand men, women, and children lived in the four parishes of the city (Saint-Pierre-des-Cusines, Daurade, Dalbade, Saint-Étienne) and seven thousand in the two parishes of the bourg (Saint-Sernin, Saint-Sernin-du-Taur). A few hundred more dwelt on the other side of the river in a suburb named Saint-Cyprien (whose parish was Saint Nicholas from 1188), whose houses clustered near the Old bridge (opened as long as anyone remembered) and the Daurade bridge (opened by 1180). A further hundred or so lived in the *salvetat* (safeguard) of Toulouse: a suburban barrier of houses, shops, and gardens that sprawled south over the alluvial flatlands in front of the Château Narbonnais. The *salvetat* belonged completely to the count of Toulouse, and so those who lived there, while enjoying liberties from his tolls and monopolies, were not citizens under the jurisdiction of the consulate. It was initially established (before 1141) as a "safe" area where village nobles and their small wars were forbidden. As this comital protection waned throughout the twelfth century, the *salvetat* was habitually abandoned in time of war, effectively "safeguarding" the Narbonne gate and the Château Narbonnais from a besieging army.[2]

Raimon VI recognized that Arnau Amalric and Milo were brazenly maneuvering him and his city into the path of the most holy war on heresy. Milo boldly summoned an ecclesiastical council at Avignon (attended by four archbishops and twenty bishops) in the middle of September with the agenda of excommunicating the count, the consuls, and the community of Toulouse. Raimon, though excused an outright anathema, was conditionally excommunicated on the following familiar crimes: not expelling heretics and their believers from his lands, not surrendering heretics (under his authority) to the crusaders, willfully dispensing wretched justice upon churches and religious houses (and then not responding to their petitions),

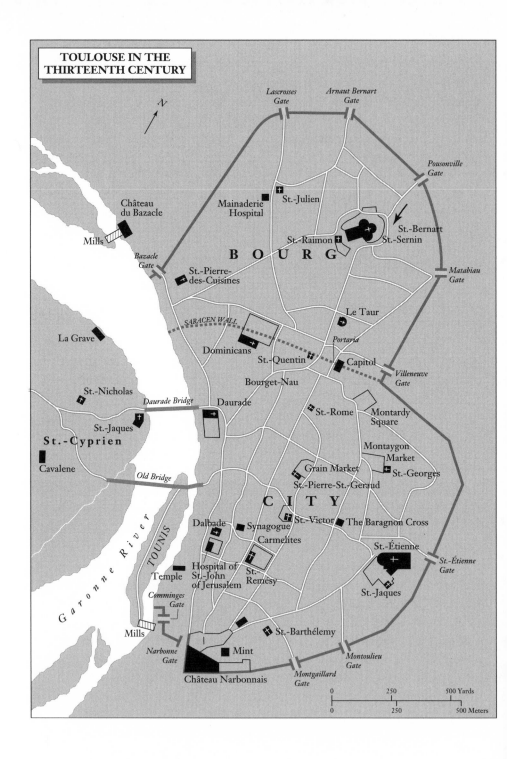

TOULOUSE IN THE THIRTEENTH CENTURY

N

Lascrosses Gate

Arnaut Bernart Gate

Pousonville Gate

Château du Bazacle

Mills

Mainaderie Hospital

St.-Julien

St.-Raimon

St.-Bernart
St.-Sernin

B O U R G

Bazacle Gate

St.-Pierre-des-Cuisines

Matabiau Gate

Le Taur

SARACEN WALL

La Grave

Portaria

Dominicans

St.-Quentin

Capitol

Villeneuve Gate

St.-Nicholas

Daurade Bridge

Daurade

Bourget-Nau

St.-Rome

Montardy Square

St.-Cyprien

St.-Jaques

Montaygon Market

Old Bridge

Grain Market

St.-Georges

Cavalene

St.-Pierre-St.-Geraud

C I T Y

Garonne River

TOUNIS

Dalbade

St.-Victor

The Baragnon Cross

Synagogue

Carmelites

St.-Étienne

Temple

Hospital of St.-John of Jerusalem

St.-Remésy

St.-Étienne Gate

St.-Jaques

Commminges Gate

Mills

St.-Barthélemy

Narbonne Gate

Mint

Montoulieu Gate

Montgaillard Gate

Château Narbonnais

| 0 | 250 | 500 Yards |
| 0 | 250 | 500 Meters |

not protecting castral churches (under his authority) from being destroyed, and not ceasing to willfully extort unjust tolls on roads, bridges, and rivers. (Raimon's excommunication by Peire de Castelnau in 1207 had listed, among the many comital offenses, extortion through unfair tolls and fees along the Rhône.) The consuls and community of Toulouse, on account of their refusal to hand over the heretics and their believers (and the goods of the heretics and their believers) to the crusaders, were placed under the interdiction of excommunication, and their city and territories were now, theoretically at least, open to seizure. Milo and Hugh, bishop of Riez, another papal legate and an Avignon participant, reported in their conciliar memorandum that the count had until All Saint's Day (Sunday, 1 November) to absolve himself of his crimes, "otherwise he himself and his lands will be subjected to the sentence of excommunication and interdict." Raimon VI, contingently condemned, decided that he too must appeal directly to Innocent III.[3]

The count of Toulouse initially visited Philip II Augustus in Paris to discuss the looming excommunication and the truculent behavior of the papal legates. The king, though vaguely concerned, gave no meaningful counsel, and so the count, having wasted two or more months in France, arrived in Rome sometime after Christmas. Milo, in the meantime, died in late December at Montpellier; his former assistant, Thedisius, replaced him as legate (and as Arnau Amalric's "instrument"). Pierre des Vaux-de-Cernay wrote that the pope greeted the count as "an unbeliever, a persecutor of the cross," and an enemy of the faith; Guilhem de Tudela sang that the pope greeted the count with gifts and "cordial friendship," even allowing him to touch the linen cloth with which Veronica wiped His face and on which His countenance (from the chest up) was imprinted. (The "Veronica" was usually displayed in Saint Peter's basilica near the door, on the right as you entered.)[4] Innocent III, evidently more sympathetic to the comital and consular pleas than what young Pierre maliciously imagined, promptly issued letters tempering the zeal of his legates. On Tuesday, 19 January 1210, he revoked the interdict against the consuls and community of Toulouse and ordered the legates to absolve them. Six days later he informed Thedisius and the bishop of Riez that, when Raimon VI was (once again) legally absolved of heretical depravity and the murder of Peire de Castelnau, then his absolution must be accepted and his seven *castra* (given as a pledge of faith almost a year earlier) summarily returned. "For similar reasons," the pope continued, "we have decided to ensure that his lands will be protected from the Christian army which went forth to expunge the heretics—in accordance with our mandate—and which has now almost destroyed its adversaries." The legates were to summon a council within three months of receiving this letter and reassess the faithfulness of the count; nevertheless, "you must await confirmation of your decision from the Apostolic See." Raimon departed Rome relatively satisfied. As he journeyed back to Saint-Gilles he visited the Emperor Otto IV in Arles and Philip II Augustus in Paris to discuss the threat of crusade; the first was politely indifferent, the second overtly inimical. Raimon, rattled by the concerted apathy of his suzerains, welcomed the spring with fear and confusion.[5]

Simon de Montfort retreated from Cabaret to the blackened hulk of Fanjeaux. He rebuilt the castral walls and regrouped his forces. He mustered thirty French knights, a few hundred mounted sergeants, and roughly a thousand foot soldiers. He protested over and over to Innocent III about the smallness of the army of God and the burden of his poverty. "I am having to hire the *soldarios* who have remained with me for a greater price than in other wars," he wrote to the pope. "I can hardly keep any of them unless they are paid twice the usual amount." These *soldarii* were an entrepreneurial group of mostly journeymen mercenaries and some Provençal nobles (who overcame their courtly qualms with monetary retainers). In late September, Vidal, abbot of Saint-Antonin de Pamiers, offered Simon the fortified town of Pamiers on the Ariège River in the county of Foix. This unforeseen gift roused His little army into a month of frenzied campaigning and conquest. The abbot and Raimon Roger, count of Foix, shared the lordship of Pamiers. Simon dismissed this arrangement without a second thought. He descended upon the county of Foix in holy righteousness. Raimon Roger de Foix, while not presently accused of protecting heretics and mercenaries, was more than guilty of such turpitude in the past. The *castrum* of Mirepoix on the Hers River was seized two days into the expedition. Three days later Simon rendered homage to the abbot for Pamiers. The next day he captured Saverdun further north along the Ariège. He then withdrew from the county of Foix and, passing through Fanjeaux, proceeded to Lombers, where fifty knights swore to be his faithful men. He galloped to nearby Albi and received the city from Guilhem, bishop of Albi. The new "lord of the Albigeois," after a cursory inspection of his domain, hurried back to Carcassonne. The army of God, campaigning in the Razés, occupied Limoux and hanged a score of recalcitrant villagers. Simon resumed his war with the count of Foix by laying siege to the castle of Preixan. Raimon Roger de Foix—stunned, staggered—surrendered the castle, gave his son Aimericas as a hostage, and sued for peace. Simon, quite exhausted, readily obliged and returned to Carcassonne with the boy.[6]

Pere II was the overlord of Raimon Roger de Foix and, once again, the predatoriness of the crusaders disgusted him. Nevertheless, largely due to papal prompting, the king of Aragon tried to reconcile himself to the holy war on heresy by accepting Simon de Montfort's homage as the new viscount of Carcassonne, Béziers, and Albi. The king invited the parvenu viscount to Montpellier in November. He equivocated for two weeks about when and how the ceremony of vassalage was to be undertaken. Pere's loathing of Simon finally got the better of him; he simply could not bring himself to accept that man as his man. Showing neither grace nor courtesy, he asked Simon to leave Montpellier. The athlete of Christ did not care one way or the other; he had written to the pope requesting recognition of his claim to the Trencavel lands; more important, he held the viscounty by martial force and God's justice.[7]

Simon de Montfort returned to Carcassonne and discovered that during his sojourn in Montpellier many nobles and knights of the Biterrois, Carcassès, and Albigeois had renounced their oaths of loyalty to him. *Castra* and castles, faithful only a few weeks earlier, repudiated the viscount and killed or imprisoned his men. The villagers of Castres and Lombers dismissed their friendship with Simon and locked up a French knight and some soldiers in a tower—although the prisoners soon escaped out of a high widow by shimmying down a rope of twisted clothes. The French knights Amaury and Guillaume de Poissy were attacked and trapped in a fortified hamlet near Carcassonne. Gaubert d'Essigny and Bouchard de Marly, in an act of vainglorious stupidity, decided to march against Cabaret with only a handful of men, and, ambushed along the Grésilhou, the former was killed and the later captured. Giraut del Pepios (de Pépieux), a knight of the Biterrois whom Simon had befriended and entrusted with guarding some *castra* in the Minervois, decried the "French from France" when one of them killed his uncle; furious with revenge and anger, he seized the village of Puisserguier. (Simon, when he first heard of the murder, tried to mollify Giraut by having his uncle's killer buried alive.) Simon quickly retook Puisserguier, but not before Giraut del Pepios fled to Minerve with two French knights as prisoners. These Frenchmen were cruelly used; their eyes were gouged out and their ears, noses, and upper lips sliced off; and, when the fun was over, they were discarded without clothes into the bitter cold and biting wind of the Minervois. One soon died in a dung heap; the other, guided by a kindly beggar, made it to Carcassonne. Raimon Roger de Foix, having caught his breath, disowned his peace with Simon and attempted, rather incompetently, to storm the half-built walls of Fanjeaux. "Almost all the local people were similarly affected with this malignancy and deserted our count," grieved Pierre des Vaux-de-Cernay. By the middle of December most of the villages and castles gained during the previous month were lost. All Simon securely held were Carcassonne, Fanjeaux, Saissac, Pamiers, Saverdun, Ambialet, and (very tenuously) Limoux. "What was the count of Christ to do?"[8]

Raimon Roger Trencavel suddenly became ill and died at Carcassonne on Tuesday, 10 November. "What crying and weeping you would have seen throughout the Carcassès!" Raimon Roger, despite rumors then and now, was not poisoned; melancholia, lack of appetite, and the harrowing awareness of how deeply He hated him—the holocaust of Béziers still smoldered, for Christ's sake!—resulted in such weakness of body and soul that the young man was unable to endure a modest bout of dysentery. "And so he had to die," sang Guilhem de Tudela.[9]

Simon de Monfort, after a morose winter inside Carcassonne, was cheered at the beginning of Lent when he heard that his wife (whom he had summoned) was approaching the Biterrois in the company of numerous French knights signed with the cross. He expectantly galloped into the Agde and, soon enough, found Alice de Montmorency, resting at the village of Pézenas on the Herault River. Simon and Alice journeyed back to Carcassonne together; however, when the couple reached Capendu just east of Carcassonne, a report reached them that the *castrum* of Montlaur in the Corbières had betrayed the viscount and attacked his soldiers. Simon, leaving his wife with an escort, went off with the French knights to Montlaur and, in a perfunctory assault, captured the village and hanged the traitors. "Then the Lord, who seemed perhaps to have been asleep, rose up to help His servants and could now be seen more manifestly to do great things for us!" Simon and the French crusaders, before returning to Carcassonne, subdued all of the Minervois except Minerve and the hamlet of Ventajou and, for good measure, uprooted and burned all the vineyards around Cabaret. The French crusaders, after a brief respite at Carcassonne, were eager to walk like Him throughout the Carcassès and Albigeois. Around Easter Simon marched the enlarged army of God into the Lauragais and, after occupying the abandoned village of Alzonne, encircled the defiant *castrum* of Bram. Three days of pointless yelling, easily avoided arrows, and taut silence ended when the soldiers of Christ charged the walls and overran the village in a matter of minutes. In retaliation for the mutilation of the two Frenchmen by Giraut del Pepios and as a warning to other obdurate *castra*, Simon dug out one hundred and ninety-nine eyes and hacked off a hundred noses. The one man allowed to keep his one eye shepherded (as cyclope chaperone) the sightless ninety-nine to Cabaret.

The count of Toulouse, the king of Aragon, and the count of Foix met near Pamiers while Simon de Montfort was slicing and carving at Bram. Raimon VI and Pere II tried to persuade Raimon Roger de Foix to make peace with Simon; the count of Foix curtly refused, and the meeting abruptly ended. A week later the army of God surprised Foix itself and, as the gates were carelessly ajar, almost captured the town in one fell swoop. The knights defending Foix slammed the gates shut at the last minute. Simon, before returning to Carcassonne, devastated the surrounding fields, vineyards, and woods. Meanwhile, Pere lingered along the Ariège and, with little or no discretion, started negotiating with Peire Roger, lord of Cabaret, Raimon, lord of Termes, and Aimeric de Laurac, lord of Montréal, about becoming their immediate suzerain and helping them in their fight against the crusaders. Simon intended to disrupt these deliberations because, while such a reworking of the ties of homage was suppositional at best, the very idea was still intolerable. He knew Pere was journeying to Montréal to meet the "Albigensian knights" (as Pierre des Vaux-de-Cernay called them), and yet, hesitant to threaten or attack the king directly, he besieged the *castrum* of Bellegarde near Montréal. The king approached Montréal and, despite the entreaties of the anxious lords within, refused to enter the *castrum* until Peire Roger handed over Cabaret to the crown of Aragon. Indeed, when Pere required that Raimon and Aimeric give him all their possessions whenever he so chose, it was clear he was never serious about receiving them as his men. The three lords refused the royal terms and retreated inside Montréal. Bellegarde, without any hope of support, quickly surrendered. The king, patently bluffing about his reason for touring the Carcassès, visited Simon at Bellegarde and asked him to make peace with Raimon Roger de Foix. Simon, going along with the sham, agreed to a truce until next Easter. Pere—composed, cocky—retired to the coolness of the Pyrénéan foothills.[10]

In the humble parish of the Dalbade in Toulouse was the little whitewashed church of the Holy Mary. (The parochial name derived from the church's plain façade: Latin *dealbo*, "to whitewash.") The Dalbade was a dependency of the Benedictine priory of Saint-Pierre de Moissac in the parish of the Daurade. Around 1200 the chaplain of the Dalbade, Vidal, protested in the court of the bishop of Toulouse that the priory unfairly raised his annual parish fee from six shillings to fifty. Vidal argued that the Dalbade had no tithes and barely survived on charges for funerals and burials. The dire poverty of his church was "due to the heretics whose perverse sects abound in the region of Toulouse and," more honestly, "due to the newly built churches in the parish that all the parishioners go to on feast days and other days." He won his case.[11] A decade later Vidal and his church, still poor, were swathed in an extraordinary miracle. It was the middle of June and the walls, recently whitewashed, were suddenly covered at dusk with innumerable crosses, inside and out, more lustrous, more silvery, than the pure walls themselves. The crosses moved incessantly, appearing, disappearing, shimmering, rippling, brightly blazing, softly glowing. They were of all sizes, perpetually overlapping, constantly splintering, forever merging. The miracle lasted fifteen days and almost everyone in Toulouse saw the crosses—except Vidal himself. He prayed and prayed until, startlingly, a host of crosses danced about him, not on the walls, but in the very air. One cross, larger than all the others, abruptly flew out of the church and, chased by the smaller crosses, soared through the streets. Vidal followed the crosses outside the city and, wondrously, saw them hover around a beautiful man with a great unsheathed sword. This sublime figure, armored with the crosses, then killed an enormous man who unexpectedly emerged from Toulouse. Vidal all but fainted at the sight. Arnau Amalric and Thedisius viewed the Dalbade crosses many times and even heard about the beautiful man. The crosses disappeared just as Raimon VI entered Toulouse after his long absence; far from being comforted by the miracle, he felt only boundless menace.[12]

Four months earlier, in compliance with papal edicts, Arnau Amalric went to Toulouse to absolve the city and the bourg. The consuls refused to negotiate with the abbot; they thought him unreasonable. Most decisively, only Thedisius had the apostolic mandate to purify them. Folc de Maselha, bishop of Toulouse, arbitrated a compromise between the consuls and the legate. The consuls agreed to pay Arnau Amalric 1,000 pounds of Toulouse (an enormous amount equal to about a tenth of the wealth of the city and bourg) in support of the crusade as an affirmation of their faithfulness to the Church. The absolution was postponed when only five hundred pounds were collected because of vicious urban riots—riots largely fomented by Folc. At the beginning of Lent the bishop founded a grand crusader confraternity to expel heretics and usurers from the city and the bourg. A multitude yielded to Christ in the city; very few did in the bourg. The holy brotherhood presently ransacked the contumacious bourg. A confraternity of sorts was soon established in the bourg to oppose the one in the city. These gangs—city adorned in white and bourg in black—even battled on armored horses. The street fighting eventually subsided and Folc was able to mediate another compromise. The remaining five hundred pounds was to be paid by early August, and, as a pledge of good faith, ten "greater good men" were sent as hostages to Pamiers. Folc de Maselha, gratified even if Arnau Amalric was not, absolved the consuls and community of Toulouse.[13]

The animosity between the brotherhoods of the city and the bourg, between "Whites" and "Blacks," still seethed when Raimon VI returned to

Toulouse in June. The count's immediate concern, though, was his purgation for the crime of heresy and the murder of Peire de Castelnau and the removal of his conditional excommunication. Thedisius visited Toulouse during the Dalbade miracle and discussed with Arnau Amalric what they should do regarding the papal injunction to purify the count. The legate, convinced that Raimon was guilty and that he had beguiled the pope with wicked lies, searched for lawful reasons to refuse absolution. Thedisius, with lawyerly sophistry, discovered a solution in the very papal injunction that seemed so indisputable. "It is our wish," Innocent III had stated in his letter, "that in the interim the count of Toulouse should implement all our mandates." The pope intended his instructions on absolution to cover only the crime of heresy and the murder of Peire de Castelnau. Raimon's other supposed sins, from illicit river fees to stealing monastic rents, were to be ignored. Thedisius, on the other hand, now interpreted these instructions to cover all of the felonies alleged against the count at the council of Avignon. Adopting the appearance of utmost fairness, the legate informed Raimon that absolution would be offered in Saint-Gilles. The count, just wanting it all to be over, was ready to reenact what he had performed a year earlier. The legate, obeying the papal instruction to hold a council to reassess the faithfulness of the count, summoned nineteen bishops, including Folc de Maselha, and seven abbots to Saint-Gilles. The count arrived during the first week of August and was unequivocally informed by the council that he had not implemented all of the papal mandates. If he could not resolve the lesser crime of unjust tolls, then how could he be trusted to fulfill his obligations on the greater crime of heresy? Absolution was denied. Raimon sobbed with shock, anger, and frustration. Thedisius and his colleagues dismissed the tears as one more deception and, without hesitation, excommunicated the count and all his supporters.[14]

Simon de Montfort, after capturing Bellegarde, returned to Carcassonne. In April and May almost three thousand crusaders from Champagne, Maine, Anjou, Brittany, Lorraine, Frisia, Gascony, and the German lands joined the army of God camped around the city. The spring floods of the Aude had receded, the roads were dry, and the warmth was invigorating. Aimeric IV, viscount of Narbonne, angered that Guilhem, lord of Minerve, repeatedly harried his lands, was ready to sign himself with the cross if an expedition was undertaken at once against the Minervois heretics. He was still fearful of the crusaders from last summer—everything about them was too volatile—but in this instance he saw a purpose to being a pilgrim. Simon, elated that the young viscount yielded to Him, was more than happy to attack Minerve rather sooner than later. The soldiers of

Christ, after an easy march, surrounded the strongly fortified *castrum* at the beginning of July. Minerve sat on a rugged limestone plateau framed by the confluence of two small southwardly flowing rivers, the Cesse on the east and the Brian on the west. These rivers, though so trifling that the Cesse was largely waterless throughout the year, had so eroded the calciferous rock over the millennia that plunging narrow ravines (eighty meters deep, fifty meters wide) naturally moated Minerve on three sides. Simon pitched his tents and pavilions on the eastern side of the Brian; one of his French knights, Guy de Lucy, camped with the Gascon crusaders on the western edge of the Cesse ravine; Aimeric bivouacked to the north, facing the thick neck of unbroken rock guarded by the village walls; and all the other crusaders settled slightly southwest of the Cesse. Minerve was soon ringed with catapults and petraries that battered the lime-mortared walls day and night. The Gascons built a hefty catapult known as a "mangonel" and Simon constructed a massive petrary wryly named *Malevoisine*, "Bad Neighbor," by the crew of fifty or more men who pulled on the ropes (and who cost an astonishing twenty-one pounds a day). After three weeks— with the walls fractured, the well empty, and a bungling attempt to burn *Malevoisine* foiled—Guilhem, lord of Minerve, came out to parley with Simon about a peace.[15]

As Simon de Montfort and Guilhem de Minerve were discussing terms, Arnau Amalric and Thedisius unexpectedly arrived in Minerve. Simon, who for all intents and purposes was the leader of the crusade since his acclamation at Carcassonne, accepted this rude assertion of legatine authority with equanimity. He openly acknowledged the abbot as the appointed lord and master of Christ's war on heresy and submitted Minerve's surrender to his arbitration. Guilhem said he would do whatever the abbot decided. Arnau Amalric, torn between wanting His enemies dead right away and the present situation that muted all cries for slaughter, searched for a way to end any talk of a compromise. He told the two lords to put their respective terms for surrender in writing; when these terms were read aloud, Simon predictably dismissed what Guilhem had written and ordered *Malevoisine* readied for launching. Arnau Amalric was delighted; unfortunately for the abbot, Guilhem unconditionally conceded his *castrum* to the army of God. Arnau Amalric, again masking zealotry with a compassionate façade, commanded that everyone in Minerve was to be spared, including heretical believers, if they agreed to be reconciled to the Church; indeed, any heretic who converted to Catholicism was reprieved as well. One of the leading French crusaders, Robert de Mauvoisin, was appalled at such leniency; he had come to kill the enemies of Christ, not show them pity. "Do not fear," smiled Arnau Amalric, "I believe very few will accept conversion." Sure enough, with more discrimination than usual in discerning the supposedly heretical, a house of good men and a house of good women were judged recalcitrant and, along with the more familiar lack of discrimination, these heretics and a hundred or more other persons were tossed into a huge flaming pyre. Afterward the corpses were buried in mud because newly arrived crusaders, as yet unaccustomed to the odor of charred flesh, retched and vomited.[16]

Arnau Amalric returned to Toulouse, Thedisius went back to Saint-Gilles, Aimeric IV departed for Narbonne, and the shrinking army of God—many crusaders retired after Minerve—marched with Simon de Montfort to Pennautier on the Hers. Guilhem de Minerve relinquished his *castrum* to Simon and, in compensation, was given a village in the Biterrois plain on the condition he loyally support the crusade. The hamlet of Ventajou, without hope of survival, surrendered and was summarily demolished. Aimeric de Laurac, lord of Montréal, frightened of attack, exchanged all his lands and *castra* for an unwalled Biterrois village. Raimon II Trencavel, the three-year-old heir of the late viscount, abjured all rights over his father's lands and titles. The boy's mother, na Agnes de Montpellier (sister of Maria), had already forfeited her dower lands of Pézenas and Tourbes for a pension.[17] Alice de Montmorency joined her husband at Pennautier and was present when he and the leading crusader nobles, such as Robert de Mauvoisin, decided that the castle of Termes should be assaulted before the end of summer. Simon appointed Guillaume de Contres, one of his long-time French companions, to defend Carcassonne in his absence; he pressed him to finish dismantling the forest of petraries that still encircled the city and swiftly cart them to Termes. Guillaume, galloping hard on his Hungarian destrier, reached Carcassonne just before moonrise. As he entered the Toulouse gate, someone above him on the parapet roared, "To arms! To arms!" Guillaume turned in his saddle and saw a hundred equine silhouettes madly dashing toward a group of petraries with blazing torches. "Knights! To arms!" he yelled and spurred his mount toward the hurtling saboteurs—saboteurs from Cabaret led by Peire Roger. A handful of petraries were set alight and others busted with axes before Guillaume and the knights of Carcassonne reached the marauders. A furious mêlée, illuminated by burning machines and a full moon, lasted throughout the night, until the men from Cabaret finally retreated. Peire Roger, nearly captured two or three times, escaped only by mimicking the new crusader battle cry: "Montfort! Montfort!"[18]

Guillaume de Contres was cheerfully welcomed by the army of God when he arrived at Termes around the middle of August with the petraries and his tale of victory over Peire Roger de Cabaret. Termes, about thirty kilometers southeast of Carcassonne, crouched at the edge of a four-hundred-meter limestone crag in the mountainous Termenès on the western edge of the Corbières. A small bourg huddled beneath the southern castral wall. A tower known as the "Termenet" sat upon a knurl two hundred meters to the northwest. This was a crumpled and corrugated landscape of precarious sinkholes and fissures, plummeting ravines and chasms, and great abrasive tongues of rock jutting out in all directions. The Sou River flowed in a gorge to the east and north of Termes, while the tiny Caulière rivulet trickled through a gully to the west. A few lonely holm oaks survived in muddy craters, and lime-loving *garigue* (rockrose) flourished in every crevice and along every ledge. There were few villages, even fewer roads, some terraced vines, and the occasional flock of famished sheep. (It took two scattered hectares of *garigue* to support one sheep.)[19] The only approach to Termes was from the south, and the soldiers of Christ awkwardly spread their tents and pavilions over the gnarled terrain. Raimon, the elderly lord of Termes, was not intimidated; his castle, wrote Pierre des Vaux-de-Cernay, "was indeed marvellously and incredibly strong and in human estimation appeared to be quite impregnable." The soldiers on the walls of Termes ridiculed His mediocre army by raucously feigning fear: "Flee from the sight of the army! Flee from the sight of the army!" Peire Roger de Cabaret and his men, undeterred by the Carcassonne debacle, ambushed crusaders journeying to Termes and, after poking out eyes, hewing off noses, and carving whatever else took their fancy, they dumped the mutilated pilgrims at the edge of the crusader camp.

During the last two weeks of August more and more crusaders reached Termes unscathed. A contingent of Bretons arrived with their own siege machines, and multitudes of Frenchmen and Germans replaced those who left after Minerve. Renaud, bishop of Chartres, Philip, bishop of Beauvais, his brother Robert, count of Deux, and Guillaume, count of Ponthieu, all made the pilgrimage into the Termenès with large martial entourages. The crusaders soon erected petraries and mangonels all around Termes, pushing and pulling them up jagged gradients, dragging them over rickety bridges, and hoisting them onto parlous ledges and spurs. Over the next two months these machines hurled stones against the walls of Termes and were extremely effective in smashing the fortifications; the men inside Termes were equally expert at repairing the damage with wooden barricades and rocks. Nevertheless, in September the tower of Termenet was captured, and by early October, even though the walls were not breached, Raimon de Termes was willing to compromise as his cisterns were dry. Simon was glad to parley as he was running out of money and food and the French crusaders were becoming increasingly anxious and agitated. In fact, during negotiations with Raimon, the bishops of Chartres and Beauvais and the counts of Dreux and Ponthieu resolved to leave. Simon and his wife begged them to stay; the bishop of Chartres relented for a few weeks; the others refused and departed. (Once again the curious fragility of crusader zeal, and the even more curious effect of sinister-looking mountains on Frenchmen, was demonstrated.) Simon, though significantly weakened, came to an agreement with Raimon. The night before the surrender of Termes, however, heavy autumnal rain filled the cisterns and Raimon revoked his capitulation. The petraries and mangonels started thumping again. The army of God, soaked by rainstorms, lashed by brutal winds, and frozen by snowfalls, was enlivened when footsore and frostbitten German crusaders from the Lorraine unexpectedly traipsed into camp. The cistern water in Termes turned foul and dysentery debilitated young and old. A sickly Raimon and his men attempted to escape during the night of Monday, 22 November. He and most of his followers were caught and the siege ended.[20]

Simon de Montfort and the army of God slowly descended out of the mountains; as they slogged to Carcassonne, not only did village after village either surrender or empty before them, but the weather became so unseasonably hot that it felt like summer. Buoyed by his success at Termes and the unusual warmth of December, Simon briefly rested at Carcassonne—to accommodate his wife and to imprison Raimon de Termes—before advancing north into the Albigeois. The men of Castres, repentant and frightened, submitted to his will; the men of Lombers, simply frightened, ran away. Simon as lord of the Albigeois effortlessly reasserted his authority over all the *castra* south of the Tarn and, secure in his honor, returned to Carcassonne for Christmas.

At the end of January 1211 Arnau Amalric and Thedisius convened a colloquium at Narbonne about His enterprise between the Garonne and the Rhône; in attendance were Simon de Montfort, Raimon Roger de Foix, Aimeric IV, Pere II, Raimon VI, and Raimon, bishop of Uzès and papal legate (and confidant of Vidal, chaplain of the Dalbade). The colloquium discussed (at Pere's request) the previous summer's peace between Raimon Roger and Simon and the possibility of making it permanent. Raimon Roger never actually agreed to the truce—it was more an amused understanding between Pere and Simon—and dismissed all compromises. (Pierre des Vaux-de-Cernay, in one of his more spiteful vignettes highlighting the wickedness of Simon's enemies, accused Raimon Roger of sawing the legs and arms off a wooden Christ on the cross and using them to pestle pepper for his food.) The colloquium heard the routine slandering of the count of

Toulouse by the papal legates. The count, as everyone well knew, only had to expel the heretics from his lands and his excommunication would be removed. Now was that really asking so very much? And yet time and time again…Raimon sighed and offered no reply. "They achieved nothing," sang Guilhem de Tudela, "not even the price of a wild rose." The colloquium ended—though not before the legates persuaded the king of Aragon to finally accept the homage of the de facto viscount of Carcassonne and Béziers. Pere acknowledged Simon as his man (after some theatrical to-ing and fro-ing) during the last week of January. He still detested the smug Frenchman, but, what with the capture of Termes, the pacification of the Albigeois, and his own forthcoming crusade against the Muslim Almohads (al-Muwahhidun) in Andalusia, the ambitions of the crown of Aragon beyond the Pyrénées were presently in abeyance.

The king of Aragon, the viscount of Carcassonne, the count of Toulouse, and the apostolic legates proceeded to Montpellier after Narbonne. Pere, smothering his disdain in political necessity, betrothed his infant son (not yet three), Jaume, to Simon's infant daughter (not yet three), Amicia. The king then remitted his boy as well as Montpellier to the custody of the viscount. This courtly exercise in love and loyalty soured when it became known that Pere was arranging the betrothal of his young sister (not yet twelve), Sancha, to Raimon's adolescent son (not yet fourteen), Raimon. (This youth, the future Raimon VII, was formerly betrothed to Pere's newborn daughter Sancha in 1205.) "What more?" Arnau Amalric and Thedisius, never missing an opportunity to play the "holy game," caught the elder Raimon unawares and presented him with a new list of things he must do if he wished to be reconciled to the Church: dismiss all mercenaries by dawn, banish Jews and usurers, eat meat only twice a week, wear only coarse dun-colored clothes, demolish castles, stop unjust tolls, visit the River Jordan as a pilgrim, become a Templar or Hospitaller, forbid nobles to live in towns, expel heretics. It was a vicious farrago whose only purpose was to humiliate and provoke the count. Raimon, wondering if this was a cruel joke, tried to laugh it off. Arnau Amalric and Thedisius were, as always, deadly earnest; they knew, even if others doubted, that the count was a vulpine charlatan and that his lands were ripe with poisonous fruit. Stupefied by the abiding malice of the legates, shaken by the omen of a bird flying to the left, Raimon rode away without saying a word. Less than a week later, on Sunday, 6 February 1211, Arnau Amalric and Thedisius again decreed the excommunication of the count, and, one obviously fettered with the other, they again proclaimed Toulouse under interdiction. Two months later, on Friday, 15 April, Innocent III, momentarily swayed by his legates, confirmed the excommunication of Raimon VI and his city.[21]

PIERRE DE NEMURS, bishop of Paris, Enguerrand III de Coucy, Robert de Courtenay, Juhel de Mayenne, and some other noble French crusaders arrived in Carcassonne around the middle of March 1211 during Lent. Simon de Montfort and the newly arrived crusaders readied themselves to besiege Cabaret. Peire Roger de Cabaret, fearing his castle would fall as easily as Termes, precipitously surrendered to his unshaven and flea-bitten prisoner Bouchard de Marly, the idiot Frenchman he had captured five months earlier, before the army of God finished packing their roncins and mules. Simon joyfully received the castle from the liberated (and newly groomed) Bouchard, and, despite the raids, hostage taking, and mutilations, he gave Peire Roger an unwalled village in the Biterrois. Simon and the French crusaders, relieved they did not have to march through lowering ravines and gorges, prepared instead to campaign against the *castrum* of Lavaur that narrowly—very narrowly—resided in the Albigeois. Lavaur was a strongly fortified town whose walls (wide enough for a trotting horseman) ascended a gentle grassy slope that, ending in a steep drop, overlooked the western bank of the Agout. Simon as viscount of Albi was nominally the suzerain of the greater lord of Lavaur, the widow na Girauta de Laurac, and her persistent indifference to his claims demanded a holy expedition. Lavaur, though, was inside the diocese of Toulouse, and, among the proprietorial rights crisscrossing the landscape, the bishop and the count of Toulouse (especially) possessed substantial honor within the town. Until now Simon had never directly threatened Raimon VI—he deliberately shied away from it, in fact—but an assault on Lavaur was a provocation that in no uncertain terms signaled he was ready to chance an escalation of the most holy war. The tenacious pressure from Arnau Amalric and Thedisius was clearly at work, as was the overbearing enthusiasm of the French crusaders, and yet Simon himself unquestionably thought the moment was finally right to walk like Him in the lands of the count of Toulouse.

The army of God, however, was presently too small to encircle Lavaur and only besieged the foremost walls. Aimeric de Laurac, former lord of Montréal and brother of Girauta, organized Lavaur's defense; he resented living in poverty in the Biterrois and, renouncing his homage to Simon during Lent, galloped to his sister's aid. Roger de Comminges, viscount of Couserans and nephew of the count of Foix, impulsively rode into the crusader camp and offered his fealty to Simon on Good Friday. The siege was neither here nor there for at least a fortnight; if anything, it favored the soldiers of Lavaur. In the middle of April a strong contingent of French crusaders appeared and siege machines soon fenced the *castrum*, including, once a wooden bridge was constructed over the Agout, the riverine side. The leading nobles in this new crusader influx were Jourdain, bishop of Lisieux, Robert, bishop of Bayeux, and Pierre de Courtenay, count of Auxerre, returning as a pilgrim after a two-year absence. (Pierre was the brother of Robert de Courtenay.) Missiles as big as millstones were hurled by great petraries day and night; leather-canopied wagons were dragged near the walls so that men could sap foundations; and hundreds of crusader clergy, orchestrated by the Cistercian Hugh, abbot of La Cour-Dieu de Orléans, fervently sang *Veni Creator Spiritus* over and over. This combination of siege craft and holy song so petrified and disheartened everyone inside Lavaur that, when the smallest breech in the walls occurred, Girauta and her brother surrendered without a fight. The soldiers of Christ entered Lavaur on Monday, 3 May, the feast of the Invention of the Holy Cross, and, herding most of the town into a nearby meadow, torched them in a colossal fire. Simon hanged Aimeric like a thief before the army of God, although the spectacle was marred when the poorly built gibbet collapsed during Aimeric's death throes. (He was too tall and heavy for the flimsy wooden frame.) Eighty of Aimeric's noble companions, now denied the gibbet, were put to the sword. Simon flaunted Girauta to the cheering crusaders and, "as she cried and wept and screamed," threw her down a well and piled stones on top.[1]

The "White" confraternity of Toulouse, white cloth crosses on their shoulders, white banners flying, and roncins loaded with supplies, paraded into the jubilant crusader camp the day after Girauta was executed. Folc de

Maselha and Arnau Amalric rallied the Whites throughout Lent. Although Raimon VI tolerated the consuls sending matériel and even mercenaries to the crusaders at Lavaur, he unsuccessfully tried to forestall what he saw as confraternal presumption. "And you, ignorant Whites, you make red that which is white," jeered the troubadour Gavaudan (courtier to Raimon) about the imprudent expeditionary force.[2] On the Sunday after Lent the bishop retaliated by asking Raimon whether, as canon law banned the celebration of divine ministrations in the vicinity of an excommunicated prince, he would mind wandering outside the city for a bit, "just as he might do for pleasure." The count, while acknowledging the truth of what the bishop said, was nevertheless stunned and infuriated, not least because he had been in Toulouse this month or more without similar requests, but mostly because Arnau Amalric was transparently goading him through a fool like Folc. Raimon rebuked the bishop and ordered him to leave the city and the bourg. "The count of Toulouse did not make me bishop," Folc proudly declared, "nor was I ordained by his hands or on his behalf." The bishop waited fifteen days—"afraid for his skin," so everyone said—before leaving on Easter Saturday (2 April) for the ongoing siege of Lavaur. Folc rushed out to meet the Whites when they arrived after Girauta's death and preached that the days of the tyrant Raimon were numbered. Folc de Maselha was, like Bertran de Born, a troubadour before he became a Cistercian and, inspiring neither envy nor admiration, was delivered into paradise by Dante in the *Commedia* where, somewhat ironically, he lamented the manipulation of canon law by cardinals and popes.[3]

Enguerrand III de Coucy, Robert de Courtenay, Juhel de Mayenne, and Pierre de Nemurs, having fulfilled their forty-day oaths to Christ, returned to France after the fall of Lavaur. Raimon de Salvanhac, a Montpellier moneylender who had funded Simon and the army of God for the past year, was repaid with treasure (money, wine, grain, bolts of dyed cloth, horses) seized at Lavaur. Simon, always impecunious, took out more loans with Raimon de Salvanhac. (A year later Simon compensated Raimon with the *castra* of Pézenas and Torves.)[4] A dazed and bedraggled young Lorraine nobleman wandered into the crusader camp and told how a large force of German crusaders marching from Carcassonne were ambushed, slaughtered, and mutilated near the *castrum* of Montgey by Raimon Roger de Foix, his son Roger Bernart, and the unforgiving Giraut del Pepios. Simon and the leading crusaders vowed to avenge the massacre at Montgey. As the *castrum* was plainly in the lands of the count of Toulouse, Raimon VI was as guilty of the murders as if he had sliced throat after throat with his own hand. (Montgey was in the archdeaconry of Vielmorez in the Lauragais in the diocese of Toulouse.) Simon recited all the misdeeds and crimes of

Raimon, ancient and modern, which demanded His vengeance upon the house of Saint-Gilles. Indeed, Simon argued, even at the siege of Lavaur the count was obviously conspiring against the soldiers of Christ: he openly refused to transport siege machines from Toulouse; he covertly dispatched knights to fight for Girauta; he hindered the White confraternity; and, during his visit to the crusader camp in April, he exuded venomous scorn when his cousins Pierre and Robert de Courtenay asked him to submit to the mandates of Arnau Amalric and Thedisius. The excommunication of Raimon VI was more than justified. With almost the same righteous thrill as two years earlier, Simon de Montfort and the small army of God marched into the Lauragais and Toulousain in May 1211.[5]

Three years before Innocent III proclaimed the crusade against the *Provinciales heretici*, a holy woman in Liège, Marie d'Oignes, had a vision of the coming war. "When this happened there had been no mention of these heretics in our lands," observed Jacques de Vitry in his biography of Marie, "but then that was the time when God spoke to her in the spirit and it was as if He were complaining that He had lost almost all His realm and had been banished like an exile from His lands." Three years into the war and Marie, "although she lived far away," had a vision of the crusaders being killed at Montgey. Amid the carnage she saw angels rejoicing as they carried the souls of the "holy martyrs of Christ" directly to paradise without the necessity of purgatory. Marie was so moved by this joyful sight that she ardently wished to join the pilgrimage against the heretics. "She could barely be restrained from doing so" and was dissuaded only by the social impropriety of such a journey. Jacques was Marie's confessor and, sympathetic to her desire to walk like Him by the Garonne, asked what she would do if she were signed with the cross. "I would honour my Lord by witnessing His name where so many impious men have denied Him by blasphemy."

Folc de Maselha, "banished like an exile from his lands," visited Marie in Liège as she lay dying during the summer of 1213. He knew of her and other holy women from Jacques and the northern crusaders. These *mulieres sanctae* came mostly from mercantile families; by fasting and praying in urban houses either alone or in the company of similar women, they strived for "celestial glory." These women, obsequious before priests, obsessed with the Eucharist, were living testaments against the heretical good women. They were "soldiers of God" in the most holy war on heresy. Jacques wrote about Marie after her death at the prompting of Folc: "When her tiny body was washed after death, it was found to be so small and shrivelled by her illness and fasting that her spine touched her belly." He dedicated her *vita* to the exiled bishop. Marie, crippled by starvation and chronic weeping, gripped with an unquenchable thirst for the "vivifying blood of Christ," was to be admired rather than imitated, wrote Jacques. What justified this admiration was the imitation (and absorption) of Christ by a woman who, so imbued with His body and blood, waged continuous war on the "Provençal heretics" through the disfiguring fervor of her existence.[6]

In the fields and vineyards around Montgey were scattered a thousand or more bloated sunburned bodies. Folc de Maselha reported that a great column of fire descended from heaven and positioned the dead crusaders with their faces up and their arms outstretched like crosses. (A mocking Raimon Roger de Foix more likely placed the corpses this way.) A wrathful Simon de Montfort obliterated the village of Montgey. The nearby *castrum* of les Cassés was besieged and the castral lords, Raimon and Bernart Rocovila, treacherously surrendered some good men and good women under their protection in exchange for safe passage to Toulouse. The soldiers of Christ, after the usual perfunctory attempt at conversion, incinerated these widowers, widows, and little girls.

Baudouin de Toulouse was the younger brother of Raimon VI; raised in France after their parents divorced in 1165, he went back to Toulouse when the old count died in 1194. (Raimon, not surprisingly, initially thought his brother was a French impostor.) Baudouin now waited in the fortified village of Montferrand—only a three-hour stroll from les Cassés—for the onslaught of the crusaders. The village guarded the Roman road (*via Aquitania*) from Toulouse to Carcassonne (and so on to Narbonne). Simon and the army of God easily encircled Montferrand with petraries toward the end of May. "Lord count Baudouin, come out in safety," shouted Jean, count of Chalon-sur-Saône, after three days of bombardment, "all the barons favor compromising with you." Baudouin came outside and, spitting up blood from old war wounds, agreed to hand over the *castrum* if his men were pardoned; Simon assented. Baudouin further promised never to fight the crusaders again and, feeling quite unwell, galloped to Toulouse. Raimon and his brother were never close—although they were close enough for the count to give him partial custody of his son and an annual stipend in September 1209—and, after an acrimonious few days, Baudouin returned to the army of God and yielded to Christ.[7]

Raimon VI, during the siege of les Cassés, rode one morning with a score of men to the *castrum* of Castelnaudary and, even though the castral lords were his men, evacuated the village and set it on fire. Castelnaudary was another important fortified village on the old Roman road, and Raimon, lacking men for its defense, desired a scorched mound of uninhabitable rubble. Simon, however, went straight to Castelnaudary after

Montferrand and, extinguishing the lingering fires, started rebuilding the walls. The army of God then proceeded north through the Lauragais plain; traversing the Agout at Lavaur, they tramped northwesterly along the river until, around early July, they forded the Tarn. With fear subduing all before them, they effortlessly occupied the Albigeois *castra* of Rabastens, Montégut, Gaillac, Cahuzac, Saint-Marcel, Laguépie, Puycelci, and Saint-Antonin. On Sunday, 5 June, by the banks of the Tarn, Raimon Trencavel, uncle of the late viscount of Albi and Carcassonne, relinquished to Simon his possessory rights over the Albigeois and Carcassès. Thibaud I, count of Bar (in the eastern Champagne) and of Luxembourg, reached Carcassonne around the middle of June with a large contingent of crusaders. (Thibaud had announced his martial pilgrimage "against the Albigensian heretics" three months earlier, on Easter Sunday.)[8] A messenger was sent into the Albigeois by Alice de Montmorency to inform her husband; he found the viscount the next afternoon resting by the Tarn, and a day later he breathlessly requested the count of Bar to meet the army of God at Montgiscard on the River Hers for a holy expedition against Toulouse.[9]

Thibaud, guided by a party of French knights, rendezvoused with Simon at Montgiscard on Wednesday, 15 June. On the following morning the army of God loaded their mules and roncins and, with carts carrying the siege machines, filed along the Roman road toward Toulouse. Raimon VI, notified by scouts about the advancing crusaders, gathered together a few hundred noble horsemen and foot soldiers to meet them. He foolishly allowed his cousin Bernart IV, count of Comminges, and Raimon Roger de Foix to accompany him. He hoped, once again, to try to negotiate with Arnau Amalric and Thedisius. A month earlier, before the sieges of les Cassés and Montferrand, he sent word to Simon and the leading crusaders that, as a peaceful compromise, he was willing to place himself and all his possessions, except Toulouse, under their protective custody and await their noble judgment on his faith. This agreement, though acceptable to many northern lords, was not agreeable to the legates—after all, it stymied their long-held plans on His behalf—nor to the incandescent "count of Christ" who crossed into the Toulousain. This time around, Raimon never even had a chance to parley because, when he was no more than an hour from Toulouse near the village of Montaudran on the Hers, Simon and a horde of French knights, "without warning, charged at him, hoping to capture and kill him and," so the king of Aragon heard a year later from the consuls of Toulouse, "they chased him for a league." Raimon and his men, taken aback by this feverish assault, fought a rearguard action all the way to the gates of Toulouse. Simon evidently thought the sauntering comital guard was an army on the march; if nothing else, the banners of the count of Foix were signs of hostility. The French knights, racing through meadows, fields, and vineyards, cut down any man, woman, or child in their path. "Near a barbican, by the edge of a meadow," sang Guilhem de Tudela, "thirty-three villagers of the land were slaughtered." The crusaders yelled abuse at the gates of Toulouse before galloping back to Montgiscard.[10]

On the parapets of Toulouse, "the flower and rose of all cities," count and consuls watched as the army of God pitched their tents and pavilions throughout the next day on the grassy flatland adjacent to the southern walls of the city. Around four thousand crusaders faced one thousand three hundred meters of gently curving wall from the Narbonne gate, where the Roman road ended, to the Saint Étienne gate near the cathedral. These fortifications were the oldest and strongest in the city: crenellated walls thirty to fifty meters high raised upon Roman and Visigothic foundations three to five meters wide.[11] This long scythe of ancient and medieval masonry was empierced with two lesser gates, the Montgaillard and Montoulieu, and overarching these portals—as with all the gates around Toulouse—towered barbicans with massive ironbound oak doors. The Narbonne gate was particularly impressive as it incorporated the walls and towers of the great comital castle, the Château Narbonnais, *lo castel Narbones*. The consuls of Toulouse, when all the tents and pavilions were erected, sent a delegation of "greater good men" into the crusader camp to discuss a compromise. Folc de Maselha, speaking for the legates, replied that the city and bourg must renounce the lordship of Raimon VI and submit to a new lord chosen by the crusaders, otherwise the whole community of Toulouse would be judged heretics and receivers of heretics. The consuls dismissed these terms as dishonorable to Toulouse and to the count; they were faithful to Christ, as the bishop well knew, but their loyalty was not so easily exploited. Folc then ordered Mascaron, provost of the cathedral of Saint-Étienne, to lead all the clergy out of Toulouse. "They obeyed and departed barefoot taking with them the Holy Sacrament." The city and bourg, though much distressed by this exodus, responded with "divine cooperation," ending all confraternal "discord and dissent." The consuls told the king of Aragon, "We have reformed ourselves, so that never were we so blessed."[12]

The early morning haze on Saturday was only just vanishing when the count of Bar and the count of Chalon assaulted the defensive outwork between the Montgaillard and Montoulieu gates. A line of leather-canopied wagons and leather-wrapped wooden towers slowly crawled toward the walls like so many drowsy brown beetles and black mantises. Trenches and ditches were hastily filled and bridged with bundles of branches and vines. The wagons and towers, though bristling with hundreds of wasted arrows and bolts, edged closer and closer until, seemingly out of nowhere, knights and soldiers surged from four hidden doorways in the walls and the crusaders, startled, shocked, and harried, immediately retreated, taking nothing with them. The men of Toulouse captured three of the biggest assault towers and set fire to them. The few petraries and catapults erected by the crusaders did no damage whatsoever to the formidable fortifications. (No "Bad Neighbor" or other large machines pounded Toulouse.) One morning some knights charged out of the Narbonne gate and raided the crusader camp while the army of God was eating. One afternoon when the crusaders were resting as usual after their midday meal—it was summer and too hot to move with a full stomach, explained Pierre des Vaux-de-Cernay—a company of Navarrois mercenaries dashed from the hidden doorways and attacked the recumbent warriors. The crusaders chased their assailants away; though many martial pilgrims were killed, more would have died if the soldiers of Christ, constantly worried about these surprise attacks, were not fully armored day and night. After two weeks the meals of the crusaders were decidedly sparse: there was no meat, little wine, small loaves of bread cost two shillings (unlike at the siege of Carcassonne, where thirty were had for a penny), and everyone survived on beans and scavenged fruit (from the rare tree or vine not uprooted a fortnight earlier). The siege of Toulouse was becoming too expensive—which was perhaps why no great petraries were used—and, as nothing was or would be achieved this summer, Simon resolved to harass the exposed lands of Raimon Roger de Foix. At dawn on Wednesday, 29 June, the feast of Saint Peter, the starving and dispirited army of God shambled away toward the Ariège.[13]

It was just after the siege of Toulouse that the ghost Guilhem appeared along the Rhône in Beaucaire. "At the moment of leaving this life," he was absolutely terrified beyond all measure, with both good and bad angels fighting over him, "but eventually the good ones prevailed and conducted him to purgatory." No agony, "no suffering is equal or comparable to death," Guilhem stressed, "and the slightest pain of purgatory is harsher than any bodily suffering." This was why the dead loathed the word "death" and preferred to say "leaving this life." Purgatory was nearer Jerusalem, he explained, "than to the place where he used to live in the world." Heaven and hell were both seen from purgatory, and he saw "the joy of the just and the sadness of the lost." Indeed, "when souls leave the body, he sees them approaching and sees where they go." Sometimes, though, the dead wander among the living for three or four days, uncertain, unsure, before angels escort them to purgatory or hell. All spirits in purgatory and heaven see everything on earth without obstruction. "Shameful deeds should therefore be avoided at all costs," Guilhem advised the living, "because they are seen by the numberless spirits." Faithfulness and modesty, most assuredly, are "fostered by so many witnesses." Guilhem, for all his heartfelt testimony about the physical and spiritual pain of "leaving this life," spared no sympathy for the "Albigensians." He saw the massacre at Béziers and the bloodshed over the past two years—as did all spirits—and he applauded how those burned in the body by crusaders "are burned more severely after death in spirit." In truth, "even the good who have not stained their faith with heresy have sinned if they have tolerated it." The holy war against the Albigensians was a foretelling of God's separation of the good from the bad on the Day of Judgment. Guilhem, of course, was himself a testament against heresy. He proved that the youth in life was the youth in death and that, whether by the Rhône or in purgatory, the continuity of his individual existence was absolutely unbreakable. Guilhem, among the first recorded visitors from purgatory, among the first to chart its landscape for the living, was also arguably the first ghost in Western culture.[14]

It was during the summer of 1211 that "Albigensian" became the name of choice used by most northern European crusaders, historians, preachers, biographers, and poets when they defined the quarry of the most holy war on heresy. The early and unexpected shift of the crusade from the lands of the count of Toulouse into the terrain of the viscount of Béziers, and the astonishingly brutal victories throughout that summer, demanded a reevaluation by northern Christian intellectuals, especially in France, as to the purpose and goal of the crusade to expunge the little foxes from Christendom. The crusade from the acclamation of Simon de Montfort until the assault on Toulouse was essentially a war of conquest and consolidation of the former Trencavel territories outside of the Carcassès and Biterrois. The *Albigenses* came into existence as a direct result of the abiding sense of disappointment in the aftermath of the first summer, when serpentine heretics in general and the *Provinciales heretici* in particular were not eliminated from the world. The Albigensians were heretics, heretical believers, mercenaries, refugee nobles, criminal mutilators, good men and good women, in short, anyone who opposed or was accused of opposing Simon de Montfort as lord of the Albigeois. The fugitive nobility in this vulpine miscellany were sometimes denounced as *fautors* or *faidits* (exiles, rebels, patrons of heretics, men without honor). The town of Albi was never considered a heretical stronghold by the crusaders, and "Albigensian" does not derive from it. Arnau Amalric, Thedisius, Jacques de Vitry, and hundreds of other northern European clergy all preached throughout 1210 that the crusade was now against the Albigensians. Undoubtedly, the carnage at Lavaur in 1211 recalled the small war thirty years earlier against "Albigensian heretics"—as it certainly did for Guilhem de Puylaurens—and so the present term was opportunely endorsed by the past. "Albigensian" was not repudiated when the crusade targeted Raimon VI and his allies; quite the contrary, it acquired new heretical meanings and broader spatial implications, and, though never adopted by the men and women who lived between the Garonne and the Rhône, it endured as the overall epithet for the crusade.

XI

RAIMON VI, ODDLY aloof during the defense of Toulouse, mustered an army throughout the late summer for an expedition against Simon de Montfort. The normally erratic martial loyalty of a Toulousain or Lauragais noble toward his count was subsumed by the exigency of combating the crusaders. Toward the end of September, when the army of God was diminished by the departure of thousands of fair-weather pilgrims, the army of Toulouse tramped the old Roman road to assail Castelnaudary. Raimon Roger de Foix, Giraut del Pepios, and Gaston VI, viscount of Béarn (in southern Gascony) and vavasor of the king of Aragon, marched alongside Raimon. Around a thousand noble horsemen—every one an *ome de paratge*, a man of honor—and another two to three thousand foot soldiers formed the core of the comital army. The Navarrois mercenaries, hired again by the count and consuls, joked and swaggered with other routiers from the Agenais and Quercy. Roncins and mules carried bread and wine. Buffalo and massive oxen dragged an enormous trebuchet. Peasants prodded and urged these beasts by loudly cursing Simon de Montfort. "Traitor! Son of a whore!" they yelled, slapping equine buttocks and bovine noses. The traitorous whoreson himself waited inside Castelnaudary with a few hundred men. Raimon and the army of Toulouse pitched their tents and pavilions on a small hillock to the north of the *castrum*. The trebuchet was positioned in the middle of the Roman road, and, with only porous sedimentary rock lying about, missile after missile impotently shattered on impact. (All respectable martial rocks were used in rebuilding the castral walls.) Bouchard de Marly, as loyal as he was foolhardy, frantically galloped from Lavaur to Castelnaudary with a hundred horsemen. Raimon Roger de Foix rode out to meet him with a much larger force and, promptly, furiously, was put to rout. He eluded capture only by crying, "Montfort! Montfort!" Raimon, shaken when hundreds of riderless horses returned from the fray, ended the siege at once and retreated to Toulouse. The great trebuchet was abandoned to wind and rain.[1]

Almost all the *castra* that surrendered to Simon throughout the summer rebelled against him during the autumn. The army of God was too small and too tired to assault these villages and castles in October and November. Robert de Mauvoisin, the bloody-minded pilgrim at Minerve, arrived at Carcassonne in December with a hundred French knights and close to a thousand foot soldiers. Simon and Robert journeyed to the Albigeois—capturing the fortified village of la Pomarède in the Lauragais on the way—and celebrated Christmas at Castres. Guy de Montfort, returning from the Holy Land with his wife, Héloïse de Ibelin, joined his brother at Castres. A swift expedition was undertaken against the village of las Toellas, whose principal lord, Frezo de Lautrac, was Giraut del Pepios's father; the village was easily overrun, the inhabitants slaughtered. A short siege in snow and slush secured the village of Cahuzac. The counts of Toulouse, Comminges, and Foix patched together an army at rebellious Gaillac for a cold January campaign in the Albigeois. Simon trudged as fast as he could to Gaillac and camped before the *castrum*. Raimon VI and his allies, taken aback, fled to renegade Montégut. The army of God followed them to Montégut. The counts withdrew to seditious Rabastens. Simon chased them to Rabastens. Raimon—his bellicosity as brittle as ever—simply gave up and retreated to Toulouse. The soldiers of Christ returned to Cahuzac.[2]

Throngs of crusaders from France, the German lands, Lombardy, the Auvergne, and even a group from the Balkans rallied at Castres during Easter. Pierre des Vaux-de-Cernay soon arrived with his uncle Guy, the new bishop of Carcassonne. On Thursday, 5 April 1212, Simon decided to attack the mountainous *castrum* of Hautpoul on the extreme northern tip of the Montagne Noire. Three days later the army of God, climbing over craggy precipices and up and up jagged slopes, camped before the outer castral walls of Hautpoul. A large petrary hurled stone after stone against the fortified tower inside the walls. On the fourth day of the siege, just after sundown, an impenetrable mist shrouded the *castrum* and the crusaders. The men and women of Hautpoul, fearing divine retribution, frantically tried to escape. The soldiers of Christ heard the castral gates open and, though fog-blind themselves, rushed the noise and killed every quivering shadow. Hautpoul, visible under a bright spring sky the next morning, was razed to the ground. The French knights who came with Robert de Mauvoisin retired after the destruction. The army of God hastened into the Toulousain and Lauragais and reoccupied Cuq, Montmaur, Saint-Félix, les Cassès, Montferrand, Avignonet, Saint-Michel-de-Lanès, and Puylaurens. At the beginning of May the villages of Gaillac, Montégut, and Rabastens penitently submitted to Simon. The *castrum* of Saint-Marcel on the River Cerou was grabbed and destroyed on Saturday, 19 May. A day later the army of God pitched their tents and pavilions near the strongly fortified village of Saint-Antonin on the river Bonnette. "The count of Montfort must know that a mob of *bordoniers* [stick carriers, pilgrims] will never take my *castel*," boasted Guilhem Peire, lord of Saint-Antonin. By nightfall the village was taken and Guilhem carted off to Carcassonne in chains. "I think you would have barely cooked an egg," quipped Guilhem de Tudela, "in the time it took to seize the place."[3]

Robert, archbishop of Rouen, Robert, bishop-elect of Laon, Guillaume, archdeacon of Paris (and a skilled engineer who fought at the siege of Termes), and two thousand martial pilgrims entered Carcassonne in late May. Guy de Montfort galloped to these *crucesignati* with a plan: lay waste the riparian Ariège, rampage up the Garonne, and, crossing the Agenais, join his brother at Penne alongside the Lot. Simon, veering into the Agenais and Quercy, risked war with John, king of England, suzerain of these lands. (Raimon VI acquired them when he married Joanna Plantagenet in 1196.) Simon and his *bordoniers*, moving northwesterly from Saint-Antonin through deserted fields and villages, reached formidable Penne on Sunday, 3 June 1212. Petraries soon crashed the ramparts and leather-canopied wagons gnawed the lower walls. Fifty-two days later, on Wednesday, 25 July, the feast of Saint James, Penne, harrowed by thirst, riddled with dysentery, and crumbling from a mighty catapult designed by the archdeacon of Paris, begged a compromise. Simon, weakened by the recent departure of the Rouen and Laon pilgrims, occupied Penne without bloodshed. Alberic, archbishop of Reims, arrived with new crusaders the next morning. Nineteen days later, on Tuesday, 14 August, the feast of the assumption of the Blessed Virgin, Simon besieged sturdy Moissac on the Tarn. "A bolt pierced my robe," exclaimed Pierre des Vaux-de-Cernay, "and missed my flesh by a finger's width or less" when he sat too close to a petrary. Twenty-five days later, on Saturday, 8 September, the feast of the birth of the Blessed Virgin, Moissac, desiccated by an unforgiving sun, perpetually pounded by petraries, and a great swathe of wall sapped away, compromised with Simon. The townspeople handed over 500 marks of silver and, as the archbishop of Reims's nephew was dismembered by routiers during the siege, three hundred hirelings were put to the sword.

The army of God then ravaged the lands of the count of Comminges and, throughout autumn, seized all remaining *castra* in the Toulousain and Lauragais except Montauban.[4]

Simon summoned a general council at Pamiers in November; apart from confirming him as a model Christian prince in forty-six (XLVI) inviolable customs, the explicit intention of the council was the transformation of the anomalous southern landscape into the pure world of northern France around Paris. "Accordingly we, Simon, count of Leicester, lord of Montfort and by God's grace viscount of Béziers and Carcassonne and lord of Albi and the Razès," in consultation with noblemen and with the archbishop of Bordeaux, the bishops of Toulouse, Carcassonne, Agen, Périgueux, Couserans, Comminges and Bigorre, "now establish the following customs to be followed in all our lands." All "houses of heretics" were to be made into churches or given to priests (X). Anyone who allowed a heretic to reside on his land, whatever the motive, "let him for this single reason lose all his land forever" (XI). No heretical believer, even if reconciled, could be a provost, *bailli*, or judge (XIV). No clothed heretic, even if reconciled, may remain in the village where he lived in perversion but, somewhat surprisingly, may live elsewhere if permitted by Simon (XV). Crucially, "no men are to be judged to have been heretical believers or to have been heretics, except on the testimony of bishops and priests" (XXV). "Succession to inheritances amongst barons and knights, also townspeople and peasants," can no longer be fractious and partible, "but will take place according to the custom and usage of France around Paris" (XLIII). The ultimate custom, "on account of the danger to the land," banned noble widows or girls in possession of castles and *castra* from marrying local men for ten years without Simon's consent, "although they may marry Frenchmen as they wish." Simon and his "good customs," while acknowledging that a generation must come and go before his lands were finally purified, nevertheless assumed the holy war on heresy was, if not quite over, then nearing the last judgment.[5]

XII

"THE LITTLE FOXES that were spoiling the vines of the Lord of Hosts in *Provincia* have been seized," Innocent III wrote to Arnau Amalric on Tuesday, 15 January 1213. The Holy Land was in much greater peril and urgently needed help. "We therefore hereby enjoin you, dear brother, to devote your earnest attention to negotiating treaties for peace and a truce with our dearest son in Christ, Pere [II] the illustrious king of Aragon, and counts and barons and other prudent men," so that the horrid war in *Provincia* will end in abiding concord. "You should thus cease to call Christians to arms," until otherwise instructed. The pope suspended the holy war on heresy. Seven months earlier the kings of Aragon, Navarre, and Castile decimated the grand army of the Almohad caliph Muhammad al-Nasir on the Andalusian plain of Las Navas de Tolosa.[1] Innocent III was elated with the victors, and Pere, once more attending to the other side of the Pyrénées, found the papal ear solicitous. Aragonese envoys—the royal notary Master Colom and Hispan, bishop of Segorbe-Albarracín—advised the pope throughout autumn and winter on the injustices of the crusaders. Simon de Montfort was accused of occupying lands never poisoned with heresy, and, as he accepted homage from persons on these lands rather than expunging or slaughtering them, he tacitly admitted these individuals were Catholic. The pope agreed and ordered all lands restored to the counts of Foix and Comminges. "Although it is necessary to cut off putrid flesh," he chided Arnau Amalric three days after he stopped the crusade, "the healing hand must be applied carefully." Instead, wantonly attacking the count of

IBERIAN PENINSULA,
1212

Christian
Muslim

Toulouse without apostolic approval was the work of "greedy hands." The count, entrusting his lands, son, and wife to the king of Aragon, was now a most biddable penitent. Innocent III enjoined his legates to once again summon a general council to review the crusade and assess the vigor of the little foxes.[2]

Pere II paraded into Toulouse with a large entourage during the first week of January 1213 unaware (though no doubt hoping) that the pope was about to suspend the crusade. He notified Arnau Amalric and Simon de Montfort that he wanted a truce and a compromise regarding Raimon VI and the consuls of Toulouse. The pridefulness of Arnau Amalric, always a worry for the pope, always a comital complaint, was now even more hectoring since his election in March 1212 as archbishop of Narbonne, and, while the new primate was a worthy pilgrim against the Almohads last summer, Pere had no great hopes of honest negotiation. Arnau Amalric, equally ignorant of papal intentions, convened a council of archbishops

(Bordeaux) and bishops (Albi, Toulouse, Comminges, Riez) on Monday, 14 January, in a village between Toulouse and Lavaur. Simon pompously offered a truce for eight days. The archbishop—though he now arrogantly liked to call himself the duke of Narbonne, adopting a nominal honor of the counts of Toulouse—asked the king to submit his requests in writing to the council. Pere, repeating what his envoys told the pope, stated that Raimon desired to be absolved; that the counts of Foix and Comminges, as well as Gaston de Béarn, were never heretics and so confiscating their lands was unlawful; and that Raimon's son was a faithful young man eager (as was his father) to go on crusade in Spain or the Holy Land. The prelates dismissed every request. "Renowned prince," they warned, "since these men have been excommunicated," it was unseemly for "royal serenity" to mediate on their behalf. The king was dismayed, though hardly surprised, and proceeded to take the excommunicated nobles and their lands under his protection. Arnau Amalric again cautioned the monarch against "incurring the stigma of excommunication by communing with the excommunicated." Pere was undeterred—especially as Master Colom arrived with reassuring news from Rome—and so on Sunday, 27 January, he accepted oaths of allegiance from Raimon, his son, and the consuls and community of Toulouse. Two weeks later he renounced his suzerainty over Simon de Montfort.[3]

Arnau Amalric and his council, troubled by the composure of the king of Aragon, dimly aware of what the royal envoys argued in Rome, dispatched a shrill and portentous letter to Innocent III on Monday, 21 January. In *Provincia*, they wrote, "the plague of heresy, its seed sown long ago, has in our times so flourished that pious worship has become entirely derided and insulted." At last, due to the holy army of crusaders wiping out this filthy plague, the Church had begun to raise its head after coming so close to ruin. Yet, remnants of this plague still thrive, "namely, in the city of Toulouse and a few *castra* where, like filth sinking into a bilge-hold, the residue of heretical depravity has collected." The count of Toulouse, an angel of Satan in his heart, comforted by the Emperor Otto IV and King John of England, relentlessly attacked the Church. Indeed, he even sent emissaries to the "king of Morocco"—that is, Caliph Muhammad al-Nasir—and begged aid "in destroying not only our land but the whole of Christendom." (Caesarius of Heisterbach, a decade later, recycled the accusation that the Almohads defeated at Las Navas de Tolosa were coming to help the "Albigensians.")[4] The count, his son, the counts of Foix and Comminges, and Gaston de Béarn deceived and used the king of Aragon. Fortunately, "that most Christian athlete of the faith, the count of Montfort, has occupied almost all their lands, treating them as enemies of God and the

Church in a holy and just war." We pray, we implore, "that you lay an axe to the root of the accursed tree and destroy it forever so that it can do no further harm." These lands, after such an effusion of Christian blood, must never be returned to their former tyrants, "as this would cause enormous offence to the faithful who have fought this fight" and eternal ruination for the Church. Garsia, bishop of Comminges, Peire, the abbot of Clairac, Guillaume, the archdeacon of Paris, Peire Marc, a clerical scribe, and Thedisius accompanied this letter to Rome.[5]

(In a letter to the Cistercian general chapter five months earlier, Arnau Amalric described the battle of Las Navas de Tolosa as a mighty Catholic Christian triumph in the great and ongoing war against "the three plagues of humanity and enemies of His Holy Church; namely, schismatics from the East, heretics from the West, and Saracens from the South." The archbishop viewed his summer pilgrimage against the Almohads as merely another aspect of the most holy war on heresy and, while Muslims in the Holy Land were conspicuously absent in his sinful pandemic, schismatic Christians hidden among the ruins of Constantinople were not. Crusaders killing Saracens near the Guadalquivir or heretics along the Garonne or schismatics by the Golden Horn were all engaged in the purification of Christendom. Unquestionably, Arnau Amalric accepted the Levantine crusades as a Christian necessity, and yet, in all his letters and sermons, the idolatrous occupation of Jerusalem never inflamed his apocalyptic vision of the ultimate war to end all wars. As he once thought invading the Trencavel lands was a chance to hack the tendrils of heresy whose roots were in Toulouse, so he now thought his expedition against the "king of Morocco" was a way of stemming—if not reversing—the poisonous allegiance of His enemies on either side of the Pyrénées. Equally, he expected some moral and political sense to be impressed upon the king of Aragon when that willful monarch realized—through the archbishop's own glorious example—that being a crusader in Andalusia demanded being signed with the cross in the Toulousain. Arnau Amalric hoped—and badly punned—that the victory of Tolosa heralded the inevitable defeat of the "Toulouse [*Tolosa*] heretics.")[6]

Innocent III issued a general letter throughout late April exhorting all Christians to be signed with the cross and go liberate the Holy Land. This extraordinary encyclical, accompanied by a summons to a great ecumenical council in Rome two years later, envisioned Latin Christendom as a world perpetually on crusade, as forever yielding to Him. "Oh, how much good has already come from this cause!" The false prophet Muhammad, "who has seduced many men from the truth by worldly enticements and the pleasures of the flesh," will be overthrown by the Crucified One. "So rouse yourselves, most beloved sons, transforming your quarrels and rivalries, brother against brother, into associations of peace and love," and fight for Him who shed His blood for you. The pope conceded that anyone, "except persons bound by religious profession, may take the cross in such a way that this vow may be commuted, redeemed or deferred by apostolic mandate when urgent need or evident expediency demands it." He allowed the possibility of walking like Him without going on a pilgrimage to the Holy Land—or *Provincia* or Spain. Much of this momentous vision derived from the crusade against the *Provinciales heretici* and the profound opportunity this enduring holy war offered to walk like Him within Christendom itself. Indeed, it was the very profundity (and convenience) of imitating the Crucified One between the Garonne and the Rhône that caused the pope to revoke all indulgences granted for crusaders in *Provincia* and Spain. He argued that the threats in both regions were diminished, "so that the immediate use of force is not necessary," and that the Holy Land was more needful. The people of *Provincia* and Spain, though, could still be signed with the cross against heretics and Saracens. A month later—and now advised by Thedisius, his companions, and their letter—the servant of the servants of God completely and fiercely reversed himself on the holy war on heresy.[7]

As far as heresy and Toulouse were concerned, "you have neither looked to your own interests nor deferred to us as you should," Innocent III rebuked the king of Aragon on Tuesday, 21 May. The people of Toulouse, "cut off from the body of the Church by the sword of excommunication," were rightly placed under interdiction. "Some are manifest heretics, many more are believers, or the supporters, receivers and defenders of heretics, while others from outside the city," driven from their hovels by Christ and His army, "have fled for refuge to the bilge-hold of error that is Toulouse." These foul locusts, if given half a chance, would devour the true faith newly planted in *Provincia.* "Your serenity," by protecting these creatures you forgot your fear of the divine, "as though you had the power to prevail against God or turn aside His hand." Your serenity, you must abandon them without delay. The bishop of Toulouse has written instructions if these ravenous insects truly wish to be reunited with the Church. "As to those who remain in the shadows of error," they must be expelled from Toulouse and their goods confiscated. "We are amazed and disturbed that by using your envoys to suppress the truth with mendacious storytelling," you extorted an apostolic mandate restoring lands to the excommunicated. This edict was canceled, "as if it were stolen." Meanwhile, a firm truce between you and Simon de Montfort must be agreed and maintained. "We intend through renewed indulgences that the faithful and those signed with the cross will rise up and eliminate this plague." The crusaders will fight the heretics and their defenders—who, knowing better, were worse than the heretics themselves. "Whatever love we have for you, we could not spare you or give way to you if you go against the enterprise of the Christian faith," admonished the pope. "There are ancient and modern examples to teach you the imminent danger if you oppose God and the Church" and dare impede His most holy war.[8]

Toulouse and the army of God were, for the most part, blithely unaware that the holy war on heresy was briefly suspended. Louis, son of the king of France, was similarly oblivious and signed himself with the cross in February. Many French knights yielded to Christ when they heard that the twenty-five-year-old prince was a crusader against the pestilential heretics. Philip II Augustus, as muted as ever about the crusade, nevertheless held a general assembly of his barons in Paris on the first Sunday of Lent (3 March) to discuss arrangements for his son's martial pilgrimage. The bishops of Toulouse and Carcassonne, having preached and promoted the crusade throughout the northern winter, were present at the assembly. Berenguer de Palou, the bishop of Barcelona, and some Aragonese knights arrived in Paris as delegates from the king of Aragon just as the assembly was meeting. Pere II desired— rather audaciously—to marry the daughter of the French king, Marie, widow of Philip de Namur; unfortunately, he was still married to Maria de Montpellier, and, largely due to whispers from the bishop of Carcassonne, it was known in the French court that the pope refused an annulment. (It did not help that Pere was widely known to be, as his son later put it, "a ladies' man.")[9] The delegation, apart from conveying a proposal of marriage, carried copies of the papal letters suspending the crusade. Philip, despite his insouciant manner toward the holy war, was furious that the king of Aragon received the homage of the count of Toulouse—this news had reached Paris!—and curtly dismissed the bishop of Barcelona. The assembly in Paris arranged for Louis and his fellow pilgrims to depart one week after the feast of the Resurrection (Sunday, 21 April). The king of France soon postponed the royal pilgrimage— as he perhaps intended to do all along—when he announced a series of summertime wars (including a possible maritime invasion) against the king of England.[10]

Manasses de Seignelay, bishop of Orléans, and his brother Guillaume de Seignelay, bishop of Auxerre, upset by the delay of Louis and his crusaders, worried that the enemies of Christ were emboldened by the Aragonese king, gathered as many knights and foot soldiers as they could and hastily journeyed to the Carcassès. At the beginning of May they surprised Simon de Montfort and the army of God at Fanjeaux. Simon was overjoyed and, after a few days' rest, led the newly arrived crusaders to the village of Muret on the west bank of the Garonne. (One pilgrim, Alard de Strépy, was a vassal of the king of England and, refusing to assail the count of Toulouse, quietly withdrew from the expedition.) Muret was an advantageous *castrum*, no more than a northeasterly morning ride from Toulouse, well watered, well pastured, "although it was somewhat poorly fortified." All through the early summer—and so just before the harvest—the crusaders trampled, cut down, and set alight the myriad orchards, fields, and vineyards encircling Toulouse. Every now and again, mercenaries and soldiers from Toulouse ventured into the burning fields and harassed the arsonists of Christ with arrows and feathered bolts. The army of God, when not annihilating fruit trees, sacked and destroyed seventeen castles and towers. While his brother was at Muret, Guy de Montfort besieged rebellious Puycelsi in the northern Albigeois. The counts of Toulouse, Foix, and Comminges and Guilem Ramon de Montcada, the seneschal of Catalonia, tried and failed to raise the siege. Guy abandoned the assault when most of his army returned to France. On Monday, 24 June, the feast of the nativity of John the Baptist, Simon, wishing his son Amaury to be a true knight of Christ, asked the bishops of Orléans and Auxerre to place the belt of knighthood around the boy before the altar of the church in Castelnaudary. "Oh, what a novel and original way of becoming a knight!" lauded Pierre des Vaux-de-Cernay. "Who in attendance could refrain from tears?"[11]

By now Pere II had read the papal letter castigating him as a liar and no better than a heretic. Simon, aware the holy war on heresy was about to be reinstated, was acutely conscious that the rest of Christendom did not know of the apostolic change of heart; the flow of midsummer pilgrims into the Carcassès was almost nonexistent. Raimon VI, gauging the moment right for an offensive against the overextended army of God, suggested to the consuls of Toulouse that an assault be made on the tiny *castel* of le Pujol, less than an hour away to the southeast. "Let us do that," said the consuls. Le Pujol was one of the seventeen castles razed by the crusaders only a few weeks earlier and, though little more than an insipid pile of stone, it was held by three of Simon's most loyal knights. The counts of Toulouse, Foix, and Comminges, a few hundred noble horsemen, and two thousand foot soldiers jubilantly marched out of the Narbonne gate. Le Pujol was soon ringed by petraries. Leather-covered wagons quickly scraped and scratched at the castral walls. The defenders dumped stones, blazing torches, and boiling water on one overly confident wagon. "Scabies is sweeter," joked the soldiers as they ran from their scalded cat, "than this hot water!" The jocular confidence of the army of Toulouse was rewarded when le Pujol, after only a few petrean knocks, tumbled into a defeated heap. Every

Frenchman, one way or another, was killed; most were swiftly butchered, a few were hanged, and the three knights were dragged by horses through the streets of Toulouse until they looked like lumps of raw meat. The king of Aragon, encouraged by this small victory, crossed the Pyrénées and, during the first week of September, promenaded through the Narbonne gate with "the flower of Catalonia and great noble warriors from Aragon." Pere II—fearing neither imminent danger nor the lack of apostolic love—intended, once and for all, the destruction of Simon de Montfort.[12]

Guilhem de Tudela ended his song when the king of Aragon resolved to fight Simon de Montfort. He sang his last lines around 1218: "And we, if we live long enough, shall see who is vanquished. And we will keep writing what we remember, so long as we have material that lasts until the war is over." He wanted to carry his song forward—there was more than enough material—but he never did (although he edited some verses as late as 1223). An anonymous troubadour in the final years of the crusade started singing where Guilhem ended and, passionately, dazzlingly, continued the *canso*. He detested the crusade and the "French from France" (a poetic irony considering his narrative rhythms emulated the *chanson de gestes* of northern France). He was most likely a soldier of Toulouse or Foix. Guilhem, though always supportive of the crusade, though always mocking *la fola erransa*, was no crude panegyrist. Baudouin de Toulouse was his sometime patron, and the shifting loyalties of this lord partially shaped his outlook. Nevertheless, there was much moral and metaphoric ambiguity in Guilhem's attitude to the crusade. He was always trying to sing his way through events that seemed dictated by a providence too brutal to be completely benign. This is where he and Pierre des Vaux-de-Cernay were very different; the cruelty of His will revealed the beneficence of His love to the Cistercian. Guilhem was like all those Provençal nobles who signed themselves with the cross; he believed in the rightness of the crusade and yet the massacres unnerved and disturbed him. The anonymous troubadour, in angry contrast, was simply furious after twenty years of holy war. He was intensely nostalgic about the world destroyed by the crusade. Everyone talks and talks in his verses, so vividly, so immediately, just as if he heard them yesterday. He lamented the erosion of *cortezia* and the loss of *paratge*. This rage and sentimentality was transformed into sublime and moving poetry: *À la recherche de temps perdu* sung by a strong-lunged warrior poet. He was less impressed with fate as a despot and saw all terror emanating from Simon de Montfort. The anonymous troubadour's verses thrill with a moral clarity so sharp and sarcastic that even Christ Himself was briefly humbled by his wrath.[13]

The king of Aragon and the counts of Toulouse, Foix, and Comminges decided to besiege Muret and, after that resounding triumph, go on to conquer all of the Carcassès. Pere II and Raimon VI even expected the king of England to support them in this campaign. John—only just absolved in July of the excommunication placed on him by the pope in November 1209—did send two envoys to Toulouse in August to discuss an expedition; in the end, "a great quantity of wind in England" conveniently stalled the Plantagenet army.[14] On Tuesday, 10 September, a host of roughly two thousand horsemen and eight thousand foot soldiers camped on a soggy meadow in front of a little rectangular bourg abutting the southwestern walls of Muret. On the left of the army was the River Louge, a sinuous tributary of the Garonne, and on the right was the great river itself. The militia of Toulouse positioned catapults and petraries before the bourg and, in next to no time, leveled the dry-built walls. Nobles and soldiers dashed over the rubble and, with the defenders retreating inside the old castral walls, the men of Toulouse hesitated in the debris of the bourg. Pere went to the consuls of Toulouse and, far from asking them to press the assault, suggested that the militia withdraw back to their tents and pavilions. "For we should be fools if we capture the French now," argued the king. Let Simon come to Muret, let him enter and, once inside, "assail the village on all sides and capture the French and all of the crusaders." The war will end, "and *paratge* will shine resplendent." Let us wait, "as we hold all the dice and won't loosen our grip until the game is played out." The consuls agreed and took the chance.[15]

Simon was at Fanjeaux when he heard about the royal and comital expedition against Muret. He anticipated such an offensive and had already prepared the army of God to go to the *castrum*. Alice de Montmorency, the night before her husband departed, dreamed that rivers of blood gushed from her arms. She awoke in terror and told Simon. "Honestly," he calmed her, "do you think I believe in dreams and auguries like a Spaniard?" Alice was not comforted. Simon—heaven forbid all omens!—raced off with about eight hundred horsemen and a few hundred foot soldiers on Tuesday, 10 September. The archbishop of Narbonne, the bishop of Toulouse, six other bishops, three abbots, and thirty French knights newly signed with the cross accompanied the army of God. Alice went northeast to Carcassonne to muster more knights and soldiers. Simon went northwest to Saverdun on the Ariège, and, though he wanted to gallop through the night to Muret, his men argued that they and their horses were too tired. He reluctantly agreed. In the morning—after making his will and sending it to the nearby Cistercian monastery at Boulbonne—he formed the soldiers of Christ into three columns in the name of the Holy and Indivisible Trinity. This tight triad marched charily north. Simon expected Pere and Raimon to attack him before he reached Muret; he definitely expected them to ambush him on the narrow mushy road to the east of the village. The soldiers of Toulouse and Aragon, gripping their dice, watched as the army of God approached the eastern bank of the Garonne. A light rainstorm passed over the crusaders and, reaching the tents and pavilions of those contemplating them, doused the evening fires. Bernart de Capuolet, prior of the Hospitallers in Toulouse, rode out with a compromise from the consuls and community of Toulouse. Folc de Maselha dismissed him. The horsemen and foot soldiers, merging three into one, ambled over a wooden bridge into Muret.[16]

The next morning the king of Aragon addressed the counts of Toulouse, Foix, and Comminges. "Lords," said Pere, "Simon has come here and he cannot escape. So, as much as I can say anything, I say be ready for battle before evening." Raimon, wary of martial platitudes, proposed barricading the camp and, if the French horsemen attacked, harry them with crossbows so that, when they swerved, "we charge and destroy them." The Catalan and Aragonese nobles shouted down such a proposal as unworthy of the king. "Lords," Raimon protested, "we shall see who leaves the field last!" At that very moment the bishops inside Muret were about to walk barefoot to Pere and beg for peace. "To arms! To arms!" thundered the Catalan, Aragonese, and Toulousain host. The prelates flinched at the sound. "The time has come for you to let us fight," Simon told them, not unkindly. And so he and eight hundred horsemen, crystal-studded helmets glistening and leonine pennants flapping, filed out of the eastern gate of Muret and, treading the marshy soil between the castral walls and the Garonne, came out on the right side of the Aragonese and Toulousain camp. Pere, sheathed in nondescript chain mail, sat upon his *milsoldor* with two thousand other horsemen over by the Louge and, expecting an attack on his left, was shocked by the sudden appearance of the crusaders. Simon, chancing the "holy game," bolted headlong toward the larger mass of horsemen. As the crusaders charged they split into their triune formation so as to assail the confused Catalans, Aragonese, and Toulousains in three waves. The first assault swept aside those horsemen who, with some presence of mind, formed a ragged line. The second assault plunged into this tumult, and Pere, flailing about like a drowning man, died as he screamed, "I am the king!" Simon and the third column darted around this equine shambles and, hacking away at disoriented knights, sprinted to the bourg, where the militia of Toulouse, unaware of the catastrophe behind them, were attacking Muret. The French knights cut down thousands of startled militiamen. Simon paused—breathless, exhilarated—and rode to where Pere was killed. He found the royal body, already stripped by the foot soldiers of Christ, naked in a field of naked bloody bodies. Simon dismounted and mourned over Pere—"a second David over a second Saul."[17]

XIII

BLACK VULTURES AND ravens circled the meadow of Muret. The knights of the Hospital of Saint John of Jerusalem were granted the body of the king of Aragon and carried the corpse to their priory in Toulouse. The crusaders gathered cartloads of weapons and marshaled hundreds of riderless horses. They buried thousands of Catalans, Aragonese, and Toulousains in a mass grave dug into the cloying river mud. "It was pitiful to see and hear the laments of the people of Toulouse as they wept for their dead," Guilhem de Puylaurens recalled half a century later. "Indeed, there was hardly a single house that did not have someone dead to mourn or a prisoner they believed to be dead." Among the humble corpses was Bernart Furner, a baker fighting in the militia, whose young wife, Petrona de Tonenquis, mourned him for more than a decade.[1] By contrast, there were almost no casualties in the army of God. "Let all Christendom give thanks to Christ for the victory of the Christians," the bishops inside Muret wrote to the pope the day after the battle, "because He has overcome an innumerable multitude of the faithless through a handful of the faithful." Arrogance and sheer incompetence by the king, or rather, a nonchalant trust in his own invulnerability, a trust nobly embodied in his knights, led to the devastation at Muret. More salaciously, though no less profligate, the king whiled away the night before battle with a mistress and, too tired to even stand for Mass next morning, was worn out all day.[2] Maria de Montpellier never mourned her husband. Innocent III, despite his recent enmity, was deeply saddened by the death of Pere II. He had crowned him at San Pancrazio Martyr in 1204, when the king promised "to defend the Catholic faith and persecute heretical depravity," as a vassal of the Church.[3] Yet, he admitted, Pere was warned against impeding His most holy war. Raimon VI, never quite persuaded by the royal charisma and confidence, escaped with his son as soon as the king was engulfed by the crusader onslaught. The two Raimons, covertly and with some difficulty, fled all the way to the English court, arriving in London at the beginning of December. Jaume, the young son of Pere, remained in the custody of Simon de Montfort.[4]

Simon de Montfort, even with so many Toulousains killed, was nowhere near strong enough to besiege Toulouse itself. He journeyed back to Fanjeaux, laden with treasure, and then on to Carcassonne. His wife greeted him with joy, mocking all portents. The overwhelming victory at Muret, far from eliciting the complete subjugation of the enemies of Christ, provoked only intense hatred in the lands of the count of Toulouse. Castles and villages along the Rhône, mostly complacent until now, openly attacked and assaulted groups of martial pilgrims traveling to Carcassonne. Simon responded by leaving in late October for a winter campaign in the marquisate of Provence. Aimeric IV, viscount of Narbonne, always worried about crusader zeal, refused to allow the army of God into his city. Simon complied—what else could he do?—and camped outside the walls. Three days later, on Saturday, 2 November, the frightened consuls of Montpellier denied the crusaders entry into their city. Simon, traveling north along the Rhône, reached Romans in the Viennois in early December. The thirty French crusaders who fought at Muret, their vows well and truly fulfilled, continued on to Lyon. The army of God was now very small, consisting only of Simon's loyal followers, hired *soldarios*, and an increasingly blasé (about the holy war, about Simon as His athlete) Arnau Amalric. Eudes III, duke of Burgundy (and pilgrim in 1209), joined Simon at Romans. The duke and his soldiers helped convince a number of ambivalent Provençal lords to submit to the victor of Muret. The archbishop of Narbonne (or rather, the duke) and the duke of Burgundy also arranged the betrothal of Amaury de Montfort and Béatrice, daughter of André-Dauphin, count of the Viennois. Simon, sometime after Christmas, received word that Aragonese and Toulousain nobles were raiding his lands in the Carcassès and Biterrois and, rather more slowly than usual, he and the army of God slogged through chill and frigid drizzle back to Carcassonne.[5]

Innocent III appointed Piero di Benevento, cardinal-deacon of Santa Maria in Aquiro, as his new legate *a latere* in January 1214. The pope ordered all prelates and clergy in the ecclesiastical provinces of Embrun, Arles, Aix, and Narbonne to warmly embrace Piero, "as if he were our own person, indeed as if we were present in him!" The legate would lead those signed with the cross in triumph against the black horseman of the plague, "namely heretical depravity." On Thursday, 23 January, he wrote to Simon de Montfort about Piero, stressing that his legate was mandated to arrange the safe return of Jaume, the infant son of Pere II, to the kingdom of Aragon, "where he will make provision for the boy's care." Earnestly, humbly, heed these mandates, "since it is unseemly that you should hold the king's son any longer." Simon was to hand over the child without delay to the legate. Any hesitation, the pope warned with ominous obscurity, and Piero will expedite matters as only he knows. Innocent III privately instructed his legate to reconcile the count of Comminges, the viscount of Béarn, and the consuls and community of Toulouse. "Even though their excesses are considerable and serious, entry to the Church should not be denied to those who knock on her doors with humility." Toulouse, once reconciled, "will live under the protection of the Apostolic See without fear of molestation by the count of Montfort or others of the Catholic faith—so long as the citizens persist in the Catholic faith and in ecclesiastical peace." Simon greeted the legate at Capestang (a *castrum* near Narbonne) during Easter and diligently handed over Jaume. A few weeks later, on Friday, 18 April, the counts of Comminges and Foix were reconciled by the legate. Seven days later the consuls of Toulouse swore oaths of loyalty to the Church, promised never to aid Raimon VI and his son, and, after surrendering one hundred twenty hostages, were reconciled by the legate. Piero di Benevento, having hobbled the black horseman, departed with Jaume for Catalonia.[6]

Raimon VI, subsidized by the English crown (10, 000 marks), departed England after Christmas and, traveling from the Atlantic along the Garonne, was in Montauban by the middle of February. Much to his surprise, he discovered his estranged brother imprisoned in the *castrum*. Baudouin de Toulouse had been given the fortified villages of Montcuq and Lolmie and some other tiny *castra* in the western Quercy a year earlier by Simon de Montfort. On the night of Sunday, 17 February, as he slept naked in a house at Lolmie—complaisantly, confidently—some village nobles and mercenaries (having first obtained the key to his room) kidnapped him. He was taken to Montcuq, where he was starved, beaten, and humiliated, and then carted (limp, half-dead) to Montauban. Roger Bernart, son of the count of Foix, and Bernat de Portella, an Aragonese knight, wanted to hang Baudouin in revenge for the death of Pere II, "since he had been present on the other side at the battle of Muret." Raimon hesitated for a few days until, more resigned than revengeful, he acquiesced to the execution of his brother. Baudouin was strung up on a walnut tree and left dangling for a week. "The brothers Templars asked for and were granted possession of his body," elegized Guilhem de Puylaurens, "which they took down from the gallows-tree and buried in the cloister at Lavilledieu near to their church." Raimon marched out of Montauban three weeks later and, with a large force of hired *soldarios*, ineptly besieged Moissac for the next three weeks before returning south of the Aveyron.[7]

Guy des Vaux-de-Cernay, bishop of Carcassonne, after a year preaching the most holy war on heresy throughout northern France with Jacques de Vitry, arrived at Montpellier with a large contingent of French crusaders at the beginning of May. "I myself accompanied the bishop," boasted Pierre des Vaux-de-Cernay. "There we found the archdeacon of Paris and other crusaders who had travelled with him from France." All the pilgrims then marched to the fortified village of Saint-Thibéry (north of Béziers) to rendezvous with Simon de Montfort. "There were about a hundred thousand of us," Pierre gleefully counted; there were, in fact, about five thousand. The suspension of the crusade had come and gone, and now, with the opportunity to walk like Him between the Garonne and the Rhône once more on offer, many northern European knights gladly yielded to Christ. The Englishman Robert Curzon, papal legate in France, and charged by Innocent III with preaching the new crusade to the Holy Land in 1213, had long since included exhortations to fight for the Crucified One alongside the Garonne as well as the Jordan.[8]

Piero di Benevento soon arrived in the "Albigensian lands"—as Pierre des Vaux-de-Cernay consistently called everything between the Garonne and the Rhône in the last third of his history—and helped Simon rally the crusaders against the thousands of angry and bedraggled Aragonese and Catalan soldiers fighting and stealing their way back over the Pyrénées. These rampaging mobs, whose violence seemed without purpose, dismayed the pilgrims, who, though more than ready "to confront pestilential heretics," were unprepared for feral gangs who did not give a tinker's toss about whether they lived or died. Simon and the army of God were unable to travel through the Bitterois and the Narbonnais without having to fight one tiny skirmish after another. Eventually these fugitive soldiers either retired inside Narbonne, escaped into the Pyrenean foothills, or simply thought ambushing the crusaders not worth the risk. The soldiers of Christ regrouped in the fields around Carcassonne at the end of May. Guy des Vaux-de-Cernay, "performing the functions of legate," and Guy de Montfort departed with most of the crusaders to slash and burn the Rouergue and Quercy. Simon traveled to Valence so his son Amaury could marry Béatrice de Viennois. Unfortunately, "it was not a good time for the wedding and the count could not stay long because of the various exigencies of war, so he took the girl to Carcassonne where the marriage ceremony was performed." Dominic de Guzmán blessed the (rushed and uncertain) newlyweds.[9]

Simon, flushed with largesse after the wedding, presented Folc de Maselha with the *castrum* of Verfeil—the village that humiliated Bernard of Clairvaux so long ago—on Wednesday, 4 June 1214.[10] In return, Folc had to supply from the village "one well-equipped noble knight." Simon in this martial obligation was redefining what it meant to be a village knight and what service such an individual rendered to his lord. Village nobles, those rambunctious *omes de paratge*, were under few obligations to the old counts of Toulouse. In general the nobility (and good men) of a village supplied the counts with food to maintain fighting men— either in long-term comital employ or temporarily hired—rather than sending well-fed (or well-equipped) warriors when needed. In each village this was a very precise yearly commitment of foodstuffs (usually good wine, good bread, and cold meat in the morning and good wine, good bread, and warm meat in the evening) for a very specific number of knights and other armed men. This lordly right was known as the *albergum*; of course, it was partible, so that all of it or fractions of it were sold, leased, and splintered among numerous nobles, peasants, and institutions such as monasteries. The horse and weapons of a knight were the responsibility of the count and not inherent aspects of what it was to be a knight. *Cabalerius* was the usual term for a Provençal knight in documents detailing the *albergum* before the crusade rather than the Parisian *miles* requested by Simon. About halfway through the war the hungry *cabalerii* disappear as documentary entities, completely replaced by the panoplied *milites*. This highlights the stark difference in equipment (and so military technique) between the northern crusaders and the southern nobility at the beginning of the crusade. Everything had changed by 1214. Two months after Folc received Verfeil a Provençal lord defined the equivalent of one "well-equipped knight," costing 800 to 1,200 shillings, as "two knights with unarmored horses or eight sergeants, and a knight [without a horse] or an archer with an armed squire [and] four sergeants." This was a very expensive and very different, very northern French way of warfare.[11]

Robert Curzon visited the crusaders toward the end of June during the siege of Morlhon (near Rodez in the Rouergue). "Everyone in the *castrum* decided to resist us," wrote Pierre des Vaux-de-Cernay, "since the *castrum* was incredibly strong and virtually inaccessible." As soon as the legate arrived the soldiers of Christ attacked the village walls with renewed vigor. "The defenders realized they could not hold out any longer and on that very day surrendered to the legate, agreeing to follow his wishes in every respect." Robert ordered Morlhon destroyed. "I cannot be silent about the fact that we found seven heretics of the sect known as Waldensian," Pierre noted with wonder. The followers of Valdes were seldom identified (as enemies, victims, or even heretics) during the war. In this rare instance, "they were led to the legate, confessing their unbelief freely and fully"—and then set on fire by the crusaders.[12]

Simon de Montfort rejoined the army of God in the western Agenais, that region bordering the lands of the English crown, and after demolishing the fortifications of every village that surrendered to him, he besieged Casseneuil on Saturday, 28 June. This was the same *castrum* on the Lot that fought off the short-lived crusade led by the count of Clermont and Auvergne in 1209. Five years later Simon positioned petraries on a limestone precipice overlooking the walls and on the flatland beneath this escarpement. Stones crashed day and night, punching ramparts and collapsing houses. The men and women of Casseneuil soon constructed their own petraries, hurling lumps of limestone at their tormentors. One night during a lull some saboteurs climbed the precipice and, as they wrecked machines, almost killed Amaury de Montfort sleeping near a petrary. John, king of England, marched an army into the Périgord in the middle of July. Rumors in camp and *castrum* said he was coming to raise the siege. John had no intention of doing such a thing; though he scorned the crusaders, he lacked the overweening bellicosity (and charisma) of Pere II. Simon knew this and shrugged off the threat. A moat (or rather a narrow tributary of the Lot) stood between the crusaders and the crumbling walls. A master engineer suggested a floating bridge be made of wood and bundles of sticks lashed to wine casks. This pontoon sank the moment it touched the water. Another floating bridge was tried, but it was too short (and wobbly for a man in armor). The master engineer then built a flat-roofed "house"; as it was gradually pushed into the water, soldiers filled the moat beneath it with dirt and wood. It was always half-in-half-out, never quite buoyant. On the roof was a five-story wooden tower faced with boiled leather to protect rows of crossbowmen. This swimming cat, despite an attempt to burn it with a flaming boat of fat and salted meat, succeeded in reaching the walls. The crusaders attacked and, accompanied by priests singing *Veni Creator Spiritus* on the precipice, captured Casseneuil on Monday, 18 August. Simon slaughtered the defenders, razed the walls, and gave the town revenues to Dominic de Guzmán.[13]

On Sunday, 7 December, Piero di Benevento and Robert Curzon summoned a general council to meet at Montpellier fifteen days after Christmas. Robert observed the Casseneuil siege in mid-July and a day or so later at

Sainte-Livrade decreed that all Simon's conquests, past and future, "were possessed in perpetuity."[14] Piero returned from Catalonia at the end of summer and, while concerned about the legality of Robert's everlasting gift to Simon, was swept along by the ardor of his fellow legate. "I ask and require you," he preached to the five archbishops, twenty-eight bishops, and hundreds of other miscellaneous clergy assembled in Montpellier, "to cast aside prejudice, hatred, or fear, and give me faithful counsel to the best of your ability. As regards the honour of God and the Holy Church, as regards peace and the expulsion of heretical filth in these lands, who should be granted and assigned Toulouse? And all the lands formerly held by the count of Toulouse? And all the lands that the army of the crusaders has occupied?" The archbishops and bishops, after perfunctory consultations with various Provençal abbots and clergy, agreed on one and only one recommendation: "that the noble count of Montfort should be chosen as prince and absolute ruler of all these lands." Piero nodded. The archbishops and bishops, having made their decision, urged the legate to give Simon all these lands immediately. Piero dissented. The Apostolic See, as was stated in many letters over many years, must first confirm the decision of the council. Bernart, archbishop of Embrun, was commissioned by the prelates to implore the vicar of Christ to approve, without reserve, without condition, the count of Christ as prince *in perpetuum* between the Garonne and the Rhône.[15]

Philip II Augustus excused himself from initially leading the crusade against the *Provinciales heretici* because two great and dangerous lions, Emperor Otto IV and King John of England, were poised to tear him limb from limb in 1209. Five summers later and these beasts were crippled by the French king: John was mauled at the battle of La Roche-aux-Moines in Anjou on Wednesday, 2 July, and Otto was savaged at the great battle of Bouvines in Flanders on Sunday, 27 July. Philip, though no longer fearful of big cats, remained forever wary of killing little foxes; nevertheless, he reluctantly allowed his son to go on crusade in the spring of 1215. Prince Louis, Philip, bishop of Beauvais, Gaucher, count of Saint-Pol, Robert, count of Sées and Alençon, Guichard de Beaujeu, Matthieu de Montmorency (brother of Alice), and a host of other French nobles assembled at Lyon on Easter Sunday (19 April). Guy des Vaux-de-Cernay, bishop of Carcassonne, was with them; once again, he had preached the crusade throughout the northern winter. The crusaders departed Lyon on Easter Monday and, resting here and there along the Rhône, reached Saint-Gilles at the beginning of May. The pilgrims, rambling southwesterly, admiring the high blue skies over the Mediterranean, fascinated by the infinite lagoons and saline marshes on the edge of the coast, arrived in Béziers a few weeks later. Simon de Montfort was rebuilding the town; though black scars were still to be seen on much of the reused stone, the holocaust of six years earlier was most noticeable in the scarce population. Piero di Benevento was worried about Louis challenging his ultimate authority over the Albigensian lands and so, as a distraction, he encouraged the newly arrived crusaders to demolish the walls of Toulouse. Arnau Amalric tried to stop similar destruction in Narbonne; Louis ordered the walls razed within three weeks. Louis, Simon, Piero, and the martial pilgrims paraded into Toulouse in early June and, ensconced in the Château Narbonnais, supervised the wrecking of the walls. The prince and the French crusaders, having fulfilled their oaths to Christ more as sightseers than soldiers, soon departed, gladly leaving the choking dust of demolition behind.[16]

"We recommend that you be praised in the Lord's name," Innocent III congratulated Simon de Montfort on Thursday, 2 April 1215, "as is your due for fighting His battles so laudably" as a true and strenuous soldier of Christ. "Go forth, soldier of Christ!" Do not wipe away the sweat of battle just yet, not before the palm of victory! The most holy war, so gloriously begun, so gloriously fought, will end in even greater glory! "Now," and the pope came to the point, "we have decided that all the lands formerly held by the count of Toulouse, together with those conquered by the crusaders and those controlled by our beloved son Piero, cardinal-deacon of Santa Maria in Aquino and apostolic legate, shall be entrusted to your prudent lordship" until the ecumenical council in November shall decree more precise and more detailed arrangements. "It will be your duty to preserve, guard, and defend these lands." Further, "you will be granted the revenues and harvests of these lands, with all other justices and approved jurisdictions," which is only right, "as you cannot carry on a military campaign from your own funds nor should you be expected to do so." We charge you, we entreat you, "do not refuse this mission on behalf of Christ, since Christ Himself accepted a mission from His Father on your behalf." The foul locusts must not be allowed to emerge from their bottomless pit and—heaven forbid!—pollute the lands so recently cleansed. We know you will accept; we know you will imitate Him. Accordingly, every lord and consul in these lands must submit to your authority and obey without exception your mandates. Aimeric IV, viscount of Narbonne, did just that; he rendered conditional homage to Simon de Montfort on Friday, 22 May. Lords and consuls who yielded to Simon de Montfort, though worthy and faithful, must do more than just bend the knee, chided Innocent III, they must zealously help the soldier of Christ and, at long last, bring the most holy war to a triumphant end.[17]

XIV

WE FIRMLY BELIEVE and simply confess that there is only one true God," declared the first canon of the Fourth Lateran Council convened by Innocent III, "Father, Son and Holy Spirit, three persons but one absolute simple essence." Seventy-one primates, four hundred twelve bishops, eight hundred two abbots, and thousands of other clergy traveled to Rome. The streets were hung with lanterns and the houses draped in purple cloth. The pope opened the council on Wednesday, 11 November, the Feast of Saint Martin, with a dawn Mass in the church of Saint John Lateran (the ancient basilica of Constantine and church of the Savior). "When the mass had been said," wrote an anonymous German cleric listening outside, "many thousands, even ten times a hundred thousand," crushed their way into the church. The pope climbed a raised platform, sang *Veni Creator Spiritus*, and preached a sermon on the sacrifice of Christ. "Unfortunately," grumbled the anonymous cleric, "I understood very little of this sermon," as the tumult was deafening. An even rowdier session occurred nine days later. At the final session on Friday, 20 November, the Feast of Saint Andrew, the pope proposed sixty-eight canons (or constitutions) and two dogmatic decrees for approval by the council. These canons enacted rules and general principles about transforming the Church and individual Christians into His true likeness and, through such compelling imitation, redeem and purify Christendom. "Although He is immortal and unable to suffer according to His divinity," continued the first canon, "He was made capable of suffering and dying

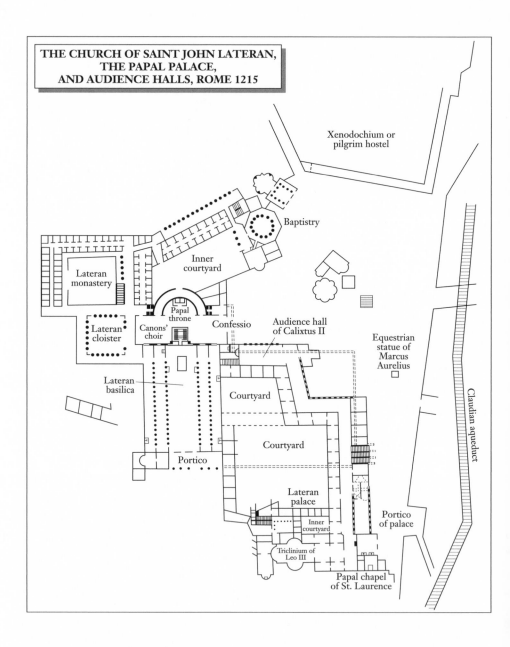

THE CHURCH OF SAINT JOHN LATERAN,
THE PAPAL PALACE,
AND AUDIENCE HALLS, ROME 1215

Xenodochium or
pilgrim hostel

Baptistry

Inner
courtyard

Lateran
monastery

Papal
throne

Lateran
cloister

Canons'
choir

Confessio

Audience hall
of Calixtus II

Equestrian
statue of
Marcus
Aurelius

Lateran
basilica

Courtyard

Courtyard

Claudian aqueduct

Portico

Lateran
palace

Inner
courtyard

Portico
of palace

Triclinium of
Leo III

Papal chapel
of St. Laurence

according to His humanity." In this legislation the boundaries between heaven and earth, soul and body, Christendom and the world were, if not completely erased, then confirmed as overlapping. "His body and blood are truly contained in the sacrament of the altar under the forms of bread and wine," concluded the first canon. In this transubstantiation of the mundane into the holy—rendered by God, performed by a priest—"we receive from God what He received from us." The divinity of Christ was literally ingested by the individual (and so absorbed into the world) as a consequence of His humanity.[1]

Raimon VI had been in Rome since January pleading his case to Innocent III about his unwarranted dispossession by the crusaders and his everlasting desire to be absolved. His son crossed the English Channel and, traveling through France disguised as a servant in the entourage of a merchant, reached him in autumn. Raimon Roger de Foix and Guy de Montfort arrived around the same time. Piero di Benevento, Robert Curzon, Folc de Maselha (accompanied by Dominic de Guzmán), Thedisius, Guy des Vaux-de-Cernay, a very taciturn Arnau Amalric, thirty or more other higher clergy from *Provincia*, and scores of lesser Provençal clerics journeyed to Rome throughout the late summer. (All conciliar participants were required to be in Rome by the Feast of All Saints on Sunday, 1 November.) Simon de Montfort remained in Toulouse. Holy wars and heresy were paramount concerns of the council. The pope's opening sermon was immediately followed by homilies from Raoul de Merencourt, patriarch of Jerusalem, on a new crusade to the Levant and from Thedisius, bishop of Agde, on the continuing threat of the "Provençal heretics." The anonymous German cleric, straining against the cacophony, barely heard the patriarch and simply had no idea what the bishop said. Raimon and his son, sidestepping clerical louts crowding every street and square, acutely conscious that most of the council despised them, nervously waited for some word on their petition. It was around the middle of November that the Toulouse question was finally discussed in a special session at the Lateran palace. "Here I must pass over many other matters whose truth I could not ascertain," the anonymous cleric wrote about this meeting *in camera*, "as I only heard rumours," and such half-truths "only gain in strength as they make the rounds." The gossip that got around—and there was constant whispering in lobbies and foyers—told a contentious tale whose outcome, for all the furtive speculation, was never in doubt.[2]

The anonymous troubadour, not surprisingly, cherished half-heard half-truths. "When the court was assembled," he sang about the session in the Lateran palace, "great debates ensued." Innocent III sat enthroned in a marble hall decorated with frescos and mosaics. Around him were seated archbishops, bishops, abbots, priests, "counts and viscounts from many places," anyone and everyone with an opinion on the county of Toulouse. Raimon VI and his son approached the pope and, dropping to their knees, begged for the return of the "lands of their forefathers." The pope, though solicitous to the son, confirmed the dispossession of the father. The two Raimons were speechless. Raimon Roger de Foix quickly marched into the middle of the paved floor. "Lord and rightful pope," he said, "I have come to your court for true justice," and pointing at young Raimon, "I am astonished that any prudent man could suffer his disinheritance." Folc de Maselha jumped up and denounced the count of Foix as a defender of heretics. "Lords," he said, "his land is the major root of heresy," with the serpents nourished and protected by him. "And your pilgrims," slashed and maimed by him, "lie thick on the field of Montgey." Listen, "outside the door are the sad cries of the sightless, of the disfigured," of all the pilgrims he cut and sliced. "He should never possess his lands again," yelled the bishop, "for he is worthless!" A noble of Foix shouted that he now wished more eyes and noses had been gouged and hacked. Raimon Roger, calming his vassal, replied that Folc's present words were like his old songs: "They kill the very soul of any who say them!" The bishop, "I promise you, is more like the Antichrist than a messenger of Rome!" The pope, furious with the count, the bishop, and the whole session, walked outside into his garden. A clutch of prelates chased after him. "Lords, excuse me," said the pope, "I am thinking." He soon returned to the hall. Everyone was screaming and arguing. A former Trencavel vassal cried out that the new viscount of Carcassonne had murdered the old. Cheers and catcalls. An archdeacon of Lyon rashly defended the count of Toulouse. Hurrahs and heckles. "Lords," and the pope silenced the hall, "judgement is made!" Innocent III acclaimed Simon de Montfort as the new lord of Toulouse, Montauban, and all the lands conquered by the soldiers of Christ.[3]

"We excommunicate and anathematise every heresy exalting itself against the holy, orthodox, and Catholic faith," asserted the council's third canon with a censorious universalism unlike any previous ecclesiastical edict. "We condemn all heretics, whatever names they may go under; indeed, although they have varying features, their tails are tied together inasmuch as they are similar in their pride." Those found suspect of heresy were struck with the sword of anathema, "unless they can prove their innocence by an appropriate purgation." Truly, "if a temporal lord, required and instructed by the Church, neglects to purify his lands of this heretical filth, he shall be bound with the bond of excommunication." If he still refused to expunge the heretics after a year, then, with apostolic approval, his lands could be possessed and purified by Catholics. "Truly, we determine to subject to excommunication those who receive, defend, or support heretics." All archbishops and bishops, in person or through archdeacons, must visit parishes at least once a year where heretics were said to live. They must compel men and women to testify about any persons "who hold secret conventicles or who differ in their life and habits from the normal way of living of the faithful." The bishop himself must summon those accused of dissenting from proper Christian norms and examine their supposed errors. "If any bishop is negligent or remiss in cleansing his diocese of the ferment of heresy," then a worthier person, one more "able to overthrow the evil of heretical depravity," will replace him. "Truly," the canon stated unequivocally, "Catholics who take the cross and gird themselves for the expulsion of heretics shall enjoy the same indulgence, and be strengthened in the same holy privilege, as is granted to those who go to the Holy Land."[4]

"All the faithful of either sex," mandated the twenty-first canon, "after they have reached the age of discernment, should individually confess all their sins in a faithful manner to their own priest at least once a year." More than a century later this far-reaching and revolutionary decree finally became the sacred routine of most Christians. In less than two decades, however, thousands of men, women, and children in the pestiferous lands of the count of Toulouse were purified (and so policed) by repeatedly confessing to inquisitors (who as Dominicans were priests). "Let the faithful reverently receive the sacrament of the Eucharist at Easter," continued the canon. If they do not, "then they shall be barred from entering a church during their lifetime and they shall be denied a Christian burial at death." A prudent and discerning priest was like a skilled doctor pouring wine and oil over the wounded. "Let him carefully inquire about the circumstances of both the sinner and the sin," so that he may discern what advice to give and what remedy to apply, "using various means to heal the sick person." He must take care "never to betray the sinner at all by word or sign or in any other way." If any priest revealed a sin disclosed to him in confession, " we decree that he is not only to be deposed from his priestly office but also to be confined to a strict monastery to do perpetual penance." This stricture was never applied to the inquisitors of heretical depravity.[5]

Innocent III announced his judgment on the count of Toulouse in a general encyclical on Monday, 14 December. "Almost the whole world knows how hard the Church has laboured through preachers and crusaders to expel heretics and mercenaries from the province of Narbonne and neighbouring lands." The Church, by God's grace, by apostolic succor, was rewarded with the expulsion of the heretics and mercenaries. The once poisonous terrain, now salubriously governed, flourished with the Catholic faith and fraternal peace. "In truth, because a new plant still needs to be watered, we have (in consultation with the sacred council) decided to make new provisions." As the count of Toulouse was found guilty of nourishing and defending heretics and mercenaries, "and as his lands will never stay safe in the true faith under his rule," he was forever excluded from his rights of dominion. He was to live outside his lands and perform appropriate penance for his sins; he was to receive 400 marks annually from the revenue of his former properties. His wife, the sister of Pere II, retained her dotal possessions in their entirety. "All the lands which the crusaders have won in their fight against the heretics and their believers, supporters, and receivers— together with Montauban and Toulouse, the most corrupted of all by the stain of heresy—are to be handed over and given to the count of Montfort." The marquisate of Provence, though, was to be governed by the Church and eventually granted to Raimon, son of the count of Toulouse. (No decision was made about the count of Foix, except that further enquires were necessary.) Finally, the many doubts and difficulties likely to arise, and the pope guessed there would be many, were to be referred the Apostolic See for adjudication, "since what has been achieved with great cost and much toil should not be lost through individual arrogance or malice."[6]

"Let the lying heretics hide away," Gervase of Tilbury cursed four folios into his universal history and a year or so after the Lateran Council, "let the tongues of the Albigensians cleave to their jaws!" He was giving an initial "description of the world" when, angry at the potential for evil in the hearts of men, he started describing the wanton lies of the Albigensians. These heretics "maintain that there are two gods: a good one from whom good things come, and an evil one by whom evil is punished." The good one, "so they say, created all that is perfect and imperishable, the heaven of heavens and angels." The evil one, so they say, "created corrupt bodies," prescribed the punishment for wrongdoing, "administers justice by the shedding of blood," and "makes the earth bring forth life under the impulse of lewd reproduction." The god of good proclaimed the gospel, lived in the apostles, and "does not punish sins but absolves them." The god of evil spoke to Moses and "reigns in our priests." The heretics extolled the apostles in preaching but damned the prophets. "For shame!" Curiously, despite this apparent consistency in belief, the Albigensians "fight amongst themselves like speckled sheep," always "at odds and opposed to each other in their opinions," forever making schisms. In the end, though, it was the Albigensian denial that "God created heaven and earth, that is, the world," and their rejection of the inseparability of matter and spirit, that so enraged

Gervase.[7] It was from this evil idea, this false seed, that the heresy flourished, acquired a form, and became a threat.

This Albigensian cosmos was the exact opposite of the Catholic universe decreed by Innocent III and his sacred council—and, of course, that was the point of Gervase's furious digression. "The origin of the world derived from a divine decree and act of creation." God ordained what was to be created by foreseeing it. "The Father created in wisdom, that is, in the Son, by the working of the Holy Spirit. One in three persons, God set what he had created in order, and once it was in order he adorned it and regulated it." This was done in the Son and with the Son. "I am Alpha and Omega; I am the beginning, who also speak to you," Gervase quoted Him. "The Son, then, is the beginning of time, the beginning of the creation of the world." As God alone was eternal, the world was sempiternal. "The beginning, therefore, is a being without a beginning: with the beginning, from the beginning, in the beginning of time, God created heaven and earth, that is, the world."[8] By denying this, an Albigensian (along with every tail-tied heretic) denied that all time and space were Christian, that all those who had lived and would live were given the revelation of Christ. Eventually, this Catholic cosmology demanded the consistent classification of Jews and Muslims as heretics, as no better than Albigensians, because they so clearly turned away from His loving embrace on the cross. Indeed, the sixty-eighth canon of the council required Jews and Muslims to dress distinctively from Christians and so end all confusion about who was and was not like Him. Gervase's Albigensian excursus (livid, convoluted, almost a parody) was one of the earliest accounts—if not the earliest—of what the *Albigenses* supposedly believed and why they deserved extermination.

Guy de Montfort returned from Rome to Toulouse and told his brother of the papal decision. Simon de Montfort immediately named himself the new count of Toulouse and required oaths of loyalty from the consuls and community of Toulouse. Apart from continuing to dismantle the outer city walls, Simon ordered the demolition of small walls within the bourg. All the chains at crossroads throughout the city and the bourg were removed as well. He also instructed that hundreds of fortified houses and stone towers belonging to the urban nobles and merchants of Toulouse—all the "greater good men"—were to be torn down. Simon commanded this leveling and clearing, according to Guilhem de Puylaurens, "so that the citizens would not rise against him in the future."[9] The Château Narbonnais, as a further precautionary measure, was ringed with large stakes of fir wood and surrounded by deep ditches to separate it from the city streets. Simon, feeling more secure, departed for France during Lent. At Melun on

Sunday, 10 April 1216, the king of France invested him and his heirs with the duchy of Narbonne, the city of Toulouse, and all the lands conquered by the crusaders, including the Trencavel territories that were never part of the French domain.

Two months later—and the most holy war far from over—Innocent III unexpectedly died at Perugia on Wednesday, 16 July 1216. He was fifty-five. He is the greatest pope of the Middle Ages and one of the most important individuals in the history of Christianity. "This bride of mine, the Roman Church," he famously preached on the first anniversary of his consecration, "did not come empty handed. She brought me a dowry precious beyond price: a plenitude of spiritual goods and a broad sweep of temporal power."[10] His vision of the limitless authority of the Apostolic See was unparalleled. Without him there would have been no Albigensian Crusade. Although the threat of heresy was a feverish obsession among Church intellectuals during the last decades of the twelfth century, the idea of a grand exterminating holy war was the singular innovation of Innocent III. Previous popes had blessed wars between Christians, but none had ever linked annihilating bloodshed with the redemptive gift of being like Him. That an apocalyptic cleansing crusade appealed to so many does not make it inevitable. Great men and great cultural shifts equally make history; indeed, the latter frequently needs the former to be fully achieved.

Historians have variously defined the twelfth century as a "renaissance," a "reformation," and a "revolution." It was the century—usually defined as "the long twelfth century" and so beginning and ending with a certain temporal elasticity—when the medieval world achieved cultural coherence around particular ideas and practices.[11] Innocent III and his policies highlight the fragility of such claims. An intellectual edifice was certainly constructed in the century before the crusade, along with a sweeping archipelago of monasteries and churches, but beneath those notional towers and outside those cloistered walls, most ordinary Christians lived and worshipped in vastly differing ways. We must always be wary of mistaking what intellectuals say a world was like for the reality of that world. Innocent III understood this and set out from the beginning of his papacy to remake Christendom in His coherent and unified image—and he did this especially through the Albigensian Crusade and the Fourth Lateran Council. The effects of the council would take a century to be wholly realized; the consequences of the crusade were immediate. Still, despite such lucidity of thought and purpose, the papal manner throughout the crusade was erratic. One moment Innocent III lauded sacred mass murder, the next he seemed to regret it. It was as if he reluctantly acknowledged that truly being like

Christ involved truly wallowing in blood. "Love God, choose the Lord, seek Him, possess Him, enjoy Him," motivated both pope in sacred council and crusader in butchering frenzy.[12] Jacques de Vitry arrived in Perugia just after Innocent III died. He saw and smelled the naked and fetid corpse, reflecting, "Brief and empty is the deceptive glory of this world."[13]

R AIMON VI DEPARTED Rome in disgust straight after the council and, reaching Genoa, waited for his son. The younger Raimon met his father in February 1216; sailing to Marseille, they planned the recovery of their lands. The father remained in port readying himself for travel to Spain. The son paraded up the Rhône throughout Easter and, gaining noble supporters and a ragtag army along the way, was joyfully welcomed into Beaucaire, the town of his birth. (Michel, archbishop of Arles, gave Beaucaire to Simon de Montfort on Friday, 30 January 1215. The older Raimon previously held it from the archbishop.) "Our beloved lord is entering the town with joy in his soul," cried the townspeople. "And now neither the Barrois [men from Bar] nor the French will have peace!" Young Raimon and his soldiers chased the French knights into the castle of Beaucaire (overlooking the town) and besieged them. "You're captured," the townspeople shouted at the castle, "every one of you!" The Frenchmen yelled back, "Easier said than done! You'll have to come and get us!" Petraries and a great battering ram soon punched and pummeled the castle walls and gates. Guy de Montfort, his nephew Amaury, and the army of God arrived on Sunday, 5 June, and assailed the outer walls of Beaucaire. Simon appeared the next day, rushing from France the moment he heard of the siege. Nobles and peasants from villages and towns all along the Rhône came to aid young Raimon. Men from Marseille, rowing against the strong river currents, singing at their oars, landed archers and foot soldiers on the riverbank. Simon's army was simply too small to stop all these reinforcements. The soldiers of Christ assaulted the town in bloody and forlorn sorties. "By God," exclaimed one crusader after such butchery, "we can set up a meat market!" The French knights flew a black flag over the castle in early August as a signal that they were starving and thirsty. They had eaten all their mules, were about to eat their horses, and if worse came to worse, "Let every man eat his comrade!" Simon—angrily, darkly—agreed to a compromise with young Raimon on Wednesday, 24 August. The French knights withdrew unharmed from the castle, but all their treasure, weapons, and (uneaten) horses were forfeited. Simon and the army of God retreated in defeat.[1]

Simon de Montfort left Beaucaire in disgust straight after the siege and, full of revenge, hastened to Toulouse. Young Raimon traveled down the Rhône to Saint-Gilles and, cheered by the townspeople, scared off the crusader garrison. The older Raimon was in Aragon and Catalonia gathering horsemen, foot soldiers, and mercenaries. Simon—rancorous, hateful— entered Toulouse in early September with the army of God. "We shall return to Provence when we have silver," he told his men, "but first we shall destroy Toulouse and leave nothing beautiful or good inside it. They have robbed me of Provence and they shall pay for its recovery!" His brother tried to dissuade him. Folc de Maselha attempted to calm him and "blunt the sharp edge of steel with silver." Simon demanded 30,000 marks from the city and the bourg. "Pay up," growled French lads, knocking on doors in every parish, "or else be tortured!" The churches were looted, the synagogue ransacked (there were about five hundred Jews in the city), and the four leprosaria robbed. Peire de Yspania, a modest merchant who owned some houses and shops in the bourg near the public baths, fled to Saint-Sernin for protection. Upon returning to his properties, he found them forfeited to Simon—they were worth 200 shillings—along with his "good leather coat, leather helmet, iron hat," bows, arrows, "and all grain and wood."[2] After a week of threats and extortions, the citizens of Toulouse cried out, "Better to die honourably than live caged in a prison!" Nobles put on chain mail and mounted armored horses; militiamen dressed in leather coats and grabbed sharp axes. Wine barrels, benches, and roof beams were heaped in front of houses and on street corners. "Montfort!" roared the French as they attacked these makeshift palisades. "Toulouse! Beaucaire!" yelled the defenders as they fought off each foray. These vicious scuffles lasted through the night. The next morning the bishop (somewhat disingenuously) and the "greater good men" tried to compromise with the count. Simon demanded hostages, money, and the devastation of Toulouse; nothing else would appease him. "Throughout every part of Toulouse," the anonymous troubadour sang of the ensuing destruction, "so great was the din, dust, crash, fear, and heat," that it seemed as if the ground was shaking, the sky thundering, and ten thousand drums beating.[3]

"Water," remarked Gervase of Tilbury, "when set in motion by its own lightness, stirs up and engenders a breeze. That is why there are strong breezes near the fast-flowing waters of the Rhône, and windy people are born there, who are empty-headed, inconstant, and extremely unreliable in their promises." This water-and-wind ascription was prompted by the turmoil along the Rhône after the victory of young Raimon at Beaucaire. All of Simon de Montfort's newly acquired towns and *castra* renounced their loyalty to him. He campaigned against these insurgents throughout 1217. He struggled to pacify the Rhône; for every village he burned, two more rebelled. It was a losing battle against such windy and inconstant people. "Whatever the nature of the air," Gervase sighed, "that will be the nature of the temperament of the human body."[4]

Raimon VI crossed the Pyrénées during August 1217 and, accompanied by the counts of Comminges and Plahars, cautiously made his way north along the Garonne. "He rode straight towards Toulouse, up hill and down valley, across combes and through great leafy woods." He soon reached the river crossing protected by the Toulouse *salvetat*. Joris, a petty Toulousain noble, suddenly galloped out of the suburban "safeguard" and attacked his old count. "Men hacked and slashed," horses tripped and fell, "but when Joris felt their strength, he took flight." The victors crossed the river with banners flying. They were now on the western riverbank and, hiding in groves and copses, trotted around the suburb of Saint-Cyprien. At dawn they reached the river shallows opposite the Bazacle gate in the bourg. Raimon was worried about being seen, "but God worked a miracle for him by clouding the sunrise in a grey mist." The nobles Uc Joan and Raimon Belenguier, wading through the Garonne on horses, greeted Raimon with *cortezia*. "Lord, thanks be to God," said Uc with a bow. "Now, come and recover Toulouse!" Raimon and his party forded the river and regrouped on the meadow outside the northern walls of the bourg. On Wednesday, 13 September, eve of the feast of the Holy Cross, the old count of Toulouse and his followers, banners and blazons flapping, cantered through the Bazacle gate. "Great and small, barons and ladies, wives and husbands" gathered around Raimon and, kneeling before him, kissed his clothing, feet, legs, arms, and fingers. "Now we have our Jesus Christ," they said to one another between tears of joy. "This is our Lord who was lost!" This rapture became more and more feverish, more and more fraught, until everyone suddenly screamed, "Toulouse! Toulouse!" Great and small ran screeching through the ruined streets and, picking up clubs and applewood cudgels, bludgeoned to death every Frenchman they found. "Today the false lord must go! And all his family and all his evil race!" The terrified crusaders retreated into the Château Narbonnais.[5]

Alice de Montmorency, alarmed by the uproar coming from the streets, wanted to know what was happening in the parishes of Toulouse. "Barons," she asked, looking out a window of the Château Narbonnais, "who are these routiers who have taken all of the town? Who is to blame?" Simon de Montfort was away incinerating villages along the Rhône, and so his countess commanded the city. "Lady," replied the seneschal Gervase de Chamigny, "it can only be count Raimon, who claims Toulouse." Alice violently clapped her hands together. "Alas!" she cried, "so much yesterday was so good!" She immediately called for a squire "fluent in many tongues" and a swift horse. "Friend, deliver the bad news to the count." Alice looked out the window again and saw men, women, and children erecting wooden barricades, piling stones across streets, and digging defensive ditches throughout the city. "I've never seen such magnificent toil," cheered the anonymous troubadour. Raimon VI and his men camped in and around Saint-Sernin in the bourg. (Viollet-le-Duc also restored Saint-Sernin in the nineteenth century, although unlike the walls of Carcassonne, this exquisite Romanesque building from 1117 has experienced *dérestauration* from his vision.)[6] The militia of Toulouse regrouped and armed men were stationed on roofs and in church towers. "And at night the whole community of Toulouse kept watch," with torches and candles in every street, "with drums and tambours and bugles playing all the time." Women and girls danced and sang, rejoicing in the return of the old count and praying for the death of the new. Alice put her hands to her ears and hoped against hope.[7]

The squire galloped hard, "travelling fast over long stages," until he found Simon de Montfort besieging the *castrum* of Crest. A medieval traveler rarely changed horses, preferring to rest his mount one day out of every three, and so the noble youth took about a fortnight to reach his lord. Simon walked out of his tent and greeted him. The squire dropped to his knees and, sighing, handed over a sealed letter. "Friend," said the count tossing the letter aside, "tell me the news—what is the state of my affairs?" The lad swallowed. "Lord, it is painful to speak." Simon stared at him. "I have lost the town?" "Yes, lord, without a doubt." "Friend, who took it from me?" "Lord, what I know is what I saw, as did other men—and that was the other count returning in joy." "Friend, with a great company?" "Lord, that I can't guess." "What are the townspeople doing?" "Lord, they labour long on ditches and trenches and wooden parapets—in my opinion, they mean to assault the Château Narbonnais." "Is the countess inside?" "Yes, lord." "Where is Guy, my brother?" "Lord, I heard that he was leading the brave company that you usually lead, intending to assault Toulouse—but I don't think he can win the fight." "Friend," said Simon, "keep this secret." He gripped the youth's shoulder. "If any man sees you so much as laugh and joke about this, I'll have you burned, hanged, and hacked in pieces." He released his hand and smiled. "And if anyone asks for news, say something smart—say no man is so bold as to invade my lands!" "Lord," said the squire, "no need to chastise me on this." Simon returned to his tent and, feigning pleasure at having heard some wonderful news, was eagerly questioned by his nobles. "His mouth was laughing," sang the anonymous troubadour, "even though his heart was aching." "Lords," and Simon launched into a rollicking denial of reality, "I do assure you that I pledge Jesus Christ my fear and gratitude—as it seems to me that no one has ever been given so much good fortune by Him. My brother has sent me a heartening letter. No man, anywhere, stands against him. And count Raimon—he's off gallivanting in Spain." The king of England wanted a treaty; Guy was happily collecting taxes in Toulouse; there were only glad tidings in the letter. The loyal French lords were pleased, "but many others felt their hearts trembling." This fear was hardly lessened when Simon immediately ended the siege of Crest and ordered His soldiers back to Toulouse.[8]

Simon de Montfort and the army of God arrived before the southern walls of Toulouse in October. Guy de Montfort met his brother and, though he reported fighting his way into the city at one point, he conceded that the Toulousains were putting up a surprisingly tough resistance. "Brother," said Simon, "it's a disgrace that unarmed men defeated you!" The new papal legate, Bertrand, cardinal-priest of Saint John and Paul, appointed by the new pope, Honorius III, accompanied the soldiers of Christ. "Lords," Bertrand addressed the crusaders, "the mandates of the Spiritual King say that the fires of hell burn in this town because it overflows with sinful criminals!" The crusaders agreed. "You will recapture the town and seize every house! No one is to be left alive, neither man nor woman!" The soldiers of Christ readied themselves to attack the walls between the Montgaillard and Montoulieu gates, exactly as they had six years earlier. "The light airs ruffling embroidered gonfalons, the jiggling harness-bells, and the glinting gold shields, warmed their hearts and fired their ardour." Admittedly, the walls were still rather shabby after Simon's efforts at pulling them down, and so they seemed easily assailed. Along the ramparts were crossbowmen, spearmen, and *ballistae* (massive crossbows firing great bolts or spears). At the base of the walls deep trenches were excavated and row upon row of sharpened holm oak stakes radiated outward. A mangonel was erected inside the walls and positioned to hurl stones over the ramparts. Noble ladies, merchant wives, and washerwomen filled buckets with stones of all sizes, as large as a dog, as small as a fist. The militia of Toulouse stood around with clubs, cudgels, and great axes. Horsemen, waiting inside the gates, were poised to charge when the crusaders did. And, soon enough, the crusaders did charge, yelling and shrieking, "Montfort! Montfort!" The mangonel crashed stones left and right into the careening French knights. The gates opened and the horsemen of Toulouse bolted out. The militia ran into the fray, waving their axes, crying and howling, "Toulouse! Toulouse!" Rocks, arrows, spears, and bolts, "dense as fine rain, darkened the clear skies." The crusader assault faltered and stumbled backward in chaos.[9]

The crusaders accused Simon de Montfort of being too adventurous with their bodies and souls. (Some Gascon nobles, fighting with the crusaders only because Simon was their new lord, privately blessed the continued success of Toulouse.) Simon, enraged and resentful, galloped out of range of the crossbows and entered the Château Narbonnais during sunset. His wife could say nothing to comfort him. "My lord count," said Foucaud de Berzy, lord of Puylaurens, in the morning, "let us now discuss and implement a scheme that men will still talk about when we are dead!" Simon and the leading crusaders were intrigued. "Let us build a new town with new buildings, newly provided with new roofs, and erect new barricades with newly felled timber. Then, when we newly occupy these new places, new people with new men will come and join us there." Simon was slightly bemused. "New Toulouse, it shall be called," said Foucaud triumphantly. New Toulouse, for all the clever talk, was merely an argument for strengthening and expanding the deserted *salvetat* in front of the Château Narbonnais. The suburban safeguard would be fortified with new stone buildings and low defensive walls on either side of the road to Carcassonne. The siege of old Toulouse was going to be long, and this permanent camp, this martial shantytown, was a shrewd necessity, especially with winter approaching. "Lords," said Simon, "this counsel pleases me." All the leading crusaders agreed, except Folc de Maselha, who noted that New Toulouse did nothing whatsoever about assailing the Toulousains on the western bank of the Garonne or boxing them inside the bourg. The point was well taken, and, although the army of God was too few to do anything but occasionally pester the northern walls of the bourg, Simon and his men immediately punted across the Garonne and occupied the exposed suburb of Saint-Cyprien. Toulouse was to be invested to the west and to the south.[10]

The crusaders proceeded to build New Toulouse throughout autumn and winter. This was largely an exercise in colonizing the *salvetat*: horses, roncins, and mules were stabled in houses; swords, chain-mail hauberks (28,000 to 50,000 links in an all-riveted full-length coat might take 1,000 hours to make), and siege engines were made in the workshops; bread was baked in the ovens; supplies were stored in sheds; flat-bottom boats were built by the score; and the leprosarium beneath the Narbonne gate became a hospital for the wounded. Thousands of tents and pavilions were pitched among the buildings and on the meadow in front of the Château Narbonnais. New Toulouse was ringed with brick and stone ramparts, trenches and ditches, iron chains and holm oak stakes. Allied to this appropriation of the *salvetat* was the sustained occupation of suburban Saint-Cyprien. The crusaders again seized houses, raised tents, and constructed defenses. Simon de Montfort and his "brave company" marched along the riverbank most days, "banner, ensigns, and lion symbol" goading the Toulousains watching on the other side. "The shimmering helmets and painted banners, the doubled escutcheons and nielloed scabbards, the marvellous shields and golden braid, glowed resplendent beside riverbank, water, and meadow." The militia of Toulouse attacked these promenades by simultaneously racing across the Old and Daurade bridges. Simon was so startled the first time this happened that he fell into the river, and, while a comrade saved him, his horse drowned in her armor. He never allowed such a fiasco to happen again. He had hundreds of punts move back and forth across the Garonne, effectively uniting New Toulouse and Saint-Cyprien, so that either suburb was always ready to aid the other. The soldiers of Christ never captured the bridges, no matter how they tried, but they did manage to fight off all incursions from the city and to hold Saint-Cyprien. Simon and his little flotilla controlled the river. In practice they dumped animal corpses near the Old bridge so as to foul the northern flow. In hunger they emptied hundreds of eel traps and salmon nets. In revenge they killed absentminded Toulousains watering their horses.[11]

The men, women, and children of Toulouse continued rebuilding the walls of the city and the bourg throughout autumn and winter. Carpenters constructed a host of petraries, trebuchets, mangonels, and *tormenta* (light catapults with mechanisms of torsional ropes like mangonels). Blacksmiths hammered out iron helmets, swords, and crossbow bolts. Tanners and leatherworkers made screens for catapult crews, parapet shelters, "vineyards" (protective leather canopies), and coats for cats. (In 1158 the tanners, represented by their own "good men," swore to faithfully supply leather to the count and the "good men of the city and bourg" in time of war.)[12] Nobles and peasants from the Toulousain, Lauragais, Albigeois, Carcassès, and even the Biterrois joined in the defense. Lords from Aragon and Catalonia arrived, seeking revenge for the death of Pere II. Raimon Roger, count of Foix, galloped into the bourg one clear autumn night. Everyone roared and cheered. Torches and bonfires glowed in the streets and squares. Drums beat, trumpets blew, tabors rolled. The crusaders shivered when they heard this resounding "tempest." "Stay calm," barked Simon de Montfort. "A flower has blossomed through you," Raimon Roger applauded the people of Toulouse. "You have cleared the clouds and spread the light." He worried, though, about traitors and cowards. "If you have a tree that leaves a bad smell," he recommended, "then tear it up and throw it far away!"[13] Raimon Roger, though fond of violent demagoguery, was right to be concerned. Although most people in Toulouse fought and labored for count and consuls, there were still some village nobles more than willing to engage in old rapacious habits. The noble Peire Guilhem de Rocovila (whose nickname was "Three Measures") proudly told the inquisitor Bernart de Caux that he kidnapped three soldiers of Toulouse during the siege and, holding them hostage for two nights, released them only after the consuls paid a ransom. He was against Simon, more or less, but chances for profit were not to be missed. (Raimon and Bernart de Rocovila, who sacrificed the good men and good women of les Cassés seven years earlier, were his brothers.) One of the freed soldiers was soon mortally wounded and, so Peire Guilhem heard, received "consolation" from a good man.[14]

As soon as the men, women, and children of Toulouse positioned the petraries, trebuchets, mangonels, and *tormenta* throughout the city, they pounded the Château Narbonnais. "More than ten thousand pulled on the ropes," rejoiced the anonymous troubadour, "and they loaded the slings with big beautiful rocks." The castle gates, "walls, barbicans, long galleries, and high windows in the Ferranda tower, were all crashed, bashed, and smashed into pieces." Although the weather became colder and the river icy and the ground frosted, the soldiers of Christ and the soldiers of Toulouse attacked each other daily, leaping trenches, hopping mud flats, so that the dead and the dying lay exposed on frigid soil or in chilly water. No one took prisoners. Simon de Montfort, for all his maneuvers and feints, was unable to capture the city. Raimon VI and the consuls, for all their missiles and arrows, were unable to dislodge the crusaders. It was a war of attrition, more in loss of life than lack of food, with each side reduced by the killing fields around Toulouse. Alice de Montmorency and Folc de Maselha traveled to France, promising to return in the spring with new pilgrims. Raimon and the consuls hired mercenaries from Navarre and Brabant. Winter was a bloody season. "In the field of the Montoulieu was planted a garden which burst forth and blossomed every day," grieved the anonymous troubadour. "It was sown with lilies; but the white and the red which budded and flowered were flesh and blood and weapons and the slosh of splattered brains. Spirits and souls, sinners and saved, the freshly killed replenished hell and paradise."[15]

After three days of torrential rain and tempest, the Garonne flooded in early May 1218. All the streets and squares, houses and churches, orchards and gardens were caked in mud and silt. The lower half of the whitewashed church of the Dalbade was honey brown. Six lepers drowned inside the Bazacle gate.

Petraries and trebuchets, sodden and swollen, fell apart. Bridges were damaged and mills swept away. Much of New Toulouse crumbled or disappeared when the waters receded. The crusader camp in Saint-Cyprien was flushed down the river. Alice de Montmorency had just arrived from France with new crusaders and all their tents and clothes were stained and soaked, all their leather and armor mildewed and rusted. In the middle of the Garonne were two slender clay islands with two small towers, and, when the river settled down, Simon resolved to assault them. The soldiers of Christ were lined up all along the western bank and a troop of catapults was placed on a flat strip of sand. Simon moored his flotilla in preparation for landing on the islands. The Toulousains did not know what to do. The flood weakened the Old bridge that crossed over the largest and most permanent island, named Tounis, while the other island was now all but impossible to reach as the surging waters had dramatically altered the depth of the river and the flow of the currents. An Aragonese squire, Peron Domingo, stripped off his armor and, clutching a rope, swam out to the tower on Tounis; he then swam back and guided two boats laden with food and weapons along the rope. The thousands watching from either riverbank said to each other in absorbed admiration, "That man's agile!" A bridge of ropes to this tower was soon made. Peron swam to the other tower and, splicing and weaving, knitted an elaborate system of ropes and pulleys to supply the defenders—a futile endeavor, as the island, dissolving into the choppy Garonne, was soon evacuated as the tower tumbled into the waves. Simon, impressed but undeterred, shattered the tower on Tounis with his catapults and, when the defenders crawled back to Toulouse along the ropes, sent crusaders over in boats to occupy the island.[16]

Simon, despite his success in the Garonne, was anxious about the siege. The newly arrived crusaders disagreed with his tactics, and, much more important, he was running out of money. The mercenaries he hired were preparing to leave unless they were paid in coin or plunder. Simon decided to build an enormous wooden tower, reinforced with iron and wrapped in many layers of leather—so many layers, in fact, that no trebuchet or flying stone could harm it. He would put four hundred knights and one hundred fifty archers inside the cat and, dragging the great brute along the southern walls of Toulouse, clear the ramparts of defenders and storm the city. "I'll either destroy Toulouse in fire and ashes," he swore, "or I'll be received as a martyr, dead and suffering!" Young Raimon arrived in old Toulouse as the mighty assault tower was being constructed in New Toulouse. Bells peeled throughout the city and the bourg, rejoicing in the return of the "bright star." Simon, even more irritated by the returning son than the returned father, hastened his carpenters and blacksmiths, so that by the middle of June he was ready to test his monstrous cat. The huge leather and wooden beast, lurching and swaying in front of the Château Narbonnais, was gingerly pushed and dragged along the walls toward the Montgaillard gate. Unfortunately, as soon as the tower was beyond the protection of the comital castle, a well-aimed trebuchet crashed through the head of the cat. The men at the base of the tower turned around and began to push the headless folly back to the castle. The expert crew of the trebuchet hurled another stone and, blasting through the wood-and-leather torso, caused the tower to crumple in a mewling heap. "By God," Simon shouted to his men, "move the cat at once or be killed!" "Anyone you put inside this thing," they yelled back, "would be better off with wounds, fever, or disease!"[17]

(A certain Raimon Escrivan saw the trebuchet destroy the cat and, amused by the absurdity of the scene, composed a cruel ditty about it. He was most likely a soldier in the militia and, though perhaps a troubadour by profession, his little song was sung for the defenders of Toulouse. "Lady Cat" and "Trebuchet" sing a duet as she assaults the walls of a town. Lady Cat begs to know why Trebuchet keeps wounding her with stones. Trebuchet glibly says the wounds are nothing. Lady Cat weeps. "Sulking Cat," teases Trebuchet, "I'll soon destroy you." "Trebuchet," screams Lady Cat, "you hurt me, you check me, leave me alone!" "Lady Cat," Trebuchet brutally ends the song, "you'll never have truce nor peace from me, therefore you must die!")[18]

Simon set about rebuilding his great cat and, quite soon, she was even bigger and stronger. "My lord," said Foucaud de Berzy, "try some other way, this cat will never be worth three dice." Simon dismissed all doubts. "I will take Toulouse before the week is out," he promised, "or I'll die trying." Curiously, what added to Simon's faith in his cat was the obvious ambition of the Toulousains to burn the creature. "We'll go and attack the cat," agreed the Toulousain nobility and militia, "and Toulouse and *paratge* will never be parted again." At dawn on Monday, 25 June, armored horsemen and foot soldiers charged out of the Montgaillard and Montoulieu gates intending to capture and burn Simon's pet. They carried ladders to scale the low walls and barricades of New Toulouse. The petraries, mangonels, and trebuchets inside the city walls distracted the Château Narbonnais with constant bombardment. "Kill them! Kill them! It's the only way!" cried the men of Toulouse. Simon was presently at Mass in the chapel of the comital castle and, though hearing and feeling the petrarian thud thud, kept on praying. A frightened squire rudely interrupted him: "This piety is disastrous!" The athlete of Christ caressed the lad's cheek and told him to be calm. He then looked to the altar and quietly prayed, "Jesus Christ the righteous, give me death on the field or give me victory." Simon walked out of the chapel and, mounting his swift horse, rode out to join the crusaders replenishing the bloody garden before the Montoulieu gate. Guy de Montfort, seeing his brother, galloped to meet him. An arrow pierced his horse's head. The animal reared up in agony and a crossbowman sent a bolt plunging straight into Guy's groin. Horse and rider made it to Simon before both fell to the ground. "Brother," joked Guy as he grimaced in pain, "this wound will make me an Hospitaller!" Simon laughed that chastity was not so easily achieved. As he bent down to help his brother a flying stone—lobbed from a mangonel worked by noble ladies, merchant wives, and little girls—crushed his helmet. Simon dropped dead.[19]

"So the man who inspired terror from the Mediterranean to the British sea fell by a single stone," wrote Guilhem de Puylaurens, "and at his fall those who had previously stood firm fell down." All the fighting in and around Toulouse instantly ceased with the death of Simon de Montfort. The soldiers of Christ and the soldiers of Toulouse were equally stunned and confused. The Toulousains soon reformed and, meeting no resistance, set fire to Simon's cat. Candles were lit and bells were rung throughout the city and the bourg of Toulouse to celebrate the death of the "cruel and murderous count." The army of God—uncertain, unsure—half-heartedly acclaimed Amaury de Montfort the new count of Toulouse, duke of Narbonne, and viscount of Carcassonne. The crusaders attempted one more desultory assault on the walls between the Montgaillard and Montoulieu gates; it failed miserably. At the end of July Amaury, his family, and all the martial pilgrims withdrew to Carcassonne with the body of Simon de Montfort.[20]

Pierre des Vaux-de-Cernay's Albigensian history changed in meaning and purpose after the death of Innocent III. In the first draft, dedicated to the pope and written before 1216, the crusade was seen as lasting no more than a decade. In later drafts, as the war went on and on, Pierre was faced with a conundrum: Why did God allow the heretics to keep on living? His answer was to reconfigure his history into a *vita* recounting the metamorphosis of Simon de Montfort into the Crucified One. Unfortunately, this inspired solution ended "suddenly, when a stone from an enemy mangonel hit the knight of Christ on the head." Pierre simply stopped writing—although not before pointing out that as the Savior was wounded five times before His death on the cross, so Simon was pierced five times by arrows before his skull was smashed.[21]

The anonymous troubadour scathingly reproached all who butchered in the name of God when he sang of the epitaph above the tomb of Simon de Montfort at Carcassonne.

The epitaph says, for those who can read it,
that he is a saint and a martyr and that he shall breathe again
and inherit and flourish in marvellous joy
and wear a crown and be seated in the Kingdom.
And me, I have heard it said that this must be so
if, by killing men and by spilling blood
and by squandering souls and by sanctioning deaths
and by trusting evil counsel and by setting fires
and by destroying barons and by dishonouring *paratge*
and by seizing lands and by nourishing pride
and by lauding evil and mocking the good
and by massacring ladies and by slaughtering children,
a man can win over Jesus Christ in this world,
then the count of Montfort wears a crown and shines in heaven.[22]

Unquestionably, the tension of being like Him from sunrise to sunset enhanced the sanctimonious tendencies of Simon de Montfort and, toward the end, produced dark moods of vengeful introspection. Yet for all the inherent brutality of being a holy soldier and a holy sacrifice without respite, especially in a war against those who deliberately turned away from Christ, it was this strenuous melding of the divine and the human in Simon that anticipated the holy kingship of Louis IX and even the holy stigmata of Francis of Assisi. Extraordinary holiness and extraordinary cruelty were never incompatible during the crusade—indeed, more often than not, they went together by necessity. The redeeming majesty of His love was revealed only through wholesale slaughter honoring Him. The tender humanity of Christ was made manifest only amid the blood of the faithless. Simon's charismatic sacrality, as much as his genuine military gifts (excluding his late obsession with cats), was the reason he was so successful for so long. It inspired the army of God; it gave them an aura of invincibility.

At the core of this army were crusaders from the first summer who signed themselves with the cross in perpetuity in imitation of Simon. This was very different from the behavior of the European knights and soldiers who settled in the Levant after 1099. These men, though acutely aware of protecting and holding the land of His birth, made a sharp distinction between their old vows as pilgrims and their new lives as settlers in the Holy Land. The Latin Christians who ruled Jerusalem until 1187 never felt compelled to imitate Him day in day out. Admittedly, what it meant to be a crusader was only incrementally clarified throughout the twelfth century, and so the glory and burden of yielding to Christ was felt more vividly in 1218 than a hundred years earlier. Nevertheless, something very new and distinct happened to the warriors who fought under Simon's banner. The exigency of always walking like Him essentially transformed them into a martial *ordo* resembling the Templars and Hospitallers. (This may partially explain why the military orders barely participated in the crusade.) Unfortunately, after Simon's death the army of God was without purpose or inspiration. Amaury de Montfort simply did not possess his father's unwavering ambition, talent, or the very real sense of being like Him every day of his life.[23]

XVI

"THE CRUSADE IS shattered," sang the anonymous troubadour. "Now is the moment to attack and destroy! Come on Toulouse and seize the opportunity, so that honour and *paratge* will never perish! Because the brave young count, who verdantly renews the world, who brilliantly colors the darkness with gold, must go through his lands, regaining them, banners flying," all the while, "destroying and killing the French."[1]

Pope Honorius III sent a flurry of letters into France and *Provincia* during the nine-month siege of Toulouse appealing for crusaders to go to the Garonne and support Simon de Montfort. He commanded the consuls and community of Toulouse to abandon the false count Raimon. Three weeks after Simon's death the pope issued an encyclical throughout France and the Holy Roman Empire exhorting all Christian knights to sign themselves with the cross against the *Provinciales heretici*, with the same privileges and indulgences as if they were fighting in the Holy Land. The pope begged Philip II Augustus to lead a holy expedition to finally cleanse the lands between the Garonne and the Rhône. The king was predictably indifferent. On Wednesday, 5 September 1218, Honorius offered Philip half the tax he was collecting from the French clergy for a crusade to Jerusalem if he would go to Toulouse and expunge the heretical serpents. Philip agreed; or rather, he agreed to allow his son to go once more on crusade.[2]

Prince Louis signed himself with the cross on Saturday, 20 November 1218, and, after gathering a thousand knights, left Paris six months later at the beginning of summer. "He was accompanied by twenty-five thousand lances, magnificent knights on horses with beautiful manes," sang the anonymous troubadour with more flash than fidelity. Louis tramped from the Rhône through the Rouergue and Albigeois into the Agenais and joined Amaury de Montfort besieging the *castrum* of Marmande on the Garonne. (The town was captured by the crusaders in 1212 and recovered by Raimon VI two years later.) The French surrounded the fortified village with tents, rich pavilions, and petraries. Marmande was too small to hold out for long against such a mighty army. After a few days the walls were breached, and, while the prince and his nobles were debating policy inside the royal pavilion, thousands of soldiers charged into the tiny village streets, killing everyone in their path. "Barons and ladies and little children and men and women, their clothes slashed, their bodies naked, were hacked and cut to pieces by sharp-edged swords," sang the troubadour. "Flesh and blood and brains and torsos and limbs and faces were carved and ripped. Livers and guts were torn out and tossed about the ground as if they had rained down from above." Marshes and meadows were soaked red. When there was no one left to kill, Marmande was set on fire. Louis was upset by the massacre, more by the unsanctioned slaughter than anything else, and as the sweet-smelling smoke was too much for him, he hastily departed for Toulouse.[3]

So many pilgrims accompanied the prince "that the hills and plains and roads and paths were swarmed, crawling with men and women." The anonymous troubadour saw crusaders from France and Berry, "along with Flemings, English, and Normans." He saw men from Champagne, Brittany, and Poitiers, "along with Germans and Bavarians." He eyed this "throng of murderers" and counted "thirteen hundred thousand." Whatever the number, and it was clearly astonishing (probably around eight thousand humans and twelve thousand animals), the martial pilgrimage meandered beside the Garonne, moving forward in short, clumsy stages. The papal legate Bertrand rode beside Louis, discussing what was to be done with the foul locusts of Toulouse. Archbishops, bishops, abbots, monks, priests, and even some Templars rode on horses or mules or trundled in carts dragged by oxen. Two thousand wagons carried weapons and siege equipment. Empty villages throughout the Toulousain greeted the soldiers of Christ. Scouts from Toulouse (including the anonymous troubadour) watched and noted the progress of this lumbering, if undeniably powerful, host.[4]

"Is it any wonder that in Toulouse," when the scouts returned, "everyone in the town was filled with fear?" The consuls immediately started organizing the militia, promising citizenship (and so emancipation) to any Toulousain or Lauragais peasant who fought for the city. In a routine all too familiar, adults and children, "singing songs and ballads," set about strengthening the fortifications of the city and the bourg. Ditches were dug, wooden stakes were shaved needle-sharp, leather "vineyards" were trailed along the ramparts, and missiles were collected for petraries, mangonels, and trebuchets. A statue of Saint Exupéry, fifth bishop of Toulouse, who reputably saved the city from the Vandals in the fourth century, was raised into the bell tower of Saint Étienne. The saint was swathed in candles and lanterns so that all could see him. Young Raimon, "always audacious," was ready to fight Louis and, if need be, Philip himself. "The king was my lord," he told a group of consuls and urban nobles, "and if he had treated me justly I would have been true to him forever." Regrettably, now "he is my enemy, strong and violent." The prince, "so long as he rides with these *bordoniers* [pilgrims], will have neither envoys nor pleasantries from me." Only when Raimon faced Louis in battle, "when night and day the blood is flowing and men are dying, when barons and warhorses tumble," then and only then was a "benevolent" royal reply assured to any query. Young Raimon was full of good humor and confidence that Toulouse would stand firm "against the arrogance of France."[5]

The anonymous troubadour ended his song with Toulouse anxiously waiting for Louis and the crusaders. He offered no explanation for stopping, just as he never explained why he started singing in the first place. Most likely, knowing the outcome of the crusade, he finished the *canso* while there still seemed to be hope for young Raimon and his city. "But the Virgin Mary will preserve them," he prayed. "She puts right all that is wrong, so that innocent blood will not be spilled." The men, women, and children "will not be afraid, for Saint Sernin guides them and God and justice and strength and the young count and the saints will defend Toulouse!"[6]

"His army was truly immense. His camp extended around the whole of Toulouse," wrote Guilhem de Puylaurens when Louis arrived during the middle of July. As the Toulousains crowded their walls they saw a vast ocean of tents and pavilions rippling in the warm air. It was a beautiful, if frightening, sight. Petraries and trebuchets soon launched rocks and stones against the walls. Cats and leather-canopied wagons moved into position. Women and little girls inside the city fired shot after shot from mangonels. Crossbowmen traded feathered bolts with one another. Every so often a boy playing on the ramparts was hit in the arm or leg by a high-flying bolt. Each side skirmished by the riverbank when watering horses. Each side cursed the other as godless cowards. A thousand clerics sang *Veni Sancte Spiritus* day and night. Yet for all this there were no crusader assaults, there were no raids from Toulouse, there was very little bloodshed. Louis seemed listless and half-hearted about killing heretics. The "throng of murderers" were keen but lacked direction. Old Raimon was his usual skittish martial self. Young Raimon was wary about the apparent royal apathy. The consuls and the militia were simultaneously poised for an attack and pleased it never came. Abruptly, after forty days, all the tents and pavilions disappeared. Louis raised his cursory siege and returned to France.[7]

Raimon VI suddenly became ill and died at the age of sixty-six in August 1222. As he lay dying the Knights of the Hospital of Saint John of Jerusalem held to his lips a robe signed with a cross; unable to speak, he softly kissed the cross of cloth before "leaving this life." The Hospitallers solemnly carried the corpse the short distance from the Château Narbonnais to their priory. The count was forbidden burial in the Hospitaller cemetery as he was excommunicated, and so his coffin was placed on a stone plinth in the priory courtyard. Young Raimon pleaded in vain with the Apostolic See that his father had repented *in extremis* and was entitled to a Christian burial. Corpse and coffin rotted away on the plinth for two centuries.[8]

Honorius III appointed Konrad von Urach, cardinal-bishop of Porto, as his new legate to France and *Provincia* in December 1219. Konrad was once abbot of Cîteaux and, imbued with almost a century of Cistercian hatred for the little foxes, he tried to enliven the most holy war with renewed purpose and design. The army of God dispersed under Amaury de Montfort and what knights and soldiers he possessed engaged in blatant brigandage to survive. A decade of ravaged fields, vineyards, and orchards in the Biterrois, Carcassès, Albigeois, Toulousain, and Lauragais left nothing but poor and struggling harvests; the land would take another generation to recover. The pope and his legate worried that many priests and even some bishops now regretted the crusade and wanted no more holy expeditions into their parishes and dioceses. Konrad created the Order of the Faith of Jesus Christ sometime between 1221 and 1222 as a way of invigorating the war on heresy. This was a new military order modeled on the Templars; just as the knights of the Temple fought Saracens, the knights of the Faith would fight depraved heretics, rebels against the Church, and the enemies of Amaury de Montfort. The Order of the Faith of Jesus Christ perhaps evolved from a confraternal militia, like the Whites of Toulouse, or from the remnants of the army of God, but, as no one seemed to join or endow this new martial *ordo*, the legatine initiative faded away. Amaury received more feasible support when Honorius III on

Thursday, 3 June 1221, confirmed him as the new count of Toulouse and then, four months later, perpetually disinherited young Raimon from any rights to the lands of his excommunicated father.[9]

On the same day Honorius III endorsed Amaury's comital rights he offered the king of France a twentieth of the annual income of every French cleric for three years if he went on crusade against the Albigensians. In December Konrad von Urach and the bishops of Lodève, Manguelone, Agde, and Béziers reiterated this exceptional gift and, even more remarkably, implied that Amaury was willing to cede all his territorial rights to Philip II Augustus. Six months later the parvenu count of Toulouse begged the king for aid against the son of the former count of Toulouse and, as an inducement, explicitly ceded all rights to his rapidly disappearing lands. On Saturday, 14 May 1222, the pope wrote to Philip and—mimicking the great exhortations of Innocent III—urged the king to be signed with the cross and to cleanse his kingdom of the heretical plague. He reaffirmed the triennial twentieth and the willingness of Amaury to relinquish his lands; he even sent a copy of his exheredation of the son of the former count of Toulouse. In June, not knowing where else to turn, young Raimon wrote to Philip, "his sole refuge," protesting his eternal dispossession and the enduring papal antipathy. Philip replied to Honorius and Raimon with uncommon speed and sympathy. He proposed that Amaury and Raimon hold a truce, reach a compromise, and conclude the war. The pope agreed. The two young men agreed. (Guilhem de Puylaurens reported that Raimon, though married to the sister of Pere II, even contemplated marrying Amaury's sister.) Konrad held a council at Saint-Flour in the Auvergne on the royal proposal in May 1223; unfortunately, the council soon ended in rancor and renewed warfare. The legate then summoned all French prelates to another council two months later at Sens in Burgundy to discuss the growing Albigensian crisis. Quite astonishingly, what precipitated this sense of urgency was Konrad von Urach's claim that an "anti-pope of the Albigensian heretics" from the region of Bulgaria, Croatia, and Dalmatia had consecrated (from a distance) a certain *Bartolomeus* (Bertolomieu) of Carcassonne as a "bishop of the heretics." Now the most holy war on heresy was to expel such Albigensian bishops and their believers.[10]

Na Aimerzens Viguier, adolescent and pregnant, was escorted by her aunt na Geralda de Cabuer from Cambiac to the village of Auriac to hear two holy "good ladies" preach in the house of na Esquiva Aldric in 1223. The girl, whose stomach was visibly swollen beneath her dress, was instructed by Esquiva as soon as she entered the house to offer three bows to the good ladies and to recite, "Bless us, good ladies, pray God for these sinners."

Later that same day more noble men and women from Auriac joined the girl in the Aldric house. The good ladies preached to this gathering and then everyone offered them the *melhoramen*, exactly as Esquiva had shown Aimerzens. This courtly moment shattered when the good ladies facetiously told Aimerzens that "because I was a pregnant adolescent," she remembered twenty-three years later, "I was carrying a demon in my belly." The wit of the good ladies provoked raucous laughter in everyone, including Aunt Geralda. The girl was so deeply disturbed, so wounded by such a blatant lack of *cortezia*, that she no longer felt able to honor the good ladies. Aimerzens, in the days and weeks that followed, was bullied by her husband to "love the heretics," just like everyone else, "but I didn't want to love them," she told the inquisitor Bernart de Caux, "after they told me I was pregnant with a demon." It was not the gravid horror of a demon growing inside her that so upset Aimerzens; such a notion of capricious growth and reproduction was the very definition of a fertile adolescent. It was the shocking abuse of *cortezia*, the shame of being mocked over such an inescapable fact of feminine existence, that severed all love and loyalty the girl had for the holy good ladies. The humiliation of na Aimerzens Viguier poignantly demonstrated how a decade or more of holy war had so changed the good men and good women, had so severely broken the world that once needed them, that the famously courtly and tempestuous culture between the Garonne and the Rhône, damned by Cistercian preaching, celebrated by troubadour song, by 1220 no longer existed.[11]

It was once simply unimaginable that a good woman might preach and openly receive the *melhoramen*. A noble adolescent needing instruction in holy decorum (and who had not been a child good woman) was equally inconceivable before the crusade. Na Aimerzens Viguier took *cortezia* seriously—her hurt and embarrassment showed that—but the former implications of courtliness and melioration were meaningless to her. The *melhoramen* was now performed in varying ways; benedictions even differed in the same village. One person might recite the older formula, "Bless me, good men, pray God for me," while another stumbled over "Lords, pray God for this sinner, that it might make me a good Christian and may lead me to a good end." Bows and genuflections, once so precisely watched and counted, swayed into either indifference or profligacy. Three adult knights implausibly offered meliorations to two little boy *bons omes* in the village of Montesquieu in 1227. Courtesies withered into clichés. A "coming together" known as the *aparelhamen* (transcribed as *apparellamentum* by inquisitorial scribes) was instituted by some good men and their noble believers; every month they secretly performed overwrought versions of *cortezia*. A lady at a Fanjeaux *aparelhamen* in 1234 bowed so feverishly, so immoderately, she fell over. "I had to leave the house with some others," a knight grinned a decade later, "because we couldn't refrain from laughing." A few good men halfway through the war even started calling themselves "deacons" and "bishops" in vain attempts at grasping fading honor and at restraining the holy chaos around them. These "bishops" were non-nobles like Bernart de la Mothe, Peire Polhan, Peire Izarn, and Bertran (also called Bernart) Marti. By copying the titles of the Catholic Church (and by exchanging their modest clothes for vivid woad-blue robes) these good men reaffirmed their rights as the "friends of God."[12] The art of living in the world formerly embodied by the holy good men, an aesthetic precisely shaped by moderation and melioration, was now garish and conceited.

All good men and good women were fugitives by 1220, sheltering in woods, hiding in cellars, wandering in fear through the countryside. They consciously tried to remain holy even when the communal structures of honor and courtesy that once needed and created them were destroyed by war. They now embodied sacred and social nostalgia. This hearth and holy sentimentality applied to those who knowingly became "believers of heretics." The good men sincerely assumed continuities with their past, and yet, no matter what they or their believers said, the sacrality they exemplified was little more than longing and regret calcifying into an increasingly passive divinity that, if anything, resembled the secluded holiness of the good women before the coming of the crusaders.

In 1652 the Toulousain scholar Guillaume Besse was given a scrap of parchment by a prebendary of Saint Étienne in Toulouse. Eight years later he published what was written on this remnant in a three-page appendix entitled "Charte de Niquinta" in his *Histoire des ducs, marquis et comtes de Narbonne*. The "Charter of Niquinta" purports to be excerpts from three Latin documents supposedly copied by the good man (and "bishop") Peire Polhan for the good man (and "bishop") Peire Izarn in August 1223 or 1233. The text is a slovenly mess and requires emendation by all who read it. It opens with a report of an assembly of good men at the Lauragais *castrum* of Saint-Félix-de-Caraman in 1167. Then an excerpt from a sermon given at this assembly by a *papa* Niquinta (or Nicetas) from Constantinople. It concludes with the demarcation of new heretical dioceses in the Toulousain, Carcassès, and Agenais (and the "consoling" of the new bishops by the Byzantine heresiarch). In May 1167, "the church of Toulouse brought *papa* Niquinta to the *castrum* of Saint-Félix." Men and women from the heretical churches of Toulouse, Albi, France, and Lombardy "gathered there to receive the *consolamentum*" from him. "You have asked me," preached Niquinta, "whether the customs of the primitive churches were heavy or light, and I say to you that the Seven Churches of Asia were divided from each other by boundaries and none of them did anything to infringe on the rights of another of them." The heretical "churches of Rome, Dragometia, Melenguia, Bulgaria, and Dalmatia have agreed boundaries," and so he advised that episcopal limits for Toulouse and Carcassonne be adjudicated. Many modern scholars extol the "Charter of Niquinta" as the resounding proof of a widespread "Cathar Church" in the twelfth and thirteenth centuries—though it never mentions Cathars (or Bogomils) or even comes close to being historically cogent. What makes these scholarly claims even more absurd (and rather embarrassing) is that no one has ever seen the original parchment except Besse. The most important document in the history of Catharism only exists as a disheveled *pièce justificative* from 1660.[13]

There is evidence that Besse forged the "Charter of Niquinta."[14] There is better evidence that the document was forged by Peire Polhan and Peire Izarn. Nobles, peasants, and monks frequently faked charters, bequests, and chronicles.[15] Such fabrication was less overt mendacity than the crafting of a "truthful" past that, for one reason or another, lacked (and so needed) documentary verification in the present. Admittedly, in 1291 a man confessed to the inquisition at Carcassonne that he blackmailed other men with counterfeit documents revealing long-dead parents or grandparents to have been heretics (he cleverly aged and darkened parchment by leaving it on the windowsill near his wife's cooking fire).[16] The two Peires were not quite so false. They merely invented a history of the good men that justified an ephemeral episcopal hierarchy. Other fugitive good men were now priests in all but name of a far-flung "Church" with a long institutional memory. Bureaucratic fiction was substituted for anarchic reality. No doubt the two Peires believed this narrative to be essentially true. What is so fascinating is that they adopted (and adapted) the accusations that Catholic intellectuals made against men such as themselves after 1220. Before the crusade no pope, Cistercian, or good man ever suggested that a heretical "Church" existed between the Garonne and the Rhône. Nor did anyone ever suggest linkages with heretics in the Byzantine Empire, and certainly not with Bosnia or Bulgaria. It was only after a decade or more of holy war that "Albigensians" were accused of having "bishops" and Balkan acquaintances. Guilhem de Tudela in one of the last revisions of his *canso* (around 1223) sang of some Carcassonne heretics as *cels de Bolgaria*, that is, as "Bulgars" or *Bolgres* (in old Provençal) or *Bougres* (in old French).[17] Confusingly, *Bolgre* or *Bougre* initially derived from the ecclesiastical province of Bourges, the southernmost archdiocese of France, whose southernmost diocese was Albi. As *Albigenses* acquired new meanings, so too did *Bougres*. Indeed, Guilhem probably first sang of "those [heretics] from Bourges" and he (or a later editor) altered it to *Bolgaria*. Of course some good men were "bishops" around this time, and like so much about these furtive individuals, they functioned within a sacred and social illusion that, while partially their own design, was mostly shaped by their persecutors.

In 1621 the English scholar Robert Burton, reflecting upon the lack of grace and charm that is the constant melancholy of scholars lost in their own thoughts, especially those that think about heresy and holy wars, remembered reading that the Dominican Thomas Aquinas halfway through a quiet supper with Louis IX unexpectedly slammed his fist upon the table and cried, "This proves the Manichaeans were wrong!"[18] A rebuke to bookish "woolgathering." A reproach to learned daydreaming of a "Cathar Church." Remarkable erudition has been lavished upon Guillaume Besse's appendix by great scholars. It adds up to nothing, no more than wishful thinking. One must already believe in a "Cathar Church" to see such an entity within the text, even if the text itself is the foundational proof underlying this belief. Everything about the "Charter of Niquinta" resembles a *ficción* by Jorge Luis Borges: a quixotic addendum (and libraries of extravagant exegesis) displaces reality with fantasy. The vanished document, whether forged by Besse, Peire Izarn, Peire Polhan, an unknown good man, or even an inquisitor, is one of the most enduring forgeries in Western culture. Even assuming that it was faked by Peire Polhan and Peire Izarn—which seems most likely—then it was preserved in a Dominican archive, filed away with other thirteenth-century apocrypha demonstrating heretical connections between the Pyrénées and the Balkans. Relying on the "Charter of Niquinta" as evidence of Catharism requires turning aside from all historical specificity and warmly embracing the intellectualist bias in the study of heresy. "Heresies," as Sir Thomas Browne gracefully encapsulated this idealist tendency in 1636, "perish not with their Authors, but like the River *Arethusa*, though they lose their currents in one place, they rise up againe in another."[19]

In 1221 some transient Waldensians "persecuted heretics" in the *castrum* of Avignonet, Michel Verger told Bernart de Caux, "and many a time I gave alms to the said Waldensians, when they were begging door to door for love of God, and since at that time the [village] church was supporting the said Waldensians, and they were with the clergy in the [village] church itself singing and reading, I thought they were good men."[20] After twelve years of the crusade, Waldensians were still not considered heretics in Avignonet; indeed, as Michel stressed, Waldensians actively harried good men and good women. This seems to have been a widespread phenomenon. Guilhem de Puylaurens knew about Waldensians preaching against heresy in village squares and was disgusted that "ignorant priests sometimes welcomed them."[21] This explains why those seven Waldensians at Morlhon freely confessed their beliefs to Robert Curzon in 1214. They assumed they were on the side of the Church in the holy war on heresy—which was why their immolation came as such a cruel surprise.

Philip II Augustus died at the age of fifty-eight on Friday, 14 July 1223. The king's revived interest in the crusade was never tested, and, whatever the outcome, his commitment was still shaped by wariness rather than ardor. Folc de Maselha told Guilhem de Puylaurens that he once heard the king prophetically say, "I know that after my death the prelates will press my son Louis to take responsibility for the Albigensian enterprise; but he is a man of delicate and feeble constitution who will not be able to sustain the labour, and will die an early death." Louis VIII, despite two rather perfunctory martial pilgrimages, was indeed more responsive than his father to the entreaties of popes and prelates regarding the most holy war. In the immediate aftermath of his father's death he dispatched 10,000 marks from the royal will to Amaury de Montfort so that the knight of Christ could defend Carcassonne and the surrounding lands from Raimon VII.[22]

On Tuesday, 23 January 1224, Arnau Amalric wrote a long letter to Louis VIII lamenting that, while Carcassonne survived being besieged, almost all the *castra* throughout the Albigeois, Carcassès, and Biterrois were deserting Amaury de Montfort. With these villages again seething with heresy, he begged the king to be signed with the cross, "in the hope that these lands may be acquired and brought back to unity with the Church through your services and those of others of the faith." A month later a wretched Amaury ceded all his lands to the king in perpetuity. The handful of crusaders still fighting as the army of God were imprisoned, ransomed, or killed by Raimon VII. Raimon II Trencavel, the sixteen-year-old son of Raimon Roger, returned from exile with his guardian, Roger Bernart, the new count of Foix. (Raimon Roger, the savage old count of Foix, died in March 1222 from an ulcer while, impenitent to the end, he besieged his former *castrum* of Mirepoix.) The king of France, although persuaded the "Albigensian lands" were in crisis, nevertheless required certain conditions to be met by the pope before he committed himself to a crusade. He requested papal letters stating that both Raimons, "namely father and son, and their heirs have been deprived by judicial sentence of the county of Toulouse in perpetuity." He requested that these lands and the viscounties of Béziers and Carcassonne be given to him and his heirs forever. He requested 60,000 pounds of Paris each year for ten years. He requested a ten-year truce with England. "And when he shall have been personally in the Albigensian lands and shall have worked in good faith at that enterprise," the pope cannot make him or his heirs stay or go back against their will. Louis was so confident of the acceptance of his terms that he informed the consuls and community of Narbonne in February, "We have decided to proceed against the Albigensian heretics and, if God wills it, secure all the Albigensian lands."[23]

Raimon VII forced Amaury de Montfort into a truce on Sunday, 14 January. Raimon orchestrated the peace in the hope that, by demonstrating his willingness to be reconciled to the Church, any justification for a royal crusade was eliminated. He was excommunicated after capturing Beaucaire in 1216 and wanted absolution. He even offered Amaury 10,000 silver marks to help him achieve everlasting peace with the Apostolic See. Amaury was irrelevant to Raimon as an adversary, but he was immensely useful as the son and heir of the great Simon de Montfort when it came to manipulating papal sentiment. Amaury's abandonment of his rights to Louis VIII—an act of petty desperation—acknowledged he was no more than an instrument in Raimon's diplomacy. Honorius III was, as Raimon hoped, enthralled by the prospect of lasting peace in *Provincia* and, envisioning no need for a royal pilgrimage, sent Konrad von Urach to Louis with a letter (dated Thursday, 4 April) saying as much. The king was told that Raimon, son of the late count of Toulouse, would remain faithful and obedient to the Church, "solely by the power of the terror you cause and without the noise of battle or the shedding of blood." The Albigensian Crusade was unnecessary, all the more so as it distracted men and resources from the new crusade of Emperor Frederick II to the Holy Land. Louis was shocked, angry, and rather hurt. "About the Albigensian enterprise," he wrote to Konrad a month later, "we have washed our hands of it!" Raimon ended the summer at Montpellier by promising Arnau Amalric on Monday, 25 August, that he would expel heretics and routiers, give the Church 20,000 silver marks to indemnify ruined churches and provide for Amaury's honor, and "equally and faithfully cause the Catholic faith to be observed throughout our land." He then sent envoys to the pope to discuss perpetuating the peace in *Provincia*, rescinding apostolic approval of Amaury as count of Toulouse, and removing his excommunication.[24]

Honorius III sent Raimon a short letter on Friday, 31 January 1225. He praised Raimon's envoys as "prudent men" and extended the peace until Easter. All other matters he left to his new legate *a latere* to both France and *Provincia*, Romanus Frangipani, cardinal-deacon of Sant'

Angelo. "Consequently, when he arrives there, you must be so reverently and obediently attentive to him," so humble and submissive to his warnings and commands, "so you may be able to deserve the favor of God and the Apostolic See." The pope's cool ambivalence after the warmth of last spring was due to his renewed conviction of the necessity of the crusade into the "Albigensian lands." He had come to distrust Raimon's sincerity about maintaining peace and expunging heretics and, no longer recoiling from the shreds of war, embraced an armed pilgrimage as the only possible path to purification and redemption. Guy de Montfort—now with a pronounced limp—was in Rome at the same time as Raimon's envoys, and, though his nephew's cause was hopeless, he spitefully slandered the son of the late count of Toulouse.[25]

Romanus Frangipani arrived in Paris during May and immediately set about cajoling Louis VIII into leading a new crusade. The king, somewhat surprisingly, was still willing to fight the heretics, although his previous conditions about going on crusade were to be partially met and the holiness of the enterprise endorsed by an ecclesiastical council. Romanus, with this in mind, summoned all the archbishops, bishops, and other prelates of France and *Provincia* to a great council at Bourges (at the confluence of the Yèvre and Auron Rivers) on Saturday, 30 November, "to again raise up the enterprise of peace and faith, which had wholly collapsed, and to uproot the heretical depravity of the Albigensian lands and surrounding regions." Raimon was invited—under royal protection for a month—to argue his faith and humility before the council. Amaury de Montfort, now the tool of Romanus and Louis, theatrically pleaded his rights as count of Toulouse and viscount of Carcassonne and Béziers before the council. Raimon, though more than ready to submit to the Church, though purging his lands at that very moment of heretics, denied that Amaury possessed any rights to Toulouse, Carcassonne, and Béziers. Romanus asked Raimon to leave while the council deliberated in closed session. Romanus and the council promptly excommunicated Raimon due to his unwillingness to carry out the mandates of the Church, namely, restoring Amaury's lands and expelling heretics. Roger Bernart de Foix and Raimon II Trencavel were also excommunicated. Romanus and the council then agreed to prevail upon Louis VIII to take up the "Albigensian enterprise" and "purge that land of heretical depravity." The king was offered a tenth of all ecclesiastical revenues for five years if he signed himself with the cross. "One and all," the French poet Philip Mousket sang about the council of Bourges a decade later, "the clergy unanimously decided that, for God's sake and for mercy, the Albigensians should be destroyed!"[26]

Arnau Amalric died two months before the council and so Raimon lost the one prelate who was sympathetic to him. This improbable shift in temperament—from ravening hatred of the father to affectionate coddling of the son—reflected the archbishop's growing disillusionment as to how the "holy game" was being played. He never retreated from the view that heretics were a greater threat to Christendom than Muslims or schismatic Greeks; he merely retreated from the conviction that the most holy war was following in the path he so savagely hacked and burned in 1209. A sacred egoism defined the man; he knew better than Him how His war was to be waged and, as his influence was waning after 1220, he wallowed in sanctimonious insouciance. Raimon was embraced in resentful animus rather than pastoral affection.

On Wednesday, 28 January 1226, Romanus Frangipani reaffirmed the excommunication of Raimon VII, Raimon Roger de Foix, and Raimon II Trencavel. On the same day Louis VIII convened a Parisian assembly of all his barons to plan the holy and royal expedition into the Albigensian lands. Two days later the king yielded to Christ and summoned all his nobles to rally at Bourges four weeks after Easter, on Sunday, 17 May—"the time when kings like to go to war," observed Guilhem de Puylaurens. Romanus preached throughout France the necessity of a martial pilgrimage to slay the "wild boar of Toulouse" uprooting the vineyard of the Lord. Honorius III declared peace between the English and French kings and prohibited all wars against the kingdom of France during the royal crusade. The crusader army that gathered at Bourges, "moved by awe of royalty and the legate's preaching," numbered around twenty thousand men. This was almost twice as many warriors as the crusader army of 1209. Yet, unlike that summer, there were no hordes of ordinary men and women wanting to walk like Him between the Garonne and the Rhône; if this pedestrian multitude is included, the army that mustered at Bourges was roughly the same size as the sprawling host that encircled Béziers seventeen years earlier. Admittedly, many "old men, boys, women, poor, and infirm" did come to Bourges signed with the cross, and Romanus Frangipani, accepting whatever monies they had put aside for the crusade, "sent them home forthwith, their vows having been fulfilled."[27]

Louis VIII and his grand army marched easterly toward Lyon and, once there, loaded equipment onto boats and heaped matériel into carts. The boats glided down the Rhône; the carts trundled along the Roman road on the eastern riverbank. On Saturday, 7 June, the eve of Pentecost, the crusaders reached Avignon in the marquisate of Provence. As the first crusaders moved through the town toward the vital bridge (completed in

1188) over the Rhône, the men and women of Avignon started worrying that the French horsemen and foot soldiers were an army of occupation; before the next contingent entered the town, the gates were swiftly shut. Louis and the rest of the crusaders were denied entry. The consuls of Avignon relented slightly; they would allow the king to enter the city with a small party, but that was all. The fears of the men and women of Avignon were to some extent justified. Louis had planned on besieging the first Albigensian town or village that refused his apostolic mandate and, more important, his royal suzerainty. The siege would be a showcase of his power and, as a consequence, spread dismay and dread. His previous martial pilgrimages were, by and large, no more than loud demonstrations of royal authority and not long-lasting campaigns of conquest and expurgation. Louis intended a similar regal exhibition this summer, though on a much more magnificent and enduring scale, indeed, one so splendid in scope that the Albigensian lands would instantly surrender to him. The trouble with Avignon was that its suzerain was the Holy Roman Emperor, and so, though obviously infected with heresy as a possession of the former counts of Toulouse, it was never considered part of the kingdom of France or an Albigensian land. The panic of Avignon provoked Louis into unleashing his might much earlier in time and place than he envisioned. A rebuke to king and Christ, however pathetic and alarmist, could not go unanswered. Louis surrounded Avignon with petraries, trebuchets, and mangonels and started a three-month siege.[28]

While the siege of Avignon was pounding away to its inevitable conclusion, Louis VIII and Romanus Frangipani asked the new archbishop of Narbonne, Peire Amielh, to go throughout the Biterrois, Carcassès, Albigeois, Lauragais, and Toulousain seeking the submission of all towns and villages. He succeeded beyond all expectations; virtually every village and town surrendered to the king before the end of summer. Even Roger Bernart de Foix tried to make peace with the king but was rebuffed. Raimon VII and the consuls of Toulouse prepared for the worst and strengthened the walls of the city and the bourg. The consuls worried that some urban and rural nobles, having secretly submitted to the king, were planning attacks within and without the city. They successfully petitioned the count to extend the *salvetat* for almost a league in all directions (a maximum radius of fourteen kilometres from the center of town); they reinstituted the older notion of the "safeguard" as a region where parochial warfare was forbidden, emphasizing the comital right to police and punish recalcitrant nobles. This preemptive measure against noble "robbers and evil-doers" was a desperate (and anachronistic) attempt at delaying the inevitable capitulation of hundreds of petty lords to the king.[29]

During the siege of Avignon two knightly troubadours from Tarascon, Tomier and Palazi, denounced the French pilgrims as warriors on a "false crusade." The French "deprived the Selpulcher of help and strength," wilfully abandoning the land of His birth to depredation. "And that is impious," heretical, and treacherous. "The false fools will never enjoy silver [*Argenza*, punning on silver and the region around Beaucaire] so secured!" The noble troubadours echoed the consuls of Toulouse in worrying about Provençal lords surrendering to the king. "We shall have mighty aid," so let no *ome de paratge* lose heart, "we shall conquer the French!" By hitting hard, "one easily conquers such mercenaries!" God will take revenge on such a sacrilegious army. "Lords," the troubadours cheered, "we are certain and confident of mighty aid!" A song of desperation (and anachronism) boldly singing that resistance to the impious French was holy and just.[30]

Avignon finally capitulated in September; though it was not an especially horrific siege for either side—there were few slaughterhouse assaults—a great many crusaders died from varying degrees of excruciating dysentery. Even Louis VIII was sick, and, though he tried to keep his illness hidden, he progressively deteriorated. The much-reduced royal expedition trudged into Béziers, Carcassonne, and Pamiers. Folc de Maselha, though exiled from Toulouse, supplied the crusaders with bread, meat, and wine when they marched through the Lauragais and Toulousain. The king avoided Toulouse completely, perhaps due to his sickness, although avoiding serious resistance and prolonged warfare was very much in character. At the approach of autumn the royal crusade departed the Albigensian lands and returned to France through the Auvergne. Louis was so weak he was unable to stay on his horse. "It was said his illness was one that could be relieved by the use of a woman," wrote Guilhem de Puylaurens. Accordingly, a close and not especially bright royal companion placed a pretty noble virgin beside the king while he was sleeping. Louis awoke, wondered what was going on, and after being told, kindly said, "No girl, it will not be so." Louis became more and more feeble—despite well-meaning cures—and died on Sunday, 8 November 1226, at Montpensier. "Rome, you killed good king Louis," the troubadour Guilhem Figueira angrily sang a few years later, "because, with your false preaching, you lured him away from Paris."[31]

The crusade of Louis VIII, though a crucial continuation of the most holy war, was a very different expedition from previous martial pilgrimages between the Garonne and the Rhône. It certainly lacked the apocalyptic chiliasm of the summer of 1209—then again, no subsequent crusading summer was so fervidly millennial. Louis definitely believed there was an Albigensian crisis, and, while this danger absolutely threatened Christendom, it was also a moment of truth for the kingdom of France. Innocent III may have tried to cajole Philip II Augustus into a crusade against the little foxes by arguing that the lands of the count of Toulouse were part of the French realm, but he never suggested that the kingdom itself was in jeopardy—except, of course, as part of a potentially poisoned Christendom. Louis quite clearly thought the heretical Albigensian lands, meaning almost everything below the Massif Central, were by their very nature a threat to his kingdom and equally to Christendom. He took it for granted that a heretic who denied the kingdom of God denied the kingdom of France. He assumed that when heretics turned away from Christ as king, they turned away from him as king. Philip, chancellor of Notre Dame in Paris, gave a sermon in the cathedral during the siege of Avignon in which he compared Christ claiming His heavenly kingdom when He ascended into heaven as no different from Louis claiming his earthly kingdom when he descended into the Albigensian lands. This was a sacred and political vision that justified and demanded the conquest and purification of the humid and heterodox south. Louis was in many ways a mediocrity in theory and in practice, and it seems apparent that his transformation of France into the kingdom of Christ through a royal crusade was only half-formed and even half-understood at his death. Nevertheless, without this profound shift in the war, the inherent divinity of his son, the future Saint Louis, would never have happened.[32]

Louis IX was twelve years old when his father died and his mother, Blanche of Castile, became the regent of France. The French crusaders, even during this slight interregnum, continued reclaiming and cleansing the Albigensian territories. Louis VIII, during his sojourn in the Biterrois and Carcassès, installed *sénéchaux* and *baillis*, royal administrators, into his newly recovered lands and reorganized them on northern French lines as the *sénéchaussées* of Beaucaire-Nîmes and Carcassonne-Béziers. This royal domain from the Rhône to the Aude was placed under the control of his cousin Imbert de Beaujeu and protected by five hundred French knights. "Chivalry," an anonymous French cleric eulogized around 1226, "whom everyone should honor," shielded all Christians by defending Holy Church, by upholding "justice for us against those who would do us harm." He wrote his little book on *chevalerie* in the vernacular, specifically encapsulating and celebrating what it meant to be a French knight returning from or preparing to go on pilgrimage to Spain, the Levant, or the Albigensian lands. Everything about a knight, from leather belt to iron helmet, from warm bath to camp bed, was imbued with holiness. The table of God and the kingdom of France would be despoiled without the order of chivalry.

"The good would never survive if the wicked did not fear knights." Christendom and France, "if there were only Saracens, Albigensians, Barbarians, and others of evil faith," would never endure—fortunately, these sacred realms were guarded by the *ordene de chevalerie*.[33]

Raimon VII seized a number of *castra* after the death of Louis VIII, assuming that either the crusade would dissipate with a boy monarch and widow regent or a compromise would be reached with the French crown if he possessed more lands by which to negotiate. Imbert de Beaujeu, rather than compromising, besieged and reoccupied the *castra* Raimon recaptured. In 1228 the archbishops of Auch and Bordeaux arrived midsummer with Gascon mercenaries and, guided by Imbert, systematically destroyed all the crops and vineyards throughout the Toulousain and Lauragais. This was not simply trampling or burning fields and vines; this was digging them up and ploughing them under, this was thousands of men with axes and shovels working every day on the devastation of the terrain. After almost twenty years of war the fragmented vineyards around Toulouse were a pitiful sight, and so this destruction, while easily achieved, was catastrophic. These harvest-time hostilities were relentless, never ceasing, never pausing, wearing and wearying Raimon and the Toulousains. At the same time the new pope, Gregory IX—Honorius III died in March 1227—requested Romanus Frangipani to pursue a compromise that would finally end the war. The legate sent the Cistercian Elie Garin, abbot of Grandselve, to Raimon with an offer of peace; Raimon accepted the offer without hesitation. A truce was arranged, meetings were held near Baziège in November, "and the defeated son of the former count of Toulouse went to France."[34]

Raimon VII, the abbot of Grandselve, some "greater good men" of Toulouse, the archbishop of Narbonne, and many other clerics and officials from France and *Provincia* gathered at Meaux (east and north of Paris by the River Marne) in January 1229 and drafted a compromise peace by the beginning of Lent. These negotiations then moved to Paris, where more revisions to the compromise occurred until, with Easter approaching, the treaty was acceptable to Romanus Frangipani and Louis IX. Raimon was now named count of Toulouse in all papal and French documents. On Holy Thursday, 12 April 1229, Raimon stood barefoot in a loose shirt in the great square of Notre Dame cathedral in the presence of Louis, Romanus, Konrad von Urach (now legate to England), a woeful Amaury de Montfort, and thousands of other French nobles, prelates, and ordinary Parisians. He was led to the altar, absolved by Romanus, and reconciled to Jesus Christ and His Church. He left the cathedral and did homage to the king. Raimon was thirty-one and Louis would be fifteen in two weeks. The compromise at Meaux was then ratified as the treaty of Paris. The most holy war was over.[35]

"Raimon, by God's grace count of Toulouse, gives greetings in the Lord's name to all those to whom this document may be presented," began the treaty of Paris. He swore devotion to the Church and servility to Louis IX. He promised to expel all heretics from his lands, "and their believers, supporters, and receivers." His *bayles*, local comital officials in towns and *castra*, were to seek out and capture heretics "and their believers, supporters, and receivers." No Jews or suspected heretics were to be *bayles*. A bounty of 2 silver marks was to be paid for two years to anyone who helped in the arrest of a suspected heretic and, if the suspect was condemned for heresy by his or her local bishop (or any other person with the requisite power), 1 silver mark was to be paid in perpetuity to the informant. All mercenaries were to be expelled. All *faidits*, so long as they were not accused of heresy, were to return and reoccupy their lands. The walls of Toulouse and of thirty *castra* (such as Fanjeaux, Castelnaudary, Montauban, Lavaur, Avignonet, Moissac, Labécède) were to be demolished. All ecclesiastical properties unjustly confiscated "before the first coming of the crusaders" were to be restored to the Church. Ten thousand silver marks were to be distributed to churches and clerics injured during the war. The abbot of Cîteaux received 2,000 marks and the abbot of Clairvaux 500 marks for the benefit of monks. The abbot of Grandselve received 1,000 marks, the abbot of Belleperche 300 marks, and the abbot of Candeil 200 marks, for new buildings. Four thousand marks endowed four masters in theology, two masters in canon law, six masters in liberal arts, and two masters in grammar in a *studium generale* (university) in Toulouse. The king of France possessed and occupied the Château Narbonnais for ten years and the count of Toulouse was to pay 6,000 marks for strengthening and manning the castle. All these astonishing sums were to be paid over four years.

Raimon VII never quite managed to pay these absurd and humiliating indemnities; yet they were nothing compared to his complete subjugation regarding his nine-year-old daughter, Joanna de Tolosa, and her inheritance. Joanna was to be married to a brother of the king; in June she was betrothed to nine-year-old Alphonse de Poitiers, and, after living in Paris for seven years, she married him. Raimon, as a consequence of this marriage, was granted all the lands within the diocese of Toulouse (essentially the Toulousain and Lauragais). He was given lands in the dioceses of Agen and Cahors. He retained some *castra* along the western bank of the Tarn. All his properties on the western side of the Rhône were forfeited to the French crown. All his properties on the eastern side, namely, the marquisate of Provence, were handed over to Romanus Frangipani and the Church in perpetuity. At Raimon's death all his lands were to go to

Alphonse or to any of Joanna's sons. If Alphonse died without children, then these lands reverted to the king of France and his heirs. Joanna had no proprietary rights. Raimon died twenty years after he swore to these terms on Monday, 27 September 1249. Alphonse and Joanna died within a few months of each other in 1271; they were childless. The lands of the count of Toulouse were immediately absorbed into the kingdom of France and became the lands of the "tongue of oc"—that is to say, Languedoc.[36]

XVII

THE YOUNG ENGLISHMAN John of Garland arrived in Toulouse as a new master of grammar in May 1229. "In the city of Toulouse," he wrote in his delightful *Dictionarius*, "still not calmed after the tumult of war, I have seen barbicans, lice, towers above deep moats, brattice, scaffolds, and hurdles erected from beams, the iron-bound gauntlet, the great round shields, the *targes* [small shields], arm guards, and petraries or *tormenta*." In a touristy aside about these discarded machines he wrote, "One of them crushed to death Simon, count of Montfort." Toulouse was littered with war debris. French poleaxes, Spanish knives, German spears, English daggers, Roman javelins, Toulousain bows, pointy-topped helmets, chain-mail rings, thigh guards, knee plates, thousands of crossbow bolts, "all of which are made so that wretched men may be destroyed." John's mind floated from topic to topic in the *Dictionarius*—the first "dictionary" in name and method—listing, digressing, explaining, as one thing provoked his contemplation of another. He was ruminating on mills, "cogs screeching as they go around," when he thought of ravaged Toulouse. Wretched men killed in war led to "naked men fulling cloth" led to dyers steeped in woad blue and kermes red, whose fingernails were "sometimes red, then black, then blue, and are therefore scorned by beautiful women (unless embraced thanks to money)." The simplicity and charm of the *Dictionarius*—"On the clothes-rack of Master John of Garland hang various garments" followed some words on the harmony of heavenly spheres—was unusual for John. The florid and bombastic style of the professor was his normal manner.

A long eccentric poem begun in Toulouse, "On the Triumph of the Church," exemplified his *scientia*; it mingled autobiography, history, tortured rhymes, a seething hatred of heretics, and a "Letter sent by the masters of Toulouse to all the universities in the world." The letter exhorted students to come south and plant the cedars of faith against the thorny forest of heretical depravity. Books banned in Paris were studied in Toulouse. Classes met on time. Wine was cheap. Good salaries were paid. Toulouse was "the promised land" of learning.[1]

The Cistercian Hélinard de Froidmont preached the inaugural sermon for the University of Toulouse on Thursday, 24 May 1229, the day of Ascension. It was his fourth sermon in Toulouse that week. "Now let us say a few things in simple speech for the simple," he bluntly announced. All erudition was harmful without faith. Learning without the love of God was worthless. "The clerics in Paris chase the liberal arts," he decried, "in Orléans, authors; in Bologna, the *Codex*; in Salerno, medicine chests; in Toledo, magic; and nowhere, virtue!" Hélinard vehemently reminded the masters and students why they taught and studied in Toulouse. Only knowledge imbued with God would defeat the wickedness of heretics.[2] Seven months later Hélinard preached the opening sermon at the council of Toulouse summoned by Romanus Frangipani. Raimon VII, Folc de Maselha, two consuls (one from the city, one from the bourg), three archbishops (Narbonne, Bordeaux, Auch), hundreds of local nobles, numerous French lords, and the university masters attended council sessions throughout November. Forty-five canons were eventually proposed and approved. They were the familiar clerical wish list, with some notable exceptions. The first canon required every prelate to commission every parish priest (assisted by reputable village men) to search every house (and underground room) for "heretics, believers, fautors, receivers, and defenders." The twelfth canon required every man over fourteen and every women over twelve to abjure heresy every year. The thirteenth canon required them to confess to a priest each year at Easter, Pentecost, and Christmas. The final canon required parish priests to read out the forty-five canons four times a year.[3] "Heretics," preached Hélinard in the closing sermon of the council, "are much worse through apostasy than pagans through idolatry." This sermon was a vivid demonstration of learning suffused with God. He quoted and glossed Euripides, Augustine of Hippo, Jerome, Porphyry, the Stoics, Egyptian priests, Ovid, and Ezekiel. He showed that modern heretics were more than just the descendants of ancient schismatics; they were the heirs of every past demonic sect—up to and including the followers of Muhammad.[4]

"What madness it is, O miserable mortals, to stir up wars!" John of Garland, while opening his epic *De triumphis ecclesiae* with this cry, desperately wanted a war—a great holy war against unbelievers and heretics. He opposed Christians fighting Christians—now that was madness!—not the faithful killing the faithless. Any war against His enemies was just and holy: "It is lawful to repress the unjust with just arms." A crusade that purged Spain and Africa was no different from a crusade that cleansed Jerusalem. Nevertheless, though the followers of Muhammad were wicked, Hydra-headed heretics were worse. "Who can tolerate deceitful heretics?" A war against them was most just, most holy. "Such depravity must be exterminated by scholar, fire, and sword!" He saluted Roland, master of theology at the university, when his colleague dug up a recently buried Waldensian and, dragging the corpse through the streets of Toulouse, burned the remains in the meadow near the Narbonne gate. John surveyed twenty years of holy war and saw only the opening maneuvers of an apocalyptic battle for Christendom. He rejoiced in the slaughter at Muret—happily imagining dead sons, brothers, fathers, and husbands drifting down the Garonne and the womanly lamentations when the bodies arrived in Toulouse—but this victory was nothing compared to victories yet to come. The great fighters in this war were, apart from scholars like himself and Roland, the Dominicans. The Order of Friars Preachers moved into a house in the bourg (with a garden in the city) in 1230.[5] John praised their ardor; they too exhumed dead heretics and incinerated the human dross. Two years later the young grammarian returned to Paris. He blamed Raimon VII for failing to pay his salary. More truthfully, Toulouse was in turmoil due to the fury of the Dominicans; the unrest only intensified when Gregory IX instructed them to be the first inquisitors into heretical depravity in 1233. John escaped Toulouse by sailing north on the Garonne. The boatmen turned on him. He pointed at a shield-shaped cloud and yelled, "Behold the sky denounces war and the heavenly avenger of the Church is not far distant!" The boatmen retreated. The southern skies, notwithstanding heavenly avengers, remained ominously overcast for more than a decade.[6]

On Thursday night, 29 May 1242, the Dominican inquisitor Guilhem Arnaut, the Franciscan inquisitor Esteve de Sant Tuberi, and nine companions were asleep in the castle of the *bayle* of Avignonet. The *bayle* Raimon de Alfaro waited outside the castle doors. He stood in darkness—the moon was a pale sliver—readying himself for murder. Earlier in the day Peire Roger de Mirepoix and a handful of noble thugs galloped north from the castle of Montségur in the Pyrénées. At dusk they reached the hamlet of Gaja-le-Seve. More men joined them, some with axes, others with clubs. Peire Roger remained in Gaja-le-Seve, ostensibly in reserve, while his savage mob bolted across the Lauragais. Around midnight the horsemen dismounted beneath the broken walls of Avignonet and raced up the village street. Raimon greeted them outside the castle and, screaming, shrieking, they smashed the wooden doors with axes. The inquisitors and their companions were butchered in a bloody frenzy. Guilhem and Esteve chanted the *Te Deum* as axes and swords overwhelmed them. "Go well! Be well!" Raimon laughed as he repeatedly clubbed their mangled corpses. One assassin cut out Guilhem's tongue as a souvenir. Another snipped off Arnaut's nose. The castle was ransacked; clothes, letters, inquisitorial registers, a box of ginger, and a fine black horse were seized. The killers swaggered down the street dressed in mendicant robes and, without a care in the world, mounted and rode for Gaja-le-Seve. "Good luck as you go," cheered Raimon. "Where's the cup?" Peire Roger quipped when his men arrived at dawn. "It's broken!" Everyone doubled up. One dolt stared blankly until, chuckling, he realized the cup was Guilhem Arnaut's skull. As Peire Roger and his louts sauntered back to Montségur, they sang of their *estor*, their little war. The *bayle* of Avignonet even spread word that Raimon VII supported the killings. The murderers hoped two decades of humiliation would be reversed in one slaughterous night. It was nostalgia drenched in naïveté and blood. "We're all free," rejoiced na Austorga de Resengas in her village square on the morning after the murders. "We're all dead," murmured her husband. Villagers throughout the Toulousain and Lauragais agreed with both of them.[7]

The Avignonet *estor* was the most pitiful brawl in three years of ill-fated wars against the French and the Church. Raimon II Trencavel, exiled at the court of Aragon for more than a decade, crossed the Pyrénées during the late summer and early autumn of 1240. The nominal viscount of Béziers and Carcassonne hoped to overthrow the *sénéchaux* and *baillis* of Louis IX. As he marched through the Razés a number of *castra* swore loyalty to him. Some nobles from the Carcassès and Minervois joined the insurgency. The royal seneschal sought out Raimon VII. The count was in the village of Pennautier on his way back to Toulouse after a summer harassing (besieging Arles, destroying crops) the count of Provence. The seneschal pleaded for help; Raimon procrastinated, saying he needed more counsel. Meanwhile, the small Trencavel army assaulted Carcassonne, quickly capturing the bourg. A month later the rebels, unable to breach the urban walls, were chased away by an expeditionary force under the royal chamberlain, Jean de Beaumont. The fugitives retreated to Montréal. "Suddenly, there was a great cry that the French had seized the town," na Airmengarta de Cornelha told Bernart de Caux six years later, "and very frightened," she hid in a house with her mother. "I heard it said and cried throughout the market square that Izarn de Vilatraver, my brother, was wounded." Airmengarta ran out of the house and, despite French soldiers pillaging Montréal, searched until Izarn was found. (Incidentally, na Airmengarta was carrying stones to catapults with other noble women just before the French overran the town.)[8] The count of Toulouse—now with an opinion on the uprising—intervened with the count of Foix and arbitrated a compromise. Raimon II Trencavel and his followers retired back over the Pyrénées. The royal chamberlain hunted down lesser *faidits* and hanged them from walnut trees. Two summers later the count of Toulouse chanced a war with the French crown. Hugh de Lusignan, count of La Marche, and Henry III, king of England, were his allies. Victory was assured. Unfortunately, nothing even vaguely victorious happened, and on Monday, 20 October 1242, Louis IX (once again) accepted the unconditional surrender of Raimon VII.[9]

Louis IX, as a consequence of these wars, extracted throughout 1243 and 1244 oaths of obedience, pledges of submission, and promises to accompany him on crusade to the eastern Mediterranean.[10] Raimon VII swore loving fealty and vowed to be signed with the cross. One thousand twenty-eight leading citizens of Toulouse swore to uphold the treaty of Paris.[11] At the end of May 1243 the newly appointed royal seneschal of Carcassonne-Béziers, Hugues d'Acris, marched against the *castel* of Montségur. "It was so strong," wrote Guilhem de Puylaurens, "because of its situation on a very high crag," a granite splinter three hundred meters high, "that it seemed unassailable." Peire Roger de Mirepoix mocked French martial vanity; he told the four hundred men, women, and children crowded on the windy summit that they would survive any siege. Many of these refugees were vagrant good men and good women who, choosing to live as heretics, reluctantly sheltered on this mountain eyrie. All the women were noble and so were most of the men. These holy émigrés still elected (or accepted) the non-noble Bertran Marti as their "bishop." Impoverished *faidits* and noble "believers" accompanied these sacred sentimentalists. Sermons on the futility of existence comforted these exiles. A great trebuchet positioned by the bishop of Albi hurled stones inside the castle. These missiles, though annoying, were easily avoided. Sympathetic villagers climbed with supplies. "For a long time the besiegers could achieve little," until some lightly armed mercenaries, guided by local men, scaled "a terrifying precipitous slope" one wintry night. The mercenaries swiftly captured a small tower on the northeastern edge of the peak. The French ascended and assailed the castle throughout February 1244. Peire Roger, more loudmouth than warrior, begged a compromise. He surrendered the castle and his life was spared. Around two hundred good men, good women, and their believers, abandoned by their valiant protector, were herded into a wooden enclosure and burned. The siege of Montségur was the last—and so the most romanticized—*estor* of a disparate group of noble thugs and holy innocents.[12]

"I fled the land for fear of the *bayles* of the count of Toulouse," Giraut Durant confessed to the inquisition at Saint-Sernin on Saturday, 30 June 1246. The *bayles* "wanted to grab me" two summers ago following an afternoon with two noble good women hiding in the woods near the village of Auriac. Giraut was no more than a boy and, though born after the peace of Paris, he sincerely wanted these furtive *bonas femnas* to be holy. "I believed them to be good women, to be truthful, to be the friends of God, to have good faith, and to have salvation through them." His notion of their sacrality was as earnestly illusory as the gifts he bought them in the woods. "I didn't give them anything," he said, "because I didn't have anything." Nevertheless, this poor dreamy adolescent was being hunted by the *bayles* of Raimon VII on account of his visits with these elderly matrons. After the murders at Avignonet the *bayles* of the count of Toulouse and the *baillis* of the king of France relentlessly searched woods and houses for good men, good women, and *faidits*. Na Nomais de Roveret, testifying a month earlier than Giraut, told Bernart de Caux that the *bayle* of the village of Vaux had recently caged and beaten her into confessing that she once "adored" a good man. "But it wasn't true!" she cried. "It was out of fear that I said so!" The same *bayle* burned her husband as a heretic in the early spring. Young Giraut's good women were caught and incinerated too—but not before telling him that he lived in such an oppressive world that even "God was a fugitive!"[13]

It is a harsh irony that the heresy of the good men investigated by inquisitors like Bernart de Caux, Joan de Sant-Peire, Friar Ferrer, Guilhem Arnaut, and Esteve de Sant-Tuberi after the crusade was no more than atrophied nostalgia for the vivid and distinctive world of the good men before war. The inquisitions into heretical depravity persecuted a heresy of pessimistic sentimentality only two decades old. Bernart de Caux once heard a heretical homily during a confession that illustrated just how woeful the cosmos really was for a good man in 1244. "When God saw His kingdom impoverished through the fall of the evil ones," so a witness heard from a good man, "He asked those standing around, 'Do any of you wish to be my son, and me to be his father?' And as nobody answered, Christ who was God's *bayle* said, 'I want to be your son, and I shall go wherever you send me.' And then God sent Christ as his son into the world to preach God's name," and that was how He came into the world. In this astonishingly poignant story about Christ as a *bayle*, there was neither hope nor salvation, merely the mournful acknowledgment that to be a good man was to exist in a world in which even He wanted to see you suffer and burn.[14]

XVIII

THE ALBIGENSIAN CRUSADE ushered genocide into the West by linking divine salvation to mass murder, by making slaughter as loving an act as His sacrifice on the cross. This ethos of redemptive homicide is what separates the crusade massacres from other great killings before the thirteenth century. A crusader not only cleansed his soul by cutting the throat of a pestilential baker from Toulouse, he cleansed the very soul of Christendom. As horrific as is any bloodshed, past or present, distinctions must be made if a category like genocide is to have any useful historical meaning. First and foremost, it is an irrevocable moral obligation to eliminate specific people from the world who, if not wiped out rather sooner than later, will poison and destroy all human existence. Second, it is a historical vision that these same specific people have always existed through time (often in secret, often behind the scenes) and, while perpetually cancerous to civilization, have only recently begun to threaten the survival of the pure. Third, those deserving to be killed in vast numbers are actually very similar to their committed killers, and it is this similarity that makes them so menacing, so difficult to sort out from the virtuous. Fourth, there is a sense of divine pleasure experienced by mass murderers, a joyful knowledge that the relations between heaven and earth are maintained by the relentless extermination of particular men, women, and children. Fifth, an especially polluted region must be conquered, colonized, and systematically purged of specific people over years, if not decades. Sixth, in the activity of causing widespread death, individuals produce more than just a smile on the godhead, they actually become the godhead themselves. This is a definition of genocide; this is a definition of the Albigensian Crusade.

That this definition closely resembles what it meant to be a medieval Christian after the most holy war is no coincidence. The crusade, far from being a Christian aberration, epitomized the sanguine beauty and bloody savagery of thirteenth-century Latin Christendom. The threat from heresy and the necessity of eliminating that threat were fundamental in creating the Christ-like world that Innocent III struggled all his life to achieve. The ability to resemble Him through day-to-day activity, so much so that you really were Christ, was the sublime religious phenomenon of the Middle Ages. No other monotheistic religion has ever celebrated or promoted such a godly imitative ideal among ordinary believers. The Albigensian Crusade offered the opportunity to walk like Him for twenty years within Europe. It was as crucial as the Fourth Lateran Council in promulgating the notion that anyone could attain this divine gift. The love of Christ necessitated great and small holocausts between the Garonne and the Rhône.

Muslims and Jews never endangered the survival of Christendom in the twelfth and thirteenth centuries in the same apocalyptic way that vulpine heretics did. This was not the case in the century after the Albigensian Crusade. The moral imperative demanding the extermination of heretics through mass murder became the ethical basis for eliminating Muslims and Jews from Christendom. Sermons justified crusades against Islam with the same metaphors and arguments as were once used to justify the most holy war against heresy. "Who is so stupid as to dare say that no one should resist infidels or evil men who desire to wipe out the worship of Christ from the world?" Humbert de Romans, former Dominican Master General, excoriated all who doubted the Saracen threat around 1272. "It is not against God and apostolic teaching for Saracens to be killed by Christians." So, "as these bestial men are touching the mount of the Holy Trinity," as they are cursing all who believe in Him with their Qur'an, "surely they deserve to die?" In fact, "Saracens sinning against the Holy Spirit do not allow His grace to reach them—in other words, they reject His preaching!" Obviously, as Muslims in rejecting Christ were no different from heretics, "they must be removed from the world!" Humbert, "as far as Jews are concerned," was more lenient. "It has been prophesied that in the end the remnant of them [that is, the Jews] will be converted." The followers of Muhammad will never convert, so they must be extinguished. "Jews must be tolerated as there is hope they may convert," so do not expunge them from the world. There was no salvation in slaughtering Jews. Redemption was achieved in killing heretics and Saracens. Eternal glory was attained in yielding and dying for Him. "The aim of Christianity is not to populate the earth but to populate heaven! Why worry if the number of Christians is lessened in the world by deaths endured for God? By this kind of death people make their way to heaven who perhaps would never reach it by another road." Mass murder and mass sacrifice were the bloody wonders of imitating Christ.[1]

Around the same time that Humbert de Romans justified exterminating Muslims from the world through crusade, another Dominican, the Jewish convert Paul Chrétien (formerly Saul of Montpellier), exhorted his Christian audience during a debate with the rabbis of Paris: "They [the Jews] deserve to be killed, just as they killed Him; and woe to those creatures that tolerate them." Paul (labelled "the heretic" in the Hebrew account of the Parisian disputations) decried the Jews for not understanding their own history, for substituting the rabbinic gibberish of the Talmud for the Christ-revealing truth of the Old Testament. "Hear me house of Jacob and all the families of the house of Israel," he exclaimed, "I will exact the very blood of your lives" if you do not renounce your faith. "You are without a faith, a people called *Bougres*, heretics, worthy of being burned!"[2] Jews were the very same pestilential heretics as those expunged by the most holy war. Paul shunned Humbert's view of the Jews; they deserved to be removed from the world as much as (if not more than) Muslims. Of course conversion was merely another way (and frequently no less murderous) of eliminating Jews. A hundred and fifty years later the Jewish historian and cabalist Judah ibn Verga linked the savage Christian violence experienced by Spanish Jews (mass conversions, interrogation by inquisitors, indiscriminate burnings) with the first savage summer of the Albigensian Crusade. The Christian persecution of Jews in the fifteenth century was already predicted (and so explained) by two hundred Jews killed during the infamous immolation of Béziers.[3] Judah was wrong about the Biterrois Jews; he was right about the most holy war. When after 1300 the idea that all time and space had always been Christian and will always be Christian was widely accepted—and Dante's *Commedia* was the most magnificent evocation of this vision—past, present, and future Jews were condemned as immutable heretics denying His eternal suffering. Anti-semiticism (rather anti-Judaism) in the Middle Ages only occurred after the Albigensian Crusade.

A distinct and highly developed Christian culture existed in the lands of the count of Toulouse before the crusaders arrived in 1209. The modern notion of an idyllic world of religious tolerance and lovelorn troubadours barely resembles historical reality. The modern fantasy of Cathars ambling over hill and dale is just plain wrong. The history of Christianity has to be rewritten, jettisoning the fiction of Catharism. The Albigensian Crusade is even more horrific and more pertinent because it was not a martial pilgrimage against a discrete religion with an organized heretical "Church." Innocent III proclaimed a holy war to cleanse the lands between the Garonne and the Rhône of men, women, and children whom he readily acknowledged looked and acted like Christians—that was the trouble. The pestilential deception of heresy—so that diseased individuals frequently did not know they were poisoned—demanded the elimination of "Provençal heretics" before their infection spread throughout Christendom. This initial justification for a campaign of extermination shifted and changed as the crusade lasted twenty summers, though the necessity of removing heretics from the world did not. When the war ended the world that had existed before the coming of the crusaders was no more than a memory. Innocent III, though dead for more than a decade, finally won his battle for Christendom.

The most holy war was only three years old when the ghost Guilhem visited his cousin in 1211, and yet Béziers, Carcassonnne, Lavaur, and a hundred more villages were already soaked in blood and scorched with fire. God's homicidal pleasure lasted another eighteen years. Mountaintop castles were assaulted. *Castrum* after *castrum* was razed to the ground. Young viscounts died of heartache. Counts were humiliated. Toulouse was besieged. Corpses fouled rivers. Great long meandering armies traipsed every summer from the Rhône to the Garonne. Vultures and ravens grew plump. Legates cried out for vengeance. Men died hearing *Veni Creator Spiritus*. Wives and little girls worked catapults. Great cats assaulted battlements. Skulls were crushed. Murder was a path to redemption. Vines and fields were devastated. A pregnant girl was mocked. Good men became heretics. A young count surrendered to a boy king. Inquisitors scoured the countryside. Heretics dangled from walnut trees. Very few who began the war lasted to the end. The world was changed forever.

Glossary

Albigenses
Albigensians

Aparelhamen (old Provençal), *apparellamentum* (Latin)
A "coming together" once a month instituted by some good men and believers after 1220.

Bon ome, bons omes (old Provençal), *bonus homo, boni homines* (Latin)
Good man, good men.

Bona femna, bonas femnas (old Provençal), *bona femina, bone femine* (Latin)
Good woman, good women.

Bona domna, bonas domnas (old Provinçal), *bona domina, bone domine* (Latin)
Good lady, good ladies.

Bolgre, bolgres (old Provençal), *Bougre, Bougres* (old French)
Initially designating a heretic from the archdiocese of Bourges and so another term for Albigensian. After 1220 included heretics from "Bulgaria" and was even used against Jews.

Castrum, castra (Latin)
Fortified village or farm.

Consolamen (old Provençal), *consolamentum* (Latin)
Consolation or comforting by a good man "in the face of death." The early inquisitors into heretical depravity quite deliberately (and confusingly) classified consolations as acts of "heretication."

Cortezia (old Provençal)
Courtliness, courtesy, decorum.

Crezen, crezens (old Provençal), *credens, credentes* (Latin)
Believers of heretics.

Crozat, crozatz (old Provencal), *crucesignatus, crucesignati* (Latin).
Crusader, crusaders.

Eretge, eretges (old Provençal), *hereticus, heretici* (Latin)
Heretic, heretics.

Inquisitiones heretice pravitatis (Latin)
Inquisitions into heretical depravity.

Melhoramen (old Provençal), *melioramen, melioramentum* (Latin)
Melioration—meaning improvement, betterment, perfection, moderation, accumulation of honor, the accretion of wisdom, and the reciprocal process of giving and receiving holiness—was the exemplification of all potential variations of *cortezia.*

Na (old Provençal)
Lady

Ome de paratge, omes de paratge (old Provençal).
Men of honor, nobility, and valor.

Paratge (old Provençal)
Honor, nobility, courtliness, sacred and social perfection.

Prodome, prodomes (old Provençal), *probus homo, probi homines* (Latin)
Prudent (or proven or tested or perfected) man, prudent men.

Provincia (Latin)
The "Province" that included the ecclesiastical province of Narbonne (containing the bishoprics of Toulouse, Carcassonne, Elne, Béziers, Agde, Lodève, Maguelonne, Nîmes, and Uzès), some of Bourges (Albi, Cahors, and Rodez), elements of Arles (Avignon and Orange), with bits of Auch (Couserans), Vienne (Viviers), and Bordeaux (Agenais). *Provincia* embraced what has become modern southern France.

Provinciales (Latin)
Persons from *Provincia.*

Provinciales heretici (Latin)
Provençal heretics.

Salvetat (old Provençal)
Safeguard of Toulouse.

Abbreviations Used in Notes and Bibliography

Albigensian Crusade
Pierre des Vaux-de-Cernay, *The History of the Albigensian Crusade*, trans. by W. A. Sibly and M. D. Sibly (Woodbridge, UK: Boydell Press, 1998).

Chronica
Guilhem de Puylaurens, *Chronica Magistri Guillelmi de Podio Laurentii*, ed. and trans. Jean Duvernoy, Sources d'Histoire Médiévale (Paris: Éditions du Centre National de la Recherche Scientifique, 1976).

Chronicle
Guilhem de Puylaurens, *The Chronicle of William of Puylaurens: The Albigensian Crusade and Its Aftermath*, trans. W. A. Sibly and M. D. Sibly (Woodbridge, UK: Boydell Press, 2003).

Crozada
Guilhem de Tudela and Anonymous Troubadour, *La Chanson de la Croisade Albigeoise (La Canso de la Crozada)*, ed. and trans. Eugène Martin-Chabot, 2nd ed. (Paris: Société d'Édition Les Belles Lettres, 1960).

Crusade
Guilhem de Tudela and Anonymous Troubadour, *The Song of the Cathar Wars: A History of the Albigensian Crusade*, trans. Janet Shirley (Aldershot, UK: Scolar Press, 1996).

Doat
Collection Doat, Bibliothèque nationale, Paris.

HGL

Claude de Vic and Joseph Vaissette, *Histoire Générale de Languedoc avec des notes et les pièces justificatives*, 5 vols. (Paris: J. Vincent, 1730–1745) ; 2nd ed., 16 vols., ed. Auguste Molinier (Toulouse: Édouard Privat, 1882–1904).

Historia Albigensis

Pierre des Vaux-de-Cernay, *Historia Albigensis*, 2 vols., ed. Pascal Guébin and Ernest Lyon, Société de l'Histoire de France (Paris: Librairie Ancienne Honoré Champion, 1926).

Layettes

Layettes du Tresor des chartes, 5 vols, ed. Alexandre Teulet, Joseph de Laborde, Elie Berger, and Henri-François Delaborde (Paris: H. Plon, 1863–1909).

MS 609

MS 609, Bibliothèque municipale, Toulouse.

PL

Patrologiae cursus completus: Series latina, 221 vols., ed. Jacques-Paul Migne (Paris: Garnier Frères, 1844–1904).

RHGF

Recueil des historiens des Gaules et de la France, 24 vols., dir. Léopold Delisle (Paris: [imprint varies], 1869–1904).

Reg. Inn

Die Register Innocenz' III: Texte und Indices, ed. Othmar Hageneder, Andrea Sommerlechner, John C. Moore, and Herwig Weigl, Historischen Instituts beim Österreichischen Kulturinstitut in Rom, 5 volumes to date, numbered according to register year (vols. 1, 2, 5, 6, and 7) (Graz: Verlag der Österreichischen Akademie der Wissenschaften, 1964–1997).

Sacrorum conciliorum

Sacrorum conciliorum nova et amplissima collectio, 54 vols, ed. Joannes Dominicus [Giovan Domenico] Mansi (Florence: Expensis Antonii Zatta, 1759–1798; Paris: H. Welter, 1901–1927).

Notes

Chapter I

1. Gervase of Tilbury, *Otia Imperialia* (Recreation for an Emperor), ed. and trans. S. E. Banks and J. W. Binns (Oxford: Clarendon Press, 2002), III, 103, pp. 759–85, especially p. 779.

2. Ibid., p. 761.

3. The Albigensian Crusade has, somewhat surprisingly, not received the same attention from scholars as crusading to the eastern Mediterranean. See Austin P. Evans, "The Albigensian Crusade," in *A History of the Crusades*, ed. Kenneth M. Setton, Robert Lee Wolff, and Harry W. Hazard (Philadelphia: University of Pennsylvania Press, 1962), 2, pp. 277–324; Pierre Belperron, *La Croisade contre les Albigeois et l'union de Languedoc à la France (1209–1249)* (Paris: Perrin, 1967); Michel Roquebert, *L'épopée Cathare: I 1198–1212: L'invasion* (Toulouse: Privat, 1970), *II 1213–1216: Muret ou la dépossession* (Toulouse: Privat, 1977), *III 1216–1219: Les Lys et La Croix* (Toulouse: Privat, 1986), *IV Mourir à Montségur* (Toulouse: Privat, 1989); Joseph R. Strayer, *The Albigensian Crusades*, with a New Epilogue by Carol Lansing (1971; Ann Arbor: University of Michigan Press, 1992); Walter L. Wakefield, *Heresy, Crusade and Inquisition in Southern France 1100–1250* (London: George Allen & Unwin, 1974); Bernard Hamilton, *The Albigensian Crusade* (London: Historical Association, 1974), and "The Albigensian Crusade and Heresy," in *The New Cambridge Medieval History: V c. 1198–c. 1300*, ed. David Abulafia (Cambridge: Cambridge University Press, 1999), pp. 164–81; Jonathon Sumption, *The Albigensian Crusade* (London: Faber and Faber, 1978); Monique Zerner-Chardavoine, *La Croisade Albigeoise* (Paris: Julliard, 1979); Michael Costen, *The Cathars and the Albigensian Crusade* (Manchester, UK: Manchester University Press, 1997); Jörg

Oberste, *Der "Kreuzzug" gegen die Albigenser: Ketzerei und Machtpolitik im Mittelalter* (Darmstadt, Germany: Primus, 2003); Elaine Graham-Leigh, *The Southern French Nobility and the Albigensian Crusade* (Woodbridge, UK: Boydell Press, 2005); and Laurence W. Marvin, *The Occitan War: A Military and Political History of the Albigensian Crusade, 1209–1218* (Cambridge: Cambridge University Press, 2008). For an excellent bibliography on the Albigensian Crusade (if not so exemplary on heresy), see Marco Meschini, Martín Alvira Cabrer, Martin Aurell, Laurent Macé, Damian J. Smith, and Kay Wagner, "Bibliografia delle crociate albigesi," *Reti Medievali Rivista* 7 (2006): 1–47.

4. *Crozada*, I, laisse 4, p. 14 [*Crusade*, p. 13]; laisse 5, pp. 16–18 [p. 13]; laisse 7, p. 22 [p. 14].

5. *Historia Albigensis*, I, § 55, p. 51 [*Albigensian History*, p. 31]. Innocent III's letter was quoted verbatim in *Historia Albigensis*, I, §§ 55–65, pp. 51–65 [pp. 31–38]. It is edited in PL 215, cols. 1354–58, and *Layettes* I, no. 841. The (almost identical) letters sent to the province of Lyon and to Philip II Augustus are in PL 215, cols. 1358–59.

6. *Historia Albigensis*, I, § 57, p. 52 [p. 31], § 57, p. 53 [p. 32], § 57, p. 54 [p. 32], § 58, p. 54 [p. 32], § 59, pp. 555–56 [p. 33].

7. Ibid., I, § 64, p. 63 [p. 37], § 60, pp. 56–60 [pp. 33–35], § 62, pp. 60–61 [pp. 35–36], p. 61 [p. 36], § 64, pp. 63–65 [pp. 37–38]. Peire de Castelnau's murder was also described by Guilhem de Puylaurens in *Chronica*, ix, p. 52 [*Chronicle*, p. 27] On the various prejudices and talents of Pierre des Vaux-de-Cernay, Guilhem de Puylaurens, and Guilhem de Tudela, see Sibly and Sibly in *Albigensian Crusade*, pp. xix–xlvi, and *Chronicle*, pp. xv–xxxvi; Duvernoy in *Chronica*, pp. 1–20; Martin-Chabot in *Crozada*, I, pp. v–xxxv; Shirley in *Crusade*, pp. 1–10; and Yves Dossat, "La croisade vue par les chroniqueurs," *Cahiers de Fanjeaux: Paix de Dieu et guerre sainte en Languedoc au XIIIe* 4 (1969): 221–59. Generally on sources for the crusade, see Kay Wagner, *Debellare Albigenses : Darstellung und Deutung des Albigenserkreuzzuges in der europäischen Geschichtsschreibung von 1209 bis 1328* (Neuried, Germany: Ars Una, 2000).

Chapter II

1. Rodulfus Glaber, *Historiarum Libri Quinque* (*The Five Books of the Histories*), ed. Neithard Bulst, trans. John France and Paul Reynolds (Oxford: Clarendon Press, 1989), 3.iv.13, pp. 114–17; 2.xii.22, pp. 92–93; 3.vii.24–25, pp. 132–37, for the destruction of the Holy Sepulchre in 1009 through deception by the Jews of Orléans and 1.iv.9, pp. 20–21, for a discussion of the Prophet Mohammad (and see especially p. 21, n. 2, where it is observed that this could be the first mention of Muhammed in northern Europe before 1100); 2.vii.13, pp. 74–75, for the eruption of Vesuvius in 993 or 994; 2.ix.17, pp. 80–82, 4.iv.9–13, pp. 186–93, for famine and hunger; 2.v.8, pp. 64–67, for the weeping crucifix in 988; 2.xi.22, pp. 88–91, on Leutard and the bees in 1000.

2. Ibid., 3.viii.26–31, pp. 139–51, specifically in reference to heresy in Orléans in 1022. See also 2.xii.22, pp. 92–93, for the heretic Vilgardus at Ravenna and on heresies in Sardinia and Spain; and for heresy at Monteforte, 4.ii.5, pp. 176–81.

3. Ademar of Chabannes, *Chronicon*, ed. Pascale Bourgain, Corpus Christianorum. Continuatio Mediaevalis 129 (Turnhout, Belgium: Brepols, 1999), III, 59, p. 180, and III, 46, pp. 165–66 for the vision of the crucifix. See Richard Landes, *Relics, Apocalypse, and the Deceits of History. Ademar of Chabannes, 989–1034* (Cambridge, Mass.: Harvard University Press, 1995), pp. 188–89, and Thomas Head, "Naming Names: The Nomenclature of Heresy in the Early Eleventh Century," in *History in the Comic Mode: Medieval Communities and the Matter of Person*, ed. Rachel Fulton and Bruce W. Holsinger (New York: Columbia University Press, 2007), pp. 91–100.

4. *Historiarum Libri Quinque*, III.viii.28, pp. 142–43, quoting 1 Corinthians 11:19.

5. Fulcher of Chartres, *Historia Hierosolymitana*, ed. Heinrich Hagenmeyer (Heidelberg: C. Winter, 1913), I.3.7, p. 136; translated by Martha McGinty in *The First Crusade*, 2nd ed., ed. Edward Peters (Philadelphia: University of Pennsylvania Press, 1998), pp. 50–53.

6. Ibid., I.3.7, p. 137 [p. 54].

7. On the First Crusade, see Jonathan Riley-Smith, *The First Crusade and the Idea of Crusading* (Philadelphia: University of Pennsylvania Press, 1986); Marcus Bull, *Knightly Piety and the Lay Response to the First Crusade* (Oxford: Clarendon Press, 1993); John France, *Victory in the East: A Military History of the First Crusade* (Cambridge: Cambridge University Press, 1994); Thomas Ashbridge, *The First Crusade: A New History* (Oxford: Oxford University Press, 2004); and Christopher Tyerman, *God's War: A New History of the Crusades* (Cambridge, Mass.: Harvard University Press, 2006), pp. 27–164. On the medieval crusades, see, for example, Carl Erdmann, *The Origin of the Idea of Crusade*, translated by Marshall W. Baldwin and Walter Goffart (Princeton, N.J.: Princeton University Press, 1977); Hans Eberhard Mayer, *The Crusades*, 2nd ed., translated by John Gillingham (Oxford: Clarendon Press, 1988); Carole Hillenbrand, *The Crusades: Islamic Perspectives* (New York: Routledge, 2000); Jean Flori, *La Guerre sainte: La Formation de l'idée de croisade dans l'Occident chrétien* (Paris: Aubier, 2001); Giles Constable, "The Historiography of the Crusades," in *The Crusades from the Perspective of Byzantium and the Muslim World*, ed. Angeliki E. Laiou and Roy Parviz Mottahedeh (Washington, D.C.: Dumbarton Oaks, 2001), pp. 1–22; Jonathan Riley-Smith, *What Were the Crusades?* 3rd ed. (New York: Palgrave Macmillan, 2002); and Christopher Tyerman, *Fighting for Christendom: Holy War and the Crusades* (New York: Oxford University Press, 2004); Paul E. Chevedden, "The Islamic Interpretation of the Crusade: A New (Old) Paradigm for Understanding the Crusades," *Der Islam* 83 (2006): 90–136; and Norman J. Housley, "The Crusades and Islam," *Medieval Encounters* 13 (2007): 189–208.

8. Guibert of Nogent, *Dei gesta per Francos et cinq autres textes*, ed. R. B. C. Huygens, Corpus Christianorum. Continuatio Mediaevalis 127A (Turnholt, Belgium: Brepols, 1996), I.1, p. 87; translated by Robert Levine as *The Deeds of God through the Franks: Gesta Dei per Francos* (Woodbridge, UK: Boydell Press, 1997), 2:28.

9. Gervase of Tilbury, *Otia Imperialia*, III, 90, pp. 734–39.

10. Élie Griffe, "Géographie Ecclésiastique de la province de Narbonnaise au moyen âge," *Annales du Midi* 48 (1938): 363–82.

11. Linda M. Paterson, *The World of the Troubadours: Medieval Occitan Society, c. 1100–c. 1300* (Cambridge: Cambridge University Press, 2003), p. 3.

12. William Chester Jordan, "The Capetians from the Death of Philip II to Philip IV," in *The New Cambridge Medieval History: V c. 1198–c. 1300*, ed. David Abulafia (Cambridge: Cambridge University Press, 1999), pp. 279–313.

13. Marcabru, "Pois l'inverns d'ogan es anatz," in *Marcabru: A Critical Edition*, ed. and trans. Simon Gaunt, Ruth Harvey, and Linda Paterson (Cambridge, UK: D. S. Brewer, 2000), pp. 496–97.

14. *Historia Albigensis*, I, § 9, pp. 8–9 [p. 10].

15. Dante Alighieri, *The Divine Comedy: I Inferno*, trans. Mark Musa (Harmondsworth, UK: Penguin, 2003), IX, p. 152.

16. Caesarius of Heisterbach, *Dialogus Miraculorum*, ed. Joseph Strange (Cologne: H. Lempertz, 1851), I, V, xxi, p. 301; translated by H. von E. Scott and C. C. Swinton Bland as *The Dialogue on Miracles* (London: George Routledge & Sons, 1929) I, V, xxi, p. 345.

17. *Historiarum Libri Quinque*, III.ix.40, pp. 165–69.

18. Gervase of Tilbury, *Otia Imperialia*, III.90, pp. 734–39; preface, pp. 14–15; II.10, pp. 298–99.

19. MS 609, fols. 18v–19r, 29v.

20. For example, Ibid., fol. 129r, for the opening of Pons de Beatueville's testimony on 16 June 1246. See Mark Gregory Pegg, *The Corruption of Angels: The Great Inquisition of 1245–1246* (Princeton, NJ: Princeton University Press, 2001), pp. 45–51.

21. Yves Dossat, *Les crises de l'Inquisition Toulousaine au XIIIe siècle* (Bordeaux: Imprimerie Bière, 1959), pp. 118–21, and his edition of both letters on pp. 325–29.

22. Richard Kieckhefer, "The Office of Inquisition and Medieval Heresy: The Transition from Personal to Institutional Jurisdiction," *Journal of Ecclesiastical History* 46 (1995): 36–61; and Pegg, *The Corruption of Angels*, pp. 32–34. Cf. John Arnold, *Inquisition and Power: Catharism and the Confessing Subject in Medieval Languedoc* (Philadelphia: University of Pennsylvania Press, 2001).

23. MS 609, fols. 180v–181r.

Chapter III

1. *Chronica*, i, p. 22 [p. 7].

2. *Historia Albigensis*, I, § 2, p. 2 [p. 5].

3. Ibid., I, § 8, p. 7 [p. 9], p. 8 [p. 9], § 9, p. 8 [p. 10], § 8, p. 7 [p. 9], § 2, p. 2 [p. 5].

4. *Chronica*, i, pp. 26–29 [pp. 10–11].

5. Bernard of Clairvaux, *Sancti Bernardi Opera VIII: Epistolae*, ed. Jean Leclercq and H. Rochais (Rome: Editions Cistercienses, 1977), Ep. 241, pp. 125–27.

6. *Gesta Pontificum Cenomannensium*, RHGF 12, p. 547.

7. Bernard of Clairvaux, *Sancti Bernardi Opera VIII: Epistolae*, Ep. 241, pp. 126–27.

8. *Vita Prima*, PL 185, col. 313.

9. Bernard of Clairvaux, *Sancti Bernardi Opera VIII: Epistolae*, Ep. 241, p. 126; Ep. 242, pp. 128–29.

10. PL 204, cols. 235–40.

11. *Historia Albigensis*, preface, § 4, pp. 3–4 [p. 6], 1, §§ 10–19, pp. 9–20 [pp. 10–15].

12. *Chronica*, prologue, p. 22, i, p. 24 [pp. 7–8].

13. Geoffroi du Breuil, *Chronicon*, RHGF 12, p. 448.

14. PL 204, cols. 235–40.

15. Geoffroi du Breuil, *Chronicon*, p. 449. Guilhem de Puylaurens's memory of "the Arian" is in *Chronica*, ii, p. 28 [p. 22]. See also Robert of Auxerre, *Chronicon*, ed. Oswald Holder-Egger, Monumenta Germaniae Historica Scriptorum 26 (Stuttgart: Anton Hiersemann Verlag, 1881), p. 245.

16. Geoffroi du Breuil, *Chronicon*, p. 449.

17. On the Cathars, see, for example, Arno Borst, *Die Katharer*. Schriften der Monumenta Germaniae Historica 12 (Deutsches Institut für Erforschung des Mittelalters.) (Stuttgart: Anton Hiersemann Verlag, 1953); Jean Duvernoy, *Le catharisme: La religion des cathares* (Toulouse: Privat, 1976); Bernard Hamilton, "Wisdom from the East: The Reception by the Cathars of Eastern Dualist Texts," in *Heresy and Literacy, 1000–1530*, ed. Anne Hudson and Peter Biller, 38–60. Cambridge Studies in Medieval Literature 23 (Cambridge: Cambridge University Press, 1994), pp. 38–60; Malcolm Lambert, *The Cathars* (Oxford: Blackwell, 1998); Malcolm Barber, *The Cathars: Dualist Heretics in Languedoc in the High Middle Ages* (Harlow, UK: Longman, 2000); Bernard Hamilton, "Introduction," *Hugh Eteriano Contra Patarenos*, ed. and trans. Janet Hamilton and Sarah Hamilton (Leiden: Brill, 2004), pp. 1–102; Claire Taylor, *Heresy in Medieval France: Dualism in Aquitaine and the Agenais, 1000–1249*. Royal Historical Society Studies in History. New Series. (Woodbridge, UK: Royal Historical Society–Boydell Press, 2005). On the Bogomils, see, for example, Dimitri Obolensky, *The Bogomils: A Study in Balkan Neo-Manichaeism* (Cambridge: Cambridge University Press, 1948); Franjo Šanjak, *Les chretiens bosniaques et le movement cathare XIIe–XVe siècles* (Brussels: Editions Nauwelaerts, 1976), and, "Dernières traces de catharisme dans les Balkans," *Cahiers de Fanjeaux: Effacement du Catharisme? (XIIIe-XIVe S.)*, 20 (1985): 119–34. Also see historiographic surveys: Mark Gregory Pegg, "On the Cathars, the Albigensians, and Good Men of Languedoc," *Journal of Medieval History* 27 (2001): 181–95, and "'Catharism' and the Study of Medieval Heresy," *New Medieval Literatures* 6 (2004): 249–69.

18. Yves de Chartres, *Prologue*, ed and trans J. Werckmeister (Paris: Les Éditions du Cerf, 1997), § 31, p. 95; and the eighth canon of the First Council of Nicaea in *Decrees of the Ecumenical Councils*, ed. and trans. Norman P. Tanner (London: Sheed and Ward, 1990), pp. 8–9.

19. Eckbert of Schönau, *Sermones contra Catharos*, PL 195, Sermo 1, cols. 11–19; and the edition of Robert Joyce Harrison in his "Eckbert of Schonau's *Sermones contra Kataros*" (PhD diss., Ohio State University, 1990), 1, pp. 1–24. Borst, *Die Katharer*, p. 240, mistakenly thought Eckbert of Schönau was the first medieval intellectual to note the etymology of *Cathari*. See the superb Uwe Brunn, *Des contestataires aux*

"cathares": Discours de réforme et propagande antihérétique dans les pays du Rhin et de la Meuse avant l'Inquisition (Paris: Institute d'Études Augustiniennes, 2006), pp. 275–364.

20. See, for example, Hrabanus Maurus (c. 780–856), *De institutione clericorum libri tres*, ed. Detlev Zimpel (Frankfurt am Main: Peter Lang, 1996), II, 58, pp. 425–34, especially 429–31; Paschasius Radbertus (786–c. 860), *Expositio in Lamentationes Hieremiae libri quinque*, ed. Beda Paulus, Corpus Christianorum. Continuatio Mediaevalis 85 (Turnhout, Belgium: Brepols, 1988), IV.15, p. 287; Humbert of Silva Candida (c. 1000–1061), *Libri tres adversus simoniacos*, ed. Elaine Golden Robison (PhD diss., Princeton University, 1972), 1.2, p. 12; Peter Damian (c. 1007–1072), *Liber qui appellatur gratissimus*, PL 145, 22, col. 133, *De Sacramentis per improbus administratis*, PL 145, 4, col. 530, and *Die Briefe des Petrus Damiani*, ed. Kurt Reindel (Munich: Monumenta Germaniae Historica, 1983), 1, no. 40, p. 455, 3, no. 146, p. 541; Landulf Senior (d. after 1085), *Landulphi Senioris Mediolanensis historiae libri quatuor*, ed. Alessandro Cutolo, *Rerum Italicarum scriptores* (Bologna: Nicola Zanichelli, 1942), "Epistula ystoriographi," p. 4; Bernold of Constance (d. 1100), *De vitandi excommunicatorum communione de reconciliatione lapsorum*, PL 148, col. 1189, and *Tractatus de reordinatione vitanda, et de salute parvulorum, qui ab excommicatis baptizati sunt*, PL 148, 8, col. 1257; and Peter Lombard (c. 1100–1160), *Commentarius in psalmos Davidicos: Psalmus XXIV*, PL 191, col. 257. See Jan Bremmer, *The Rise and Fall of the Afterlife: The 1995 Read-Tuckwell Lectures at the University of Bristol* (New York: Routledge, 2002), pp. 67–69, 164, for an erudite discussion of heretical nomenclature that nevertheless remains mired in misguided assumptions about "Catharism."

21. Alain de Lille, *De fide catholica liber quatuor*, PL 210, col. 366.

22. Eberwin of Steinfeld, Ep. 472, PL 182, cols. 676–80; and Bernard of Clairvaux, *Sancti Bernardi Opera II: Sermones super Cantica Canticorum 36–86*, ed. Jean Leclercq, C. H. Talbot, and H. Rochais (Rome: Editions Cistercienses, 1958), Sermo 65, pp. 172–77. Both are translated in *Heresies of the High Middle Ages: Selected Sources Translated and Annotated*, ed. Walter Leggett Wakefield and Austin P. Evans (New York: Columbia University Press, 1991), pp. 126–38.

23. Wibald of Corvey, Ep. 167, in *Monumenta Corbeiensia*, ed. Philip Jaffé, Bibliotheca Rerum Germanicarum (Berlin: Weidmann, 1864), 1, p. 278.

24. John of Ford, *Super Extremam Partem Cantici Canticorum Sermones CXX*, ed. Edmund Mikkers and Hilary Costello, Corpus Christianorum. Continuatio Mediaevalis 18 (Turnholt, Belgium: Brepols, 1970), 2, Sermo 85, pp. 580–86, especially 582–83; translated by Wendy Mary Beckett in *Sermons on the Final Verses of the Song of Songs* (Kalamazoo, MI: Cistercian Publications, 1984), 6, pp. 21–35, especially 26–29.

25. MS 609, fols. 45v, 22r, 157v.

26. *Historia Albigensis*, 1, § 13, pp. 13–14 [p. 12].

27. Paul Ourliac, "Juges et justiciables au XIe siècle: Les *boni homines*," *Recueil de mémoires et trauvaux publié par la Société d'histoire du droit et des institutions des anciens pays de droit écrit* 16 (1994): 17–33.

28. Pegg, *The Corruption of Angels*, pp. 95–96.

29. Monique Bourin-Derreau, *Villages médiévaux en bas-Languedoc: Genèse d'une sociabilité (Xe–XIVe siècle)* (Paris: L'Harmattan, 1987) 1, pp. 315–26, details the return of the *boni homines* and *probi homines*; John Hine Mundy, *Liberty and Political Power in Toulouse 1050–1230* (New York: Columbia University Press, 1954), p. 32, and Mundy, *Society and Government at Toulouse in the Age of the Cathars* (Toronto: Pontifical Institute of Medieval Studies, 1997), appendix 4, p. 386, for the names of these *probihomines de Tolosa et burgo*.

Chapter IV

1. Marcabru, "Cortesamen vuoill comensar," in *Marcabru: A Critical Edition*, pp. 202–3.

2. On this incredibly complex issue of land tenure, see, for example, Bourin-Derruau, *Villages médiévaux en bas-Languedoc*; Aline Durand, *Les paysages medievaux du Languedoc: Xe–XIIe siècles*, 2nd ed. (Toulouse: Presses universitaires du Mirail, 2003); Hélène Débax, *La féodalité languedocienne XIe–XIIe siècles: Serments, hommages et fiefs dans le Languedoc des Trencavel* (Toulouse: Presses universitaires du Mirail, 2003); and Fredric L. Cheyette, *Ermangard of Narbonne and the World of the Troubadours* (Ithaca, NY: Cornell University Press, 2001), especially pp. 127–68.

3. *Chronica*, prologue, p. 24 [p. 8]

4. *Cartulaires des Templiers de Douzens*, ed. Pierre Gérard, Élisabeth Magnou, and Philippe Wolff (Paris: Bibliothèque Nationale, 1965), A, no. 8, pp. 18–19. See Malcolm Barber, "The Templar Preceptory of Douzens (Aude) in the Twelfth Century," in *The World of Eleanor of Aquitaine: Literature and Society in Southern France between the Eleventh and Thirteenth Centuries*, ed. Marcus Bull and Catherine Léglu (Woodbridge, UK: Boydell Press, 2005), pp. 37–56.

5. Marcabru, "Lo vers comens cant vei del fau," in *Marcabru: A Critical Edition*, pp. 420–21.

6. Marcabru, "Lo vers comenssa," in *Marcabru: A Critical Edition*, pp. 404–5.

7. MS 609, fols. 225r, 159r.

8. Ibid., fol. 159r.

9. Ibid., fols. 55v, 20r, 184r, 57r.

10. Ibid., fols. 143v–144r, 143v, 85v.

11. Ibid., fol. 184v.

12. Arnaut Daniel, "Si.m fos amors de joi donar tant larga," in *The Poetry of Arnaut Daniel*, ed. and trans. James J. Wilhelm (New York: Garland, 1981), 17, pp. 72–73.

13. Marcabru, "Dirai vos e mon latin," in *Marcabru: A Critical Edition*, XVII, pp. 230–31.

14. For example, MS 609, fol. 237r.

15. Ibid., fols. 133v, 120r, 20v, 184v.

16. *Historia Albigensis*, 1, § 13, p. 14 [p. 12].

17. Jacqueline Caille, *Medieval Narbonne: A City at the Heart of the Troubadour World* (Aldershot, UK: Ashgate, 2005), pp. 17–18. The kermes insect (*Kermes ilicis*) thrived on the leaves of the holm oaks that grew between the Garonne and the

Rhône. Woad (*Isatis tinctoria*) is an herb of the mustard family and was cultivated in the Lauragais and Albigeois. See William F. Leggett, *Ancient and Medieval Dyes* (Brooklyn: Chemical Publishing Co., 1944), pp. 31–41, 69–82.

18. *Historia Albigensis*, 1, § 17, p. 18 [p. 14].

19. On Cistercian avoidance of birdflesh, see Giles Constable, *The Reformation of the Twelfth Century* (Cambridge: Cambridge University Press, 1998), p. 187.

20. See the collected articles on food and cooking utensils between the Garonne and Rhône in the Middle Ages in *Dossier Spécial: Cusine Médiévale: Archéologie du Midi Medieval*, nos. 15–16 (1997–1998): 135–340.

21. On food as gifts to the good men, see Pegg, *The Corruption of Angels*, pp. 114–18.

22. *Historia Albigensis*, 1, § 13, pp. 13–14 [p. 12].

23. *Cartulaires des Templiers de Douzens*, A, no. 6, pp. 15–16.

24. MS 609, fols. 11v, 14v.

25. Ibid., fols. 133v, 198r.

26. *Historia Albigensis*, 1, §§ 20–24, pp. 21–27 [p. 18].

27. Marcabru, "Per savi teing ses doptanza," in *Marcabru: A Critical Edition*, XXXVII, pp. 466–69.

28. Girault de Borneil, "La flors el vergan," in *The* Cansos *and* Sirventes *of the Troubadour Girault de Borneil: A Critical Edition*, ed. and trans. Ruth Verity Sharman (Cambridge: Cambridge University Press, 1989), XXVIII, pp. 168–72. See also Linda M. Paterson, *Troubadours and Eloquence* (Oxford: Oxford University Press, 1975), pp. 88–144.

29. Girault de Borneil, "Si.m sentis fizels amics," in *The* Cansos *and* Sirventes *of the Troubadour Girault de Borneil: A Critical Edition*, XXX, pp. 181–85.

30. Girault de Borneil, "La flors el vergan," in *The* Cansos *and* Sirventes *of the Troubadour Girault de Borneil: A Critical Edition*, XXVIII, pp. 168–69, 172.

31. Girault de Borneil, "A penas sai comenssar," in *The* Cansos *and* Sirventes *of the Troubadour Girault de Borneil: A Critical Edition*, XXXIII, pp. 196–97.

32. Giles Constable, "The Language of Preaching in the Twelfth Century," *Viator* 25 (1994): 131–52, especially 139, 146, and 152. See David d'Avray, *Medieval Marriage Sermons: Mass Communication in a Culture without Print* (Oxford: Oxford University Press, 2001), pp. 1–30.

33. *Acta concilii Lumbariensis*, RHGF 14, pp. 430–434 [*Heresies of the High Middle Ages*, pp. 189–94].

34. *Chronicon universale anonymi Laudunensis*, ed. Georg Waitz, Monumenta Germaniae Historica Scriptores 26 (Stuttgart: Anton Hiersemann Verlag, 1881), pp. 447–49 [*Heresies of the High Middle Ages*, pp. 200–202].

35. Walter Map, *De nugis curialium*, ed. Montague R. James (Oxford: Oxford University Press, 1914), pp. 60–62 [*Heresies of the High Middle Ages*, pp. 203–4].

36. *Chronicon universale anonymi Laudunensis*, p. 449 [p. 203].

37. *Corpus Iuris Canonici*, ed. Aemilius Friedberg (Leipzig: B. Tauchnitz, 1879; reprint Graz: Akademische Druck-u. Verlagsanstalt, 1959), 2, cols. 780–82.

38. Étienne de Bourbon, *Anecdotes Historiques. Légendes et Apologues tirés du recueil inédit d'Etienne de Bourbon, Dominicain du XIIIe siècle*, ed. Richard Albert Lecoy de la

Marche (Paris: Librairie Renouard, 1877), IV, p. 293 [*Heresies of the High Middle Ages*, p. 210]. See Peter Biller, "Goodbye to Waldensianism?" *Past and Present* 192 (2006): 3–33.

39. MS 609, fol. 120r.

40. Girault de Borneil, "Nos.s pot sufrir ma lenga q'ill non dia," in *The* Cansos *and* Sirventes *of the Troubadour Girault de Borneil: A Critical Edition*, LXVIII, pp. 439–41.

41. See especially Giles Constable, *Three Studies in Medieval Religious and Social Thought* (Cambridge, UK: Cambridge University Press, 1998), pp. 143–248.

42. Bernard of Clairvaux, *Sancti Bernardi Opera V: Sermones II*, ed. Jean Leclercq and H. Rochais (Rome: Editions Cistercienses, 1972), *Serm. in natali s. Benedicti*, pp. 7–8.

43. Ibid., *Serm. 2 in die Pentecostes*, p. 168.

44. Bernard of Clairvaux, *Sancti Bernardi Opera II: Sermones super Cantica Canticorum 36–86*, Serm. 66, p. 185, translated by Killian Walsh and Irene M. Edmonds in *On the Song of Songs III* (Kalamazoo, MI: Cistercian Publications, 1979), p. 202

Chapter V

1. Gervase of Canterbury, *Chronicle of the Reigns of Stephen, Henry II, and Richard I*, ed. William Stubbs, Rolls Ser. 73 (London: Longman, 1879), 1, pp. 269–71.

2. Robert of Torigni, *Chronica*, in *Chronicles of the Reigns of Stephen, Henry II and Richard I*, ed. Richard Howlett, Rolls Ser. 82 (London: Eyre and Spottiswoode, 1889), 4, p. 255; Geoffroi du Breuil, *Chronicon*, RHGF 12, p. 443; Roger of Howden, *Gesta regis Henrici Secundi Benedicti Abbati*, ed. William Stubbs, Rolls Ser. 49 (London: Longmans, Green, Reader, and Dyer, 1867), 1, pp. 35–36; Ralph of Diceto, *Opera Historica*, ed. William Stubbs, Rolls Ser. 68 (London: Longman, 1876), 1, pp. 353–54; and Ralph of Coggeshall, *Chronicon Anglicanum*, ed. Joseph Stevenson, Rolls Ser. 66 (London: Longman, 1875), p. 17. See Richard Benjamin, "A Forty Years War: Toulouse and the Plantagenets, 1156–96," *Historical Research* 61 (1988): 270–85, especially 274–76; Nicholas Vincent, "England and the Albigensian Crusade," in *England and Europe in the Reign of Henry III (1216–1272)*, ed. Björn Weiler and Ifor Rowlands (Aldershot, UK: Ashgate, 2002), pp. 67–71; and R. I. Moore, "Les Albigeois d'apres les chroniques Angevines," in *La Croisade Albigeoise: Actes du Colloque du Centre d'Études Cathares Carcassonne, 4,5, et 6 Octobre 2002* (Balma, France: Imprimerie des Capitouls, 2004), pp. 81–90.

3. Benjamin, "A Forty Years War," 270.

4. RHGF 16, pp. 158–59.

5. Cheyette, *Ermangard of Narbonne*, pp. 253–343, especially p. 274.

6. *Liber feudorum maior: Cartulario real que se conserva en el Archivo de la Corona de Aragón*, ed. Francisco Miguel Rosell (Barcelona: Es Propiedad, 1955), 2, n. 854, pp. 329–30.

7. HGL 8, cols. 341–44.

8. Epistola 73, PL 211, cols. 371–72; and see Epistola 75, PL 211, col. 375.

9. *Decrees of the Ecumenical Councils*, pp. 211–25, especially pp. 211, 224–25.

10. HGL 6, pp. 19–21.

11. William of Newburgh, *Historia Rerum Anglicarum*, in *Chronicles of the Reigns of Stephen, Henry II and Richard I*, ed. Richard Howlett, Rolls Ser. 82 (London: Longman, 1885), 2, p. 491.

12. Thomas N. Bisson, *Medieval France and Her Pyrenean Neighbours: Studies in Early Institutional History* (London: Hambledon Press, 1989), pp. 215–36.

13. *Historia Albigensis*, 1, § 27, pp. 30–31 [p. 21].

14. 29 May 1207, PL 215, cols. 1166–68; and RHGF 13 p. 140.

15. *Crozada*, 1, laisses 7–8, pp. 20–25 [p. 14]. The letter was probably the one dated 28 March 1208, *Layettes*, 1, no. 843.

16. *Crozada*, 1, laisse 8, p. 22 [p. 14].

17. Bertran de Born, "Ges de far sirventes no.m tartz," in *The Poems of the Troubadour Bertran de Born*, ed. and trans William D. Paden, Tilde Sankovitch, and Patricia H. Ståblein (Berkeley: University of California Press, 1986), pp. 250–51.

18. Bertran de Born, "Be.m plai lo gais temps de pasor," in *The Poems of the Troubadour Bertran de Born*, pp. 338–43.

19. Bertran de Born, "Un sirventes on motz non faill," in *The Poems of the Troubadour Bertran de Born*, pp. 122–23.

20. Bertran de Born, "Gerr'e trebailh vei et afan," in *The Poems of the Troubadour Bertran de Born*, pp. 460–61.

21. Dante Alighieri, *De vulgari eloquentia*, ed. and trans. Steven Botterill (Cambridge: Cambridge University Press, 1996), pp. 52–53.

22. Bertran de Born. "Gerr'e trebailh vei et afan," in *The Poems of the Troubadour Bertran de Born*, pp. 460–61.

23. Ibid.

24. Paul Ourliac, *Études d'histoire du droit médiéval* (Paris: A. et J. Picard, 1979), pp. 243–52; and Élisabeth Magnou-Nortier, "La foi et les *convenientiae.* Enquête lexicographique et interprétation sociale," in *Littérature et société au Moyen Âge: Actes du colloque des 5 et 6 mai 1978* (Amiens: Université de Picardie, 1978), pp. 249–62. See Adam J. Kosto, *Making Agreements in Medieval Catalonia: Power, Order, and the Written Word, 1000–1200* (Cambridge: Cambridge University Press, 2001), pp. 19–23.

25. *The Canso d'Antioca: An Occitan Epic Chronicle of the First Crusade*, ed. and trans. Carol Sweetenham and Linda M. Paterson (Aldershot, UK: Ashgate, 2003), pp. 218–19, where the poet (who may or may not have been Gregory Bechada) had Ademar, bishop of le Puy and legate of the First Crusade, end a sermon with these rousing words.

26. *Crozada*, 1, laisse 1, pp. 8–9 [p. 11].

27. Dante Alighieri, *The Divine Comedy: I Inferno*, XXVIII, pp. 325–29.

28. C. 23 q. 2 d. p. c. 2, *Decretum Gratiani* in *Corpus Iuris Canonici*, 1, col. 895. On Gratian, see John T. Noonan, "Gratian Slept Here: The Changing Identity of the Father of the Systematic Study of Canon Law," *Traditio* 35 (1979): 145–72, and Anders Winroth, *The Making of Gratian's Decretum* (Cambridge: Cambridge University Press, 2000), pp. 1–32. On Augustine of Hippo and just war, see Robert A. Markus, "Saint Augustine's Views on the 'Just War,' " in *The Church and War*, ed. W. J. Shiels, Studies in Church History 20 (Oxford: Basil Blackwell, 1983), pp. 1–15.

29. C. 24 q. 3 c. 26, *Decretum Gratiani*, col. 997; and see C. 24 q. 3 c. 27–29, cols. 997–98. See Winroth's discussion of Causa 24 in his *The Making of Gratian's Decretum*, pp. 34–76.

30. Dante Alighieri, *The Divine Comedy: III Paradise*, trans. Mark Musa (Harmondsworth, UK: Penguin, 2003), X, p. 122.

31. In general, see Causa 23 of Pars Secunda of the *Decretum Gratiani*, cols. 889–965. See Frederick H. Russell, *The Just War in the Middle Ages* (Cambridge: Cambridge University Press, 1975), pp. 55–85, and H. E. J. Cowdrey, "Christianity and Morality of Warfare during the First Century of Crusading," in *The Experience of Crusading: Western Approaches*, ed. Marcus Bull and Norman Housley (Cambridge: Cambridge University Press, 2003), i, pp. 175–92, especially 186–87.

32. PL 214, cols. 537–39; and *Regesta Pontificum Romanorum*, ed. Augustus Potthast (Berlin: Decker, 1874) i, no. 643, p. 61. See Walter Ullmann, "The Significance of Innocent III's Decretal (Vergentis)," in *Études d'histoire de droit canonique dédiées à Gabriel le Bras*, ed. Pierre Petot (Paris: Sirey, 1965) i, pp. 729–41; and Othmar Hageneder, "Studien zur Dekretale 'Vergentis' (X.V.7.10): Ein Beitrag zur Häretikergesetzgebung Innocenz III," *Zeitschrift der Savigny-Stiftung für Rechtsgeschichte* 49 (1963): 138–73. Graham-Leigh, *The Southern French Nobility and the Albigensian Crusade*, pp. 68–69, discusses the pope's letter to Viterbo and notes that according to the seventeenth-century Toulousain historian Pierre Gabriel, *Series praesulum Magalonensium et Monspeliensium* (Toulouse: Jean Boude, 1665), pp. 267–68, the clause dispossessing all descendants was excised when a version of the letter accompanied the cardinal-legate Giovanni di Santa Prisca during a visit to Provincia in 1200.

33. *Codex Diplomaticus Regni Croatiae, Dalmatiae et Slavoniae*, ed. T. Smiciklas (Zagreb: Officina Societatis Typographicae, 1905), 3, pp. 14–15.

34. C. 24 q. 3 c. 39, *Decretum Gratiani*, col. 1002; and Isidore of Seville, *Isidori Hispalensis Episcopi Etymologiarum sive Originum Libri XX*, ed. W. M. Lindsay (Oxford: Oxford University Press, 1911), VIII.v.28; translated by Stephen A. Barney, as *The Etymologies of Isidore of Seville* (Cambridge: Cambridge University Press, 2006), VIII.v.22, p. 176.

35. Reg. Inn. 1: 336, in *Contemporary Sources for the Fourth Crusade*, ed. and trans. Alfred J. Andrea (Leiden: Brill, 2000), pp. 9–19. On the Third Crusade, see Tyerman, *God's War*, pp. 341–477.

36. Reg. Inn. 8: 134, in *Contemporary Sources for the Fourth Crusade*, pp. 168–76. On Zara and the Fourth Crusade, see Alfred J. Andrea and Ilona Motsiff, "Pope Innocent III and the Diversion of the Fourth Crusade Army to Zara," *Byzantinoslavica* 33 (1972): 11–18; Othmar Hageneder, "Innozenz III. unde die Eroberung Zadars (1202): Ein Neuinterpretation des Br. V 160 (161)," *Mitteilungen des Instituts für österreichische Geschichtsforschung* 100 (1992): 197–213; and Thomas F. Madden, *Enrico Dandolo and the Rise of Venice* (Baltimore: Johns Hopkins University Press, 2003), pp. 133–54. On Constantinople and the Fourth Crusade, see Donald E. Queller and Thomas F. Madden, *The Fourth Crusade: The Conquest of Constantinople* (Philadelphia: University of Pennsylvania Press, 1997), pp. 119–205; Jonathan Phillips, *The Fourth Crusade and the Sack of Constantinople* (London: Jonathan Cape, 2004),

pp. 127–280; Alfred J. Andrea, "Innocent III, the Fourth Crusade, and the Coming Apocalypse," in *The Medieval Crusade*, ed. Susan J. Ridyard (Woodbridge, UK: Boydell Press, 2004), pp. 97–106; and Tyerman, *God's War*, 447–562. Cf. Bernard Hamilton, "The Albigensian Crusade and the Latin Empire of Constantinople," in *Urbs Capta: The Fourth Crusade and Its Consequences*, ed. Angeliki Laiou (Paris: Lethielleux, 2005), pp. 335–44.

37. PL 215, cols. 361–62.

38. HGL 8, cols. 558–59.

39. PL 215, cols. 1469–70.

40. PL 217, col. 658.

41. *Historia Albigensis*, 1, § 61, p. 60 [p. 35].

Chapter VI

1. PL 215, cols. 1545–46; the pope's letter is dated Tuesday, 3 February 1209.

2. On the church doors of Saint-Gilles, see Richard Hamann, *Deutsche und französische Kunst im Mittelalter* (Marburg a. Lahn: Kunstgeschichtliches Seminar, 1923), pp. 1–9; and M. C. Maguelone, "Les ports de Saint-Gilles au moyen âge," part 1, *Cahiers d'études cathares* 33 (1982): 42–60, and part 2, 34 (1983): 15–38, 43–65, and 77–79.

3. All the accusations against Raimon VI and the mandates of Arnau Amalric imposed on the count were recorded as *Processus negotii Raymundi Comitis Tolosani*, PL 216, cols. 89–98.

4. On these events, see *Historia Albigensis*, 1, §§ 67–81, pp. 65–81 [pp. 38–46], and *Crozada*, 1, laisse 10–11, pp. 30–33 [pp. 15–16].

5. *Historia Albigensis*, 1, § 82, pp. 81–82 [pp. 45–47], and *Crozada*, 1, laisses 8–13, pp. 22–41 [pp. 14–17]. Cf. Walter L. Wakefield, *Heresy, Crusade and Inquisition in Southern France 1100–1250* (London: George Allen & Unwin, 1974), p. 112 n. 1.

6. *Crozada*, 1, laisses 13–14, pp. 38–44 [pp. 17–18].

7. *Historia Albigensis*, 1, § 82, pp. 81–82 [p. 47], and *Crozada*, 1, laisse 13, pp. 36–40 [p. 15].

8. *Crozada*, 1, laisse 8, p. 24 [p. 14], and Jacques de Vitry, Sermons 1 and 2, in *Crusade Propaganda and Ideology: Model Sermons for the Preaching of the Cross*, ed. and trans. Christoph T. Maier (Cambridge: Cambridge University Press, 2000), pp. 83–127, especially pp. 86–87, 88–89, 94–95, 124–27.

9. On the needs of men and animals during medieval campaigns, see John H. Pryor, "Introduction: Modelling Bohemond's March to Thessalonike," in *Logistics of Warfare in the Age of the Crusades: Proceedings of a Workshop Held at the Centre for Medieval Studies, University of Sydney, 30 September to 4 October 2002*, ed. John H. Pryor (Aldershot, UK: Ashgate, 2006), pp. 1–24, and John Haldon, 'Roads and Communications in the Byzantine Empire: Wagons, Horses, and Supplies," in Pryor, *Logistics of Warfare*, pp. 131–58. These are both remarkable essays.

10. HGL 8, no. 132.

11. On Pere II and Maria de Montpellier, see Damian J. Smith, *Innocent III and the Crown of Aragon: The Limits of Papal Authority* (Aldershot, UK: Ashgate, 2004),

pp. 39–40, 70–74. On Montpellier, see Kathryn L. Reyerson, *The Art of the Deal: Intermediaries of Trade in Medieval Montpellier* (Leiden: Brill, 2002), especially 47–78.

12. *Historia Albigensis*, I, § 83, p. 86 [p. 48].

13. *Crozada*, I, laisse II, pp. 30–33 [p. 16].

14. Jacques de Vitry, Sermon 2, in *Crusade Propaganda and Ideology*, pp. 126–27.

Chapter VII

1. PL 216, cols. 137–38 [*Chronicle,* as appendix A, p. 127]. This letter from late August 1209 was Arnau Amalric and Milo's report to Innocent III on the crusade's first two months.

2. *Crozada*, I, laisse 18, pp. 52–53 [p. 20].

3. PL 216, col. 138 [*Chronicle,* p. 127].

4. *Crozada*, I, laisse 15, pp. 44–47 [pp. 18–19], and *Historia Albigensis*, I, §§ 84–88, p. 86–89 [pp. 48–50].

5. Henri Vidal, *Episcopatus et pouvoir épiscopal à Béziers à la veille de la Croisade Albigeoise 1152–1209* (Montpellier: n.p., 1951), pp. 20–32; and Graham-Leigh, *The Southern French Nobility and the Albigensian Crusade*, pp. 63, 144.

6. *Crozada*, I, laisses 16–17, pp. 48–53 [p. 19], and *Historia Albigensis*, I, § 89, p. 90 [p. 50].

7. *Crozada*, I, laisse 17, pp. 50–53 [p. 19].

8. *Crozada*, I, laisses 18–19, pp. 52–55 [p. 20], and *Historia Albigensis*, I, § 90 p. 91 [p. 50].

9. *Crozada*, I, laisses 19–21, pp. 54–59 [pp. 20–21].

10. Ibid., I, laisses 22–23, pp. 60–65 [pp. 21–22].

11. Caesarius of Heisterbach, *Dialogus Miraculorum*, I, V, xxi, p. 302 [*The Dialogue on Miracles*, I, pp. 345–46].

12. *Glossa ordinaria* to the *Decretum*, ed. Augustin Caravita and Prosper Caravita (Venice: Apud Iuntas, 1605), C. 23 q. 5 c. 32 ad v. *omnes.* See James A. Brundage, "Holy War and the Medieval Lawyers," in *The Holy War,* ed. Thomas Patrick Murphy (Columbus: Ohio State University Press, 1976), pp. 99–140, especially pp. 123 and 139 n. 167.

13. PL 216, cols. 138–39 [*Chronicle,* pp. 127–128].

14. *Historia Albigensis*, I, § 91 p. 93 [p. 51].

Chapter VIII

1. *Crozada*, I, laisse 23, pp. 62–64 [p. 22]. On the submission of Narbonne, see Guillaume de Catel, *Mémoires de histoire de Languedoc* (Toulouse: Arnaud Colomiez, 1633), p. 792, and Graham-Leigh, *The Southern French Nobility and the Albigensian Crusade*, pp. 52–53.

2. *Crozada*, I, laisses 23–24, pp. 62–65 [p. 22], and *Historia Albigensis*, I, § 93, p. 95 [p. 52].

3. Lucy MacClintock, "Monumentality versus Suitability: Viollet-le-Duc's Saint Gimer at Carcassonne," *Journal of the Society of Architectural Historians* 40

(1981): 218–35, especially 219–22. On Viollet-le-Duc's architectural theories, see Millard Fillmore Hearn, "Viollet-le-Duc: A Visionary among the Gargoyles," in his *The Architectural Theory of Viollet-le-Duc: Readings and Commentary* (Cambridge, MA: MIT Press, 1990), pp. 1–19, and Yves-Marie Froidevaux, "Viollet le Duc restaurateur et son influence," in *Actes du Colloque International Viollet le Duc*, Paris 1980, ed. Pierre-Marie Auzas (Paris: Nouvelles Editions Latines, 1982), pp. 145–51.

4. On the crossbow, see Alan Williams, *The Knight and the Blast Furnace: A History of the Metallurgy of Armour in the Middle Ages and the Early Modern Period* (Leiden: Brill, 2003), pp. 919–20.

5. *Historia Albigensis*, I, §§ 94–95, p. 95–96 [p. 52].

6. On petraries, trebuchets, and other catapults, see Paul E. Chevedden, "The Invention of the Counterweight Trebuchet: A Study in Cultural Diffusion," *Dumbarton Oaks* 54 (2000): 71–116, and David Stewart Bachrach, "English Artillery 1189–1307: The Implications of Terminology," *English Historical Review* 121 (2006): 1408–30.

7. *Crozada*, I, laisse 25, pp. 66–69 [p. 23], and *Historia Albigensis*, I, § 96, pp. 96–98 [p. 53].

8. *Crozada*, I, laisses 25–26, pp. 66–69 [p. 23], and *Historia Albigensis*, I, § 97, pp. 98–99 [pp. 53–54].

9. *Crozada*, I, laisses 26–30, pp. 68–77 [pp. 23–24].

10. *Crozada*, I, laisses 25, 30, pp. 66–67, 74–77 [pp. 24–25], and *Historia Albigensis*, I, § 98, p. 99 [p. 54].

11. *Crozada*, I, laisses 31–33, pp. 76–83 [pp. 25–26]; *Historia Albigensis*, I, §§ 98–99, pp. 99–100 [pp. 54–55]; *Chronica*, xiv, p. 62 [p. 34]; and PL 216, CVIII, col. 139 [*Chronicle*, p. 128].

12. *Crozada*, I, laisses 33–35, pp. 80–89 [pp. 26–27]; *Historia Albigensis*, I, §§ 100–107, pp. 100–111 [pp. 55–59]; *Chronica*, xiv, p. 62 [p. 34]; and PL 216, CVIII, col. 139 [*Chronicle*, pp. 128–29].

13. *Crozada*, I, laisse 34, p. 84 [p. 26]; *Historia Albigensis*, I, §§ 108–11, pp. 112–16 [pp. 59–62]; and MS 609, fols. 160r–160v.

14. *Historia Albigensis*, I, §§ 112–13, pp. 116–18 [pp. 62–63].

15. *Crozada*, I, laisses 36, p. 88 [p. 27]; *Historia Albigensis*, I, §§ 114–15, pp. 118–19 [pp. 63–64]; and PL 216, CIX, col. 141. On Cabaret, see Marie-Élise Gardel, ed., *Cabaret: Histoire et Archeologie d'un Castrum. Les Fouilles du site médiéval de Cabaret à Lastours (Aude)* (Carcassonne, France: CVPM, 1999).

16. PL 216, CVIII, col. 141 [*Chronicle*, p. 129].

17. *Historia Albigensis*, I, § 109, pp. 113–114 [p. 60]. On the views of Innocent III and continuous holy war, see PL 215, CCXXXII–CXXXIII, cols. 1546–47.

18. PL 216, CVIII, col. 141 [*Chronicle*, p. 129].

Chapter IX

1. *Crozada*, I, laisse 39, pp. 96–98 [p. 29]. On the "greater good men" and the consulate of Toulouse, see Mundy, *Liberty and Political Power in Toulouse*, pp. 30–73,

149–58; and Mundy, *Society and Government at Toulouse*, appendix 4, pp. 391–416, for lists of all the consuls from 1189 until 1280.

2. On the parishes of Toulouse, see John H. Mundy, "The Parishes of Toulouse from 1150 to 1250," *Traditio* 46 (1991): 171–204; and Mundy, *Liberty and Political Power in Toulouse*, p. 127.

3. PL 216, CVII, cols. 126–28, and *Historia Albigensis*, 1, § 138–39, pp. 143–45 [p. 76].

4. Gervase of Tilbury, *Otia Imperialia*, III, 25, pp. 606–7.

5. *Crozada*, 1, laisse 43, p. 106 [p. 31]; *Historia Albigensis*, 1, §§ 137–40, pp. 140–46 [pp. 74–77]; and PL 216, CLIII, col. 173 [Albigensian Crusade, pp. 306–7].

6. *Crozada*, 1, laisse 41, pp. 100–104 [pp. 29–30]; *Historia Albigensis*, 1, §§ 116–20, pp. 120–24 [pp. 64–66]; and PL 216, CIX, col. 141.

7. *Historia Albigensis*, 1, § 121, pp. 124–25 [pp. 67–68].

8. *Crozada*, 1, laisse 41, pp. 102–4 [p. 30], and *Historia Albigensis*, 1, §§ 122–36, pp. 125–40 [pp. 68–74].

9. *Crozada*, 1, laisse 40, p. 100 [p. 29], and HGL 5, col. 36.

10. *Historia Albigensis*, 1, §§ 146–50, pp. 151–54 [pp. 80–82].

11. John Hine Mundy, *Studies in the Ecclesiastical and Social History of Toulouse in the Age of the Cathars* (Aldershot, UK: Ashgate, 2006), pp. 13–44, especially pp. 42–44 for an edition of Vidal's lawsuit.

12. *Historia Albigensis*, 1, § 160, pp. 163–65 [pp. 86–87].

13. *Crozada*, 1, laisses 45–47, pp. 108–13 [p. 32]; *Historia Albigensis*, 1, § 162, pp. 165–66 [pp. 87–88]; *Chronica*, xv, pp. 64–67 [pp. 35–36]; and HGL 8, cols. 612–19 for a letter the consuls sent to Pere II of Aragon in July 1211 describing the previous summer.

14. *Crozada*, 1, laisse 58, p. 140–45 [p. 37]; *Historia Albigensis*, 1, §§ 163–64, pp. 166–69 [pp. 88–89]; and *Layettes*, 1, no. 930, pp. 352–53.

15. *Crozada*, 1, laisses 48–50, pp. 114–19 [pp. 32–33], and *Historia Albigensis*, 1, §§ 151–59, pp. 154–63 [pp. 82–86].

16. *Crozada*, 1, laisses 50–55, pp. 118–31 [pp. 32–34], and *Historia Albigensis*, 1, §§ 168–69, pp. 170–72 [pp. 90–91].

17. Doat 75, fols. 3–8, 16–18.

18. *Crozada*, 1, laisse 56, pp. 132–37 [p. 36], and *Historia Albigensis*, 1, §§ 171–73, pp. 173–76 [pp. 91–92].

19. Henri Gaussen, "A View from Canigou: Nature and Man in the Eastern Pyrenees," *Geographical Review* 26 (1936): 190–204.

20. *Crozada*, 1, laisses 56–57, pp. 132–45 [pp. 36–37], and *Historia Albigensis*, 1, §§ 170–91, pp. 172–93 [pp. 91–100].

21. *Crozada*, 1, laisses 59–61, pp. 132–45 [pp. 37–39]; *Historia Albigensis*, 1, §§ 192–212, pp. 193–211 [pp. 101–9]; *Chronica*, xvi, p. 66 [p. 37]; and PL 216, cols. 410–11.

Chapter X

1. *Crozada*, 1, laisses 62–71, pp. 154–75 [pp. 39–43]; *Historia Albigensis*, 1, §§ 213–16, 223–30, pp. 211–16, 223–30 [pp. 110–12, 115–18]; *Chronica*, xvi, p. 68 [pp. 38–39]; and

Alberic [Aubri] de Troisfontaines, *Chronica Albrici monarchi Trium Fontium, a monaco novi monasterii Hoiensis interpolate*, ed. Paulus Scheffer-Boichorst, Monumenta Germaniae Historica Scriptorum 23 (Hanover, Germany: Hahnian, 1874), p. 892.

2. Gavaudan, "A la pus longa nuech de l'an," in *Il trovatore Gavaudan*, ed. and trans. Saverio Guida (Modena, Italy: Mucchi, 1979), p. 397.

3. *Crozada*, I, laisses 62–71, pp. 154–75 [pp. 39–43]; *Historia Albigensis*, I, §§ 221–22, pp. [pp. 114–15]; *Chronica*, xvi, pp. 68–70 [*Chronicle*, pp. 39–40]; and Dante Alighieri, *The Divine Comedy: III Paradise*, IX, pp. 108–9. See Nicole M. Schulman, *Where Troubadours Were Bishops: The Occitania of Folc of Marseille (1150–1231)* (London: Routledge, 2001).

4. HGL 8, cols. 604–8.

5. *Crozada*, I, laisses 69–72, pp. 168–77 [pp. 42–43]; *Historia Albigensis*, I, §§ 217–20, pp. 216–20 [pp. 112–13]; and *Chronica*, xvi, p. 70 [*Chronicle*, p. 39].

6. Jacques de Vitry, *Vita Mariae Oigniacensis*, ed. Daniel von Papebroeck, *Acta Sanctorum… editio novissima* (Paris: Palmé, June 1867), 5, pp. 542–72, especially §§ pp. 547–50, §82, p. 586; translated by Margot H. King as *The Life of Marie d'Oignes by Jacques de Vitry* (Saskatoon, Canada: Peregrina, 1986), especially pp. 2–4, 79–80, 103.

7. *Crozada*, I, laisses 72–75, pp. 174–83 [pp. 43–44]; *Historia Albigensis*, I, §§ 231–36, pp. 230–37 [pp. 119–22]; *Chronica*, xii, p. 58 [p. 31]; and HGL 8, col. 573.

8. *Catalogue des actes des comtes de Bar de 1022 à 1239*, ed. Marcel Grosdidier de Matons (Bar-le-Duc, France: Contant-Laguerre, 1922), nos. 201, 241; and *Historia Albigensis*, I, § 237, p. 237 n. 7.

9. *Crozada*, I, laisses 76–78, pp. 182–89 [pp. 44–46]; *Historia Albigensis*, I, § 237, pp. 236–37 [p. 122]; HGL 8, col. 609; and *Layettes*, 5, no. 185.

10. *Historia Albigensis*, I, § 238, pp. 237–39 [pp. 122–23], and HGL 8, cols. 612–19.

11. On the Roman and Visigothic ramparts of Toulouse, see Michel Labrousse, *Toulouse antique des origines a l'établissement des Wisigoths*, Bibliothèque des écoles française d'Athènes et de Rome 212 (Paris: Éditions E. de Boccard, 1968), pp. 273–76.

12. *Crozada*, I, laisse 79, p. 190 [p. 46]; *Historia Albigensis*, I, § 234, p. 233 [p. 120]; and HGL 8, col. 615.

13. *Crozada*, I, laisses 80–84, pp. 190–203 [pp. 46–48]; *Historia Albigensis*, I, §§ 239–43, pp. 239–44 [pp. 123–25]; and HGL 8, col. 615.

14. Gervase of Tilbury, *Otia Imperialia*, III, 103, pp. 759–85.

Chapter XI

1. *Crozada*, I, laisses 90–106, pp. 210–38 [pp. 50–55]; *Historia Albigensis*, I, §§ 251–80, pp. 250–76 [pp. 129–40]; and *Chronica*, xviii, p. 74 [pp. 42–43].

2. *Crozada*, I, laisses 107–11, pp. 238–48 [pp. 55–56], and *Historia Albigensis*, I, §§ 286–93, pp. 283–88 [pp. 143–45].

3. *Crozada*, I, laisses 107–11, pp. 238–48 [pp. 55–56], and *Historia Albigensis*, I, §§ 294–300, 2, §§ 301–17, pp. 288–93, 1–18 [pp. 145–54].

4. *Crozada*, I, laisses 111–26, pp. 246–80 [pp. 56–63], and *Historia Albigensis*, 2, §§ 317–62, pp. 18–62 [pp. 153–69].

5. *Crozada*, 1, laisse 127, p. 280 [p. 63]; *Historia Albigensis*, 2, §§ 362–65, pp. 62–65 [pp. 169–71]; and HGL 8, cols. 625–35 [*Albigensian Crusade*, appendix H, pp. 321–29].

Chapter XII

1. The battle of Las Navas de Tolosa lasted from early morning until sunset on Monday, 16 July 1212. Alfonso VIII, king of Castile and Leon, PL 216, CLXXXII, 699–703, sent a detailed (and rapturous) letter to Innocent III describing the battle. See Ambrosio Huici Miranda, *Las grandes batallas de la Reconquista durante las invasiones africanas (almoravides, almohades y benimerines)* (Madrid: Instituto de Estudios Africanos, Consejo Superior de Investigaciones Científicas, 1956), pp. 219–327; Smith, *Innocent III and the Crown of Aragon*, pp. 110–15; and Martín Alvira Cabrer, "'Le triomphe de la croix': La bataille de Las Navas de Tolosa (16 Juillet 1212)," in *Les grandes batailles méridionales; "Mieux vaut mort que vif vaincu" (1209–1271)*, ed. Laurent Albaret and Nicolas Gouzy (Toulouse: Privat, 2005), pp. 62–72.

2. PL 216, CII, cols. 613–14, CCXII, 739–40, CCXIII, 741–43, CCXV, 744–45, partially translated by Sibly and Sibly in *Albigensian Crusade*, appendix F, pp. 308–11.

3. *Historia Albigensis*, 2, §§ 367–91, pp. 65–87 [pp. 172–81], and PL 216, XLII, cols. 839–43. Smith, *Innocent III*, p. 121 n. 65, notes that Colom was certainly in Toulouse with Pere II on Thursday, 24 January 1213.

4. Caesarius of Heisterbach, *Dialogus Miraculorum*, 1, V, xxi, p. 303 [p. 347].

5. *Historia Albigensis*, 2, § 392–98, pp. 65–96 [pp. 181–84], and PL 216, XLI, cols. 836–39.

6. RHGF 19, pp. 250–54, especially p. 253.

7. *Studien zum Register Innocenz' III*, ed. Georgine Tangl (Weimar: H. Böhlaus Nachf., 1929), pp. 88–97, especially p. 94; Louise Riley-Smith and Jonathon Riley-Smith, *The Crusades: Idea and Reality 1095–1274* (London: Edward Arnold, 1981), pp. 118–24.

8. *Historia Albigensis*, 2, § 401–12, pp. 65–96 [pp. 186–89], and PL 216, XLVIII, cols. 849–52.

9. *Llibre dels Fets del rei en Jaume*, ed. Jordi Bruguera (Barcelona: Barcino, 1991) 2, viii, p. 12; translated by Damian Smith and Helena Buffery as *The Book of Deeds of James I of Aragon: A Translation of the Medieval Catalan Llibre dels Fets* (Aldershot, UK: Ashgate, 2003), p. 23.

10. *Historia Albigensis*, 2, § 417–21, pp. 109–14 [pp. 191–94].

11. Ibid., 2, § 422–36, pp. 114–27 [pp. 194–98].

12. *Crozada*, 2, laisses 132–35, pp. 3–13 [pp. 66–68], and *Chronica*, xix, pp. 76–78 [pp. 43–45].

13. *Crozada*, 1, laisses 130–31, pp. 286–91 [pp. 64–65].

14. Vincent, "England and the Albigensian Crusade," p. 74.

15. *Crozada*, 2, laisses 137–38, pp. 16–23 [pp. 68–69], and *Historia Albigensis*, 2, § 446, pp. 138–39 [p. 203–4].

16. *Crozada*, 2, laisse 138, p. 22 [p. 69]; *Historia Albigensis*, 2, §§ 449–56, 473, pp. 140–68 [pp. 204–7, 215]; *Chronica*, xx, pp. 78–82 [pp. 45–47]; and *Llibre dels Fets*, 2, ix, p. 13 [p. 23].

17. *Crozada*, 2, laisses 138–41, pp. 22–36 [pp. 69–71]; *Historia Albigensis*, 2, §§ 457–83, pp. 148–76 [pp. 207–17]; *Chronica*, xxi, pp. 82–87 [pp. 47–49]; and *Llibre dels Fets*, 2, ix, pp. 13–14 [*The Book of Deeds of James I*, pp. 24–25].

Chapter XIII

1. Mundy, *Men and Women at Toulouse*, appendix 1, no. 55, p. 140.

2. *Llibre dels Fets*, 2, ix, p. 14 [p. 25].

3. Innocent III crowned Pere II on Thursday, 11 November 1204. PL 215, col. 550. *Reg. Inn. III*, 7, no. 229, pp. 406–9, especially p. 407. See Smith, *Innocent III*, pp. 43–78.

4. *Crozada*, 2, laisse 141, p. 36 [p. 71]; *Historia Albigensis*, 2, § 481, p. 174 [p. 217]; *Chronica*, xxi, p. 87 [p. 49]; *Llibre dels Fets*, 2, ix, p. 14 [p. 25]; and PL 215, cols. 503–4.

5. *Historia Albigensis*, 2, §§ 487–93, pp. 179–85 [pp. 220–22].

6. PL 216, CLXVII, CLXX, CLXVI, CLXXII, cols. 955–60; HGL 8, nos. 172, 172, cols. 643–51; *Chronica*, xxiii, pp. 88–90 [pp. 51–52]; and *Llibre dels Fets*, 2, x, pp. 14–15 [pp. 25–26].

7. *Historia Albigensis*, 2, §§ 495–500, 504, pp. 186–93, 198–99 [pp. 222–25], and *Chronica*, xxii, pp. 86–88 [pp. 50–51].

8. *Historia Albigensis*, 2, § 508, pp. 202–4 [pp. 229–30].

9. Ibid., 2, §§ 509–12, pp. 205–7 [pp. 230–31].

10. HGL 8, no. 176, cols. 653–54.

11. On the *albergum, cabalerii*, and *milites*, see Mundy, *Society and Government*, pp. 87–93; and Cheyette, *Ermengard of Narbonne*, pp. 158–67. On the equivalent of a "well-equipped knight," see *Recueil des actes des comtes de Provence appartenant à la maison de Barcelone: Alphonse II et Raimond Bérenger V (1196–1245)*, ed. Fernand Bênoit (Monaco: Impr. de Monaco, 1925), 2, no. 18 (August 1214).

12. *Historia Albigensis*, 2, § 513, pp. 207–8 [p. 231].

13. Ibid., 2, §§ 514–41, pp. 208–36 [pp. 231–41].

14. HGL 8, no. 177, cols. 654–55.

15. Mansi, *Sacrorum conciliorum*, 22, cols. 950–51; and *Historia Albigensis*, 2, §§ 542–49, pp. 236–42 [pp. 241–45].

16. *Crozada*, 2, laisses 141–42, pp. 34–39 [pp. 71–72], and *Historia Albigensis*, 2, §§ 550–53, 560–66, pp. 242–47, 252–57 [pp. 246–48, 250–53].

17. *Layettes*, 1, nos. 1113, 1115, 1116; *Historia Albigensis*, 2, §§ 554–59, pp. 248–52 [pp. 248–50]; HGL 8, no. 180, cols. 658–660.

Chapter XIV

1. *Decrees of the Ecumenical Councils*, pp. 230–71, especially pp. 230–31; PL 217, Sermon V, cols. 673–80; the text of the anonymous German cleric is edited in Stephan Kuttner and Antonio García y García, "A New Eyewitness Account of the Fourth Lateran Council," *Traditio* 20 (1964): 115–78; translated by Constantin Fasolt

in *Medieval Europe: Readings in Western Civilization*, ed. Julius Kirshner and Karl F. Morrison (Chicago: University of Chicago Press, 1986), pp. 369–76. See Brenda Bolton, "A Show with Meaning: Innocent III's Approach to the Fourth Lateran Council, 1215," in *Innocent III: Studies on Papal Authority and Pastoral Care* (Aldershot, UK: Ashgate, 1995) XI, pp. 53–67.

2. Kuttner and García, "A New Eyewitness Account," 155.

3. *Crozada*, 2, laisses 143–52, pp. 40–89 [pp. 72–83]; *Historia Albigensis*, 2, §§ 570–72, pp. 259–63 [pp. 253–55]; and *Chronica*, xxiv, pp. 92–94 [pp. 53–55].

4. *Decrees of the Ecumenical Councils*, pp. 233–35, 237–40.

5. Ibid., p. 245.

6. *Layettes*, I, nos. 1132; HGL 8, no. 188, cols. 686–87; RHGF 19, p. 598 [*Albigensian Crusade*, appendix F, pp. 311–12].

7. Gervase of Tilbury, *Otia Imperialia*, I.2, pp. 30–31; I.1, pp. 18–29; I.2, pp. 30–31; I.1, pp. 18–19.

8. Ibid., I.1, pp. 18–19.

9. *Chronica*, xiv, pp. 92–3 [p. 54].

10. PL 217, col. 665.

11. On the "renaissance," see Charles Homer Haskins, *The Renaissance of the Twelfth Century* (Cambridge, MA: Harvard University Press, 1927); on the "reformation," see Constable, *The Reformation of the Twelfth Century*; and on the "revolution," see Robert I. Moore, *The First European Revolution, c. 970–1215* (Oxford: Blackwell, 2000). See Richard William Southern, *The Making of the Middle Ages* (New Haven: Yale University Press, 1953).

12. PL 217, col. 762 D. See Leonard E. Boyle, "Innocent III's View of Himself as Pope," in *Innocenzo III: Urbs et Orbis. Atti del Congresso Internazionale Roma, 9–15 settembre 1998*, ed. Andrea Sommerlechner (Rome: Presso le Società alla Biblioteca Vallicelliana, 2003), I, pp. 5–17; and Brenda Bolton, "Signposts from the Past: Reflections on Innocent III's Providential Path," in Sommerlechner, *Innocenzo III*, pp. 21–55.

13. RHGF 19, p. 646; *Historia Albigensis*, 2, § 573, pp. 264–65 [pp. 255–56]; and Jacques de Vitry, *Lettres de Jacques de Vitry (1160/70), évêque de Saint-Jean d'Acre*, ed. R. B. C. Huygens (Leiden: Brill, 1960), I, pp. 73–74.

Chapter XV

1. *Crozada*, 2, laisses 151–71, pp. 78–197 [pp. 82–105].

2. Eugène Martin-Chabot, "Mésaventures d'un donat," in *Mélanges d'histoire du moyen-âge dédiés à la mémoire de Louis Halphen* (Paris: Presses universitaires de France, 1951), pp. 501–6; and Mundy, *Society and Government at Toulouse*, pp. 357–59.

3. *Crozada*, 2, laisses 171–80, pp. 198–263 [pp. 106–17], and *Chronica*, xxvii, pp. 98–99 [pp. 58–59].

4. Gervase of Tilbury, *Otia Imperialia*, II.12, pp. 338–39.

5. *Crozada*, 2, laisses 181–83, pp. 264–83 [pp. 119–23]. On the *salvetat*, see Mundy, *Society and Government at Toulouse*, pp. 18–20.

6. Louis Peyrusse, "Viollet-le-Duc à Saint-Sernin ou le génie de la restauration," in *Saint-Sernin de Toulouse. Trésors et Métamorphoses. Deux siècles de restaurations 1802–1989. Toulouse, Musée Saint-Raymond, 15 septembre 1989–14 janvier 1990* (Toulouse: Musée Saint-Raymond, 1990), pp. 109–19.

7. *Crozada*, 2, laisses 183–85, pp. 282–301 [pp. 123–25].

8. Ibid., laisse 186, pp. 300–309 [pp. 128–30].

9. *Crozada*, 3, laisses 187–88, pp. 8–25 [pp. 130–34].

10. Ibid., laisses 189–90, pp. 26–35 [pp. 134–37].

11. Ibid., laisses 190–91, pp. 34–73 [pp. 137–44]. On chain-mail see Williams, *The Knight and the Blast Furnace*, p. 30.

12. Mundy, *Liberty and Political Power in Toulouse*, pp. 32, 247 n. 25.

13. *Crozada*, 3, laisses 190–91, pp. 34–73 [pp. 137–44].

14. MS 609, fol. 66v.

15. *Crozada*, 3, laisses 192–98, pp. 144–27 [pp. 144–55].

16. Ibid., 3, laisses 198–202, pp. 128–73 [pp. 155–64].

17. Ibid., 3, laisses 202–3, pp. 172–75 [pp. 164–67].

18. Raimon Escrivan, "Senhors, l'autrier vi ses falhida," in *Chrestomathie Provençale (Xe–XVe siècles)*, ed. Karl Bartsch and Eduard Koschwitz (Marburg, Germany: N.G. Elwert, 1904), cols. 343–44.

19. *Crozada*, 2, laisses 180–86, pp. 264–309, 3, laisses 187–207, pp. 8–227 [pp. 117–76]; *Historia Albigensis*, 2, §§ 601–12, pp. 296–316 [pp. 271–77]; and *Chronica*, xxviii, pp. 100–105 [pp. 59–62].

20. *Chronica*, xxviii, pp. 103–5 [pp. 61–62].

21. *Historia Albigensis*, 2, §§ 612–20, pp. 315–23 [pp. 277–79]. See Christopher M. Kurpiewski, "Writing beneath the Shadow of Heresy: The *Historia Albigensis* of Brother Pierre des Vaux-de-Cernay," *Journal of Medieval History* 31 (2005): 1–27.

22. *Crozada*, 3, laisse 208, p. 228 [p. 176].

23. Cf. Jonathan Riley-Smith, "Peace Never Established: The Case of the Kingdom of Jerusalem," *Transactions of the Royal Historical Society*, fifth ser., 28 (1978): 87–102.

Chapter XVI

1. *Crozada*, 3, laisse 208, pp. 234–35 [p. 178].

2. *Crozada*, 3, laisses 210–13, pp. 252–321 [pp. 181–94]; *Regesta Honorii Papae III*, ed. Pietro Pressutti (1888; reprint, Hildesheim, Germany: George Olms Verlag, 1978), 1, nos. 940, 944–46, 949–50, 959, 1006, 1577, 1578, 1583; and Richard Kay, *The Council of Bourges, 1225: A Documentary History* (Aldershot, UK: Ashgate, 2002), pp. 6–7.

3. *Crozada*, 3, laisse 212, pp. 282–91 [pp. 186–89], and *Chronica*, xxx, pp. 106–9 [pp. 64–65].

4. *Crozada*, 3, laisse 213, pp. 292–93 [p. 189].

5. Ibid., laisse 213, pp. 294–303 [p. 189–91].

6. Ibid., laisse 214, pp. 320–21 [p. 194].

7. *Chronica*, xxx, pp. 106–9 [pp. 64–65].

8. Ibid., xxxii, pp. 112–13 [p. 67].

9. HGL 8, no. 211, cols. 738–43; *Regesta Honorii Papae III*, 1, nos. 2511, 3431, 3441, 3451, 3452, 3486; Alan John Forey, "The Military Orders and Holy War against Christians in the Thirteenth Century," *English Historical Review* 104 (1989): 1–24, especially 5–7; and Kay, *The Council of Bourges*, pp. 9–10.

10. HGL 6, pp. 546–48, HGL 8, no. 220, cols. 759–60; *Regesta Honorii Papae III*, 1, nos. 3774, 3950; RHGF 19, pp. 718–21; *Chronica*, xxxii, p. 114 [p. 68]; and Mathew Paris, *Chronica majora*, ed. Henry Richards Luard, Rolls Ser. 57 (London: Longman, 1876), 3, pp. 78–79, partially edited and translated by Kay in *The Council of Bourges*, pp. 548–49].

11. MS 609, fol. 239v.

12. Ibid., fols. 2r–3v, 4r–5v, 62r, 110r, 124r–125v, 164r, 237v. See Pegg, *The Corruption of Angels*, pp. 92–103.

13. Guillaume Besse, *Histoire des ducs, marquis et comtes de Narbonne, autrement appellez Princes des Goths, Ducs de Septimanie, et Marquis de Gothie. Dedié à Monseigneur l'Archevesque Duc de Narbonne* (Paris: Antoine de Sommaville, 1660), pp. 483–86. Besse obtained the parchment from "M. Caseneuue, Prebendier au Chapitre de l'Eglisle de Sainct Estienne de Tolose, en l'an 1652." Antoine Dondaine defended the historical value of the "Charter of Niquinta" in his "Les actes du concile albigeois de Saint-Félix de Caraman," in *Miscellanea Giovanni Mercati 5, Studi e Testi* 125 (Vatican City: Biblioteca apostolica vaticana, 1946), pp. 324–55. Bernard Hamilton, "The Cathar Council of S. Félix Reconsidered," *Archivum Fratrum Praedicatorum*, 48 (1978): 23–53, is generally assumed to have demonstrated the veracity of Besse's appendix as evidence for a "Cathar Church," an argument he elegantly restated in his "Introduction" to *Hugh Eteriano* Contra Patarenos, pp. 79–98. See the exemplary essay collection *L'histoire du Catharisme en discussion: Le "concile" de Saint-Félix (1167)*, ed. Monique Zerner (Nice: Centre d'Études Médiévales Faculté des Lettres, Arts et Sciences Humaines Université de Nice Sophia-Antipolis 2001).

14. Yves Dossat, "Remarques sur un prétendu évêque cathare du Val d'Aran en 1167," *Bulletin philologique et historique (jusqu'à 1715), années 1955 et 1956* (1957): 339–47, and, "A propos du concile cathare de Saint-Félix: Les Milingues," *Cahiers de Fanjeaux: Cathares en Languedoc*, 3 (1968): 201–14, argued that the "Charter of Niquinta" was a seventeenth-century forgery (probably by Besse). Monique Zerner cautiously agrees with Dossat in her "La charte de Niquinta, l'hérésie et l'erudition des années 1650–1660," in *L'histoire du Catharisme en discussion: Le "concile" de Saint-Félix (1167)*, pp. 203–48. Michel Roquebert responded to Zerner's doubts about the "Charter of Niquinta" with hostility in his "Le 'déconstructionisme' et le études cathares'," in *Les cathares devant l'histoire: Mélanges offerts à Jean Duvernoy*, ed. Martin Aurell (Quercy: L'Hydre, 2005), pp. 105–33. Zerner replied to Roquebert (and others) in her "Mise au point sur Les Cathares devant L'historie et retour sur L'histoire du Catharisme en discussion: Le débat sur le Charte de Niquinta n'est pas clos," *Journal des Savants* (2006): 253–73.

15. Giles Constable, "Forgery and Plagiarism in the Middle Ages," *Archiv für Diplomatik* 29 (1983): 1–41; and Paul Meyvaert, "Medieval Forgers and Modern

Scholars: Tests of Ingenuity," in *The Role of the Book in Medieval Culture: Proceedings of the Oxford International Symposium, 26 September–1 October 1982*, ed. Peter Ganz, Bibliologia. Elementa ad librorum studia pertinentia 3 (Turnhout, Belgium: Brepols, 1986), 1, pp. 83–96.

16. Doat 26, fol. 142v–147v. See Alan Friedlander, *The Hammer of the Inquisitors: Brother Bernard Délicieux and the Struggle Against the Inquisition in Fourteenth-Century France*, (Leiden: Brill, 2000), pp. 9–11.

17. *Crozada*, 1, laisse 2, p. 10 [p. 12]. On *Bougres*, see Monique Zerner, "Du court moment où appela les hérétiques de 'Bougres.' Et quelques déductions," *Cahiers de Civilization Médiévale* 32 (1989): 305–24.

18. Robert Burton, *The Anatomy of Melancholy*, ed. Thomas C. Faulkner, Nicolas K. Kiessling, and Rhonda L. Blair (Oxford: Clarendon Press, 1989) 1, p. 305. Burton read about the "woolgathering" of Thomas Aquinas in Battista Fregoso, *Baptistae Fulgosii Factorum, doctorumque memorabilium libri IX. Aucti et restituti. Index copiosisimus omnium nominum de quibus passim in historia agitur* (Antwerp: I. Bellerum, 1565), VIII, p. 612.

19. Sir Thomas Browne, *Religio Medici* in *Selected Writings*, ed. Geoffrey Keynes (London: Faber and Faber, 1968), p. 12.

20. MS 609, fol. 136r.

21. *Chronica*, prologue, p. 24 and n. 2. Cf. Mundy, *Society and Government at Toulouse*, p. 84.

22. *Chronica*, xxxii, pp. 114, 116 [pp. 67, 70]; "Memorial of Louis VIII Reviewing and Ending the Negotiations 5 May 1224," in Kay, *The Council of Bourges*, pp. 338–39.

23. HGL 8, nos. 231, 233–34, cols. 782–86, 789–90; "Louis Petitions Honorius to Grant His Conditons. Late January or February 1224," in Kay, *The Council of Bourges*, pp. 326–31.

24. HGL 8, nos. 229, 239, cols. 779–80, 804–7; and "Memorial of Louis VIII Reviewing and Ending the Negotiations 5 May 1224," pp. 340–41.

25. "The Pope Announces Romanus' Legation to Raymond 5 May 1224," and "Prolongation of the Truce in Provence," in Kay, *The Council of Bourges*, pp. 340–45.

26. "Romanus Authorizes Sequestration of Delinquent Chapters' Goods 17 May 1227," in Kay, *The Council of Bourges*, pp. 408–9; Philip Mousket, *Chronique rimée de Philippe Mouskès*, ed. Baron Frédéric-Auguste-Ferdinand-Thomas de Reiffenberg (Brussels: M. Hayez, 1838), 2, pp. 486–88, and in Kay, *The Council of Bourges*, p. 311. In general, see Kay, *The Council of Bourges*, especially pp. 77–136.

27. HGL 8, no. 244, cols. 817–818; *Chronica*, xxxiii, p. 118 [p. 71]; "Annals of Dunstable," in Kay, *The Council of Bourges*, pp. 294–95; and "Chronicle of Tours," in Kay, pp. 304–5.

28. *Chronica*, xxxiii–xxxiv, p. 118 [pp. 71–72]. On the bridge at Avignon, see Gervase of Tilbury, *Otia imperialia*, III.103, pp. 782–83, and *Avignon au Moyen Age: Textes au Moyen Age*, ed. Hérve Aliquot (Aubanel, France: Avignon, 1988), pp. 25–29. On the seige, see *Avignon au Moyen Age*, pp. 43–52.

29. Mundy, *Liberty and Political Power in Toulouse*, pp. 126–28, 342–43 n. 34.

30. Tomier and Palazi, "De chantar farai," in Vincenzo de Bartholomaeis, *Poesie provenzali storiche relative all' Italia*. Istituto storico italiano per il Medio Evo (Rome: Tipografia del Senato, 1931), 2, pp. 55–56. See Palmer A. Throop, "Criticism of Papal Crusade Policy in Old French and Provençal," *Speculum* 13 (1938): 390–93.

31. *Chronica*, xxxiii, pp. 120–25 [pp. 72–75]; Guilhem Figueira, "D'un sirventes far en est son que m'agenssa," in *Los Trovadores: Historia y Textos*, ed. Martín de Riquer (Barcelona: Editorial Planeta, 1975), 3, p. 1274.

32. Christoph T. Maier, "Crisis, Liturgy, and the Crusade in the Twelfth and Thirteenth Centuries," *Journal of Ecclesiastical History* 48 (1997): 628–57, especially 652–53, and Nicole Bériou, "La prédication de croisade de Philippe le Chancelier et d'Eudes de Châteauroux en 1226," *Cahiers de Fanjeaux: La prédication en Pays d'Oc (XIIe–début XVe siècle)* 32 (1997): 85–109. See David Traill, "Philip the Chancellor and the Heresy Inquisition in Northern France, 1235–1236," *Viator* 37 (2006): 241–54.

33. *Ordene de Chevalerie* in *Le Roman des Eles by Raoul de Houdenc. The Anonymous Ordene de Chevalerie*, ed. and trans. Keith Busby (Amsterdam: J. Benjamins, 1983), pp. 117, 174–75. See Richard W. Kaeuper, *Chivalry and Violence in Medieval Europe* (Oxford: Oxford University Press, 1999), pp. 72–73.

34. *Chronica*, xxxvi–xxxvii, pp. 128–33 [pp. 78–79]; and, for example, HGL 8, no. 277, cols. 900–901. On the vineyards around Toulouse, see Gilles Caster, "Le vignoble suburbain de Toulouse au XIIe siècle," *Annales du Midi* 78 (1966): 201–17.

35. *Chronica*, xxxvii, pp. 134–35 [p. 80]; HGL 8, nos. 270, 272, cols. 878–83, 893–94.

36. HGL 8, no. 271, cols. 883–93 [*Chronicle*, appendix C, pp. 138–44].

Chapter XVII

1. John of Garland, *The Dictionarius*, ed. and trans. Barbara Blatt Rubin (Lawrence, KS: Coronado Press, 1981), pp. 47–63, and his *De triumphis ecclesiae: A Latin Poem of the Thirteenth Century*, ed. Thomas Wright (London: JB. Nichols for the Roxburghe Club, 1856), p. 131. See Louis John Paetow's introduction to his editon of the *Morale Scolarium of John of Garland (Johannes de Garlandia): A Professor in the Universities of Paris and Toulouse in the Thirteenth Century* (Berkeley: University of California Press, 1927), pp. 77–145.

2. PL 212, cols. 603–10.

3. Mansi, *Sacrorum conciliorum*, XXIII, cols. 192–204.

4. PL 212, cols. 692–700. See also Beverly Mayne Kienzle, "Mary Speaks against Heresy: An Unedited Sermon of Hélinard for the Purification, Paris, B.N. ms. lat. 14591," *Studi erudiri* 32 (1991): 291–308, and her *Cistercians, Heresy, and Crusade in Occitania 1145–1229: Preaching in the Lord's Vineyard* (Woodbridge, UK: York Medieval Press, Boydell, 2001), pp. 185–93.

5. Mundy, *Liberty and Political Power in Toulouse*, p. 62. Guilhem Pelhisson, *Chronique (1229–1244) suivie du récit des troubles d'Albi (1234)*, ed. and trans. Jean Duvernoy (Paris: Éditions du Centre National de la Recherche Scientifique, 1994), pp. 38–41, and translated into English by Walter Wakefield in his *Heresy, Crusade*

and Inquisition in Southern France 1100–1250, pp. 207–36. See Bernard Gui, *Bernardus Guidonis de foundatione et prioribus conventuum provinciarum Tolosanae et Provinciae ordinis predictorum*, ed. Paul A. Amargier, Monumenta ordinis fratrum praedictorum historica 24 (Rome: Institutum historicum fratrum praedicatorum, 1961), pp. 32–33.

6. John of Garland, *De triumphis ecclesiae*, pp. 92–105. See Louis John Paetow, "The Crusading Ardor of John of Garland," in *The Crusades and Other Historical Essays Presented to Dana C. Munro by His Former Students*, ed. Louis John Paetow (New York: F. S. Croft, 1928), pp. 207–22.

7. Doat 22, fols. 248r–258r, 286v–287r; Doat 24, fols. 163v–164v; and MS 609, fols. 5v, 37r–37v, 139–140v. See Yves Dossat, "Le massacre d'Avignonet," *Cahiers de Fanjeaux: Le Credo, la Morale et l'Inquisition*, 6 (1971): 343–59.

8. MS 609, fols 183r–183v.

9. William Chester Jordan, *Louis IX and the Challenge of the Crusade: A Study in Rulership* (Princeton, NJ: Princeton University Press, 1979), p. 16; and Wakefield, *Heresy, Crusade, and Inquisition in Southern France*, pp. 158–61.

10. Pacts of submission were forced on the Lusignans (*Layettes*, 2, nos. 2980–81), on Raimon VII (*Layettes*, 2, nos. 2995–96, 3013), on Aimeric, viscount of Narbonne (*Layettes*, 2, no. 3014), and on Roger Bernart, count of Foix (*Layettes*, 2, no. 3015). Written pledges were extracted, for example, from Raimon II Trencavel (*Layettes*, 3, no. 3616; HGL, 8, cols. 1212–14), Bertran, brother of Raimon VII (*Layettes*, 2, no. 3057), Raoul, bishop of Angouléme, and Guilhem, abbot of Corona (*Layettes*, 2, no. 3110). See, especially, Jordan, *Louis IX and the Challenge of the Crusade*, p. 16 and n. 10.

11. On 23 February 1243. Mundy edited this oath in his *Society and Government at Toulouse*, appendix 3, pp. 368–84.

12. *Chronica*, xliv, pp. 172–77 [pp. 107–8]; On Montségur, see Yves Dossat, "Le 'Bûcher de Montségur' et les Bûchers de l'Inquisition," *Cahiers de Fanjeaux: Le Credo, la Moral, et l'Inquisition* 6 (1971): 361–78; Michel Roquebert, "Montségur: Le castrum de 1204–1244: L'apport des sources écrites," in *Heresis: Actes de la 3e Session d'Histoire Médiévale de Carcassonne organisée par le C.N.E.C./Centre René Nelli, 28 août—1er september 1990*, ed. Nicolas Gouzy (Berne: Peter Lang, 1992), pp. 343–58; and André Czeski, "Montségur (Ariège): Quelques renseignements fournis par les résultats de l'ensemble des fouilles," in Gouzy, *Heresis: Actes de la 3e Session d'Histoire Médiévale de Carcassonne*, pp. 369–403.

13. MS 609, fols. 94v, 246r.

14. Doat 22, fol. 26r.

Chapter XVIII

1. Humbert de Romans, *Opus tripartitum*, in *Fasciculus rerum expetendarum et fugiendarum*, ed. Edward Brown (London: Richard Chiswell, 1690), 2, pp. 191–8; Louise Riley-Smith and Jonathon Riley-Smith, *The Crusades*, pp. 103–17.

2. Joseph Shatzmiller, *La deuxième controverse de Paris: Un chapitre dans la polemique entre Chrétiens et Juifs au Moyen Age* (Paris: Editions E. Peters, 1994),

pp. 11, 13, 22, 44 n.8, 58. See William Chester Jordan, *The French Monarchy and the Jews: From Philip Augustus to the Last Capetians* (Philadelphia: University of Pennsylvania Press, 1989), pp. 160–1; Jeremy Cohen, *Living Letters of the Law: Ideas of the Jew in Medieval Christianity* (Berkeley: University of California Press, 1999), pp. 334–42; and Joseph Shatzmiller, "The Albigensian Heresy as Reflected in the Eyes of Contemporary Jewry," [Hebrew] in *Culture and Society in Medieval Jewry: Studies Dedicated to the Memory of Haim Hillel Ben-Sasson*, ed. Menachem Ben-Sasson and Roberto Bonfil (Jerusalem: Merkaz Zalman Shazar le-toldot Yisra'el, 1989), pp. 333–52.

3. Solomon ibn Verga, *Liber Schevet Jehuda*, edited by Meir Wiener (Hanover: Sumptibus C. Rümpleri, 1855), 1, p. 113. See David Nirenburg, *Communities of Violence: Persecution of Minorities in the Middle Ages* (Princeton, N.J.: Princeton University Press, 1996), pp. 231–49, and "Mass Conversions and Genealogical Mentalities: Jews and Christians in Fifteenth-Century Spain," *Past and Present* 174 (2002): 3–41.

Bibliography

This bibliography contains full citations for printed works only. References to manuscript sources are given only in the notes.

Primary Sources

Acta concilii Lumbariensis. RHGF 14, pp. 430–34.

Ademar of Chabannes. *Chronicon.* Edited by Pascale Bourgain, Corpus Christianorum Continuatio Mediaevalis 129. Turnhout, Belgium: Brepols, 1999.

Alain de Lille. *De fide catholica liber quatuor.* PL 210, cols. 305–430.

Alberic [Aubri] de Troisfontaines. *Chronica Albrici monarchi Trium Fontium, a monaco novi monasterii Hoiensis interpolate.* Edited by Paulus Scheffer-Boichorst. Monumenta Germaniae Historica Scriptorum 23. Hanover, Germany: Hahnian, 1874.

Arnaut Daniel. *The Poetry of Arnaut Daniel.* Edited and translated by James J. Wilhelm. New York: Garland, 1981.

Avignon au Moyen Age: Textes au Moyen Age. Edited by Hérve Aliquot. Aubanel, France: Avignon, 1988.

Bernard Gui. *Bernardus Guidonis de foundatione et prioribus conventuum provinciarum Tolosanae et Provinciae ordinis predictorum.* Edited by Paul A. Amargier. Monumenta ordinis fratrum praedictorum historica 24. Rome: Institutum historicum fratrum praedicatorum, 1961.

Bernard of Clairvaux. *Sancti Bernardi Opera II: Sermones super Cantica Canticorum 36–86.* Edited by Jean Leclercq, Charles Talbot, and Henri Rochais. Rome: Editions Cistercienses, 1958.

————. *Sancti Bernardi Opera V: Sermones II.* Edited by Jean Leclercq and Henri Rochais. Rome: Editions Cistercienses, 1968.

————. *Sancti Bernardi Opera VIII: Epistolae.* Edited by Jean Leclercq and Henri Rochais. Rome: Editions Cistercienses, 1977.

————. *On the Song of Songs III.* Translated by Killian Walsh and Irene M. Edmonds. Kalamazoo, MI: Cistercian Publications, 1979.

Bernold of Constance. *De vitandi excommunicatorum communione de reconciliatione lapsorum.* PL 148, cols. 1182–1218.

————. *Tractatus de reordinatione vitanda, et de salute parvulorum, qui ab excommicatis baptizati sunt.* PL 148, cols. 1256–66.

Bertran de Born. *The Poems of the Troubadour Bertran de Born.* Edited and translated by William D. Paden, Tilde Sankovitch, and Patricia H. Ståblein. Berkeley: University of California Press, 1986.

The Book of Deeds of James I of Aragon: A Translation of the Medieval Catalan Llibre dels Fets. Translated by Damian Smith and Helena Buffery. Aldershot, UK: Ashgate, 2003.

Caesarius of Heisterbach. *The Dialogue on Miracles.* 2 vols. Translated by H. von E. Scott and C. C. Swinton Bland. London: George Routledge & Sons, 1929.

————. *Dialogus Miraculorum.* 2 vols. Edited by Joseph Strange. Cologne: H. Lempertz, 1851.

The Canso d'Antioca: An Occitan Epic Chronicle of the First Crusade. Edited and translated by Carol Sweetenham and Linda M. Paterson. Aldershot, UK: Ashgate, 2003.

Cartulaires des Templiers de Douzens. Edited by Pierre Gérard, Élisabeth Magnou, and Philippe Wolff. Paris: Bibliothèque Nationale, 1965.

Catalogue des actes des comtes de Bar de 1022 à 1239. Edited by Marcel Grosdidier de Matons. Bar-le-Duc, France: Contant-Laguerre, 1922.

Chrestomathie Provençale (Xe–XVe siècles). Edited by Karl Bartsch and Eduard Koschwitz. Marburg, Germany: N. G. Elwert, 1904.

Chronicon universale anonymi Laudunensis. Edited by Georg Waitz. Monumenta Germaniae Historica Scriptorum 26. Stuttgart: Anton Hiersemann Verlag, 1881.

Codex Diplomaticus Regni Croatiae, Dalmatiae et Slavoniae. Vol. 3. Edited by T. Smiciklas. Zagreb: Officina Societatis Typographicae, 1905.

Contemporary Sources for the Fourth Crusade. Edited and translated by Alfred J. Andrea. Leiden: Brill, 2000.

Corpus Iuris Canonici. 2 vols. Edited by Aemilius Friedberg. Leipzig: B. Tauchnitz, 1879; reprint Graz: Akademische Druck-u. Verlagsanstalt, 1959.

Crusade Propaganda and Ideology: Model Sermons for the Preaching of the Cross. Edited and translated by Christoph T. Maier. Cambridge: Cambridge University Press, 2000.

Dante Alighieri. *De vulgari eloquentia.* Edited and translated by Steven Botterill. Cambridge: Cambridge University Press, 1996.

————. *The Divine Comedy: I Inferno.* Translated by Mark Musa. Harmondsworth, UK: Penguin, 2003.

————— . *The Divine Comedy: III Paradise.* Translated by Mark Musa. Harmondsworth, UK: Penguin, 2003.

Decrees of the Ecumenical Councils. Edited and translated by Norman P. Tanner. London: Sheed and Ward 1990.

Eberwin of Steinfeld, *Epistola 472: Everwini Steinfeldensis praepositi ad S. Bernardum. De haereticis sui temporis.* PL 182, cols. 676–680.

Eckbert of Schönau. *Sermones contra Catharos.* PL 195, cols. 11–102.

————— . *Sermones contra Kataros.* 2 vols. Edited by Robert Joyce Harrison. PhD diss., Ohio State University, 1990.

Étienne De Bourbon. *Anecdotes Historiques. Legendes et Apologues tirés du recueil inédit d'Etienne de Bourbon, Dominicain du XIIIe siècle.* Edited by Richard Albert Lecoy de la Marche. Paris: Librairie Renouard, 1877.

Fulcher of Chartres. *Historia Hierosolymitana.* Edited by Heinrich Hagenmeyer. Heidelberg: C. Winter, 1913.

Gavaudan. *Il trovatore Gavaudan.* Edited and translated by Saverio Guida. Modena, Italy: Mucchi, 1979.

Geoffroi du Breuil. *Chronicon.* RHGF 12, pp. 421–451.

Gervase of Canterbury. *Chronicle of the Reigns of Stephen, Henry II, and Richard I.* 2 vols. Edited by William Stubbs. Rolls Series 73. London: Longman, 1879.

Gervase of Tilbury. *Otia Imperialia* (Recreation for an Emperor). Edited and translated by S. E. Banks and J. W. Binns. Oxford: Clarendon Press, 2002.

Gesta Pontificum Cenomannensium. RHGF 12, pp. 539–557.

Girault de Borneil. *The* Cansos *and* Sirventes *of the Troubadour Girault de Borneil: A Critical Edition.* Edited and translated by Ruth Verity Sharman. Cambridge: Cambridge University Press, 1989.

Guibert of Nogent. The *Deeds of God through the Franks: Gesta Dei per Francos.* Translated by Robert Levine. Woodbridge, UK: Boydell Press, 1997.

————— . *Dei gesta per Francos et cing autres textes.* Edited by R. B. C. Huygens. CCCM 127A. Turnholt, Belgium: Brepols, 1996.

Guilhem de Montanhagol. *Les Poésies de Guilhem de Montanhagol: Troubadour Provençal du XIIIe Siècle.* Edited and translated by Peter T. Ricketts. Toronto: Pontifical Institute of Medieval Studies, 1964.

Guilhem de Puylaurens. *Chronica Magistri Guillelmi de Podio Laurentii.* Edited and translated by Jean Duvernoy. Paris: Éditions du Centre National de la Recherche Scientifique, 1976.

————— . *The Chronicle of William of Puylaurens: The Albigensian Crusade and Its Aftermath.* Translated by W. A. Sibly and M. D. Sibly. Woodbridge, UK: Boydell Press, 2003.

Guilhem de Tudela and Anonymous Troubadour. *La Chanson de la Croisade Albigeoise* (*La Canso de la Crozada*). 3 vols. Edited by Eugène Martin-Chabot. Les Classiques de l'Histoire de France au Moyen Age. Paris: Société d'Édition Les Belles Lettres, 1957–1961.

Guilhem de Tudela and Anonymous Troubadour. *The Song of the Cathar Wars: A History of the Albigensian Crusade.* Translated by Janet Shirley. Aldershot, UK: Scolar Press, 1996.

Guilhem Pelhisson. *Chronique (1229–1244) suivie du récit des troubles d'Albi (1234).* Edited and translated by Jean Duvernoy. Paris: Éditions du Centre National de la Recherche Scientifique, 1994.

Gratian, *Decretum.* 4 vols. Edited by Augustin Caravita and Prosper Caravita. Venice: Apud Iuntas, 1605.

Heresies of the High Middle Ages: Selected Sources Translated and Annotated. Edited by Walter Leggett Wakefield and Austin P. Evans. New York: Columbia University Press, 1991.

Hrabanus Maurus. *De institutione clericorum libri tres.* Edited by Detlev Zimpel. Frankfurt am Main: Peter Lang, 1996.

Humbert de Romans. *Opus tripartitum. Fasciculus rerum expetendarum et fugiendarum.* 2 vols. Edited by Edward Brown. London: Richard Chiswell, 1690.

Humbert of Silva Candida. *Libri tres adversus simoniacos.* Edited by Elaine Golden Robison. PhD diss., Princeton University, 1972.

Isidore of Seville. *The* Etymologies *of Isidore of Seville.* Cambridge: Cambridge University Press, 2006.

———. *Isidori Hispalensis Episcopi Etymologiarum sive Originum Libri XX.* Edited by W. M. Lindsay. Oxford: Oxford University Press, 1911.

Jacques de Vitry. *Lettres de Jacques de Vitry (1160/70), évêque de Saint-Jean d'Acre.* Edited by R. B. C. Huygens. Leiden: Brill, 1960.

———. *The Life of Marie d'Oignes by Jacques de Vitry.* Translated by Margot H. King. Saskatoon, Canada: Peregrina, 1986.

———. *Vita Mariae Oigniacensis.* Edited by Daniel von Papebroeck. *Acta Sanctorum…editio novissima 25.* Paris: Palmé, 1867.

John of Ford. *Super Extremam Partem Cantici Canticorum Sermones CXX.* 2 vols. Edited by Edmund Mikkers and Hilary Costello. Corpus Christianorum. Continuatio Mediaevalis 17–18. Turnholt, Belgium: Brepols, 1970.

———. *Sermons on the Final Verses of the Song of Songs.* Translated by Wendy Mary Beckett. Kalamazoo, MI: Cistercian Publications, 1984.

John of Garland. *De triumphis ecclesiae: A Latin Poem of the Thirteenth Century.* Edited by Thomas Wright. London: JB. Nichols for the Roxburghe Club, 1856.

———. *Dictionarius.* Edited and translated by Barbara Blatt Rubin. Lawrence, KS: Coronado Press, 1981.

———. *Morale Scolarium of John of Garland (Johannes de Garlandia): A Professor in the Universities of Paris and Toulouse in the Thirteenth Century.* Edited by Louis John Paetow. Berkeley: University of California Press, 1927.

Landulf Senior. *Landulphi Senioris Mediolanensis historiae libri quatuor.* Edited by Alessandro Cutolo. *Rerum Italicarum scriptores.* Bologna: Nicola Zanichelli, 1942.

Layettes du Tresor des chartes. 5 vols. Edited by Alexandre Teulet, Joseph de Laborde, Elie Berger, Henri-François Delaborde. Paris: H. Plon, 1863–1909.

Le Roman des Eles by Raoul de Houdenc. The Anonymous Ordene de Chevalerie. Edited and translated by Keith Busby. Amsterdam: J. Benjamins, 1983.

Liber feudorum maior: Cartulario real que se conserva en el Archivo de la Corona de Aragón. 2 vols. Edited by Francisco Miguel Rosell. Barcelona: Es Propiedad, 1955.

Llibre dels Fets del rei en Jaume. 2 vols. Edited by Jordi Bruguera. Barcelona: Barcino, 1991.

Los Trovadores: Historia y Textos. 3 vols. Edited by Martín de Riquer. Barcelona: Editorial Planeta, 1975.

Marcabru. *Marcabru: A Critical Edition.* Edited and translated by Simon Gaunt, Ruth Harvey, and Linda Paterson. Cambridge, UK: D. S. Brewer, 2000.

Mathew Paris. *Chronica majora.* Edited by Henry Richards Luard. Rolls Series 57. London: Longman, 1876.

Monumenta Corbeiensia. Edited by Philip Jaffé. Bibliotheca Rerum Germanicarum. Berlin: Weidmann, 1864.

Paschasius Radbertus. *Expositio in Lamentationes Hieremiae libri quinque.* Edited by Beda Paulus. Corpus Christianorum. Continuatio Mediaevalis 85. Turnhout, Belgium: Brepols, 1988.

Patrologiae cursus completus: Series latina. 221 vols. Edited by Jacques-Paul Migne. Paris: Garnier Frères, 1844–1904.

Peter Damian. *Die Briefe des Petrus Damiani.* 4 vols. Edited by Kurt Reindel. Munich: Monumenta Germaniae Historica, 1983–1993.

———. *Liber qui appellatur gratissimus.* PL 145, cols. 99–169.

———. *De Sacramentis per improbus administratis.* PL 145, cols. 523–30.

Peter Lombard. *Commentarius in psalmos Davidicos: Psalmus XXIV.* PL 191, cols. 251–62.

Philip Mousket. *Chronique rimée de Philippe Mouskès.* 2 vols. Edited by Baron Frédéric-Auguste-Ferdinand-Thomas de Reiffenberg. Brussels: M. Hayez, 1838.

Pierre des Vaux-de-Cernay. *Historia Albigensis.* 2 vols. Edited by Pascal Guébin and Ernest Lyon. Société de l'Histoire de France. Paris: Librairie Ancienne Honoré Champion, 1926.

———. *The History of the Albigensian Crusade.* Translated by W. A. Sibly and M. D. Sibly. Woodbridge, UK: Boydell Press, 1998.

Ralph of Coggeshall. *Chronicon Anglicanum.* Edited by Joseph Stevenson. Rolls Series 66. London: Longman, 1875.

Ralph of Diceto. *Opera Historica.* 2 vols. Edited by William Stubbs. Rolls Series 68. London: Longman, 1876.

Recueil des actes des comtes de Provence appartenant à la maison de Barcelone: Alphonse II et Raimond Bérenger V (1196–1245). Edited by Fernand Bênoit. Monaco: Impr. de Monaco, 1925.

Recueil des historiens des Gaules et de la France, 24 vols. Directed by Léopold Delisle. Paris: (imprint varies), 1869–1904.

Regesta Honorii Papae III. 2 vols. Edited by Pietro Pressutti. 1888; reprint, Hildesheim, Germany: George Olms Verlag, 1978.

Regesta Pontificum Romanorum. 2 vols. Edited by Augustus Potthast. Berlin: Decker, 1874.

Die Register Innocenz' III: Texte und Indices. 5 volumes to date, numbered according to register year (vols. 1, 2, 5, 6, and 7). Edited by Othmar Hageneder, Andrea Sommerlechner, John C. Moore, and Herwig Weigl. Historischen Instituts beim Österreichischen Kulturinstitut in Rom. Graz: Verlag der Österreichischen Akademie der Wissenschaften, 1964–1997.

Robert of Auxerre. *Chronicon.* Edited by Oswald Holder-Egger. Monumenta Germaniae Historica Scriptorum 26. Stuttgart: Anton Hiersemann Verlag, 1881.

Robert of Torigni. *Chronica.* In *Chronicles of the Reigns of Stephen, Henry II and Richard I.* Vol. 4. Edited by Richard Howlett. Rolls Series 82. London: Eyre and Spottiswoode, 1889.

Rodulfus Glaber. *Historiarum Libri Quinque (The Five Books of the Histories).* Edited by Neithard Bulst. Translated by John France and Paul Reynolds. Oxford: Clarendon Press, 1989.

Roger of Howden. *Gesta regis Henrici Secundi Benedicti Abbati.* 2 vols. Edited by William Stubbs. Rolls Series 49. London: Longmans, Green, Reader, and Dyer, 1867.

Sacrorum conciliorum nova et amplissima collectio. 54 vols. Edited by Joannes Dominicus [Giovan Domenico] Mansi. Florence: Expensis Antonii Zatta 1759–1798; Paris: H. Welter, 1901–1927.

Solomon ibn Verga, *Liber Schevet Jehuda.* 2 vols. Edited by Meir Wiener. Hanover: Sumptibus C. Rümpleri, 1855–1856.

Studien zum Register Innocenz' III. Edited by Georgine Tangl. Weimar: H. Böhlaus Nachf., 1929.

Walter Map. *De nugis curialium.* Edited by Montague R. James. Oxford: Oxford University Press, 1914.

William of Newburgh. *Historia Rerum Anglicarum.* In *Chronicles of the Reigns of Stephen, Henry II and Richard I.* Edited by Richard Howlett. Rolls Series 82. London: Longman, 1885.

Yves de Chartres. *Prologue.* Edited and translated by J. Werckmeister. Paris: Les Éditions du Cerf, 1997.

Secondary Sources

Andrea, Alfred J. "Innocent III, the Fourth Crusade, and the Coming Apocalypse." In *The Medieval Crusade,* edited by Susan J. Ridyard, 97–106. Woodbridge, UK: Boydell Press, 2004.

Andrea, Alfred J., and Ilona Motsiff. "Pope Innocent III and the Diversion of the Fourth Crusade Army to Zara." *Byzantinoslavica* 33 (1972): 11–18.

Arnold, John. *Inquisition and Power: Catharism and the Confessing Subject in Medieval Languedoc.* Philadelphia: University of Pennsylvania Press, 2001.

Ashbridge, Thomas. *The First Crusade: A New History.* Oxford: Oxford University Press, 2004.

D'Avray, David, *Medieval Marriage Sermons: Mass Communication in a Culture without Print.* Oxford: Oxford University Press, 2001.

Bachrach, David Stewart. "English Artillery 1189–1307: The Implications of Terminology." *English Historical Review* 121 (2006): 1408–30.

Baldwin, John W. *The Government of Philip Augustus: Foundations of French Royal Power in the Middle Ages.* Berkeley: University of California Press, 1991.

Barber, Malcolm. "The Albigensian Crusades: Wars Like Any Other?" In *Dei gesta per Francos: Crusade Studies in Honour of Jean Richard,* edited by Michel Balard, Benjamin Z. Kedar, and Jonathon Riley-Smith, 45–56. Aldershot, UK: Ashgate, 2001.

————. *The Cathars: Dualist Heretics in Languedoc in the High Middle Ages.* Harlow, UK: Longman, 2000.

————. "The Templar Preceptory of Douzens (Aude) in the Twelfth Century." In *The World of Eleanor of Aquitaine: Literature and Society in Southern France between the Eleventh and Thirteenth Centuries,* edited by Marcus Bull and Catherine Léglu, 37–56. Woodbridge, UK: Boydell Press, 2005.

Bartholomaeis, Vincenzo de. *Poesie provenzali storiche relative all' Italia.* 2 vols. Istituto storico italiano per il Medio Evo. Rome: Tipografia del Senato, 1931.

Belperron, Pierre. *La Croisade contre les Albigeois et l'union de Languedoc à la France (1209–1249).* Paris: Perrin, 1967.

Benjamin, Richard. "A Forty Years War: Toulouse and the Plantagenets, 1156–96." *Historical Research* 61 (1988): 270–85.

Bériou, Nicole. "La prédication de croisade de Philippe le Chancelier et d'Eudes de Châteauroux en 1226." *Cahiers de Fanjeaux: La prédication en Pays d'Oc (XIIe–début XVe siècle)* 32 (1997): 85–109.

Berlioz, Jacques. "*Exemplum* et Histoire: Césaire de Heisterbach (v. 1180–v. 1240) et la Croisade Albigeoise." *Bibliothèque de l'Ecole des Chartes* 147 (1989): 49–86.

Besse, Guillaume. *Histoire des Comtes de Carcassonne.* Béziers, France: Arnaud Estradier Marchan Libraire de Carcassonne, 1645.

————. *Histoire des ducs, marquis et comtes de Narbonne, autrement appellez Princes des Goths, Ducs de Septimanie, et Marquis de Gothie. Dedié à Monseigneur l'Archevesque Duc de Narbonne.* Paris: Antoine de Sommaville, 1660.

Biller, Peter. "Goodbye to Waldensianism?" *Past and Present* 192 (2006): 3–33.

————. "Through a Glass Darkly: Seeing Medieval Heresy." In *The Medieval World,* edited by Peter Linehan and Janet L. Nelson, 308–26. London: Routledge, 2001.

Bird, Jessalynn. "The Victorines, Peter the Chanter's Circle, and the Crusade: Two Unpublished Crusading Appeals in Paris, Bibliothéque Natonale, MS Latin 14470." *Medieval Studies* 48 (2004): 5–28.

Bisson, Thomas N. *Medieval France and Her Pyrenean Neighbours: Studies in Early Institutional History.* London: Hambledon Press, 1989.

————. "The Organized Peace in Southern France and Catalonia, ca. 1140–ca. 1233." *American Historical Review* 82 (1977): 290–311.

————. "Unheroed Pasts: History and Commemoration in South Frankland before the Albigensian Crusades." *Speculum* 65 (1990): 281–308.

Bolton, Brenda. "A Show with Meaning: Innocent III's Approach to the Fourth Lateran Council, 1215." In *Innocent III: Studies on Papal Authority and Pastoral Care*, II: 53–67. Aldershot, UK: Ashgate, 1995.

————. "Signposts from the Past: Reflections on Innocent III's Providential Path." In *Innocenzo III: Urbs et Orbis. Atti del Congresso Internazionale Roma, 9–15 settembre 1998*, edited by Andrea Sommerlechner I: 21–55. Rome: Presso le Società alla Biblioteca Vallicelliana, 2003.

Borst, Arno. *Die Katharer*. Schriften der Monumenta Germaniae Historica 12. Deutsches Institut für Erforschung des Mittelalters. Stuttgart: Anton Hiersemann Verlag, 1953.

Bourin-Derruau, Monique. *Villages médiévaux en bas-Languedoc: Genèse d'une sociabilité (Xe–XIVe siècle)*. 2 vols. Paris: L'Harmattan, 1987.

Boyle, Leonard E. "Innocent III's View of Himself as Pope." In *Innocenzo III: Urbs et Orbis. Atti del Congresso Internazionale Roma, 9–15 settembre 1998*, edited by Andrea Sommerlechner, I: 5–17. Rome: Presso le Società alla Biblioteca Vallicelliana, 2003.

Bremmer, Jan. *The Rise and Fall of the Afterlife: The 1995 Read-Tuckwell Lectures at the University of Bristol*. New York: Routledge, 2002.

Browne, Sir Thomas. *Selected Writings*, edited by Geoffrey Keynes (London: Faber and Faber, 1968).

Brundage, James A. "Holy War and the Medieval Lawyers." In *The Holy War*, edited by Thomas Patrick Murphy, 99–140. Columbus: Ohio State University Press, 1976.

Brunn, Uwe. *Des contestataires aux "cathares": Discours de réforme et propagande antihérétique dans les pays du Rhin et de la Meuse avant l'Inquisition*. Paris: Institute d'Études Augustiniennes, 2006.

Bruschi, Caterina. "Magna diligentia est habenda per inquisitorem: Precautions before Reading Doat 21–26." In *Texts and the Repression of Medieval Heresy*, edited by Peter Biller and Caterina Bruschi, 81–110. York Studies in Medieval Theology IV. Woodbridge, UK: York Medieval Press-Boydell, 2003.

Bull, Marcus. *Knightly Piety and the Lay Response to the First Crusade*. Oxford: Clarendon Press, 1993.

Burton, Robert. *The Antomy of Melancholy*. Edited by Thomas C. Faulkner, Nicolas K. Kiessling, and Rhonda L. Blair. Oxford: Clarendon Press, 1989.

Bynum, Caroline Walker. *Wonderful Blood: Theology and Practice in Late Medieval Northern Germany and Beyond*. Philadelphia: University of Pennsylvania Press, 2007.

Cabrer, Martín Alvira. " 'Le triomphe de la croix': La bataille de Las Navas de Tolosa (16 Juillet 1212)." In *Les grandes batailles méridionales: "Mieux vaut mort que vif vaincu" (1209–1271)*, edited by Laurent Albaret and Nicolas Gouzy, 62–72. Toulouse: Privat, 2005.

————. "El *venerable* Arnaldo Amalarico (h. 1196–1225): Idea y realidad de un cisterciense entre dos cruzadas." *Hispania Sacra* 98 (1996): 569–91.

Caille, Jacqueline. *Medieval Narbonne: A City at the Heart of the Troubadour World.* Aldershot, UK: Ashgate, 2005.

Cameron, Averil. "How to Read Heresiology." *Journal of Medieval and Early Modern Studies* 33 (2003): 471–92.

Campanini, Massimo. "L'eresia nell'Islàm e nel Cristianesimo: Ismailiti Assassini e Catari Albigesi." *Isla'm* 28 (1989): 165–75, 235, 37.

Caster, Gilles. "Le vignoble suburbain de Toulouse au XIIe siècle." *Annales du Midi* 78 (1966): 201–17.

Catel, Guillaume de. *Mémoires de histoire de Languedoc.* Toulouse: Arnaud Colomiez, 1633.

Cazes, Jean-Paul. "Un village castral de la plaine lauragais: Lasbordes (Aude)." *Archéologie du Midi Medieval* 8–9 (1990–1991): 3–25.

Chevedden, Paul E. "The Invention of the Counterweight Trebuchet: A Study in Cultural Diffusion." *Dumbarton Oaks* 54 (2000): 71–116.

——— . "The Islamic Interpretation of the Crusade: A New (Old) Paradigm for Understanding the Crusades." *Der Islam* 83 (2006): 90–136.

Cheyette, Fredric L. *Ermangard of Narbonne and the World of the Troubadours.* Ithaca, NY: Cornell University Press, 2001.

Cohen, Jeremy. *Living Letters of the Law: Ideas of the Jew in Medieval Christianity.* Berkeley: University of California Press, 1999.

Colin, Marie-Geneviève. "Formes and fonctions de l'habitat castral en France métidionale: Présentation d'un project collectif de recherche." In *Société Mediévale Occitane: Historiens et Archéologues. Actes de la 3e Session d'Histoire Médiévale de Carcassonne organisée par le C.N.E.C/Centre René Nelli, Villegly et Carcassonne, 28 août–1er septembre 1990,* edited by Nicolas Gouzy, 63–68. Berne, Switzerland: Peter Lang SA, 1992.

Constable, Giles. "Forgery and Plagiarism in the Middle Ages." *Archiv für Diplomatik* 29 (1983): 1–41.

——— . "The Historiography of the Crusades," in *The Crusades from the Perspective of Byzantium and the Muslim World,* edited by Angeliki E. Laiou and Roy Parviz Mottahedeh, 1–22. Washington DC: Dumbarton Oaks, 2001.

——— . "The Language of Preaching in the Twelfth Century," *Viator* 25 (1994): 131–52.

——— . *The Reformation of the Twelfth Century.* Cambridge: Cambridge University Press, 1998.

——— . *Three Studies in Medieval Religious and Social Thought.* Cambridge: Cambridge University Press, 1998.

Costen, Michael. *The Cathars and the Albigensian Crusade.* Manchester: Manchester University Press, 1997.

Cowdrey, H. E. J. "Christianity and Morality of Warfare during the First Century of Crusading." In *The Experience of Crusading: Western Approaches,* edited by Marcus Bull and Norman Housley, 1: 175–92. Cambridge: Cambridge University Press, 2003.

Czeski, André. "Montségur (Ariège): Quelques renseignements fournis par les résultats de l'ensemble des fouilles." In *Heresis: Actes de la 3e Session d'Histoire*

Médiévale de Carcassonne organisée par le C.N.E.C./Centre René Nelli, 28 août–1er september 1990, edited by Nicolas Gouzy, 369–403. Berne: Peter Lang, 1992.

Débax, Hélène. *La féodalité languedocienne XIe–XIIe siècles: Serments, hommages et fiefs dans le Languedoc des Trencavel*. Toulouse: Presses Universitaires du Mirail, 2003.

Desazars, M. le baron. *Histoire authentique des inquisiteurs tués à Avignonet en 1242*. Toulouse: Privat, 1869.

Devic, Claude and Joseph Vaissette, *Histoire Générale de Languedoc avec des notes et les pièces justificatives*. 5 vols. Paris: J. Vincent, 1730–1745. 16 vols. 2nd ed. Edited by Auguste Molinier. Toulouse: Édouard Privat, 1882–1904.

Dondaine, Antoine. "La hiérarchie cathare en Italie. I. Le 'de heresi catharorum.' " *Archivum Fratrum Praedicatorum* 19 (1949): 306–12.

———. "La hiérarchie cathare en Italie. II. Le 'Tractatus de hereticis' d'Anselme d'Alexandria." *Archivum Fratrum Praedicatorum* 20 (1950): 308–24.

———. "Les actes du concile albigeois de Saint-Félix de Caraman," in *Miscellanea Giovanni Mercati*, 324–55, Studi e Testi 125. Vatican City: Biblioteca Apostolica Vaticana, 1946.

Dossat, Yves. "A propos du concile cathare de Saint-Félix: Les Milingues," *Cahiers de Fanjeaux: Cathares en Languedoc* 3 (1968): 201–214.

———. "La croisade vue par les chroniqueurs." *Cahiers de Fanjeaux: Paix de Dieu et guerre sainte en Languedoc au XIIIe* 4 (1969): 221–59.

———. "Le 'Bûcher de Monségur' et les Bûchers de l'Inquisition." *Cahiers de Fanjeaux: Le Credo, la Morale, et l'Inquisition* 6 (1971): 361–78.

———. "Le massacre d'Avignonent." *Cahiers de Fanjeaux: Le Credo, la Morale, et l'Inquisition* 6 (1971): 343–59.

———. *Les crises de l'Inquisition Toulousaine au XIIIe siècle (1233–1273)*. Bordeaux: Imprimerie Bière, 1959.

———. "L'inquisiteur Bernard de Caux et l'Agenais." *Annales du Midi* 63 (1951): 75–79.

———. "Remarques sur un prétendu évêque cathare du Val d'Aran en 1167." *Bulletin philologique et historique (jusqu'à 1715), années 1955 et 1956* (1957): 339–47.

Dossier Spécial. Cusine Médiévale: Archéologie du Midi Medieval 15–16 (1997–1998): 135–340.

Durand, Aline. *Les paysages medievaux du Languedoc: Xe–XIe siècles*. 2nd ed. Toulouse: Presses universitaires du Mirail, 2003.

Duvernoy, Jean. *Cathares, Vaudois et Beguins, dissidents du pays d'Oc*. Domaine Cathare. Toulouse: Privat, 1994.

———. *Le catharisme: La religion des cathares*. Toulouse: Privat, 1976.

———. "Le registre de l'inquisiteur Bernard de Caux, Pamiers, 1246–1247." *Bulletin de Société ariégeoise Sciences, Lettres, et Arts* 45 (1990): 5–108.

Erdmann, Carl. *The Origin of the Idea of Crusade*. Translated by Marshall W. Baldwin and Walter Goffart. Princeton, NJ: Princeton University Press, 1977.

Evans, Austin P. "The Albigensian Crusade." In *A History of the Crusades*, edited by Kenneth M. Setton, Robert Lee Wolff, and Harry W. Hazard, II: 277–324. Philadelphia: University of Pennsylvania Press, 1962.

Fine, John V. A. *The Early Medieval Balkans: A Critical Survey from the Sixth to the Late Twelfth Century.* Ann Arbor: University of Michigan Press, 1983.

——— . *The Late Medieval Balkans: A Critical Survey from the Late Twelfth Century to the Ottoman Conquest.* Ann Arbor: University of Michigan Press, 1987.

——— . "Mid-Fifteenth Century Sources on the Bosnian Church: Their Problems and Significance." *Medievalia et Humanistica*, n.s. 12 (1984): 17–31.

Flori, Jean. *La Guerre sainte: La Formation de l'idée de croisade dans l'Occident chrétien.* Paris: Aubier, 2001.

Forey, Alan John. "The Military Orders and Holy War against Christians in the Thirteenth Century." *English Historical Review* 104 (1989): 1–24.

Fortanier, Jean Ramière de. *Chartes de Fránchises du Lauragais: Thèse pour le doctorat de l'Université de Toulouse.* Université de Toulouse, Faculté des Lettres. Toulouse: Imprimerie Touloise, 1939.

France, John. *Victory in the East: A Military History of the First Crusade.* Cambridge: Cambridge University Press, 1994.

——— . *Western Warfare in the Age of the Crusades, 1000–1300.* Ithaca, NY: Cornell University Press, 1999.

Fregoso, Battista. *Baptistae Fulgosii Factorum, doctorumque memorabilium libri IX. Aucti et restituti. Index copiosisimus omnium nominum de quibus passim in historia agitur.* Antwerp: I. Bellerum, 1565.

Friedlander, Alan. *The Hammer of the Inquisitors: Brother Bernard Délicieux and the Struggle Against the Inquisition in Fourteenth-Century France.* Leiden: Brill, 2000.

Froidevaux, Yves-Marie. "Viollet le Duc restaurateur et son influence." In *Actes du Colloque International Viollet le Duc, Paris 1980*, edited by Pierre-Marie Auzas, 145–51. Paris: Nouvelles Editions Latines, 1982.

Gabriel, Pierre. *Series praesulum Magalonensium et Monspeliensium.* Toulouse: Jean Boude, 1665.

Gardel, Marie-Élise, ed. *Cabaret: Histoire et Archeologie d'un Castrum. Les Fouilles du site médiéval de Cabaret à Lastours (Aude).* Carcassonne, France: CVPM, 1999.

——— . "Les fouilles archéologiques du 'château cathare' de Cabaret à Lastours (Aude)." *Heresis* 1 (1983): 33–47.

Gaussen, Henri. "A View from Canigou: Nature and Man in the Eastern Pyrenees." *Geographical Review* 26 (1936): 190–204.

Graham-Leigh, Elaine. "Hirelings and Shepherds: Archbishop Berenguer of Narbonne (1191–1211) and the Ideal Bishop." *English Historical Review* 116 (2001): 1183–1102.

——— . *The Southern French Nobility and the Albigensian Crusade.* Woodbridge, UK: Boydell Press, 2005.

Griffe, Élie. "Géographie Ecclésiastique de la province de Narbonnaise au moyen âge." *Annales du Midi* 48 (1938): 363–82.

Hageneder, Othmar. "Innocenz III. unde die Eroberung Zadars (1202): Ein Neuinterpretation des Br. V 160 (161)." *Mitteilungen des Instituts für österreichische Geschichtsforschung* 100 (1992): 197–213.

——— . "Studien zur Dekretale 'Vergentis' (X.V.7.10): Ein Beitrag zur Häretikergesetzgebung Innocenz III." *Zeitschrift der Savigny-Stiftung für Rechtsgeschichte* 49 (1963): 138–73.

Haldon, John. "Roads and Communications in the Byzantine Empire: Wagons, Horses, and Supplies." In *Logistics of Warfare in the Age of the Crusades: Proceedings of a Workshop Held at the Centre for Medieval Studies, University of Sydney, 30 September to 4 October 2002,* edited by John H. Pryor, 131–58. Aldershot, UK: Ashgate, 2006.

Hamann, Richard. *Deutsche und französische Kunst im Mittelalter.* Marburg a. Lahn: Kunstgeschichtliches Seminar, 1923.

Hamilton, Bernard. *The Albigensian Crusade.* London: Historical Association, 1974.

——— . "The Albigensian Crusade and Heresy." In *The New Cambridge Medieval History: V c. 1198–c. 1300,* edited by David Abulafia, 164–181. Cambridge: Cambridge University Press, 1999.

——— . "The Albigensian Crusade and the Latin Empire of Constantinople." In *Urbs Capta: The Fourth Crusade and Its Consequences,* edited by Angeliki Laiou, 335–44. Paris: Lethielleux, 2005.

——— . "The Cathar Council of S. Félix Reconsidered." *Archivum Fratrum Praedicatorum* 48 (1978): 23–53.

——— . "The Cathars and Christian Perfection." In *The Medieval Church: Universities, Heresy, and the Religious Life. Essays in Honour of Gordon Leff,* edited by Peter Biller and Barrie Dobson, 5–23. Woodbridge, UK: Ecclesiastical History Society, Boydell Press, 1999.

——— . Introduction to *Hugh Eteriano* Contra Patarenos. Edited and translated by Janet Hamilton and Sarah Hamilton, 1–102. Leiden: Brill, 2004.

——— . "The State of Research: The Legacy of Charles Schmidt to the Study of Christian Dualism." *Journal of Medieval History* 24, no. 2 (1998): 191–214.

——— . "Wisdom from the East: The Reception by the Cathars of Eastern Dualist Texts." In *Heresy and Literacy, 1000–1530,* edited by Anne Hudson and Peter Biller, 38–60. Cambridge Studies in Medieval Literature 23. Cambridge: Cambridge University Press, 1994.

Harrison, Ellen, and Richard Abels. "The Participation of Women in Languedocian Catharism." *Medieval Studies* 61 (1979): 214–51.

Haskins, Charles Homer. *The Renaissance of the Twelfth Century.* Cambridge, MA: Harvard University Press, 1927.

Head, Thomas. "Naming Names: The Nomenclature of Heresy in the Early Eleventh Century." In *History in the Comic Mode: Medieval Communities and the Matter of Person,* edited by Rachel Fulton and Bruce W. Holsinger, 91–100. New York: Columbia University Press, 2007.

Hearn, Millard Fillmore. *The Architectural Theory of Viollet-le-Duc: Readings and Commentary.* Cambridge, MA: MIT Press, 1990.

Hillenbrand, Carole. *The Crusades: Islamic Perspectives*. New York: Routledge, 2000.

Housley, Norman J. "The Crusades and Islam." *Medieval Encounters* 13 (2007): 189–208.

Jimenez, Pilar. "Relire la Charte de Niquinta: 1) Origine et problématique de la Charte." *Heresis* 22 (1994): 1–26.

———. "Relire la Charte de Niquinta: 2) Sens et portée de la charte." *Heresis* 23 (1994): 1–28.

Jordan, William Chester. "The Capetians from the Death of Philip II to Philip IV." In *The New Cambridge Medieval History: V c. 1198–c. 1300*, edited by David Abulafia, 279–313. Cambridge: Cambridge University Press, 1999.

———. *The French Monarchy and the Jews. From Philip Augustus to the Last Capetian*. Philadelphia: University of Pennsylvania Press, 1989.

———. *Louis IX and the Challenge of the Crusade: A Study in Rulership*. Princeton, NJ: Princeton University Press, 1979.

Jorré, Georges. *Le Terrefort Toulousain et Lauragais: Histoire et Géographie agraire*. Toulouse: Edouard Privat, 1971.

Kaeuper, Richard W. *Chivalry and Violence in Medieval Europe*. Oxford: Oxford University Press, 1999.

Kay, Richard. *The Council of Bourges, 1225: A Documentary History*. Aldershot, UK: Ashgate, 2002.

Kieckhefer, Richard. "The Office of Inquisition and Medieval Heresy: The Transition from Personal to Institutional Jurisdiction." *Journal of Ecclesiastical History* 46 (1995): 36–61.

Kienzle, Beverly Mayne. *Cistercians, Heresy, and the Crusades in Occitania 1145–1229: Preaching in the Lord's Vineyard*. Woodbridge, UK: York Medieval Press, Boydell, 2001.

———. "Mary Speaks against Heresy: An Unedited Sermon of Hélinard for the Purification, Paris, B.N. ms. lat. 14591." *Studi eruidiri* 32 (1991): 291–308.

Kosto, Adam J. *Making Agreements in Medieval Catalonia: Power, Order, and the Written Word, 1000–1200*. Cambridge: Cambridge University Press, 2001.

Kurpiewski, Christopher M. "Writing beneath the Shadow of Heresy: The *Historia Albigensis* of Brother Pierre des Vaux-de-Cernay." *Journal of Medieval History* 31 (2005): 1–27.

Kuttner, Stephan, and Antonio García y García. "A New Eyewitness Account of the Fourth Lateran Council." *Traditio* 20 (1964): 115–78.

Labrousse, Michel. *Toulouse antique des origines a l'établissement des Wisigoths*. Bibliothèque des écoles française d'Athènes et de Rome 212. Paris: Éditions E. de Boccard, 1968.

Lamarrigue, Anne-Marie. *Bernard Gui (1261–1331): Une historien et sa méthode*. Paris: Honore Champion, 2000.

———. "La Croisade albigeois vue par Bernard Gui." *Journal des Savants* (1993): 201–33.

Lambert, Malcolm. *The Cathars*. Oxford: Blackwell, 1998.

———— . *Medieval Heresy: Popular Movements from the Gregorian Reform to the Reformation.* Oxford: Blackwell, 1992.

Landes, Richard. *Relics, Apocalypse, and the Deceits of History. Ademar of Chabannes, 989–1034.* Cambridge, Mass.: Harvard University Press, 1995.

Leggett, William F. *Ancient and Medieval Dyes.* Brooklyn: Chemical Publishing Co., 1944.

Le Goff, Jacques. *Saint Louis.* Paris: Gallimard, 1996.

Lucas, Adam. *Wind, Water, Work: Ancient and Medieval Milling Technology.* Leiden: Brill, 2006.

MacClintock, Lucy. "Monumentality versus Suitability: Viollet-le-Duc's Saint Gimer at Carcassonne." *Journal of the Society of Architectural Historians* 40 (1981): 218–35.

Macé, Laurent. *Les comtes de Toulouse et leur entourage: Rivalités, alliances et jeux de pouvoir XIIe–XIIIe siècles.* Toulouse: Privat, 2003.

———— . "Raymond VII of Toulouse: The Son of Queen Joanne, 'Young Count' and Light of the World." In *The World of Eleanor of Aquitaine: Literature and Society in Southern France between the Eleventh and Thirteenth Centuries,* edited by Marcus Bull and Catherine Léglu, 137–156. Woodbridge, UK: Boydell Press, 2005.

Madden, Thomas F. *Enrico Dandolo and the Rise of Venice.* Baltimore: Johns Hopkins University Press, 2003.

Magnou-Nortier, Élisabeth. "La foi et les *convenientiae.* Enquête lexicographique et interprétation sociale." In *Littérature et société au Moyen Âge: Actes du colloque des 5 et 6 mai 1978,* edited by Danielle Buschinger, 249–62. Amiens: Université de Picardie, 1978.

Maguelone, M. C. "Les ports de Saint-Gilles au moyen âge." Part 1. *Cahiers d'études cathares* 33 (1982): 42–60.

———— . "Les ports de Saint-Gilles au moyen âge." Part 2. *Cahiers d'études cathares* 34 (1983): 15–38, 43–65, 77–79.

Maier, Christoph T. "Crisis, Liturgy, and the Crusade in the Twelfth and Thirteenth Centuries." *Journal of Ecclesiastical History* 48 (1997): 628–57.

———— . *Preaching the Crusades: Mendicant Friars and the Cross in the Thirteenth Century.* Cambridge: Cambridge University Press, 1994.

Markus, Robert A. "Saint Augustine's Views on the 'Just War.' " In *The Church and War,* edited by W. J. Shiels. *Studies in Church History* 20, 1–15. Oxford: Blackwell, 1983.

Martin-Chabot, Eugène. "Mésaventures d'un donat." In *Mélanges d'histoire du moyen-âge dédiés à la mémoire de Louis Halphen,* 501–6. Paris: Presses Universitaires de France, 1951.

Marvin, Laurence W. "The Massacre at Béziers July 22, 1209: A Revisionist Look." In *Heresy and the Persecuting Society in the Middle Ages: Essays on the Work of R.I. Moore,* edited by Michael Frassetto, 195–226. Leiden: Brill, 2006.

———— . *The Occitan War: A Military and Political History of the Albigensian Crusade, 1209–1218.* Cambridge: Cambridge University Press, 2008.

———— . "War in the South: A First Look at Siege Warfare in the Albigensian Crusade, 1209–1218." *War in History* 8 (2001): 373–395.

Mayer, Hans Eberhard. *The Crusades*, 2nd ed. Translated by John Gillingham. Oxford: Clarendon Press, 1988.

Merlo, Grado G. "Crociate contro gli 'Infidele' e repressione anticlericale nel medioevo." *Acme* 57 (2004): 55–69.

——. *Eretici e inquisitori nella società piemontese del Trecento: con l'edizione dei processi tenuti a Giaveno dall'inquisitore Alberto De Castellario (1335) e nelle Valli di Lanzo dall'inquisitore Tommaso Di Casasco (1373).* Torino: Claudiana, 1977.

——. *Eretici ed Eresie medievali.* Bologna: Il Mulino, 1989.

——. *"Militia Christi* come impegno antiereticale (1179–1233)." In *"Militia Christi" e crociata nei secoli XI–XIII: Atti della undecima Settimana internazionale di studio,* 355–84. Milan: Miscellanea del centro di studi mediovali, 1992.

Meschini, Marco. "Innocenz III. und der Kreuzzung als Instrument im Kampf gegen die Häresie." *Deutsches Archiv für Erforschung des Mittelalters* 61 (2005): 537–583.

Meschini, Marco, Martín Alvira Cabrer, Martin Aurell, Laurent Macé, Damian J. Smith, and Kay Wagner. "Bibliografia delle crociate albigesi." *Reti Medievali Rivista* 7 (2006): 1–47.

Meyvaert, Paul. "Medieval Forgers and Modern Scholars: Tests of Ingenuity." In *The Role of the Book in Medieval Culture: Proceedings of the Oxford International Symposium, 26 September—1 October 1982,* edited by Peter Ganz, 1 : 83–96. 2 vols. Bibliologia. Elementa ad librorum studia pertinentia. Turnhout, Belgium: Brepols, 1986.

Miranda, Ambrosio Huici. *Las grandes batallas de la Reconquista durante las invasiones africanas (almoravides, almohades y benimerines).* Madrid: Instituto de Estudios Africanos, Consejo Superior de Investigaciones Científicas, 1956.

Molinier, Charles. "La question de l'ensevelissement du comte de Toulouse Raimond VI en terre sainte (1222–1247)." *Annales de la faculté des lettres de Bordeaux,* n.s. 2 (1885): 1–92.

——. *L'Inquisition dans le Midi de la France au XIIIe et au XIVe siecle: Étude sue les sources de son histoire.* Paris: Librairie Sandoz et Fischbacher, 1880.

Moore, Robert I. "Afterthoughts on *The Origins of European Dissent.*" In *Heresy and the Persecuting Society in the Middle Ages: Essays on the Work of R.I. Moore,* edited by Michael Frassetto, 291–326. Leiden: Brill, 2006.

——. "Les Albigeois d'apres les chroniques Angevines." In *La Croisade Albigeoise: Actes du Colloque du Centre d'Études Cathares Carcassonne, 4,5, et 6 Octobre 2002,* 81–90. Balma, France: Imprimerie des Capitouls, 2004.

——. *The First European Revolution c. 970–1215.* Oxford: Blackwell, 2000.

——. *The Formation of a Persecuting Society: Authority and Deviance in Western Europe 950–1250.* 2nd ed. Oxford: Blackwell, 2007.

——. "Heresy as Disease." In *The Concept of Heresy in the Middle Ages (11th–13th C.): Proceedings of the International Conference, Louvain May 13–16, 1973,* edited by W. Lourdaux and D. Verhelst, 1–11. Medievalia Lovaniensia, Series I–Studia IV. The Hague: Leuven University Press-Martinus Hjhoff, 1976.

——. "Nicétas, émissaire de Dragovitch, a-t-il traversé les Alpes?" *Annales du Midi* 85 (1973): 85–90.

———— . *The Origins of European Dissent.* London: Allen Lane, 1977.

———— . "St. Bernard's Mission to the Languedoc in 1145." *Bulletin of the Institute of Historical Research* 47 (1974): 1–10.

Muessig, Carolyn. "Les sermons de Jacques de Vitry sur les Cathares." *Cahiers de Fanjeaux: La prédication en Pays d'Oc (XIIe-début XVe siècle)* 32 (1997): 69–83.

Mundy, John H. "Charity and Social Work in Toulouse 1100–1250." *Traditio* 22 (1966): 203–88.

———— . "The Farm of Fontanas at Toulouse: Two Families, a Monastery, and a Pope." *Bulletin of Medieval Canon Law* (1981): 29–40.

———— . "Hospitals and Leprosaries in Twelfth- and Early-Thirteenth-Century Toulouse." In *Essays in Medieval Life and Thought Presented in Honor of Austin Patterson Evans*, edited by Benjamin Nelson et al., 181–205. New York: Columbia University Press, 1955.

———— . *Liberty and Political Power in Toulouse 1050–1230.* New York: Columbia University Press, 1954.

———— . *Men and Women at Toulouse in the Age of the Cathars.* Studies and Texts 101. Toronto: Pontifical Institute of Medieval Studies, 1990.

———— . "The Parishes of Toulouse from 1150 to 1250." *Traditio* 46 (1991): 171–204.

———— . *The Repression of Catharism at Toulouse.* Studies and Texts 74. Toronto: Pontifical Institute of Medieval Studies, 1985.

———— . *Society and Government at Toulouse in the Age of the Cathars.* Studies and Texts 129. Toronto: Pontifical Institute of Medieval Studies, 1997.

———— . *Studies in the Ecclesiastical and Social History of Toulouse in the Age of the Cathars.* Aldershot, UK: Ashgate, 2006.

———— . "Village, Town, and City in the Region of Toulouse," in *Pathways to Medieval Pathways*, edited by J.A. Raftis, Papers in Medieval Studies (Toronto: Pontifical Institute of Medieval Studies, 1981) 2, pp. 141–190.

Nirenberg, David. *Communities of Violence: Persecution of Minorities in the Middle Ages.* Princeton, NJ: Princeton University Press, 1996.

———— . "Mass Conversions and Genealogical Mentalities: Jews and Christians in Fifteenth-Century Spain." *Past and Present* 174 (2002): 3–41.

Noonan, John T. "Gratian Slept Here: The Changing Identity of the Father of the Systematic Study of Canon Law." *Traditio* 35 (1979): 145–72.

Oberste, Jörg. *Der "Kreuzzug" gegen die Albigenser: Ketzerei und Machtpolitik im Mittelalter.* Darmstadt, Germany: Primus, 2003.

Ourliac, Paul. *Études d'histoire du droit médiéval.* Paris : A et J. Picard, 1979.

———— . "Juges et justiciables au XIe siècle: Les *boni homines*." *Recueil de mémoires et trauvaux publié par la Société d'histoire du droit et des institutions des anciens pays de droit écrit* 16 (1994): 17–33.

Paden, William D. "Old Occitan as a Lyric Language: The Insertions from Occitan in Three Thirteenth-Century French Romances." *Speculum* 68 (1993): 36–53.

———— . "The Troubadours and the Albigensian Crusade: A Long View." *Romance Philology* 49 (1995): 168–91.

Paetow, Louis John. "The Crusading Ardor of John of Garland." In *The Crusades and Other Historical Essays Presented to Dana C. Munro by His Former Students*, edited by John Louis Paetow, 207–22. New York: F. S. Croft, 1928.

Paterson, Linda M. *Troubadours and Eloquence*. Oxford: Oxford University Press, 1975.

———. *The World of the Troubadours: Medieval Occitan Society, c. 1100–c. 1300*. Cambridge: Cambridge University Press, 2003.

Pegg, Mark Gregory. " 'Catharism' and the Study of Medieval Heresy." *New Medieval Literatures* 6 (2004): 249–69.

———. *The Corruption of Angels: The Great Inquisition of 1245–1246*. Princeton, NJ: Princeton University Press, 2001.

———. "Heresy, Good Men, and Nomenclature." In *Heresy and the Persecuting Society in the Middle Ages: Essays on the Work of R. I. Moore*, edited by Michael Frassetto, 227–39. Leiden: Brill, 2006.

———. "Le corps et l'autorité: La lèpre de Baudouin IV." *Annales ESC* 45 (1990): 265–87.

———. "On the Cathars, the Albigensians, and Good Men of Languedoc." *Journal of Medieval History* 27 (2001): 181–95.

———. "Questions About Questions: Toulouse 609 and the Great Inquisition of 1245–6." In *Texts and the Repression of Medieval Heresy*, edited by Peter Biller and Caterina Bruschi, 111–26. York Studies in Medieval Theology IV. Woodbridge, UK: Boydell, 2003.

Petit-Dutaillis, Charles. *Étude sur la vie et le règne Louis VIII (1187–1226): Thèse présente a la Faculté des Lettres de Paris*. Paris: Librairie Émile Bouillon, 1894.

Peyrusse, Louis. "Viollet-le-Duc à Saint-Sernin ou le génie de la restauration." In *Saint-Sernin de Toulouse. Trésors et Métamorphoses. Deux siècles de restaurations 1802–1989. Toulouse, Musée Saint-Raymond, 15 septembre 1989–14 janvier 1990*, 109–19. Toulouse: Musée Saint-Raymond, 1990.

Phillips, Jonathan. *The Fourth Crusade and the Sack of Constantinople*. London: Jonathan Cape, 2004.

Portet, Pierre. "Permanences et mutations dans un terroir du Lauragais de l'après-croisade: Fanjeaux, vers 1250–vers 1340." *Annales du Midi: Paysages, habitat et vie rurale dans le Languedoc médiéval* 99 (1987): 479–93.

Pryor, John H. "Introduction: Modelling Bohemond's March to Thessalonike." In *Logistics of Warfare in the Age of the Crusades: Proceedings of a Workshop Held at the Centre for Medieval Studies, University of Sydney, 30 September to 4 October 2002*, edited by John H. Pryor, 1–24. Aldershot, UK: Ashgate, 2006.

Queller, Donald E., and Thomas F. Madden. *The Fourth Crusade: The Conquest of Constantinople*. Philadelphia: University of Pennsylvania Press, 1997.

Reyerson, Kathryn L. *The Art of the Deal: Intermediaries of Trade in Medieval Montpellier*. Leiden: Brill, 2002.

Riley-Smith, Jonathan. *The First Crusade and the Idea of Crusading*. Philadelphia: University of Pennsylvania Press, 1986.

———. "Peace Never Established: The Case of the Kingdom of Jerusalem." *Transactions of the Royal Historical Society*, fifth series, 28 (1978): 87–102.

———. *What Were the Crusades?* 3rd ed. New York: Palgrave Macmillan, 2002;

Riley-Smith, Louise, and Jonathan Riley-Smith. *The Crusades: Idea and Reality 1095–1274*. London: Edward Arnold, 1981.

Rist, Rebecca. "Papal Policy and the Albigensian Crusades: Continuity or Change?" *Crusades* 2 (2003): 99–108.

———. "Papal Protection and the Jews in the Context of Crusading, 1198–1245." *Medieval Encounters* 13 (2007): 281–309.

Roach, Andrew. *The Devil's World: Heresy and Society 1100–1300*. Harlow, UK: Longman, 2005.

Roquebert, Michel. "Le 'déconstructionisme' et le études cathares." In *Les cathares devant l'histoire: Mélanges offerts à Jean Duvernoy*, edited by Martin Aurell, 105–33. Quercy, France: L'Hydre, 2005.

———. *L'épopée Cathare*. Vol. 1, *1198–1212 L'invasion*. Vol 2, *1213–1216: Muret ou la dépossession*. Vol 3, *1216–1219: Les Lys et La Croix*. Vol. 4, *Mourir à Montségur*. Toulouse: Privat, 1970–1989.

———. "Montségur: Le castrum de 1204–1244: L'apport des sources écrites." In *Heresis: Actes de la 3e Session d'Histoire Médiévale de Carcassonne organisée par le C.N.E.C./Centre René Nelli, 28 août—1er september 1990*, edited by Nicolas Gouzy, 343–58. Berne: Peter Lang, 1992.

Runciman, Steven. *The Medieval Manichee: A Study of the Christian Dualist Heresy*. Cambridge: Cambridge University Press, 1982.

Russell, Frederick H. *The Just War in the Middle Ages*. Cambridge: Cambridge University Press, 1975.

Russell, Jeffrey Burton. "Interpretations of the Origins of Medieval Heresy." *Medieval Studies* 25 (1963): 26–53.

Šanjek, Franjo. "Dernières traces de catharisme dans les Balkans." *Cahiers de Fanjeaux: Effacement du Catharisme? (XIIIe–XIVe s.)*, 20 (1985): 119–34.

———. *Les chretiens bosniaques et le movement cathare XIIe–XVe siècles*. Brussels: Editions Nauwelaerts, 1976.

Sarret, Jean-Pierre. "La communauté villageoise de Montségur au XIIIe siècle (Ariège)." *Archéologie du Midi Medieval* 2 (1984): 111–22.

Schulman, Nicole M. *Where Troubadours Were Bishops: The Occitania of Folc of Marseille (1150–1231)*. London: Routledge, 2001.

Segl, Peter, ed. *Die Anfänge der Inquisition im Mittelalter, mit einem Ausblick auf das 20. Jahrhundert und einem Beitrag über religiöse Intoleranz im nichtchristlichen Bereich*. Bayrether Historische Kolloquien 7. Cologne: Böhlau Verlag, 1993.

Selwood, Dominic. *Knights of the Cloister: Templars and Hospitallers in Central-Southern Occitania c. 1100–c.1300*. Woodbridge, UK: Boydell Press, 1999.

Shatzmiller, Joseph. *La deuxième controverse de Paris: Un chapitre dans la polemique entre Chrétiens et Juifs au Moyen Age*. Paris: Editions E. Peters, 1994.

———. "The Albigensian Heresy as Reflected in the Eyes of Contemporary Jewry." [Hebrew] In *Culture and Society in Medieval Jewry: Studies Dedicated to the*

Memory of Haim Hillel Ben-Sasson, edited by Menachem Ben-Sasson and Roberto Bonfil, 333–52. Jerusalem: Merkaz Zalman Shazar le-toldot Yisra'el, 1989.

Sivéry, Gérard. *L'economie du royaume de France au siècle de Saint Louis (vers 1180–vers 1315)*. Lille: Presses Universitaires de Lille, 1984.

Smith, Damian J. *Innocent III and the Crown of Aragon: The Limits of Papal Authority*. Aldershot, UK: Ashgate, 2004.

Southern, Richard William. *The Making of the Middle Ages*. New Haven: Yale University Press, 1953.

Strayer, Joseph R. *The Albigensian Crusades*. With a New Epilogue by Carol Lansing. Ann Arbor: University of Michigan Press, 1992.

Sumption, Jonathon. *The Albigensian Crusade*. London: Faber and Faber, 1978.

Taylor, Claire. *Heresy in Medieval France: Dualism in Aquitaine and the Agenais, 1000–1249*. Royal Historical Society Studies in History. New Series. Woodbridge, UK: Royal Historical Society–Boydell Press, 2005.

Théry, Julien. "L'hérésie des bons hommes: Comment nommer la dissidence religieuse non vaudoise ni béguine en Languedoc (XIIe–début du XIVe siècle)?" *Heresis: Hérétiques ou Dissidents? Réflexions sur l'Identité de l'Hérésie au Moyen Âge* 36–37 (2002): 75–117.

Thouzellier, Christine. *Catharisme et Valdéisme en Languedoc a la fin du XIIe et au début du XIIIe siècle. Politique pontificale: Controverses*. Publications de la Faculté des Lettres et Sciences Humaines de Paris. Série Recherches 27. Paris: Presses Universitaires de France, 1966.

———. *Hérésie et Hérétiques: Vaudois, Cathares, Patarins, Albigeois*. Storia e Letteratura, Raccolta di Studi e Testi 116. Rome: Edizioni di Storia e Letteratura, 1969.

Throop, Palmer A. "Criticism of Papal Crusade Policy in Old French and Provençal." *Speculum* 13 (1938): 379–412.

Traill, David. "Philip the Chancellor and the Heresy Inquisition in Northern France, 1235–1236." *Viator* 37 (2006): 241–54.

Tyerman, Christopher. *Fighting for Christendom: Holy War and the Crusades*. New York: Oxford University Press, 2004.

———. *God's War: A New History of the Crusades*. Cambridge, MA: Harvard University Press, 2006.

Ullmann, Walter. "The Significance of Innocent III's Decretal 'Vergentis'." In *Études d'histoire de droit canonique dédiées à Gabriel le Bras*, edited by Pierre Petot, 1: 729–41. Paris: Sirey, 1965.

Ulrich, Jörg. "Das Glaubensbekenntnis der Katharer von Lombers (1165)." In *Frömmigkeit—Theologie—Frömmigkeitstheologie: Contributions to European Church History. Festschrift für Berndt Hamm zum 60. Geburtstag*, edited by Gudrun Litz, Heidrun Munzert, and Roland Liebenberg, 17–29. Leiden: Brill, 2005.

Vidal, Henri. *Episcopatus et pouvoir épiscopal à Béziers à la veille de la Croisade Albigeoise 1152–1209*. Montpellier: n.p., 1951.

Vincent, Nicholas. "England and the Albigensian Crusade." In *England and Europe in the Reign of Henry III (1216–1272)*, edited by Björn Weiler and Ifor Rowlands, 67–71. Aldershot, UK: Ashgate, 2002.

Wagner, Kay. *Debellare Albigenses : Darstellung und Deutung des Albigenserkreuzzuges in der europäischen Geschichtsschreibung von 1209 bis 1328.* Neuried, Germany: Ars Una, 2000.

Wakefield, Walter L. *Heresy, Crusade and Inquisition in Southern France 1100–1250.* London: George Allen & Unwin, 1974.

Williams, Alan. *The Knight and the Blast Furnace: A History of the Metallurgy of Armour in the Middle Ages and the Early Modern Period.* Leiden: Brill, 2003.

Winroth, Anders. *The Making of Gratian's Decretum.* Cambridge: Cambridge University Press, 2000.

Zanella, Gabriele. *Itinerari ereticali: Patri e catari tra Rimini e Verona.* Instituto storico italiano per il Medio Evo. Studi storici 153. Rome: Nella sede dell'Istituto 1986.

Zerner-Chardavoine, Monique. *La Croisade Albigeoise.* Paris: Julliard. 1979.

Zerner, Monique. "Du court moment où appela les hérétiques de 'Bougres.' Et quelques déductions," *Cahiers de Civilization Médiévale* 32 (1989): 305–24.

——— , ed. *Inventer l'hérésie? Discours polémiques et pouvoirs avant l'Inquisition.* Nice: Centre d'Études Médiévales Faculté des Lettres, Arts et Sciences Humaines Université de Nice Sophia-Antipolis, 1998.

——— , ed. *L'histoire du Catharisme en discussion: Le "concile" de Saint-Félix, 1167.* Nice: Centre d'Études Médiévales Faculté des Lettres, Arts et Sciences Humaines Université de Nice Sophia-Antipolis, 2001.

——— . "Mise au point sur Les Cathares devant l'historie et retour sur l'histoire du Catharisme en discussion: Le débat sur le Charte de Niquinta n'est pas clos." *Journal des Savants* (2006): 253–73.

Index

Villemur, 66
viridefolium, 19

Waldensians, 20, 45–46, 138, 171–72
    harassing good men during war, 171
Walter Map, 45
wars, 53. *See also justum bellum*
    glorification of, 54
    purpose of, 55
    in Toulouse, 95
Wibald of Corvey, 24
William of Newburgh, 53

woad, 38, 169, 182
woolgathering by scholars, especially in
    relation to heresy, 171
women. *See also mulieres sanctae*
    cortezia and, 35–36, 38, 168
    as heretics, 34–38, 40
    melhoramen and, 36–38, 168

Yves de Chartres, 22

Zara, 58, 88